THE AMERICAN FEDERATION OF LABOR

THE AMERICAN FEDERATION OF LABOR

HISTORY, POLICIES, AND PROSPECTS

BY

LEWIS L. LORWIN

[*1933*]

AUGUSTUS M. KELLEY • PUBLISHERS
CLIFTON 1972

First Edition 1933
(Washington, D. C.: The Brookings Institution, 1933)

Reprinted 1972 by
Augustus M. Kelley Publishers
REPRINTS OF ECONOMIC CLASSICS
Clifton New Jersey 07012

I S B N 0 678 00880 9
L C N 70-174559

PRINTED IN THE UNITED STATES OF AMERICA
by SENTRY PRESS, NEW YORK, N. Y. 10013

Each investigation conducted under the auspices of The Brookings Institution is in a very real sense an institutional product. Before a suggested project is undertaken it is given thorough consideration, not only by the Director and the staff members of the Institute in whose field it lies, but also by the Advisory Council of The Brookings Institution. As soon as the project is approved, the investigation is placed under the supervision of a special Committee consisting of the Director of the Institute and two or more selected staff members.

It is the function of this Committee to advise and counsel with the author in planning the analysis and to give such aid as may be possible in rendering the study worthy of publication. The Committee may refuse to recommend its publication by the Institution, if the study turns out to be defective in literary form or if the analysis in general is not of a scholarly character. If, however, the work is admittedly of a scholarly character and yet members of the Committee, after full discussion, can not agree with the author on certain phases of the analysis, the study will be published in a form satisfactory to the author, and the disagreeing Committee member or members may, if they deem the matter of sufficient importance, contribute criticisms for publication as dissenting footnotes or as appendices.

After the book is approved by the Institute for publication a digest of it is placed before the Advisory Council of The Brookings Institution. The Advisory Council does not undertake to revise or edit the manuscript, but each member is afforded an opportunity to criticize the analysis and, if so disposed, to prepare a dissenting opinion.

DIRECTOR'S PREFACE

The American Federation of Labor has, to some extent, entered the knowledge and experience of every well-informed person of the present generation. Unfortunately most of us have had our view of it limited to some particular one of its constituent unions or even a particular local, to some striking personality from its leader group, or to some episode in the annals of organized labor which has attracted wide public attention. Few of us have any adequate conception of the course of historic evolution by which the Federation has come to its present position or of the complexity and wide ramifications of its organization and activities.

The present volume makes a serious effort to remedy this gap. It starts from the premise that the organization of labor is a matter of deep interest and concern not only to wage earners and employers but to society as a whole. It views the American Federation of Labor not as a mere intra-mural force in factory or shop limiting itself to industrial questions, but as something much more far-reaching, shaping and molding many other human relations which are the very essence of our individual and social life.

The writing of such an interpretive history is a delicate and difficult task. The author has not only given it his mature and sympathetic thought but he has also availed himself of the criticisms and suggestions of a great many other students of the labor problem both within and outside of labor union ranks. In the closing chapter he has not shirked the task of stating the issues and difficulties which confront the Federation, but has done it always with a friendly and constructive purpose. It is hoped that the book may furnish an answer to many questions which the work of the Federation has raised: such as why it exists despite the opposition of employers; why it is not more radical despite the efforts of socialists and communists; what it has done for the wage earners for whom it claims to speak; what has been its contribution to American life in general; and whether it has fulfilled its mission or what its future may be.

The committee from the staff of the Institute of Economics which co-operated with the author in the preparation of this volume included Leverett S. Lyon and Isador Lubin.

E. G. Nourse
Director

Institute of Economics
May 1933

AUTHOR'S ACKNOWLEDGMENTS

The author wishes to thank Mr. William Green, president of the American Federation of Labor, for permission to use the records in the archives of the American Federation of Labor, the personal correspondence of Samuel Gompers, the minutes of the meetings of the Executive Council, and other unpublished materials. He is under obligation to Mr. Felix Frankfurter for enabling him to use the minutes of the War Labor Policies Board. He is also indebted to Dr. Leo Wolman for permission to draw upon an unpublished manuscript prepared for the President's Committee on Recent Social Trends, from which some of the material on employers' activities used in Chapters IV and IX was obtained. The author wishes to thank the many trade union officials and students of labor problems for their helpful criticisms and suggestions, particularly Miss Florence C. Thorne, of the American Federation of Labor; Mr. David J. Saposs, of Brookwood Labor College; Mr. M. H. Hedges, director of research of the International Brotherhood of Electrical Workers; Mr. Otto C. Beyer, of the Railway Employees' Department; Professor Sumner H. Slichter; Mr. Edward F. McGrady, legislative representative of the A. F. of L.; Mr. Spencer Miller, Jr., director of the Workers' Education Bureau; and Miss Fannia M. Cohn, of the International Ladies' Garment Workers' Union. Amber Arthun Warburton assisted the author in the preparation of Appendixes A and B and in revising the manuscript.

Lewis L. Lorwin

CONTENTS

APPENDIX B

INTRODUCTION

The American Federation of Labor represents the most significant organized effort of American wage earners to supply an answer to the question of the worker's place in the national economy. This question, which is the essence of the so-called labor problem, is a summation of the numerous problems arising from the three major processes involved in the worker's economic function. The first of these processes—the finding of a place in production and determining the physical conditions under which work should be carried on—raises problems of vocational guidance, training for a job, enforcing safety and sanitation in the shop, reducing fatigue, and others similar in character.

The second process concerned with obtaining a share of the product commensurate with the worker's effort, gives rise to questions of methods of wage payment, hours of work, adequate living standards, minimum wage legislation, security and steadiness of income, efficiency schemes, morale and good-will of workers, and many related ones. The third process, consisting of the effort to mold the social environment for the purpose of helping the worker solve the problems referred to above, leads to questions of collective versus individual bargaining, social insurance, child labor legislation, the need or desirability for radical changes in economic and social institutions, and the relative value of various methods for achieving such purposes.

It is part of the dynamics of modern industrialism that the employer-employee relationship based on private property and individual responsibility brings into life these complex and intricate problems. It is a further manifestation of the same dynamics that in order to meet these problems the individual worker is impelled to oppose antagonistic employers, hostile legislation, and an unfriendly public opinion steeped in the philosophy of natural rights and laissez faire, and to build up independent organizations based upon the opposite concept of group standards and collective action. Such has been the historic process in all industrial countries. The American Federation of Labor is the American counterpart of the Trade Union Congress in Great Britain, the Confederation of Labor in France, and the Federation of Trade Unions in Germany.

In seeking an answer to his problems through his own organizations, the worker starts with the local union, which is an association of wage earners in the same shop or in a number of shops of the same trade in the same locality. This unit is the foundation of the labor movement. All the workers in the United States who are organized are members of such local unions, which number about 30,000, and which are scattered in hundreds of cities and towns throughout the 48 states and the District of Columbia.

The isolated local unions from their earliest days showed a tendency to combine into larger units along various lines. In the United States, the local unions of different trades in the same city or town were the earliest to combine for purposes of common action and mutual aid. The next step was the association of different local and trade unions in the same community into city labor councils. A further development was the combination of local unions of the same trade in different cities to form national trade unions. For many purposes city labor councils and national trade unions could function independently. But at an early stage in their history they felt the need for a further consolidation of forces which resulted in the formation of general national labor associations and federations.

A national labor association presupposes a group consciousness on the part of the workers and a recognition of common national purposes. Historically, such a consciousness has been aroused by such concrete conditions as political oppression, unemployment, immigration, anti-union and anti-strike legislation, and combinations of employers. Such larger group consciousness has also been stimulated by idealistic and humanitarian protests against the wage system and by the preoccupation of small groups of workers with schemes for reforming the system or for replacing it with another.

In the United States, as in other countries, national labor associations express this larger group consciousness in concrete aims and purposes. Generally, these purposes have been four in number—to aid each other in organizing and in strikes; to promote trade union ideas by educational campaigns; to obtain favorable labor laws; and to act together in matters of general economic and social policy.

The character of a national labor association depends upon the way in which these different purposes are related and the methods used for their attainment. The history of labor movements in different countries is the story of the changes in the relative importance of these aims and in the ways in which they were pursued. The differences in the national labor organizations of different countries have been the result of the way in which these issues were settled.

These differences in aims and methods have been the subject of great controversies which have been particularly acute in the case of the American Federation of Labor. The distinct features of the A. F. of L., as compared with those of European organizations, have brought it into conflict with those who had formed their notions of the nature of a labor movement on the basis of European experience. When not attacked, these differences were puzzling to many students of labor movements. The issues raised are of general interest because the activities of the American Federation of Labor affect not only wage earners but all groups of the nation, and because its present policies and its development in the near future will have an important bearing on the economic and social life of the United States.

This book is concerned with these issues. The main questions considered are: How did the Federation acquire the character it has? How has it changed its policies from time to time? What has been its record of achievement or failure in relation to the purposes it has had? What effect has it had on the American labor movement? How does it operate, and what policies does it pursue at present? What changes are likely to occur in it as a result of current economic trends?

To answer these questions in as objective a manner as possible, the historic record of the Federation is presented first. This is followed by a description and analysis of current policies and problems. The final chapter is an attempt to supply an interpretation of the past and to present an anticipation of what may be expected in the years ahead.

PART I

FOUNDATIONS, 1864-98

CHAPTER I

ORIGINS

The idea of a national association of labor unions in the United States can be traced to the fourth decade of the nineteenth century. After the Civil War it resulted in several short-lived organizations which paved the way for the American Federation of Labor.

I. PIONEERS

The first effort to form a national labor association after 1861 sprang from the desire of the few existing unions, especially the trades assemblies, which were similar to the city central councils of today, to help each other in extending organization and in carrying on negotiations with employers. Such were the aims of the delegates from eight trades assemblies who met in Louisville, Kentucky in September 1864 to project the International Industrial Assembly of North America. They adopted a constitution providing for a general strike fund, but could not muster enough support to launch the organization.

More far-reaching were the aims of the National Labor Union which was formed in August 1866. In a series of annual congresses held between 1866, and 1872, which brought together the representatives of most of the labor organizations then in existence, the National Labor Union elaborated a number of demands which later became part of the accepted program of organized labor in America: arbitration instead of strikes, the eight-hour day, regulation of apprenticeship, a national bureau of labor statistics, a federal department of labor, exclusion of Oriental immigrants, and the abolition of the contract system of prison labor.

The National Labor Union fixed its main attention on the legal eight-hour day, on the establishment of co-operative stores and workshops, and on monetary reform for the purpose of providing cheap credit. It expressed the ideas and attitudes of the mechanics, the all-round journeymen-craftsmen, who resented the industrial and social developments of the post-Civil War years, the increasing subdivision of labor, the coming of the machine, the first growth of corporate wealth, and the widening economic and social distinctions in American life which threatened them with the loss of economic independence and status. Because of the newness of these developments, the mechanic did not believe they were permanent or inevitable. Hence his interest in cheap money which would provide him with capital for the financing of productive co-operatives and make him a self-employed producer.

However, the National Labor Union could work out neither a basis of organization nor a plan of labor action. It regarded trade unions as secondary and transitory forms of organization. Logically, it turned to politics as the main method of reform. But it could not reconcile the growing trade unions and the miscellaneous reformers who flocked to it and so came to an end in 1872. During its brief existence, however, it helped to clarify the concept of the wage earners as an economic group having problems of national significance.

II. NATIVE MOLDS AND FOREIGN MODELS

In 1872, when the National Labor Union collapsed, there were already three distinct ideas regarding the form and objectives of a national labor association. The unions of skilled workers—such as the printers, molders, blacksmiths, and coopers—wanted a national combination to aid each other in strikes, to encourage the purchasing of union goods, and to help in obtaining special laws affecting labor. Other small groups of organized workers concerned with larger economic and social questions—such as the concentration of wealth, the growing power of corporations, and the economic status of labor—carried forward the program of social reform outlined by the National Labor Union. Still further to the left a few unions and groups, largely composed of immigrant workers imbued with the ideas of the First International,[1] aimed to establish a national labor association on a socialist basis.

Between 1873 and 1880 these three concepts divided the small forces of organized labor.[2] The intellectual confusion and internal division, aggravated by the long industrial depression, by the activities of revolutionary refugees from Europe, and by the influence of secret fraternal and agrarian societies such as the Patrons of Husbandry, defeated at least half a dozen efforts to form a national labor body during this period.[3]

But out of the travail of these years emerged three national organizations which were to contest the leadership of organized labor during the two following decades. In December 1877 the socialist groups, aroused by the great railroad strikes of 1877 and by the wide-

[1] For history and ideas of the First International, see Lewis L. Lorwin, *Labor and Internationalism,* Chap. II.

[2] For the labor organizations formed during this period, see Appendix A, pp. 473-75.

[3] The Industrial Congress, 1873-75; the Industrial Brotherhood, 1874-75; the Sovereigns of Industry, 1874-75; the Junior Sons of '76; the Knights of Labor, 1869-78 (first phase); the National Greenback Labor Party, formed in 1878.

spread movement towards independent labor politics in the country, patched up their differences and formed the Socialist Labor Party with a platform advocating class struggle, independent political action, and the co-operative commonwealth as the ultimate goal. In January 1878 the Order of the Knights of Labor, which had been organized in 1869, established itself as a national organization with a program which re-stated the practical demands of American labor developed between 1866 and 1872. In addition, it elaborated the idea of productive and distributive co-operation as a means of doing away with the wage system. The Order of the Knights, though socialistic in sentiment, opposed socialist politics. It also condemned craft and trade unions as too narrow in scope and spirit, and proclaimed the need of a universal organization of all workers skilled and unskilled on the principle that an "injury to one is the concern of all."

The third organization, which was started in 1881, was sponsored by the surviving craft unions. The latter were willing to come to some agreement with the Knights, but in view of the Order's declared policy against craft organization, they turned to the idea of a distinct trade union national organization.

The craft unions were influenced in large measure by the example of the British unions and were helped by a group of men who came forward as spokesmen of practical trade unionism. Some of these men—like Adolph Strasser and P. J. McGuire—had been active in socialist organizations between 1872 and 1878 in the hope of building up a class conscious labor movement on a Marxian basis. Others, like Samuel Gompers, had been on the fringe of the socialist movement, meeting with socialists in small groups and clubs, such as "The Ten Philosophers,"[4] for the discussion of questions of trade union structure and strategy. These men, tired of factional squabbles, small politics, and the futile agitation of ephemeral organizations, and anxious to get a new foothold in American life, turned to the unions with the idea of rebuilding them.[5] They brought to their task an aggressive faith in the value of trade unions, in the importance of strong treasuries for fighting and protective purposes, and in the need of a national federation to promote the common legislative interests of labor.

In 1879, with the first signs of business revival, the Typographical Union appointed a committee which drew up a plan for a "Continental Federation of Trades." During 1880 some correspondence was carried on with the craft unions on the subject. The movement received a further impulse early in 1881 when a self-constituted committee, of which Mark W. Moore, a printer from Terre Haute, Indiana, was secretary, sent out a circular letter to labor organizations asking them to elect delegates to a proposed Amalgamated Trades Congress to be held in Terre Haute on August 2, 1881. The 21 delegates who responded were a mixed group of disaffected Knights of Labor, socialists, and officials of trade unions. The conference appointed a committee of five which proposed another meeting for the purpose of bringing together the isolated unions in a general organization that would carry on propaganda for trade union principles

[4] See Samuel Gompers, *Seventy Years of Life and Labor*, Vol. I, pp. 87-88.

[5] Strasser and Gompers assumed leadership in rebuilding the Cigarmakers' Union in 1878-79; P. J. McGuire reorganized the Carpenters' Union in 1881.

and labor legislation. The British Trade Union Congress and its Parliamentary Committee were upheld as models for the American unions.

A conference, attended by 107 delegates, was held in Pittsburgh on November 15, 1881. About 60 of these delegates came from local and district assemblies of the Knights of Labor and from the Amalgamated Labor Union, a dissenting group within the Order of the Knights; over 40 represented six national trade unions;[6] the remainder were from local unions and city trade councils. The Committee on Plan of Organization, of which Samuel Gompers was chairman, recommended that the new organization be known as the "Federation of Organized Trades Unions of the United States of America and Canada." This title excluded the unskilled. The Knights argued against the omission and forced a change of name to "Federation of Organized Trades and Labor Unions of the United States of America and Canada."

But here the concessions of the trade unionists ended. The attempts of the Knights to inject proposals of social reform were ruled out by the chairman of the conference. The platform, supplementary resolutions, and constitution were drawn up entirely by the trade unionists. The platform declared that a struggle between capital and labor was going on in the nations of the civilized world which would work disaster to the toiling millions unless they combined for mutual protection and benefit. The resolutions summed up the main demands of the skilled workers for child labor laws, employers' liability laws, apprentice laws, lien laws, the exclusion of Chinese im-

[6] The Typographical Union; the Amalgamated Association of Iron and Steel Workers; the Molders' Union; the Cigarmakers' Union; the Carpenters' Union; and the Glass Workers' Union.

migrants, the abolition of prison and foreign contract labor, and a law allowing the trade unions to incorporate. The constitution was copied almost verbatim from that of the British Trade Union Congress and its Parliamentary Committee.

As the program of the Federation was entirely political, its chief provision was for a legislative committee of five which was to try to secure legislation "favorable to the industrial classes."[7] Provisions were made for a tax of three cents per member per year and for annual meetings. The secretary of the Legislative Committee was made secretary of the Federation.

III. KNIGHTS AND CRAFT UNIONS

When the Federation of Organized Trades and Labor Unions was formed as a possible rival to the Knights of Labor, the outlook was not particularly bright for either. But within the five years that followed America witnessed a widespread labor upheaval, which resulted in the rapid and remarkable growth of the Knights, and in the emergence of the labor movement as a new and potent force.

These developments in the labor world were part of the profound transformation in American life connected with the coming of the Economic Revolution. In industry, the features of the revolution were the rapid change in methods due to the increasing use of steam as motive power and to the introduction of machinery, the unprecedented growth of invested capital, the in-

[7] The committee included Richard Powers of the Seamen's Union as president; Samuel Gompers of the Cigarmakers' Union as first vice-president; Charles F. Burgman of the San Francisco unions; Alexander C. Rankin of the Pittsburgh Iron Molders as treasurer; and W. H. Foster of the Cincinnati Trades and Labor Assembly as secretary.

creasing numbers of wage earners, rising productivity and increased volume of output.[8] Transportation and communication also made rapid progress through the building of new railways,[9] the linking of independent lines into large systems, and the adaptation of the telephone, the telegraph, the cable, and the postal service to the needs of business.

It was the cumulative economic and social effects of these changes, their accelerated pace after 1880, and the business depression of 1884-86 that produced the profound labor upheaval of these years. Observers at the time contended that the wage earners benefited by the changes through increased consumption, additional comforts and educational opportunities, and facts since available confirm their contention to some extent.[10] But what impressed the workers was not the larger purchasing power gained through falling prices due to higher technical efficiency and monetary causes, but the fact that money wages and wage rates were stationary or were reduced. Though industry expanded and the number of workers increased, the displacements of labor by machinery and the changes in industrial methods seriously affected the workers. Old skills and habits were destroyed, and large numbers were thrown temporarily out of jobs.

[8] The number of wage earners in manufactures more than trebled from 1860 to 1890, and the output increased fivefold. The number of manufacturing establishments increased from 253,852 in 1880 to 355,405 in 1890; the number of factory employees was 2,732,595 in 1880 and 4,251,613 in 1890. The value of product was $5,369,579,000 in 1880 and $9,372,437,000 in 1890. *Twelfth Census of the United States, Manufactures*, Pt. I, Vol. VII, p. 47.

[9] The railway mileage increased from 93,267 in 1880 to 163,597 in 1890.

[10] See David A. Wells, *Recent Economic Changes;* also Alvin H. Hansen, "Factors Affecting the Trend of Real Wages," *American Economic Review*, March 1925.

The hosts from the farms and small towns and the hundreds of thousands of new immigrants who poured into America from Eastern and Southern Europe, bringing with them lower economic and social standards,[11] threw the labor market into a state of chaotic and depressing competition.

Provoking also were the generally unhealthy, unsafe, and humiliating working conditions in the growing industries. Employers, many of whom were rising from the ranks of labor, were imbued with a hard and rugged practicality. In their haste to develop their business, they had no patience with nor sympathy for labor demands which meant to them a waste of time and money. Confronted with falling prices and severe competition, they wanted above everything else a large supply of cheap and docile labor. Working hours were long, and discipline in the shops was rigid and arbitrary, often enforced by ignorant and arrogant foremen and managers. Efforts to organize were resisted and employers generally refused to deal either with unions or with committees of their own employees.

Under the stress of these developments, a wave of labor unrest began to make itself felt. In 1884 there were numerous strikes by miners, steel workers, cigarmakers, printers, textile workers, longshoremen, railroad shopmen, and others, some of which were fought bitterly. As most of these strikes were lost, workers seized upon the boycott as a weapon, and the year 1885 saw several hundred boycotts carried on by workers in various sections of the country, largely against wage cuts and against the "iron clad"—the demand of employers that

[11] The total number of immigrants to the United States increased from 2,812,191 during the decade of 1870-80 to 5,246,613, during 1880-90.

their employees sign agreements not to join any labor organization.

In this movement the workers turned to the Knights of Labor, for several reasons. The Order claimed an interest in all workers, skilled and unskilled, and stressed the ideal of solidarity. Though deprecating strikes, it bent to the logic of the situation and came to the support of strikers, even when the latter failed to observe the rules regulating strikes. Though the Knights collected little money, they tried to raise as much as possible through voluntary contributions and assessment of members. The five members of their General Executive Board were vested with authority to intervene in strikes and to carry on negotiations with employers; and this centralization of authority made them a target for appeals and demands.

The faith of the workers in the Order was especially stirred by its spectacular success in several railway shop strikes during 1884 and 1885. As a result the Order loomed up as the leader of the labor masses. Its membership took a leap forward.[12] Employers began to fear it; politicians took note of it; economists described it as the "most powerful and most remarkable labor organization of modern times;"[13] while the press of the country painted it in terms of exaggeration which could not but intensify the hopes and hatreds which centered around it.[14]

In contrast to the progress of the Knights was the condition of the Federation of Organized Trades and Labor

[12] The membership of the Order increased from 19,422 in October 1881 to 42,517 in July 1882; it was 51,914 on July 1, 1883; 71,326 on July 1, 1884; and 111,395 on July 1, 1885.

[13] Richard T. Ely, *The Labor Movement of America*, 1886, p. 75.

[14] See Selig Perlman, *A History of Trade Unionism*, pp. 88-89, for the story about the Knights which appeared in the *New York Sun* and which was widely copied and reprinted in 1885.

Unions. Within a year following the Pittsburgh convention of 1881 it dwindled to an insignificant body. Only 19 delegates arrived at its second convention assembled in Cleveland in November 1882. The strongest trade union at the time—the Amalgamated Association of Iron and Steel Workers—withdrew when the article advocating a protective tariff was dropped from the constitution. Only a few unions, largely interested in the use of the label,[15] namely, the International Cigarmakers' Union, the United Brotherhood of Carpenters and Joiners, and the International Typographical Union, showed real concern for the success of the Federation. Samuel Gompers, who became chairman of the Legislative Committee in 1883, was active in its behalf, but regardless of his efforts the Federation could make no headway. Its conventions were attended by only a score or so of faithful delegates. Few unions joined between 1882 and 1885 and its annual income ranged between $400 and $725. The attempts of its Legislative Committee to gain the ear of Congress and of the Republican and Democratic Parties for labor measures were futile.

In view of the relative position of the two organizations, it looked for a while as if there was a chance for an amicable adjustment between the Knights and the craft unions. Large numbers in the latter were in sympathy with the spirit and purposes of the Order. Many local unions were also local assemblies of the Order, and many of the trade union leaders such as Adolph Strasser, P. J. McGuire, Frank K. Foster, and Samuel Gompers were members of the Knights of Labor. In their turn the Knights found that, in many of the strikes precipitated by unskilled and semi-skilled workers during

[15] For discussion of the label, see Chap. XIV.

1883 and 1884, the aid of the more skilled workers holding the strategic posts in industry was essential for victory. For this reason they were inclined to take a more friendly attitude toward trade unionism.

Beginning with 1885, however, the relations between the Knights and the craft unions began to change. The cause was the rapid growth of the Order, through which the unions lost in numbers and cohesion. Many local unions, dazzled by the growing power and glamor of the Order, joined it in a body, and this drift from the craft unions was accelerated by the aggressive tactics of the Knights. Carried away by their growth, by their successes in strikes, boycotts, and collective bargaining, the Knights were becoming more and more certain that the Order was the inclusive organization for all workers,[16] into which the unions would be forced even against their will. The friction between the Knights and the craft unions was intensified further by the activities of the socialists[17] who tried to control the Order of Knights and some of the unions.

IV. THE NEW ALLIANCE

The rift between the Knights and the trade unions was widened as a result of the eight-hour movement of

[16] During 1885 the Knights also began their proselyting activities abroad, organizing a number of assemblies in England, Belgium, and other countries.

[17] A particular case in which socialists, Knights, and trade unionists came into conflict was the factional struggle in the International Cigarmakers' Union which resulted in 1887 in the formation of a dual union—the Progressive Cigarmakers' Union. As the seceding cigarmakers were supported by the Knights and the socialists, the International Cigarmakers' Union under Strasser and Gompers became definitely hostile to both. For details, see John R. Commons and associates, *History of Labor in the United States,* Vol. II, pp. 400-01; also Norman J. Ware, *The Labor Movement in the United States, 1860-95,* Chap. XI.

1886, which stirred the country to its very depths and which was the climax of the social storm which had been gathering for years. That the protest against the depressing economic conditions of the period assumed the form of a general strike for the eight-hour day was due to the Federation of Organized Trades and Labor Unions. Hovering on the brink of death, the Federation turned to the heroic measure of a universal strike which had been suggested a decade before by the Industrial Brotherhood. At its convention in Chicago in 1884 a resolution was adopted to the effect that from and after May 1, 1886 eight hours should constitute a day's work. The resolution was reaffirmed at the Washington convention of the Federation in December 1885, but no provision was made to put it into effect. It was more in the nature of a gamble on the state of mind of the workers by an organization which had nothing to lose and everything to gain.[18]

Owing to its definiteness and concrete character, the call of the Federation gave direction to the explosive impulses of the day. The Knights of Labor, overwhelmed by numerous strikes and jealous of the Federation, opposed the movement and tried to stem it. But in vain. The main argument for the shorter working day was work for the unemployed. The agitation, carried on by local trade unions, by assemblies of the Knights, and by radical socialists who saw in it a means for arousing revolutionary ideas, began to assume large proportions in March 1886. By May 1 some 350,000 workers were on

[18] The Washington convention of the Federation was attended by 18 delegates from 7 national unions and 5 city centrals. The national unions were those of the carpenters, cigarmakers, furniture workers, printers, granite cutters, and journeymen tailors. The income of the Federation for 1884-85 was $584.

strike. The movement assumed its largest proportions in Chicago, under the leadership of radical socialists of the Chicago Central Labor Union, resulting in the bomb explosion on Haymarket Square on May 4, 1886.

When the agitation for the eight-hour day was rising towards its climax, five officials of trade unions, including P. J. McGuire, A. Strasser, and W. H. Foster, issued a circular complaining of the damage done to trade unions in general by the "malicious" element in the Knights of Labor, and calling a conference of trade unions at Philadelphia for May 18 to consider the situation. When the conference met, there were present 22 representatives from 19 trade unions, with an estimated membership of some 140,000.[19] The delegates present felt that the craft unions had a "historical basis" and "were best qualified to regulate their own internal affairs." They objected to the way in which the Knights were expanding at their expense, capturing whole locals and taking in expelled members of unions; and complained against the general officers of the Order for opposing trade unions and for not showing enough regard for trade union officials.

The delegates to the conference declared that their chief aim was to protect the skilled trades from sinking

[19] There were at the conference the seven unions affiliated with the Federation of Organized Trades and Labor Unions. The other unions represented bakers, bricklayers, iron molders, iron and steel workers, boilermakers, miners and mine laborers, lasters, metal workers, nailers, shoe stitchers, and New York stereotypers. Most of these unions had grown since 1881 and had taken important steps forward in raising the wages of their members and in building up their organizations. The Iron and Steel Workers' Association had effective trade agreements with employers; so did the Iron Molders' Union. The Miners' National Federation was on the eve of concluding its first general agreement with employers in the Central Competitive Field covering the states of Ohio, Indiana, and Illinois.

to the level of "pauper labor." Still, they professed faith in "the solidarity of all labor interests" and willingness to "establish harmonious relations" with the Order. For that purpose they appointed a committee of five to draw up a "treaty" as a basis of negotiations with the Knights. The committee formulated a drastic proposal which demanded that the Knights cease organizing trades in which there were unions without the consent of the latter, disband their trade assemblies, and refrain from interfering in strikes or from issuing labels in competition with the craft unions. If enforced, this agreement would have shorn the Order of its industrial features and made it subsidiary to the unions.

Though a considerable number of Knights favored a conciliatory policy toward the unions, the General Assembly of the Order which met at Richmond, Virginia on October 4, 1886 and which brought together over 800 delegates representing over 700,000 workers, proud of its reputation and influence, ignored the trade unions and their "treaty." It added injury to insult by admitting the Progressive Cigarmakers' Union into the Order and expelling all cigarmakers belonging to the International Cigarmakers' Union.

These decisions stirred the trade unions to action. On November 10, 1886 the trade union committee of five issued a call to all the trade unions of the country for a convention to be held at Columbus, Ohio on December 8, 1886 for the purpose of drawing "the bonds of unity much closer together between all the trades unions of America" by means of "an American federation or alliance of all national and international trades unions." In response 42 delegates from 25 labor organizations assembled at Columbus on the appointed day.[20] Moved by a common feeling of the menace of the Knights, these delegates agreed to form themselves into an American federation of labor for mutual aid and assistance. The Federation of Organized Trades and Labor Unions met at Columbus at the same time and decided to merge with the new federation.

Thus came into being the American Federation of Labor. Its constitution embodied some of the features of the former Federation of Organized Trades and Labor Unions, modified by the experiences of the five years of struggle. The direction of the new organization was placed in the hands of an executive council, composed of five officers—a president, two vice-presidents, a secretary, and a treasurer. This council was to watch and to initiate "legislative measures directly affecting the interests of the workers." In addition, it was to "secure the unification of all labor organization," to assist in boycotts, and to extend voluntary financial aid in strikes and lockouts. The new organization was based on national and international unions and was pledged to the "strict recognition of the autonomy of each trade"—an idea which grew out of the struggle of the unions against the encroachments of the Knights. The Federation was also to include city centrals and state federations. Its revenue was to be raised from a per capita tax of one-half of a cent per month, or six cents per year, and from

[20] The 13 national unions represented were: those of the iron molders, typographers, German-American typographers, granite cutters, stereotypers, miners and mine laborers, journeymen tailors, journeymen bakers, furniture workers, metal workers, carpenters and joiners, and cigarmakers. The other twelve organizations included local unions of barbers, waiters, bricklayers, and the city centrals of Baltimore, Chicago, St. Louis, Philadelphia, and New York.

charter fees. The president of the Federation was made a full-time officer with a salary of $1,000 a year and traveling expenses. Gompers was elected to the position unanimously and P. J. McGuire was made secretary.

At the time the Columbus convention of 1886 was designated as the first convention of the American Federation of Labor. It was regarded as a new departure, quite distinct from the Federation of Organized Trades and Labor Unions. But the close relation between the two federations in composition, character, and leadership was recognized a few years later, and in 1889 the American Federation of Labor decided to regard the Federation of Organized Trades and Labor Unions as the earlier stage in its own history and to date its origin from 1881. While this decision, prompted by a desire to find strength in age, did some violence to the historic record, it gave point to the complex process which brought the American Federation of Labor into being.

CHAPTER II

FORMATIVE YEARS

Out of the stress of 1884-86 the United States entered a period of comparative prosperity and political calm which lasted till 1892. Then came the depression of 1893-96 accompanied by political and social unrest culminating in the Bryan campaign. During the first half of the period the Knights lost most of their economic strongholds, while the American Federation of Labor made some progress. During the second half the Federation was in an uncertain condition owing to the business depression. But in the course of these experiences the distinctive program and techniques which were to dominate the A. F. of L. in its later course were evolved.

I. A. F. OF L. VERSUS KNIGHTS

It is generally agreed that the decline of the Knights after 1887 was the result of three main factors. One was the heterogeneity of the Order. From 1878 on the Knights of Labor had admitted to membership all elements of society, barring only lawyers, bankers, and saloon keepers. Well into the eighties, however, the Order remained primarily a wage earners' organization. But after 1886 it spread into the agricultural sections of the country, and its membership became diluted with farmers, shopkeepers, and small employers. These elements had little interest in the problems which agitated the wage earners. The resulting friction accelerated the desertion of the Order by the industrial membership.

A second factor was the failure of the Order to carry out its program of co-operation. Most of the co-operative enterprises started by the Knights between 1884 and 1886 failed, thus undermining one of the main props of the Order. A third factor was the attack upon the Order by employers, the churches, and the courts. Employers' activities,[1] convictions of Knights during 1886-87 on charges of criminal conspiracy and rioting, and the hanging of the five Chicago "anarchists" on November 11, 1887 had a disintegrating effect on the Order as well as on the unions. After 1887 the Knights suffered also from internal splits as a result of personal and political issues, and their membership fell from 700,000 in 1886 to about 200,000 in 1890.

The decline of the Knights marked the final failure of the journeyman-craftsman to shape American society after his own image. Beginning with the liberal and hopeful period of the sixties, through the depressed and desperate seventies, and into the turbulent decade of the eighties, the craftsman-mechanic had held to his basic ideas of individual independence, of self-employment through co-operative industry, and of the elevation of the wage earner to a higher social status. After the disastrous experience of 1873-77, the mechanic-craftsman enlarged his outlook and made common cause with the unskilled laborer. It was this alliance that gave the Order of the Knights its broad character and large spirit, and imbued the labor movement of the eighties with its religious fervor. The wide gap between the skilled craftsman and the laborer could be bridged only by a sentimental humanitarianism which declared that "an injury to one is

[1] The first national employers' associations to provide mutual protection against unions and strikes—the Stove Founders' National Defense Association, the United Typothetæ of America, and the National Association of Builders—were formed between 1884 and 1887.

the concern of all" and which held aloft the idea of the solidarity of all labor.

The mechanic felt that the Order, though sentimental and idealistic, was building on solid foundations. As a matter of fact, he saw only one aspect of the industrial revolution—the coming of the unskilled laborer. He overlooked the other phase—the transformation of the craftsman into the specialized skilled worker. The leaders of the Knights treated the skilled worker as an anachronism with the result that the latter rose to defend his right to be.

The Knights also erred in their estimate of the unskilled workers. Mainly foreign born, the product of recent waves of immigration, unacquainted with the institutions of their new home, working and living under deplorable conditions, the unskilled of America represented an amorphous mass. They had come to America from many lands to better their lives, and they firmly believed what they had been told—that America was the land of individual enterprise and opportunity. Their uprising in 1884-86 was the result of their first contact with industrialism in general and with its ugly harshness in the America of the eighties. But after their first shock and violent reaction, they rebounded into the channels of life which presumably led to the expected goal of individual gains, and left the Order to its own fate. The craftsman-mechanic, frustrated by the rising specialized worker whom he had fought and by the unskilled whom he had befriended, turned again to the middle class and once more sought salvation in the general movement of political reform, this time in the National People's Party.

While the Order of the Knights was disintegrating,

the American Federation of Labor was taking its first slow steps. Its main assets at this time included the loyalty of a number of craft unions and the interest of various groups of skilled workers in bettering their condition, enhanced by the energy and "stick-to-it-iveness" of one man—Samuel Gompers. The events of 1883-86 had carried him to a prominence in labor circles which stimulated his ambition for a public career. He saw in the Federation the opportunity for that large leadership to which he felt himself born, and he seized upon it with an eagerness born of an exuberant faith in his own powers and a genuine desire to "serve his class," for which he was ready to sacrifice personal comforts and the well-being of his family. He determined to make the Federation his life work.

Gompers' perseverance gave the Federation the first attributes of an organization. With the aid of Cigarmakers' Local Union No. 144, he fitted out an office on East Tenth Street in New York, in a small and meagerly furnished room. Dues came in slowly and there was not always enough money to buy paper or ink. Gompers' salary of $1,000 a year was paid irregularly.

Gompers' strategy consisted in trying to make the name of the Federation known. He participated in all the important labor activities of the day. He appeared before various labor organizations as speaker, acted as general organizer for any union which asked his help, and used every occasion to bring the Federation to public notice. It was in this way that the name of Gompers became linked with the Federation, making it almost a personal organization.

Regardless of his efforts, little progress was made during 1887-88, and the question of reconciliation with the

Knights was raised. This seemed especially desirable at the time. As a result of the strike movements of 1886-87 a condition of dual unionism had developed in the mining industry, the boot and shoe industry, the building trades, the iron and steel industry, and the brewery industry. Trade assemblies of the Knights competed with the trade unions for membership and control, and in many strikes Knights took the place of trade unionists and vice versa.

Negotiations were begun in 1888, but they failed in 1889, for the same reasons as in 1886. The Knights proposed an agreement based on a mutual recognition of working cards and labels, and on the mutual exclusion of suspended or expelled members. The Federation insisted that there must be only one jurisdiction in each trade or craft, and that the unions could not share control with other organizations. The Federation demanded that the Order revoke the charters of its trade districts and become a purely benevolent, educational, and humanitarian society, in return for which the Federation was ready to have all working people become members of the Order. The Knights rejected this demand, and from then on the Federation became increasingly hostile toward the Order.

Unable to make much headway, the Federation turned again to the idea of the eight-hour day. At its convention in 1888 it decided in favor of another general eight-hour movement similar to that of 1886, to begin on May 1, 1890. A campaign begun early in 1889 took the form of mass meetings held simultaneously in the industrial cities. But when the negotiations with the Knights fell through and the condition of the unions did not improve, Gompers became skeptical about the success of a general movement. It was then decided to change the method and to select one trade which should carry through a campaign for the eight-hour day with the aid of the other unions. The carpenters' union was selected. An assessment of two cents levied on each member of the Federation brought in over $12,000. On May 1, 1890 the Brotherhood of Carpenters and Joiners carried out a widespread strike for the eight-hour day which was moderately successful. An attempt to repeat this with the miners in 1891 fell through because the United Mine Workers, weakened by strikes and internal disorganization, failed at the last moment to act as agreed.

Though slowly, the Federation made some progress during 1889-91. Membership figures are of little significance for these years, as records were badly kept and the Federation consistently tried to exaggerate its membership. However, the number of national unions affiliated with the Federation increased, and total income grew from $4,512 in 1888 to $23,849 in 1890, falling to $17,702 in 1891. The president's salary was increased to $1,500 a year in 1889; a paid secretary was added to the staff the same year with the election of Christopher Evans; and a two-room office was rented at 26 Clinton Street, New York City.

Politically the Federation was of little importance during these years. But the willingness of state governors and city mayors to address its conventions after 1889 was evidence that it was gaining a place in public consideration.[2]

[2] At a banquet given during the 1889 convention of the Federation held in Boston, P. J. McGuire noted in his talk the change from the past when labor agitators were "a much despised class," often without a meal or a place to sleep, and the year 1889 when they had mayors and governors to greet them, and banquets in honor of the movement. See *Report of the Proceedings of the Ninth Annual Convention of the American Federation of Labor*, 1889, p. 43.

II. THE BREAK WITH THE SOCIALISTS

Though progress was slow, the leaders of the Federation in 1890 believed that the future belonged to them, if they could only keep the trade unions clear of entangling alliances. This conception, already in evidence in the negotiations with the Knights in 1889, became clarified in the conflict of the Federation with the Socialist Labor Party in 1890.

This conflict was related to the developments which had taken place in the socialist movement between 1886 and 1890, as a result of which the Socialist Labor Party had started to organize trade unions and to take a direct part in trade union activities. In New York, supported by the unions of German and Russian-Jewish immigrant workers, the socialists organized the Central Federated Union in opposition to the Central Labor Union because the latter had been unfriendly to the Socialist Labor Party in the local political campaigns of 1887 and 1888. After a brief existence the Central Federated Union, which had been chartered by the American Federation of Labor, merged with the Central Labor Union and returned its charter to Gompers. However, another quarrel soon ensued. The socialists withdrew from the Central Labor Union, reorganized the Central Federated Union, and asked Gompers to return its charter to them. Gompers refused on the ground that the Central Federated Union had admitted to membership the English-speaking section of the Socialist Labor Party, which in his opinion was not a bona fide labor union. The socialists protested, and sent Lucien Sanial as a delegate to the Detroit convention of the American Federation of Labor in 1890 to contest Gompers' decision.

The controversy at the Detroit convention was bitter.

The cause of the socialists was supported by the unions of bakers, brewery workers, furniture workers, and boot and shoe workers, under the leadership of Thomas J. Morgan, a machinist by trade, and a delegate from the Central Labor Union of Chicago. The struggle ended in the socialists' defeat. The claim that their party was different from other political parties and that it should be treated as a workers' party was rejected by the convention. Gompers, McGuire, and Frank K. Foster carried the day with the argument that the admission of the Socialist Labor Party would open the door to other political parties and would submerge the unions in politics. Gompers and McGuire, although both claimed to be in sympathy with socialist ideas, were convinced that it was not wise for the unions to identify themselves with socialism since it had been vilified in America, especially since 1886, as a doctrine of class hatred and violence and as an importation of foreigners.[3]

III. STORM AND STRESS

Five years of patient plodding had brought the Federation its first small successes. As it presented itself in 1892 it was a loose association of some 40 national unions, of which from 25 to 30 paid dues and sent delegates to the annual conventions. Most of these unions had been organized since 1885, had small memberships, existed

[3] The desire of the Americanized members of the Federation to clear the trade unions of the stigma of being a "foreign product" asserted itself at the Detroit convention in yet another way. As a large proportion of the membership of the Federation was German, it was the habit of some of the delegates to address the conventions in the German language. At Detroit, Gompers, as chairman, for the first time refused to recognize a point-of-order made in German, and a demand by a number of delegates to have the proceedings of the convention printed in German was voted down.

on low dues, and lacked most of the benefits which were regarded as an essential part of a solid trade union.

Among the stronger unions affiliated with the Federation were the United Brotherhood of Carpenters and Joiners with a membership of some 57,000; the Cigarmakers' Union with some 27,000 members; the Iron and Steel Workers' Union with over 24,000 members; the Iron Molders' Union with a membership of about 23,000; the Typographical Union with 28,000 members; and two or three smaller but compact craft unions, such as the Granite Cutters. These organizations had come out of the decade of the eighties with more centralized power, with some sick benefit and strike funds, and with control established over sections of their respective trades. The iron and steel workers were operating on a basis of agreements with their employers in Pennsylvania. The Typographical Union had achieved notable success in Chicago, where Local No. 16 was recognized by the Daily Newspaper Association and had secured the closed shop and the eight-hour day for machine compositors. The carpenters and several other building trades unions had local agreements with building contractors in a number of cities and had organized building trades councils for greater control over the local labor supply. In 1891 the Iron Molders' Union had signed a national trade agreement with the Stove Founders' National Defense Association providing for conciliation of all disputes, without resort to strikes or lockouts, pending adjudication—the first of its kind in the history of American trade unionism.

Supported by these unions, the Federation was trying to become the unifying agency for the scattered elements of organized labor. Its income from per capita tax and supplies in 1892 was over $15,000, and its total revenue $17,834. President Gompers, now receiving $1,800 a year, was stressing organization work. In the year ending October 31, 1892, 277 charters were issued to local unions, city centrals, and state federations in 32 states, and eight new national unions were chartered.

This course of development, however, was suddenly interrupted by the economic and political events which began to develop in the summer of 1892. Towards the end of June the workers in the Carnegie steel mills of Homestead, Pennsylvania, went out on strike.[4] Homestead is a steel town, its population of about 12,000 being composed almost exclusively of steel workers and their families. When the Company tried to bring in armed guards the townspeople resisted and a battle ensued in which several men on both sides were killed.[5] The guards were driven away, but the state militia was called in. The strike was finally declared off in November, and the Association of Iron and Steel Workers lost its power over a part of the industry.

During July and August the tension created by the Homestead trouble was increased by three other strikes, one by the metal miners in the Coeur d'Alene district of Idaho, one by the railroad switchmen in Buffalo, and

[4] The workers were members of the Amalgamated Association of Iron and Steel Workers with which the Carnegie Company had a three-year agreement on wage scales and hours of work. In 1891 and 1892 prices of pig iron had been falling, and the company asked for a reduction in wage rates of 10 per cent per ton. The union would agree to a reduction of 4 per cent per ton only. See Selig Perlman, *A History of Trade Unionism*, p. 133.

[5] It was in the excitement aroused by these events that Alexander Berkmann, a young Russian immigrant, fired at Henry C. Frick, director of the Carnegie mills. Berkmann was a disciple of John Most and Emma Goldman and was influenced by the general faith among anarchists during this period in the "propaganda by deed."

one by the coal miners in Tennessee. In each case there were collisions between strikers and armed guards, and state militia was used at the request of the employing corporations. All three strikes were lost.

While organized labor was aroused by these industrial events, it was also stirred by political developments. In July 1892 the People's Party was formed at Omaha, Nebraska to consolidate the forces of agrarian and industrial discontent for the "impending revolution" against monopoly and corporate wealth. The agrarian leaders won over the Knights of Labor on a comprehensive platform of reforms, including the nationalization of railroads and telegraphs, a national income tax, labor legislation, and the free coinage of silver. In the elections of 1892 the People's Party polled over a million votes.

Discouraged by the loss of the strikes described above and aroused by the political agitation, organized workers began to question again whether the trade unions had not proved impotent against corporate wealth, and whether new methods of labor action were not called for. Different answers emerged. An extreme position was taken by the new leaders of the Socialist Labor Party, Daniel De Leon and Hugo Vogt, who came to the fore in 1892. De Leon, interpreting Marx's theories of surplus value and of the progressive pauperization of the proletariat, argued that the workers as a class could not improve their condition under capitalism, that the unions were futile, and that the only way open to the workers was to support the Socialist Labor Party. A less extreme group of socialists who had the support of many trade unionists were willing to admit that the unions had done useful work, but argued that under the new conditions unionism needed to be supplemented by political action. Still a third answer was the demand for a greater consolidation of all labor organizations, as had already been suggested in 1888, for common industrial and political action.

Though disturbed by these issues, the Federation voted at its Philadelphia convention in December 1892 that no great change of method was necessary to "meet the new weapons of capital." But within six months came the panic of 1893. Again, as 20 years before, America found itself suddenly thrust from a peak of prosperity into an abyss of economic misery and unemployment. Again hundreds of thousands of workers were in search of food and work, and unions began losing their membership.

It was under these circumstances that the 1893 convention of the Federation held in Chicago faced a demand for a new departure in program and policy which would have made the Federation socialistic and political in character. The demand came up in the form of a resolution introduced by Thomas J. Morgan, secretary of the Machinists' Union, which cited the example of Great Britain where the principles of independent labor politics had been accepted that year by the Trade Union Congress, and specified eleven points as a program for a political labor movement. The most debatable item was plank ten, which declared for the collective ownership by the people of all the means of production and distribution.

After a long debate it was decided by a vote of 2,244 to 67 to submit the resolution to the unions affiliated with the Federation with the request that they instruct their delegates to the 1894 convention on the subject. This large vote registered to some extent the radical temper of the delegates, but it was also due to the fact that the socialists profited by the struggle for the presidency which developed in the convention. A move to unseat Gompers was started by some delegates opposed to him on personal grounds. Both sides solicited the votes of the socialist delegates. Gompers was elected with the help of the socialists, but by a narrow margin of 1,314 against 1,222 votes cast for John McBride of the United Mine Workers.

During 1894 the tide of discontent ran higher as a result of the continued depression and unemployment. In the labor world it reached its highest mark when the strike of the employees of the Pullman Company, caused by a wage reduction, broke out on May 11 and was followed on June 26 by the sympathetic strike of the American Railway Union.[6] Few strikes in American labor history aroused such wide sympathy and such national concern. A sympathetic boycott spread throughout the Northwest. Trains carrying Pullman cars were stopped all along the way, and by July 1894 freight and passenger service to Chicago was seriously interrupted. The Knights of Labor endorsed the strike and the Farmers' Alliance offered to feed the strikers. Large numbers of workers were eager to rally to the support of the strikers, and some proposed a general strike.[7]

[6] The American Railway Union had been formed in 1893 under the leadership of Eugene V. Debs to unite all railroad workers in one organization.

[7] The idea was stimulated when President Cleveland sent federal troops into Chicago, and when on July 7, 1894 Debs and several other officers of the American Railway Union were indicted, arrested, and held under $10,000 bail on the charge of having violated an injunction issued against them. It should be noted that between 1892 and 1894 the general strike was used on several occasions in Europe and became a topic of discussion in labor circles.

On July 9 Gompers received a telegram from the Chicago trade unions insisting that it was his duty to go to Chicago at once and call a general strike. Gompers convened a meeting of the Executive Council of the Federation in Chicago for July 12 and telegraphed to the executives of the affiliated national unions to meet the Council there.

The conference appointed a committee of five, with Gompers as chairman, to bring in a recommendation. Gompers, who was afraid that a general strike would disrupt the unions and the Federation, persuaded the conference to endorse the statement which he drew up advising the unions affiliated with the American Federation of Labor to refrain from participating in any general or local strikes. The main reason given was that, since Debs had been charged with contempt of the United States Court for disobeying an injunction and since President Cleveland had ordered federal troops into Chicago, the working classes in the popular mind had become arrayed in open hostility to federal authority, and so were now called upon to prove that they were as patriotic and law abiding as any other class of citizens. Also, it was declared worse than folly to call men out on a strike against the massed array of "armed force and brutal moneyed aristocracy." All workers connected with the American Federation of Labor who were out on sympathetic strikes were advised to return to work.

This declaration killed the movement for a general strike.[8] Gompers was severely criticized in radical circles for his failure to support the railway strike, regardless of consequences.

[8] The American Railway Union was defeated and Debs was later sentenced to six months in Woodstock jail.

Having steered the Federation clear of a general strike, Gompers and his group determined to have it out with the socialists. Gompers, Frank K. Foster, J. P. McGuire, Strasser, and others had a genuine fear of the disruptive role of politics, and a strong dislike for the socialist leadership of the day. Daniel De Leon, Hugo Vogt, and Lucien Sanial, the dominant triumvirate of the Socialist Labor Party, had shown their disdain for trade unionism and their ruthless methods of fighting their opponents. As editor of *The People* from 1892, De Leon had kept up a running fire of personal abuse against Gompers and the American Federation of Labor in general. Gompers, in De Leon's language, was an "entrapped swindler," the trade union officials "labor fakirs," and the American Federation of Labor a "cross between a wind bag and a rope of sand." While attacking the Federation, De Leon was exemplifying his methods of "rule or ruin" by his activities in District Assembly No. 49 of the Knights of Labor, with whose help he was trying to gain control of the Order. While many socialists in the unions did not approve of these tactics, an endorsement of socialist ideas threatened to give De Leon and his party a basis for their operations in the Federation.

When the 1894 convention of the Federation met in Denver and took up the main issue before it—that of the political program and plank ten—both socialists and anti-socialists were in a fighting mood. The debate lasted five days. The program was taken up plank by plank, and the first nine were passed in modified form. When plank ten advocating the collective ownership of the means of production was reached, the anti-socialists began ridiculing it by proposing various substitutes. In the confusion created by parliamentary maneuvers the plank was defeated and as a climax the convention voted down the preamble in favor of political action as well as the resolution to adopt the program as a whole. Many delegates voted against the resolution though otherwise instructed by their unions.

The socialists had their revenge in the elections. Gompers, deprived of their support, was defeated for the office of president by a combination of delegates opposed to him for political and personal reasons.[9] John McBride of the United Mine Workers was elected by a vote of 1,170 against 976. August McCraith, a Boston printer, was elected secretary in place of Christopher Evans, and the headquarters of the Federation were transferred from New York to Indianapolis.

The 1894 convention also marked the end of negotiations for agreement with the Knights of Labor. Relations with the Knights had been strained during the Pullman strike as James R. Sovereign, the grand master workman of the Order, had favored a general strike and criticized the Federation for its failure to act. Furthermore, the Order was interested in political action, while the Federation was not. As a matter of fact, there could be no agreement between the two organizations since the unions insisted on exclusive control of all trade matters.[10] Gom-

[9] Against Gompers were delegates who favored free silver and populism. The Federation had endorsed free silver at several of its conventions, and some of the influential labor leaders, like P. J. McGuire, were much concerned with the issue, in which Gompers showed but little interest.

[10] At the conferences held in 1894 the Knights proposed common action in strikes and in fixing wage scales, mutual recognition of working cards and labels, an annual congress of representatives from all national labor organizations to consider general industrial plans, and the endorsement of the People's Party.

pers, representing the Federation, made no effort to find a compromise.[11]

The socialists made an attempt to revive the discussion of the political program a year later at the convention in New York City. But the majority of the delegates were against them. The convention of 1895 adopted and inserted in the constitution of the Federation a declaration that "party politics shall have no place in the conventions of the American Federation of Labor." Gompers, who was now openly at war with the socialists, came back as president of the Federation though by a very close vote of 1,041 against 1,023 for McBride.

During 1896 the Federation was again threatened by political dissensions, this time on account of the Bryan campaign. Some of its member unions were either allied with the Democratic Party or affected by the passion and enthusiasm aroused by Bryan throughout the country. But others were protectionist in attitude, and their officials were for McKinley. The situation was complex, and there were accusations that Gompers and other members of the Executive Council were violating the nonpartisan policy of the Federation. Gompers managed to keep from being drawn publicly into the political controversy, though in his own words he had to become "a clam on the subject" and "play the hypocrite."[12]

[11] That Gompers was not interested in any agreement with the Knights is clear from a letter to McGuire in which he wrote: "Talk of harmony with the Knights of Labor is bosh. They are just as great enemies of the trade unions as any employer can be, only more vindictive. It is no use trying to placate them, or even to be friendly." Samuel Gompers, *Seventy Years of Life and Labor*, Vol. I, p. 284.

[12] Gompers was suspected of leaning towards the Republican Party. In a letter to Benn Tillett, a British labor leader, dated Nov. 4, 1896, he wrote: "Since both of them [presidential candidates] are blessed with the same Christian name, I cannot be charged with being partisan if I shout to you 'Hurrah for William.' "

Though there was some personal criticism of Gompers at the 1896 convention, he was re-elected president, for the first time unanimously. Frank Morrison was elected secretary in place of McCraith, and the headquarters of the Federation were moved to Washington. The Federation had weathered the stress of depression and the storm of industrial and political upheaval. It was entering a new phase in its history.

IV. FORGING A PROGRAM

When Gompers arrived in Washington early in 1897 and installed his offices in three small rooms, the Federation had been in existence for ten years. During this time the American labor movement had subsided from a high peak of about a million members to a level of some 400,000, and had left the Knights of Labor with their large social schemes on the rocks. It had become much narrower, centering around the Federation with its fluctuating membership, the several unaffiliated unions of bricklayers, plasterers, sheet metal workers, and the Railroad Brotherhoods.

During this decade the wage earners had made but little progress. The economic gains of 1889-92 had been lost in 1894-95; in 1896 wage rates in most industries were somewhat lower than in 1892, and total money earnings were less as a result of unemployment. Average annual earnings in manufacturing were about $406.[13] Hours of work ranged between 54 and 63 a week and were even longer in the sweated trades; union members in only a few skilled trades, such as granite and stone cutting and newspaper printing, had a shorter working week.

[13] See Paul H. Douglas, *Real Wages in the United States, 1890-1926*, pp. 96, 101, 135, 143, 392-93.

Socially and culturally, the industrial wage earner had fallen below the status of the former journeyman-mechanic. His position in shop and factory was insecure; and housing conditions were extremely bad in the congested sections of the large cities where he lived. In the mining towns the workers lived largely in company houses and traded at "company stores." The vast majority sought respite and recreation in saloons. Educational limitations upon the employment of children existed only in a few states and even there were not strictly enforced. Child labor was extensive.

Federal labor legislation had made some small progress. A bureau of labor statistics had been established by President Cleveland in 1887. The eight-hour law had been extended to letter carriers in 1888 and to those employed on government contracts in 1892. A series of amendments had been secured to strengthen the Chinese Exclusion Act of 1882, and the Alien Contract Labor Law of 1885, forbidding American employers to import foreign workingmen under a previous contract of labor, had been enacted. A law prohibiting the contract system of convict labor in federal prisons had been passed in 1893. Labor Day had been made a legal holiday in the District of Columbia and in the territories.[14]

State labor legislation had also made some advances. Thirty-two states had established bureaus of labor statistics by 1896. A dozen states and a number of cities had eight-hour laws which were applicable to workers employed by the state or municipality and by contractors on public works. Massachusetts had taken the lead in enacting legislation providing safeguards against hazards

[14] The idea of Labor Day was first suggested by P. J. McGuire on May 8, 1882, at a meeting of the Central Labor Union of New York.

in factories, prohibiting night work for women, limiting the working hours of women workers, regulating tenement house industries, and extending employers' liability for industrial accidents. New York, Ohio, Rhode Island, Missouri, and several other states followed in one or another of these legislative acts.[15] Offsetting these favorable developments, however, was the weakening of the legal status of labor organizations, as evidenced by court decisions and the use of injunctions in industrial disputes.[16]

The Federation itself could point to but few achievements during this period. But in 1897-98 matters began to change for the better. Improving business led to a number of partly successful strikes. The most notable among these was that of the soft coal miners, which put the United Mine Workers on the industrial map and led to the agreement of 1898 establishing the Interstate Joint Conference as an instrument of collective bargaining in the mining industry.[17] A further impetus to collective bargaining and to the idea of the trade agreement was given in 1898 by the Syracuse agreement between the United Typothetæ of America and the Typographical Union providing for the gradual reduction of hours in the trade from ten to nine and for the equalization of union wage scales in competitive districts.

Politically also the Federation registered some slight progress. In 1898 the Executive Council was received by President McKinley, and in his message to Congress

[15] See John R. Commons and John B. Andrews, *Principles of Labor Legislation*, pp. 249, 251, 274, 326-27, 357, 364-66.

[16] For discussion, see pp. 116-23. As early as 1896 the platform of the Democratic Party denounced "government by injunction." In 1898 the American Economic Association published a book by William H. Dunbar on *Government by Injunction*.

[17] See Arthur E. Suffern, *The Coal Miners' Struggle for Industrial Status*, pp. 70-76.

that year the President inserted a series of recommendations in favor of labor legislation, including that of an industrial commission to study the relations of labor and capital. It was the first time a president of the United States had recognized a labor organization to that extent. Observers of economic life affirmed that the Federation was becoming more firmly established.[18] In his report to the 1898 convention, Gompers emphasized this fact and included a section on "the philosophy of trade unionism." By adopting that report, the convention declared itself conscious of the principles which the Federation had been evolving. Since these principles were to guide the Federation after 1898, it may be well to summarize them here.

A. Philosophy

As expressed by its leading exponents, and as embodied in the decisions of conventions, the philosophy of the Federation was a composite product of three decades of American labor experience. It was a compound of a modified Marxism, of the ideas of Ira Steward,[19] and of a group egotism evolved in the industrial struggles of the trade unions. From Marxism the A. F. of L. inherited the idea of a world struggle between employers and workers. But in order to dissociate itself from the socialists, the Federation had shorn this concept of its extreme character. The Federation endorsed merely the idea that the labor movement was a movement of wage earners and that employers and workers must struggle over their

[18] See Morton A. Aldrich, *The American Federation of Labor*, 1898.

[19] Ira Steward was a machinist by trade. He formulated the theory of the eight-hour day as the main method for increasing wages and for doing away in time with the wage system.

relative shares of the total national output. The economic struggle, however, need not assume a violent character and might be suspended at times by mutual agreement.

In denying the Marxian idea of class struggle, the Federation also rejected its implications of an inevitable social cataclysm eventuating in a socialist state. But the concept of social change was strong in the Federation. The belief persisted that the trade unions were slowly modifying property and other economic relations and would in time bring about a new and higher social order. During the early nineties Gompers and McGuire believed that in the end the labor movement would work out some form of collectivism. In 1898 the Federation still declared that the aspirations of the trade unionists and the socialists were akin. Specific references to "ultimate aims" were avoided, however, being considered futile and impracticable.

In contrast to "ultimate aims," the Federation stressed the need and possibility of immediate improvements—higher wages; shorter hours; cleaner, healthier, and safer shops; better treatment; more education; more of the comforts of life for the workers and their families. More ardently than anything else, the Federation advocated shorter hours of labor. The eight-hour day remained its main passion. Little, if any, thought was given to processes of production, except to the extent of promising a "fair day's work for a fair day's wage." Keenly sensitive to the wide inequalities of distribution, the spokesmen of the Federation assumed that the share of the worker could be endlessly enlarged without encroaching upon the rightful share of the other "legitimate" factors in industry. No effort was made to define the latter clearly, but the Federation shared the widespread popular feeling against exorbitant profits, over-capitalization, and monopolistic privileges.

The Federation stressed the primacy of economic method and of trade union organization. During the ten years from 1886 to 1896 this idea grew clearer and stronger. It was deduced from the principle that economic power is the basis of all power, and from the conviction that the workers as a group must have their own distinctive organization. The trade union was glorified as the soundest basis of all workers' progress, as "the primary school" of the worker in technical education and in the science of self-government, as the mechanism which could be used cautiously for day-by-day advance, and as the "germ of growth and expansion to the loftiest heights of human aspiration."

This emphasis on trade unionism carried with it a strong distrust of the state. The Federation rejected the proposal for compelling corporations by law to deal with unions and fought against the compulsory arbitration of labor disputes. But if the state was not to aid the trade unions in their tasks, it was also not to hinder them by special restrictions. The Federation demanded the repeal of the conspiracy laws, and an amendment of the Sherman Anti-Trust Law to exempt trade unions from its provisions.

But the leaders of the Federation were too realistic to deny all intervention by the state in economic matters. The Federation endorsed measures for the further democratization of government, such as the popular election of United States senators, the Australian ballot, Civil Service reform, direct legislation in state and municipal governments by means of the initiative and referendum, postal savings banks, and compulsory education. In 1897 the Federation also demanded amendments to the Constitution of the United States and of the several states to deprive the courts of power to set aside laws duly enacted by the legislature.

The ideas of the Federation on the state and on the potentialities of the trade union influenced its stand on politics and political parties. It was kept from a clear-cut political policy by the ups and downs of political reform and by the fear that politics would disrupt the unions. By 1896 the separate unions had different political interests, and some of the trade union officials, especially in the city central councils and in the state federations, had become involved in Democratic and Republican politics. But the Federation had difficulty in maintaining a purely negative position on political action. The workers had special interests to defend, and the faith that the labor movement was a growing power which would slowly transform society, vague as it was, colored the procedure of the Federation. McGuire in 1896 assured the convention of the Federation that labor would control the state within 40 years. These contradictory currents were partly reconciled in the convention of 1898 by the adoption of two resolutions, one of which reaffirmed the opposition of the Federation to all partisan politics, while the other urged the workers to use the ballot independently regardless of party, in order to elect men from the ranks of the workers, preferably trade unionists.

B. Techniques and Structure

The "philosophy" of trade unionism outlined above was bound up with a specific technique. In so far as the individual unions were concerned, this technique meant high dues, a system of benefits, large strike funds, the cautious use of the strike and boycott, the avoidance of the sympathetic strike, and the most extensive possible use of the label. It meant sustained work in organizing, expertness in negotiations, a restrained militancy, preparations for striking combined with a willingness to compromise, trade agreements providing for conciliation and voluntary arbitration, and centralized authority within each union for the purposes of enforcing discipline among the workers, negotiating with employers, and carrying out the terms of contracts.

The Federation as a central body stressed strict trade autonomy, resorting only to advice and exhortation to achieve greater uniformity. The Federation left the unions free to adopt such benefits as they wished, to fix their dues, to provide for strike funds, and to take the initiative in strikes and boycotts. Year after year the Federation at its conventions urged the weaker unions to strengthen their organization by following the example of the older and more successful unions, and tried to inculcate a regard for the sanctity of trade agreements.

Central control over the use of the boycott and the label was sought by the Federation. In 1894 it started the "We Don't Patronize List" in the *Federationist*, enumerating all boycotts approved by the convention or by the Executive Council. No boycott could be included unless approved by the Executive Council of the Federation, and the Executive Council was required not to approve the application of a trade union for a boycott until the firm concerned had been given opportunity to present its side of the case. In 1898 a rule was passed limiting the number of firms which one international union might put on the list simultaneously. The Federation likewise assumed the right to endorse labels, the control of which was in the hands of the individual trade unions, and established a general A. F. of L. label which was to be used by the unions in conjunction with their own labels.

The Federation exercised its greatest power in the matter of jurisdiction. Animated by opposition to dual unionism, it insisted that only its charter gave an individual union rights and privileges. Whenever disputes arose between unions over their claims, the Federation alone was the supreme arbiter, either through the convention, the Executive Council, or specially designated committees.

On the basis of the techniques described, the Federation shaped its form of organization. As an association of trade unions, it had no directly affiliated individual members, except those enrolled in the local trade and federal labor unions. These were regarded as temporary organizations, merely as recruiting unions for workmen who were to be organized as soon as possible into national unions of their various crafts. The primary units of the Federation were the national unions, and the Federation's policy was definitely and systematically to form compact national unions in every trade, and to make them the units of power in the trade union world, with undivided authority over their local unions.

The Federation also encouraged the formation of city centrals and state federations. The place of these organizations, however, was secondary in its scheme. In no case were they to interfere with the jurisdiction of the national unions or with their trade functions. Their voting power at conventions of the Federation was limited to one for each organization regardless of membership or importance. While the Federation required every local union to belong to its national union, it did not compel any union to belong to the city centrals or state federations.

In affiliating federal labor unions, city centrals, state federations, and national unions, the Federation regarded itself as a federal association modelled after the government of the United States. It aimed to supplement, not to supplant, the powers of the trade unions. At first the leaders tried to develop a sense of voluntary discipline in the affiliated unions. By 1896, however, they advanced the idea that the resolutions and decisions of the annual conventions carried certain binding obligations. The degree of authority was left undefined, however, and the Federation reserved as its only means of compulsion the right to suspend or expel an affiliated organization.

The co-ordinating office of the Federation in Washington was directed by the Executive Council consisting of the president, the secretary, the treasurer, and six vice-presidents.[20] This council of nine had to attend to a wide range of duties, such as investigating boycotts, advising in case of industrial disputes, helping to settle strikes when requested to do so. It had the task of furthering organization. The members of the Council, with the exception of the president and secretary, were paid only for time spent on official duties. The main work fell to the president and secretary who in 1898 were full-time officers with salaries of $1,800 and $1,000 respectively.

C. An American Synthesis

The system of unionism which the Federation developed between 1886 and 1898 has been characterized as craft, job-conscious, business, and wage-conscious unionism. Undoubtedly, most of the unions of the Federation

[20] Until 1898 the Council had four vice-presidents, but in that year two more were added.

were craft unions. The Federation was also conscious of the business aspects of trade unions. Repeatedly Gompers referred to them between 1893 and 1898 as the "business organizations of the workers." But all the designations referred to fail to express the composite character of the trade unionism of this period. Aside from job and business consciousness, the Federation had a larger social interest. Wage consciousness was combined with the idea of a gradual elevation in the social position of the workers. Gompers coined the vague phrase "pure and simple unionism," to describe the mixed elements of craft unionism, inchoate syndicalism, social meliorism, vague humanitarianism, and practical opportunism which entered into the make-up of the Federation.

The course of the Federation at this time was paralleled by national union developments in Europe. The nineties witnessed the differentiation of national labor organizations in all advanced industrial countries. The German trade unions in 1893, though hampered by police regulations, formed the General Commission of Trade Unions. In 1895 the French syndicates laid the foundations of the General Confederation of Labor on the basis of complete independence from all political parties. In the same year the British Trade Union Congress extended greater power and cohesion to the separate unions. Later, in 1899, many of the older British unions took steps towards closer economic co-operation through the formation of the British Federation of Trade Unions. In 1898 national trade union commissions were formed in Belgium and Sweden, giving greater autonomy to the trade unions in their relations with the socialist parties. Between 1892 and 1898 similar arrangements were made in several other European countries.

The leaders of the Federation, especially Gompers, who took a great interest in these developments, thought that unionism in America was following the general trend of labor abroad. As a matter of fact, these developments soon proved divergent. The British Trade Union Congress organized the British Labor Party. In France, the General Confederation of Labor evolved towards revolutionary syndicalism, while in Germany, Austria, Belgium, and the Scandinavian countries, trade unionism became definitely allied with the socialist parties.[21]

The Federation made repeated efforts to participate in the international trade union movement which was beginning. It took part in developing the idea of an international Labor Day (May first), in establishing the acceptance of card transfers by unions of different countries, in exchanging delegates to conventions, and in promoting the formation of a distinctly trade unionist international organization. By 1898, however, the growth of socialist influence in the unions abroad discouraged the Federation. Reassured by signs of its own stability at home, which Gompers had been interested in bolstering through international contacts, it dropped plans for international labor action. It maintained a general attitude in favor of world peace, gave its support to struggles for national liberation such as were taking place in Cuba and Russia, and took a stand against "imperialism," opposing the annexation of Hawaii and the Philippines. Aroused by the frequent use of the armed forces of the country in strikes, it opposed a "huge standing army" and expressly discouraged its members from enlisting in the state militia or in the national guard.

The Federation wavered on the question of immigra-

[21] Lewis L. Lorwin, *Labor and Internationalism*, pp. 82-83.

tion, as a large part of its membership was composed of immigrants who favored free entrance to the United States. Until 1897 the conventions of the Federation voted that no further restriction of immigration was necessary. In that year a majority of the trade unions affiliated with the Federation voted for the first time in favor of a reasonable measure of restriction.

The evolution of "pure and simple unionism" between 1886 and 1898 must be explained in terms of the interests and outlook of the skilled worker. Aware of the economic value of his skill, he stressed the ideas of craft and of job-control. Working by the piece or hour, he was interested in wage and piece rates. Conscious of his bargaining difficulties, he wanted to strengthen them by limiting the supply of labor through apprenticeship regulations and the restriction of immigration. Certain that he had the power to improve his condition by group action, he had only a mild interest in schemes for a perfect society in the distant future. Conscious of his relative weakness in the social scheme of the nation, he distrusted the state and tended to be non-political and anti-socialist.[22]

The skilled worker found the international union the most appropriate instrument for his purposes. It embodied the idea of skill, craft, solidarity, monopolistic power, and protection against insecurity due either to scarcity of jobs or to arbitrariness of employers. It promised quick returns for limited obligations.

In their fight against the Knights of Labor between 1881 and 1890, the craft unions developed that strong fear of dual unionism which prompted them to emphasize trade autonomy as a basic principle. As a result the Ameri-

[22] For further discussion, see Chap. XVII.

can Federation of Labor was charged primarily with being the watchful guardian of the jurisdictional rights of each international trade union. Secondarily, it was to be the legislative representative of the interests of all the workers in trade and industrial matters. These were the two main objectives which it developed in the course of its formative years.

PART II

NATIONAL EXPANSION, 1899-1914

CHAPTER III

THE FIRST ADVANCE

In 1898 the American Federation of Labor was a small and limited organization. Its constituent unions were small, and most of them were struggling to achieve a sound basis of finance, discipline, and collective action. Only about half of the organized workers of the country were affiliated with it.[1]

The Federation also had to face persistent opposition. The Socialist Trade and Labor Alliance[2] was a source of trouble among the workers in the garment, coal, and textile industries. Inside the Federation, a socialist minority continued to ridicule the philosophy of "pure and simpledom." The Western Federation of Miners,[3] disappointed by the failure of the Federation to aid the striking metal miners of Leadville in 1897, withdrew, and in May 1898 organized the Western Labor Union as a sectional rival to the A. F. of L.

But firmly resisting these opposing forces, the American Federation of Labor emerged in 1898 as the most

[1] The unions of bricklayers, plasterers, the Railroad Brotherhoods, and several others refused to join the Federation. The affiliation of the Railroad Brotherhoods with the Federation had seemed likely for a while but received a setback as a result of disagreement over the Erdman Act in 1897-98. The Federation opposed the Act because it presumably provided for compulsory arbitration. Though the Federation later withdrew its opposition, the Brotherhoods were alienated.

[2] The Socialist Trade and Labor Alliance was organized by Daniel De Leon in December 1895 as a rival to the A. F. of L. and as a means of "saturating" the labor movement with socialism. Its membership in 1898 was variously estimated at 15,000 to 30,000.

[3] The Western Federation of Miners was organized in 1893 in Butte, Mont., after some bitter strikes in the copper mines of the state. It was an industrial union advocating methods of class struggle and socialism.

comprehensive and promising labor organization in America. It had attained a certain cohesion of program and outlook. Its leaders—Gompers, P. J. McGuire, James Duncan, James O'Connell, John Mitchell, John B. Lennon, and Frank Morrison—worked in unison. These men had the support of loyal trade unionists in the industrial centers of the country, who were ready to aid locally.

I. PROSPERITY AND UNION PROGRESS

The prosperity ushered in by the Spanish American War stimulated the first advance of the A. F. of L. The workers saw a chance in the rising labor market, and a wave of organizing enthusiasm as intense as that of 1885-86 swept the country. The methods evolved during the preceding decade bore fruit. Strikes were successful, especially in the building trades where the weapon of the sympathetic strike was applied. The label helped the unions in the food, service, and several other industries because of the support of the organized workers who took "union principles" seriously. The combined action of unions in allied trades locally, through councils,[4] and through city centrals, was an important factor in strengthening unionism in separate trades as well as in whole localities. In San Francisco, Chicago, Indianapolis, and a number of other cities, unionism attained a position of economic and political power.

Though driven primarily by economic motives for improving conditions of working and living, the trade unionism of the day had a large idealistic element in it. Drawn together by a sense of craft fellowship, the workers felt themselves comrades in a cause in which

[4] For analysis of building trades and other councils, see pp. 375-91.

all things big and small—strikes, dues, picnics, committee meetings, organizing campaigns, and scraps with the "bosses"—had importance. Traveling journeymen, "floaters," and "boomers" carried the gospel of unionism from place to place. Organizers braved their difficult task for small pay, finding compensation in the satisfaction of service to "the cause." Officers served enthusiastically though many of them were paid only for time lost and at the rate of the trade. For the mass of more alert workers unionism offered a new way of more intense and interesting living;[5] for men capable of leadership, it offered a field of public activity; to the ambitious and aggressive, it was a chance for a personal career.

These combined forces carried the A. F. of L. forward. Its membership doubled between 1898 and 1900 and trebled between that year and 1904. From some 278,000 in 1898 it increased to 1,676,200 in 1904, or by a million and a half. The constituent elements of the Federation in 1904 were 114 international unions, 828 directly affiliated locals, 549 city centrals, and 29 state

[5] At meetings of international unions today, those "heroic" days of unionism are often recalled. Characteristic is the story of how the first union of lathers was organized in Cedar Rapids, Iowa. The message was brought to their doors by a "floater" who dropped off a slow moving freight train. Soon after his arrival, he began to talk unionism. One of the men who later became an officer of the union described it as follows: "We met in a humble home—only a few chairs in the house. However, nothing like that could stop our enthusiasm. We used the floor for chairs with our backs against the wall. How proud we were when our charter arrived and a meeting was called to install officers. I felt for the first time that I was a man entitled to some of the comforts of life. . . . The same feeling went over all the lathers that evening. Past differences were forgotten. We pledged each other to devote ourselves to the upbuilding of the lathing business." See *Proceedings of the Sixteenth Convention of the Wood, Wire, and Metal Lathers' International Union,* September 1929, p. 73.

federations. Elated by its growth, the Federation in 1904 for the first time published a chart showing membership figures since 1881.

With growing numbers, financial resources increased. Though the per capita tax remained four cents per year, the receipts of the Federation rose from $18,639 in 1898 to $115,220 in 1901, $247,800 in 1903, and $220,995 in 1904.

Since only a small part of the increase in revenue went to office salaries,[6] the Federation was able to extend its activities. In 1900 it put 20 paid organizers into the field, at a cost of $16,400. By 1904 it had increased its force to 99, at a cost of $84,904. More and more the Federation complied with appeals for organizers by groups of workers who found themselves blocked by local opposition or by lack of funds. It raised three assessments in these years: $9,411 for the cigarmakers in 1900; $30,357 for the machinists in 1901-02; and $4,560 for strikers in San Francisco in 1902. In most of the important industrial struggles and in many lesser ones, one or more members of the Executive Council took part as mediators. To meet more adequately the increased demands for the services of the Executive Council, and to give representation to the new unions, the number of vice-presidents was increased to six in 1899 and to eight in 1903, making an Executive Council of eleven.

In this first advance of the A. F. of L. union gains were widely scattered. But the greatest progress was made by the workers in the building trades, in mining, in some metal trades, in personal service, and by long-

[6] The salaries of the president and secretary were increased in 1904 to $3,000 and $2,500 respectively.

shoremen and teamsters.[7] This was due in part to the nature of the industries and in part to the readiness of large groups of workers in these industries to apply the weapons of unionism vigorously.

II. MILITANCY AND PEACEFUL RECOGNITION

Partly as a result of these conditions, partly in reaction to the arbitrariness then prevailing in industrial relations, the unionism developed during these years

NUMBER OF STRIKES AND WORKERS INVOLVED, 1893–1904[a]

Period	Total Number of Strikes	Average Number of Strikes Per Year	Total Number of Workers Involved	Average Number of Workers Involved Per Year
1893–98	7,029	1,171	1,684,249	280,708
1899–1904	15,463	2,577	2,564,782	427,464

[a] For a classification of strikes by five-year periods between 1881 and 1905, see Paul H. Douglas, "An Analysis of Strike Statistics, 1881–1921," *Journal of the American Statistical Association*, September 1923, Vol. 18, pp. 866–77. The strike statistics of these years tell only part of the story for they do not reveal the bitterness of some of the conflicts.

was marked by a fighting spirit, often by violence, and in some cases by a tendency to use power too readily. The complaints of employers against "walking delegates," "business agents," and jurisdictional fights were often not merely an expression of the employers' impatience with violations of presumed absolute rights to run their business as they pleased, but of real injury inflicted by unions in the first flush of success.

Though supporting the militancy of the unions, the leaders of the Federation were not enthusiastic about strikes. Their aim was to establish collective relations

[7] See Appendix A, pp. 476-83.

with employers on a large scale as peaceably as possible and to obtain public approval for unionism. An opportunity for assistance in attaining this end seemed to them to present itself in the National Civic Federation which was started in Chicago in 1896 and which became a national organization in 1900. Born of the industrial turmoil of the nineties, the Civic Federation planned to bring together capitalists, employers, workers, and philanthropists on certain broad principles. Its industrial department set itself the threefold task of convincing the public that strikes and lockouts could and should be avoided, of inducing employers and workmen to enter into trade agreements, and of maintaining a commission which would always be available for mediation in disputes. The Civic Federation, being voluntary in character, did not require an individual employer to pledge himself to observe these principles in his dealings with his own workers and welcomed the non-union employer presumably in the hope of "educating" him.

At the time it seemed that this concept of industrial relations might find a wide response. The trend toward industrial consolidation during these years[8] had created a considerable reaction against competition as "the death of trade." Many manufacturers, with their eyes on expanding markets, domestic and foreign, were ready for reasonable arrangements with unions if promised security against strikes. The possible services of the Civic Federa-

[8] Fully 40 per cent of the total manufacturing output of the country was by the end of 1903 under the control of large combinations. See Henry R. Seager and Charles A. Gulick, *Trust and Corporation Problems,* pp. 60-62; see also Victor S. Clark, *History of Manufactures in the United States, 1860-1914,* 1928, Vol. II, pp. 540-43. By 1903 large corporations had obtained a dominating position in a number of important industries, their primary purpose being monopoly power in producing and selling their products.

tion in making contacts with large employers and in gaining the ear of the public loomed large in the eyes of the Federation leaders. Gompers, John Mitchell, O'Connell, and a number of other trade unionists joined the Civic Federation, to the consternation of the socialists and other radicals to whom such collaboration with employers was a violation of the principle of class struggle.

A. The Steel Strike

The value as well as the limitations of such contacts was shown in the two big industrial battles of these years. The iron and steel strike of 1901 was called by the Amalgamated Association of Iron and Steel Workers in the belief that the first stages of forming the United States Steel Corporation afforded an opportunity to organize the non-union steel and tin-plate mills entering into the merger. The companies offered the union several compromises, but the union officials were unbending. Contrary to their expectations, the managements of the steel mills were not eager for peace at any price. The officials of the union, headed by T. J. Shaffer, president of the Amalgamated, called a strike.[9] The Amalgamated had for over 20 years been an extreme craft union. Its members were the highly skilled craftsmen of the industry—the puddlers and rollers—and its total membership in 1901 was not over 10,000 out of a total of some 160,000 workers employed in the industry at the time. Faced by a powerful company, the leaders of the Amalgamated were willing to use radical tactics and began agitating for a sympathetic strike of miners and rail-

[9] Included in the suspension were workers in the plants of the Illinois Steel Company, where the trade agreement with the union had not yet expired.

road men. It appeared also that Shaffer was laying wider plans for a national labor council, with power to throw its whole weight behind any strike, to supersede the A. F. of L.

Gompers and Mitchell associated themselves with the National Civic Federation to settle the strike by mediation. On July 27, 1901 a conference was arranged between Shaffer, officials of the United States Steel Corporation, and J. Pierpont Morgan. According to Gompers' account, Morgan affirmed that he was not hostile to organized labor and gave his assurances that within two years the corporation would be ready to sign a contract with the union for all its plants. At this conference Shaffer and the secretary of the union made a tentative agreement with J. P Morgan, Charles M. Schwab, and E. H. Gary granting the union the wage scale demanded, but specifying that the union was not to organize the non-union mills. This agreement was rejected by the executive board of the union. Later, Gompers, John Mitchell, and Ralph M. Easley, secretary of the National Civic Federation, secured the corporation's assent to unionize some additional mills. They urged the officials of the Amalgamated to accept the compromise. Shaffer failed to accept this offer before the time limit expired, and so the struggle continued. In the end the union was forced to accept an agreement covering fewer mills than any of the previously proposed settlements included. The loss of the strike seriously weakened the union.

Shaffer denounced Gompers and Mitchell for failing to support his union. He claimed that neither the A. F. of L. nor the United Mine Workers contributed a cent and that the strike had been lost for lack of money and lack of co-operation by other organizations. He further asserted that the steel workers had been led to expect the miners and the trainmen to join in a sympathetic strike. Gompers replied that the A. F. of L. had not helped to raise funds because Shaffer had issued a broadcast appeal for money without asking A. F. of L. endorsement. Mitchell denied that he had ever made any promise to call out the miners, saying that such a step was contrary to his policy.[10]

B. The Coal Strike

The anthracite strike of 1902 was caused by the demand of the hard coal miners for an eight-hour working day, a 20 per cent increase in wages, payment according to weight of coal mined, and recognition of the union. Efforts of the Civic Federation to mediate between the operators and the miners failed, regardless of the willingness of John Mitchell to negotiate.[11]

On May 12 over 150,000 miners walked out on strike. There were demands that the soft coal miners join in a sympathetic strike, but Mitchell opposed this, as it would have involved a breach of contract. The soft coal miners were assessed $1.00 a week and contributed over 2 million dollars for the support of the strikers. The total amount raised by the miners, other trade unions, and the public was $2,645,324.

The strike assumed the character of a great social

[10] Gompers and Shaffer were not on friendly terms, which fact may have contributed to the lukewarm attitude of the former and the obstinacy of the latter. The Civic Federation claimed credit for having prevented sympathetic strikes by the miners and railroad men.

[11] The well-known statement of George F. Baer, president of the Philadelphia and Reading Co., is worth recalling: "The rights and interests of the laboring man will be protected and cared for not by the labor agitators but by the Christian men to whom God has given control of the property rights of the country."

struggle. The public, though suffering serious discomfort from the coal shortage, gave it remarkable support. All classes responded to appeals for funds. Lawyers offered their professional services to the strikers without fee. Men prominent in many walks of life appeared on the same platform with Mitchell and Gompers to plead the cause of the miners. The strike became a protest of the people against the oppression of "the trusts."

Public sympathy played a part in the settlement of the strike. It strengthened the hands of President Roosevelt in appointing the Anthracite Coal Commission in October 1902 and forced J. Pierpont Morgan to bring pressure on the operators to accept arbitration. Though the Commission's award was only a partial victory for the miners,[12] it gave the United Mine Workers a stronger foothold in the anthracite coal fields and a new impetus for development. It was the first public recognition of the economic and social wrongs of a large group of workers, an important victory for the American Federation of Labor.

III. PROBLEMS OF GROWTH

The growth of these years put the A. F. of L. to the test of showing how it was going to lead its developing unions in accordance with the ideas which it had developed. Many questions of policy had to be considered. But the most important were those dealing with structure, strategy, and politics.

[12] The award, which was to run for three years, granted the miners a nine-hour day, a 10 per cent increase in wages, and the right to elect their own check weighmen; it also established a board of conciliation. It failed, however, to grant union recognition. For a detailed story of the strike and negotiations, see Elsie Glück, *John Mitchell*, Chap. VI.

A. Union Structure

First in order of interest was the question of trade union structure. Prior to 1900 the unions were so small and there were so many unorganized workers that there seemed no reason to worry about boundaries. In issuing charters the A. F. of L. gave only casual consideration to possible future jurisdictional conflicts between unions. The Executive Council often recognized craft lines where differentiation in skill was hard to find and marked off minute craft subdivisions. Many of the unions chartered were based on such fine craft distinctions that a high mortality rate and increased liability to jurisdictional disputes with the larger and more successful unions were inevitable.[13]

Even during the period before 1899 the procedure of the Federation caused some friction. Matters became serious when the A. F. of L. entered its period of rapid growth. As one national union after another was organized, the area of free organizing became more and more limited. The problem of jurisdictional limitations was further complicated by changes in materials, tools, and industrial processes. From 1899 on jurisdictional disputes absorbed more and more of the time of the A. F. of L. conventions.[14]

In 1899 the craft unions sought to entrench themselves behind a resolution introduced by James O'Connell, president of the Machinists' Union, guaranteeing to each craft absolute self-government and complete jurisdiction over its members wherever employed. In

[13] Of the 69 national unions chartered between 1899 and 1904 from local trade and federal labor unions, only 37 survived after 1904.

[14] For further discussion of the character and extent of jurisdictional disputes, see pp. 341-44.

1900, however, further experience with jurisdictional fights produced a reaction, and the A. F. of L. convention of that year urged that narrow conceptions of autonomy be abandoned and that disputes be settled through amalgamation. The convention also instructed the Executive Council not to grant charters in the future without a clear definition of jurisdiction.

The attempt to reconcile opposing trends resulted in 1901 in the so-called Scranton Declaration. This declaration modified the O'Connell resolution of 1899 by recognizing the exceptional cases in which workers should be enrolled in the "paramount" organization in the industry; by recommending the alliance and federation of kindred crafts; and by suggesting the possibility of amalgamations, though qualifying this suggestion by referring to all deviations from craft principles as perhaps temporary and by rejecting the use of compulsory methods for their enforcement.[15]

[15] In view of the importance of this declaration, its main sections are reproduced here in full:

1. As the magnificent growth of the A. F. of L. is conceded by all students of economic thought to be the result of organization on trade lines, and believing it neither necessary nor expedient to make any radical departure from this fundamental principle, we declare that as a general proposition the interests of the workers will be best served by adhering as closely to that doctrine as the recent great changes in methods of production and employment make practicable. However, owing to the isolation of some few industries from thickly populated centres where the overwhelming number follow one branch thereof, and owing to the fact that in some industries comparatively few workers are engaged over whom separate organizations claim jurisdiction, we believe that jurisdiction in such industries by the paramount organization would yield the best results to the workers engaged therein, at least until the development of organization of each branch has reached a stage wherein these may be placed, without material injury to all parties in interest, in affiliation with their national unions. Nothing in this declaration is intended or shall be construed as a reversal of any decision rendered by former Executive Councils or previous conventions on questions of jurisdiction.

The resolution, however, did not decrease the friction between unions. In 1903 the Executive Council reported upon some 30 cases, a large proportion of which had to be reviewed by the convention. Gompers complained that there was scarcely an affiliated organization which was not engaged in a dispute with one or more other unions and that the bitter inter-union wars were hurting innocent employers. He warned that unless they changed their course, the unions would destroy one another.

To some extent the Executive Council was responsible for this situation. Its policy was a vacillating one. Only when unions threatened to stop paying per capita taxes to the Federation unless their wishes were complied with did the Executive Council attempt a firmer stand. Also, the Council was less liberal in interpreting the Scranton Declaration than the conventions, the latter showing greater readiness during these years to modify the principle of craft autonomy.

In the conflict over the jurisdictional issues, the unions of the cigarmakers, printers, plumbers, metal polishers, molders, and some smaller unions which feared absorption by the larger ones, clung to craft ideas. The officers of the Federation—Gompers, Morrison, Lennon, and O'Connell, supported them. The opposition consisted

---

2. We hold that the interests of the trade union movement will be promoted by closely allying the subdivided crafts, giving consideration to amalgamation and to the organization of district and national trade councils to which should be referred questions in dispute, and which should be adjusted within allied crafts' lines.

3. The A. F. of L., being a voluntary association, cannot and should not adopt methods antagonistic to or in conflict with established trade union laws, and in order to carry out the above recommendations, and in full recognition of its logical position, the A. F. of L. pledges its officers to aid and assist in the adjustment of such craft encroachments as disputants may be willing to submit to its arbitrament.

of the unions which had been forced to adopt broader methods of organization and included such groups as the miners, the brewery workers, longshoremen, and hod-carriers. These had the support of the socialists.[16] The constituents of the two groups, however, were not always guided by the general attitude of their group. The carpenters, for instance, at times supported amalgamation merely because of a desire to grow at the expense of other unions.[17]

B. Organizing the Unskilled

Closely related to the question of jurisdiction was the problem of handling the unskilled worker. During the depression of 1893-96, when the Knights of Labor were definitely out of the picture and unskilled laborers were applying for skilled jobs and acting as strike-breakers, the A. F. of L. began to claim an interest in the unskilled. In 1897 Gompers called the attention of the A. F. of L. convention to the fact that "the artisan of yesterday was the unskilled laborer of to-morrow," having been displaced by "the invention of new machines and the division and subdivision of labor." During the following years the A. F. of L. repeatedly declared that its task was to organize not only the skilled craftsmen, but the unskilled workers as well.

The Federation undertook to organize the unskilled workers in three ways: in trade and federal labor unions; in existing craft unions by virtue of the employment of the unskilled as helpers to craftsmen; and in some international unions whose membership consisted primarily of the unskilled.[18] Through these three channels

[16] Some claimed it was an alignment of Irish against Germans.

[17] See Appendix B, 508-09.

[18] Such were the Building Employees' International Union, the Cement Workers' Union, the Hod-Carriers and Building Laborers' Union, and

a stream of unskilled labor poured into the Federation between 1899 and 1904, but it was not large enough to offset the dominance of the skilled. The more important place in this scheme was assigned to the local trade and federal labor unions, which were expected to gather in the largest number of the unskilled.[19]

These unions, however, suffered from a confusion of thought and purpose which could not but cause friction. They were regarded both as a haven of refuge for unskilled workers and as a recruiting ground for trade unions generally. Skilled and unskilled were thrown together pell-mell. Every now and then blocks of workers were withdrawn to form special craft unions. Thus they were prevented from developing a sense of cohesion, without which they could not hope to further the interests of the unskilled.

Discontent among federal labor unions came to the fore at the 1901 convention. They demanded that they be allowed fuller representation at conventions, that they be given a greater return for dues paid into the Federation, that greater efforts be made to organize unskilled workers. There was also some agitation for a separate international union of laborers, and two attempts to form such a union were made in 1901 by seceding locals. The leaders of the Federation took energetic steps to thwart this movement and refused to make any changes in the voting system of the federal unions. Only on one point did they meet the federal unions even partially. The 1902 convention voted to establish a defense fund for strikes and lockouts, for the sole use of the federal unions, by setting aside five

---

the Union of Maintenance of Way Employees, which were organized in 1903 and 1904.

[19] For organization of these unions, see Chap. XII.

cents per member per month from dues paid by these unions.

Another phase of the same problem was that of the colored worker. In 1900 the question of accepting negro helpers and laborers in Southern local unions became acute. Gompers recommended organizing them into separate federal labor unions, and the suggestion was incorporated into the A. F. of L. constitution. Since Southern city centrals objected also to seating delegates from negro locals, the A. F. of L. authorized the formation of negro city centrals, if there were enough local unions of colored workers.[20]

C. Strikes and Boycotts

No less important were the issues regarding union strategy. The affiliated unions agreed that the A. F. of L. should render financial aid in strikes. The question, however, was how extensive it should be and what form it should take. The unions opposed a central strike fund, which Gompers favored. In 1899 the leaders of the Federation succeeded in having a new article incorporated in the constitution, providing for a voluntary defense fund. Organizations having contributed five cents per member per month for one year were to be eligible to receive aid from it. But the delegates from the larger international unions opposed even so slight a degree of centralized power, and as a result the fund was discontinued in 1900. To offset financial weakness, suggestions for altering the strategy of striking were made from time to time. The most serious demand was for

[20] The division of identical crafts between two organizations was never countenanced by the A. F. of L. except when the race issue was raised.

sympathetic strikes or for mass strikes by workers in related industries.[21] But these ideas ran counter to the principle of the sanctity of trade agreements.

The A. F. of L. was partially successful in its efforts to control boycotting. In 1899 Gompers warned labor to use the boycott with fairness and discretion, lest the weapon become both ridiculous and useless. Accordingly the convention of that year disapproved of boycotts conducted by local unions without A. F. of L. sanction, and adopted a recommendation that only boycotts endorsed by the Executive Council of the A. F. of L. be supported by the workers. Between 1899 and 1904 the Executive Council exercised an increasing influence in the conduct of boycotts. The Federation endorsed the principle of the label and issued appeals to workers to buy label-marked goods. But it discouraged the "universal" union label which was demanded by some unions.[22]

D. Politics and Socialism

During 1899-1904 there continued within the A. F. of L. political differences between the adherents of the two main political parties; the dissenters in sympathy with third party movements; and the socialists. The Socialist Party, organized in 1901 as a rival of the Socialist Labor Party, condemned the methods of De Leon, and set itself to winning the trade unions by co-operation, persuasion, and patience.[23] At the New Orleans convention of 1902, the socialists almost imposed upon the A. F. of L. a resolution to the effect "that the A. F. of L. advise the working people of America to organize their economic and political power to secure for labor the full

[21] For further discussion, see Chap. XIII.

[22] See Chaps. XIII and XIV.

[23] See M. Hillquit, *A History of Socialism in the United States.*

equivalent of its toil." This resolution was defeated by a vote of only 4,899 to 4,171. The narrowness of the margin made a deep impression. For a year after, the resolution of 1902 was cited as proof of the growing leaning of the A. F. of L. to socialist doctrines.[24]

Encouraged, the socialists brought to the Boston convention of 1903 resolutions for the public ownership of the means of production and for supporting only those political candidates who demanded for the workers the full product of their toil. The Committee on Resolutions reported unfavorably on them.[25] The contest for the election of president was also lost. Ernest Kreft, the socialist candidate, received only 1,236 votes against 12,449 for Gompers.

Impressed by this experience, the socialists changed their tactics. At the 1904 convention they were quite willing to drop definite commitment to socialist doctrines and only urged trade unionists to study economic conditions. Max Hayes, one of the leading socialist delegates at A. F. of L. conventions, declared that the socialists had come to realize that socialism would win not by passing resolutions, but by agitation. If the union doors were only kept open to study and discussion, the workers would reach conclusions favorable to socialism.[26]

[24] As a matter of fact the large vote at New Orleans was due to the support of the delegates from the United Mine Workers, the carpenters, and brewery workers, who cast 1,855, 799, and 291 votes respectively.

[25] The socialists in the galleries staged a noisy demonstration. Gompers ordered the galleries cleared, and Mitchell rebuked the socialists for trying to dictate to the unions.

[26] The discussion degenerated into the airing of personalities and in recriminations, but it had the effect of putting the socialists on the defensive for the time being. Victor Berger had published an article in his paper under the caption "Are They Traitors?" which he answered in the affirmative with regard to Gompers and Mitchell because they had dined with Charles W. Eliot and several bankers at the Exchange Club.

To hold together and to lead the medley of organizations which formed the A. F. of L., with their different trade interests, industrial experiences, methods of procedure, and attitudes of mind, called for shrewd and flexible leadership. Gompers supplied that leadership by following the line of least resistance. He insisted on uniformity of policy and centralized authority only where absolutely essential. He bent to the will of the strong international unions when inevitable. By assuring trade autonomy, he won the support of the majority of the union leaders, who thus were made secure in their own domains. This method of co-operation and compromise was the essence of the "Gompers' policies" which became the outstanding feature of the Federation.

CHAPTER IV

ATTACK AND COUNTER-ATTACK

The five years of growth in the life of the A. F. of L. were followed by as many years of strain and retrogression. Membership declined from 1,676,200 in 1904 to 1,482,870 in 1909. The industrial depression, anti-union employers, and internal friction put the A. F. of L. on the defensive, forcing it to make several important changes in structure and policy.

I. EMPLOYERS' OFFENSIVE

Most serious in its effects was the widespread offensive of anti-union employers. As early as 1900 John Kirby, Jr. had organized a local association of manufacturers in Dayton, Ohio to fight the unions and succeeded in making Dayton an "open shop" city. Between 1901 and 1905 he helped to organize similar associations in Elmira, Akron, Columbus, Detroit, St. Louis, Indianapolis, and Chicago, and began agitation for a national association of employers.

Kirby's activities soon received support from another source. The National Association of Manufacturers, which since its organization in 1895 had been concerned with questions of trade expansion, was converted in 1903 by its president, David M. Parry, to a policy of belligerency against trade unions. While claiming that it was not opposed to organized labor as such, the Association declared against methods which were of the very essence of the trade unionism of the day.

Soon afterward the National Association of Manufacturers helped to organize the Citizens' Industrial Association of America, with a more inclusive membership. The methods of the latter for gaining adherents were realistic. An organizer would be dispatched into a city to prepare ground. A few employers would be interested and brought into a meeting to elect temporary officers. A general call would then be issued through the press. At the second meeting a committee to secure more members would be appointed and the merchants would be solicited. The patronage of the united business men would force the timid or the reluctant. If necessary, the purchasing power of the general public was mobilized, and if a merchant refused to join the association "to protect his city" and preferred instead "to obey the labor unions," the organizers were instructed to "let the public know it."[1]

A third foe of the unions was the American Anti-Boycott Association organized in 1902. In that year an especially effective boycott was being carried on by the United Hatters of America against several hat manufacturers in Danbury, Connecticut.[2] Two of these manufacturers, of whom D. E. Loewe was one, took the first step in organizing the American Anti-Boycott Association. Their first efforts met with little success. The employers were timid, reluctant, or indifferent. Daniel Davenport, a lawyer of Bridgeport, Connecticut, was employed to enlist members. He collected 27 manufacturers, representing 12 industries, for an initial meeting on September 18, 1902. By April 1903, 100 charter members had been secured, and field men were employed to enlarge the organization.[3]

[1] *The Square Deal*, Citizens' Industrial Association, Vol. I, No. 1, p. 1.

[2] See pp. 81-82.

[3] Walter Gordon Merritt, *History of the League for Industrial Rights.*

The three employers' associations gained membership mainly among the owners of small and medium-sized firms and factories. These employers reacted strongly against "trusts" and denounced trade unions as "labor trusts." The associations were more successful in the Middle and Far West where trade unionism was beginning to spread. Highly individualistic employers of the West emerged in a somewhat embittered mood from their first contacts with labor organizations. Western communities were especially susceptible to the tales of graft, violence, and union tyranny which spread out of Chicago and New York, where unions, especially those of building trades workers and teamsters, had from time to time obtained the whip hand and abused their powers.[4]

The grievances of the employers were the closed shop, the boycott, the limitations of the right to hire and fire, violence in strikes, alleged corrupt labor leadership, union rules restricting output, union opposition to machinery, and limitation of apprentices. The unions clung to these rules and "rights" and showed little interest in the employers' complaints. Experience with American industry did not indicate that employers, if left alone, would be concerned about the welfare of the workers. The working rules on which the unions insisted had evolved gradually, giving the workers some security of employment and assurance of human treatment. The na-

[4] These employers gained support from individualists in high position. It was in 1902 that President Charles W. Eliot of Harvard called a scab "a very good type of modern hero," and aroused vigorous protest from the A. F. of L. convention of that year. See *Report of the Proceedings of the Twenty-Second Annual Convention of the American Federation of Labor*, 1902, p. 157

tional unions tried to embody these rules in trade agreements in order to make them the accepted custom of the trade. The A. F. of L. sanctioned these rules as indispensable devices for which no equally effective substitutes were offered.[5] The Federation laid the blame for violence and graft on employers and their methods of combating unionism.[6]

In addition to the national employers' associations, several trade associations took the warpath against unionism. In 1901 the National Metal Trades Association broke with the Machinists' Union,[7] and in 1904 the National Founders' Association refused to deal with the Molders' Union.[8] In 1905 came the break between the National Erectors' Association and the Bridge and Struc-

[5] The A. F. of L. objected to the term "closed shop" and drew a distinction only between the union shop open to all organized workers and the non-union shop closed to union members.

[6] At the 1902 convention of the A. F. of L. a resolution was introduced to investigate the giving of bribes by employers and their acceptance by union officials. It was dismissed because the evil was said to be exceptional. For discussion of violence, see also pp. 102-05.

[7] In 1900 the National Metal Trades Association had entered into a national agreement with the Machinists' Union providing for the introduction of the 54-hour week within a year, for conciliation, and for the right of the employer to employ non-union as well as union members. When the time came to renew the agreement, the union demanded the same pay for the shorter week. The Association refused to negotiate on this point. Both sides charged bad faith, and the union called a general strike in May 1901 which was widely effective. The National Metal Trades Association then adopted a set of principles which became the standard program of the anti-union movement. Between 1906 and 1908 the Association helped its members to fight 157 strikes, spending over $169,000 for the purpose.

[8] The National Founders' Association had difficulty with the union owing largely to the complex nature of the industry, to the disparity in the size and financial strength of the plants, and to the competitive conditions in the trade. The annual conferences of the union and the employers' association between 1900 and 1904 made little headway in dealing with a number of vexatious questions concerning minimum wage rates, apprentices, and reduction of hours.

tural Iron Workers' Union[9] because of a strike against the American Bridge Company.

In each of these cases the union officials to some extent provoked the open shop attitude. Besides, the trade agreement was a new device, and the machinery for the adjudication of disputes was rudimentary. The unions were inclined to regard an agreement as a temporary stopping point and often did not hesitate to repudiate or break one in order to take advantage of a favorable situation. The A. F. of L. tried to inculcate the concept of the sanctity of agreements, but it was far from uniformly successful. On the other hand, employers had many ways of evading the terms of an agreement even if they did not break it formally and were often unyielding in negotiations over the interpretation of terms.

Drawn together by common interest, the employers' associations referred to above co-operated in their anti-union activities.[10] In 1907 the National Council for Industrial Defense for political and lobbying purposes was organized by the National Association of Manufacturers and became active in Washington. In the same year James Van Cleave, president of the Association, urged the raising of a large fund by employers to "free the country from industrial oppression" by the unions.

[9] The National Erectors' Association was composed of large firms, and the union called strikes against many of these firms in 1902, forcing them to unionize operations at one point after another. After a general strike against it, the American Bridge Company entered into a national agreement with the union which was to run from May 1, 1903 to Jan. 1, 1905, providing for a union shop, but forbidding sympathetic strikes.

[10] The men active in these organizations were James Emery, counsel for the National Association of Manufacturers; Marshall Cushing, legislative representative for the National Metal Trades Association; Walter Gordon Merritt and Daniel Davenport of the Anti-Boycott Association; and Walter Drew, counsel for the National Erectors' Association.

A spectacular phase of this anti-union campaign was the success of the Anti-Boycott Association in the Danbury Hatters' Case[11] and the Buck Stove and Range Company controversy. In the latter an injunction was obtained by the company against the officials of the A. F. of L. enjoining them from publishing the name of the company in the "We Don't Patronize List" and from doing anything else that might injure the business of the company.[12] This case attracted special attention because of the persons involved. James Van Cleave, president of the Buck Stove and Range Company, was president of the National Manufacturers' Association,

[11] In their attempt in 1902 to force the firm of Loewe and Company to sign a closed shop agreement, the United Hatters had instituted a strike followed by a very effective secondary boycott. The boycott was extensively advertised, and union organizers traveled about dissuading retailers and customers from buying the Loewe hats. By 1903 the company estimated that its net losses amounted to over $88,000. With the aid of the Anti-Boycott Association, the company filed suit for damages under the Sherman Act. The Circuit Court dismissed the complaint. Financed by the Anti-Boycott Association, the company appealed to the Supreme Court of the United States, which on Feb. 3, 1908 handed down a unanimous decision declaring the boycott an illegal restraint of trade, under the *common law*, and also within the meaning of the Sherman Act. Two years later the Circuit Court assessed damages amounting to $232,000 against the United Hatters. The individual members of the union were held liable and their property attached. The Supreme Court upheld this proceeding in 1915, reiterating its earlier decision that the boycott violated the Sherman Act.

[12] The defendants were the A. F. of L., its officers, and the Molders' Union. Gompers, Morrison, and Mitchell were sentenced to jail for contempt of court, for giving publicity to the boycott in the *American Federationist*, and for entertaining motions relating to the boycott at conventions of the A. F. of L. and the United Mine Workers after the injunction was issued. The officers of the Federation endeavored to contest this case on the grounds that it was an infringement of the constitutional right of freedom of speech and of the press. However, before the issue could be fought to a finish, a change occurred in the management of the company, and the new management reached an amicable settlement with the Molders' Union and with the A. F. of L. The United States Supreme Court later dismissed the case on technical grounds.

while the persons enjoined were Gompers, Morrison, and Mitchell. It symbolized a pitched battle between capital and labor.

The anti-union employers' associations did not confine themselves to fighting trade unions by means of assisting financially in trade disputes, maintaining blacklists, giving joint support in litigation, or lobbying against measures sponsored by trade unions in Congress and in state legislatures. They also aimed to mold public opinion in favor of the open shop and indirectly to influence the attitude of upholders of the law and of the courts.

The need for public support caused the A. F. of L. to lean more upon the National Civic Federation. In a period when the very existence of unions was being attacked by employers, and when large struggles were precipitated which the A. F. of L. was powerless to support, the Civic Federation offered the useful possibility of warding off at least preventable struggles. It provided a forum to argue labor's case before what the labor leaders conceived to be a highly influential portion of the public.

That the Civic Federation could be used by the A. F. of L. for such purposes was due to certain differences of interest and opinion within the employing and middle-class groups themselves. In the first place, there were sectional differences. The National Civic Federation, despite its origin in Chicago, was largely an Eastern institution with headquarters in New York City. Of the 17 employer representatives on its Executive Committee in 1906, eight came from New York City, three from Boston, one from Philadelphia, and three from the Middle West. The same preponderance of New Yorkers existed among the representatives of the public. Secondly, there were differences in the occupations of the members. The National Civic Federation contained a large philanthropic and professional element—clergymen, editors, sociologists, professors of political economy. The men who both owned and managed their own businesses were in a minority. On the other hand, it contained many men of great wealth with large holdings and responsible positions in great corporations. Some were directors, vice-presidents, or general managers. It was often difficult to ascertain whether the capitalists represented philanthropists or captains of industry. Very often they acted, quite inconsistently, in the two capacities. The bankers and men in Wall Street, more remote from the scene of industrial struggles, seemed readier at times to concede, at least in general terms, the justice of organized labor's claims.

That Gompers, Mitchell, and other labor leaders over-estimated the value of repeated hearings before distinguished audiences of the Civic Federation cannot be disputed. They overlooked the twofold interests of the philanthropist-capitalist, and the ease with which responsibility for ultimate decisions could be shifted around among industrial and financial magnates and their subordinates. Furthermore, if open-mindedness towards trade unionism and benevolence towards employees were advocated by the Civic Federation, so was concern for the public interest. Labor and the public were continuously played off, one against the other.[13]

[13] At the time when he was president of the National Civic Federation, August Belmont, addressing a Civic Federation meeting, defended the rupture of relations between the Interborough Rapid Transit Company (over which he presided) and the Amalgamated Association of Street Railway Employees, on the grounds that the public interest could not tolerate interruptions of the service.

Indeed, allowing for differences in composition, geographic distribution, and ideas, a certain similarity can be detected between the National Civic Federation and the anti-union employers' associations. Both were protests against militant unionism, and against corrupt business unionism. The Civic Federation proceeded with more sophisticated or enlightened methods; but it was bent on pulling the teeth of aggressive unionism. It had no tolerance for the sympathetic strike or for the strategic strike which ignored contracts. It was concerned with settling strikes—and often settlements it applauded were disastrous to unionism.[14] It did not assist labor in organizing a single non-union industry, although large non-union interests were represented in it. This similarity in purpose, however, was over-shadowed by differences in method. The national employers' associations frequently assailed the National Civic Federation for allowing itself to be the cat's paw of organized labor.

II. THE CHALLENGE OF THE I. W. W.

The A. F. of L. was also subjected to a new attack by the radical labor forces, this time under the lead of the Western Federation of Miners. The latter, at loggerheads with the A. F. of L. since 1897, was further alienated by Gompers' connection with the National Civic Federation.[15]

The break between the two organizations was to a large extent the result of economic sectionalism. The hardy miner of the Rocky Mountain region, self-asser-

[14] For example, the stockyards strike in 1904 and the Interborough strike in New York in 1905.

[15] When Mark Hanna died in April 1904, Gompers acted as president of the Civic Federation until December 1904, when August Belmont was elected to the post. At the 1905 convention of the A. F. of L. a resolution censoring union officials for participation in the Civic Federation was rejected without debate.

tive and daring, impatient under restraint and violent in mood, skeptical of property rights in a country where riches were often the result of mere luck, and not much given to respect for the social distinctions of a settled community, was inclined to follow leaders with radical programs. Such leaders came to the fore in the industrial battles of the miners between 1893 and 1899. They supplied the Western Federation of Miners with the trinity of principles—industrial unionism, socialism, and class-conscious politics—which marked it off from the A. F. of L., and which drew a line between Eastern and Western unionism.

In 1902 the Western Federation of Miners had formed the American Labor Union with the idea of developing it into a rival of the A. F. of L. Early in 1905 the situation seemed propitious for a larger move. Unions were being attacked by employers' associations in various cities. In Chicago labor was aroused by the prolonged strikes of teamsters and packing house employees. Demands were made on Gompers to call a conference of all reform and trade union forces, in order to organize resistance. Gompers' refusal to take any steps on the ground that such a gathering might retard or imperil the trade union movement by irresponsible utterances aroused considerable irritation. Last, but not least, was the bitterness engendered by jurisdictional conflicts. The trouble between the A. F. of L. and the brewery workers was passing through a particularly acute stage, and there was much talk of a possible break.[16]

Spurred by these conditions, the Western Federation

[16] In 1903 the convention of the A. F. of L. ruled that the Union of Steam Engineers and the Union of Stationary Firemen should have jurisdiction over all members of their respective crafts wherever they were employed. The Brewery Workers' Union refused to relinquish the right to organize engineers and firemen working in breweries.

of Miners, the Socialist Trade and Labor Alliance, the Socialist Labor Party, the American Labor Union, and some members of the Socialist Party called an industrial congress which met in Chicago in June 1905 and launched the Industrial Workers of the World. The philosophy of this new organization represented an interesting synthesis of socialism, industrial unionism, and revolutionary tactics. Instead of the A. F. of L. motto of a "fair day's wage for a fair day's work," the I. W. W. inscribed on its banner the socialist watchword "abolition of the wage system." The preamble of the new organization declared that "the army of production must be organized, not only for the every-day struggle with capitalists, but to carry on production when capitalism shall have been overthrown." Convinced that the trade unions were no longer able to cope with the growing power of the employing class because they pitted one group of workers against another, the I. W. W.s declared for industrial unions. They advocated mass strikes on the principle that "an injury to one is an injury to all." By devising a scheme of organization which arranged all workers into 13 departments, grouped by industries or groups of industries, the I. W. W.s were sure that they were forging a more effective weapon for the wage battles of the workers, and that they were also "forming the structure of the new society within the shell of the old."

The forces which the I. W. W. gathered at Chicago appeared considerable, but were far from homogeneous.[17] Only a small number of A. F. of L. locals were represented. The I. W. W. did not attract a single international A. F. of L. union with the exception of the United Metal Workers, which had seceded from the A. F. of L. in 1904.

[17] There were 203 delegates representing 43 organizations claiming about 143,000 members. See Paul F. Brissenden, *The I. W. W.*, pp. 68-73.

Apart from the Western Federation of Miners, which under the able leadership of William D. Haywood, was a splendid fighting unit, the component elements of the I. W. W. were of minor account. The American Labor Union was a loose organization with a membership of some 16,000. The Socialist Trades and Labor Alliance, headed by Daniel De Leon, was little more than a name.

Though the A. F. of L. and its constituent unions had attained a fair degree of stability, Gompers and his associates felt that the I. W. W. was a potential menace. Its platform of industrial unionism might attract the two leading industrial unions in the A. F. of L., the Brewery Workers and the United Mine Workers. A number of locals of the United Mine Workers had sent delegates to the Chicago convention and had joined the I. W. W. The A. F. of L. was thus faced with the danger of dualism in one of its most important unions. Conditions were similar in a number of other unions where there were wavering elements.

For these reasons the A. F. of L. leaders launched a counter-attack. Gompers decried both the I. W. W. and the Western Federation of Miners. He denounced the promoters of the new movement as a group of socialists bent on disrupting the A. F. of L. He indiscriminately identified all socialists with the I. W. W. In vain did Max Hayes, representing the moderate socialists inside the trade unions, plead that no socialist would endorse the "revolutionary and almost unintelligible" preamble of the I. W. W. and that the majority of socialist trade unionists, like himself, were determined to remain loyal to the A. F. of L. Gompers refused to see any distinctions. Instructions were issued by the Executive Council to the constituent unions to fight the I. W. W.

III. RECOURSE TO NON-PARTISAN POLITICS

Declining membership, employers' offensive, increasing injunctions, and the menace of the I. W. W. forced the leaders of the A. F. of L. to reconsider the situation and to turn attention to the possibilities of political action. Their unsatisfactory record in the field of legislation[18] suggested the need of a new departure. Also, the spectacular success of the British trade unions in electing 52 labor members to Parliament in the general elections of December 1905 made a deep impression on American trade union leaders.

True to his policy of being both cautious and dramatic, Gompers summoned a conference of the executive heads of the international unions to meet in Washington in March 1906 to consider ways and means for obtaining legislation favorable to labor. At this conference a Bill of Grievances was drawn up, for presentation to the President, the Senate, and the Speaker of the House. Complaint was made against the failure of the government to enforce the eight-hour law, to restrict the manufacture and sale of products made by convict labor, to grant relief from "the constantly growing evil of induced and undesirable immigration"; against violations of the Chinese Exclusion Law; and against misuse of the writ of injunction and of the Sherman Anti-Trust Act.

A program was formulated demanding labor legislation and large economic and political reforms. The main industrial demands were: sanitary inspection of shops, mines and houses; one day's rest in seven; abolition of the sweat shop; liability of employers for injury or loss of life; limitation of the use of injunctions in labor dis-

[18] Between 1900 and 1905 no important labor laws were enacted by Congress.

putes; eight hours and prevailing wage rates on government work; abolition of the contract system on public work. The general demands were for child labor laws in all the states; free schools and textbooks; playgrounds; the initiative, referendum, and recall; woman suffrage; municipal ownership of public utilities; nationalization of the telephone and telegraph; United States government postal savings banks; and issue of money by the government—free from manipulation by private bankers for gain.

The Bill of Grievances concluded: "We have waited long and patiently and in vain for redress. There is not any matter of which we have complained but for which we have in an honorable and lawful manner submitted remedies. . . . Labor brings these, its grievances, to your attention because you are the representatives responsible for legislation and for failure of legislation. . . . Labor now appeals to you, and we trust that it may not be in vain. But if perchance you may not heed us, we shall appeal to the conscience and the support of our fellow citizens."[19]

The A. F. of L. decided to wage its main fight on the issue of the injunction, and caused to be introduced into the House of Representatives the Pearre bill, regulating the use of injunctions. Neither this bill nor any other labor-sponsored measures made progress, and so in July 1906 Gompers, O'Connell, and Morrison, as the "Labor Representation Committee" of the Executive Council, issued a circular to "organized labor and its friends" setting forth the political program of the A. F. of L. Central bodies and local unions were urged to

[19] *Proceedings of the 26th Annual Convention of the A. F. of L.*, 1906, p. 32.

formulate plans to further this program and to nominate candidates who would unquestionably stand for the enactment into law of labor and progressive measures. Wherever both parties ignored labor's legislative demands, a straight labor candidate was to be nominated. If a congressman or state legislator had proved himself "a true friend to the rights of labor" he was to be supported and no candidate nominated against him. This plan was justified by quotations from the decisions of the 1897 convention at which "the A. F. of L. most firmly and unequivocally" had favored "the independent use of the ballot by the trade unionists and workmen united regardless of party, that we may elect men from our own ranks to make new laws and administer them."

Throughout the summer of 1906 the *Federationist* printed the records of candidates. The Labor Representation Committee solicited funds and received a total of $8,056, of which $7,834 was spent. The efforts of the A. F. of L. centered particularly upon the defeat of Congressman Charles E. Littlefield of Maine, who had made himself peculiarly objectionable to labor.

After the elections Gompers claimed the results of the campaign had been "magical." Littlefield's margin had been appreciably cut. Labor questions had been discussed during the campaign as never before. The Republican majority in the House was reduced from 112 to 50. However, the House of Representatives, after the elections of 1906, turned out even less friendly to labor than before.

When the Labor Representation Committee began its campaign, the A. F. of L. appeared to be drifting into independent politics. But its officers assured the convention of 1906 that the policy pursued did not deviate from the political policy endorsed by the Federation in the past. The conventions of 1886, 1895, 1899, 1901, and 1902 were cited to prove the point. The policy was represented as an application of the principle of non-partisan political action. The convention was a bit uncertain on the subject. The Committee on the President's Report made a somewhat vague report on the question, recommending "independent voting, and the formation of such organizations outside the trade union as, in the judgment of the membership of each locality may be deemed most effective." Some delegates pressed for a more definite plan. Others tried to interpret this as a roundabout suggestion for the formation of a political labor party. The committee then overcame its hesitations and explained that there was no need for endorsing any particular plans, that they merely wanted to leave the unions free to do as they pleased. They non-concurred in the proposition to endorse any political party, or to form a new political party. This explanation was accepted by the convention. The principle of non-partisan politics, summed up in the dictum "to defeat labor's enemies and to reward its friends," received official sanction.

Thus the A. F. of L. once again took a definite stand against an independent labor party. The reason was the old fear of the disruptive effects of politics on trade unions. The limited funds which the Labor Representation Committee collected, the lack of interest on the part of many unions, the opposition of many union leaders connected with the regular parties—all tended to strengthen the hands of those opposed to labor politics. A no less potent reason was the fear of the A. F. of L. leaders of playing into the hands of the socialists.

A year later, in August 1907, came the injunction of the Buck Stove and Range Company against Gompers,

Mitchell, and Morrison, and in February 1908 the first United States Supreme Court decision in the Danbury Hatters' case. Organized labor throughout the country was aroused. Requests for energetic action poured into the offices of the A. F. of L. The Executive Council called a protest conference of union officers and of representatives of several farmers' organizations for March 16, 1908 in Washington. The conference drew up a "Protest to Congress," and an address to organized labor and farmers, warning them that organized labor was determined to defeat its enemies in the coming elections. The Executive Council then drew up a list of demands which were presented to the platform committees of the Democratic and Republican conventions. The chief demand was for an anti-injunction plank.

Though this plank was "moderate" in character, the Republicans had no use for it. Their candidate for the presidency, William H. Taft, was known in labor circles as the "father of injunctions" and was characterized by Gompers as "the injunction standard-bearer." The Democrats, on the other hand, interested in the labor vote, incorporated in their platform an anti-injunction plank approved by their candidate, William Jennings Bryan.

Gompers vigorously attacked the Republican platform and candidate. Though asserting that the trade unions must not interfere with the freedom to vote according to individual choice, he threw the weight of his influence and that of the Federation in favor of Bryan and the Democratic Party.

Though the Republicans were victorious in the elections, the psychological effect of labor's first entry into a national political campaign was considerable. The fact that the A. F. of L. acted as a practical ally of the

Democratic Party without causing serious internal dissensions[20] brought it into the political arena. It was a new factor to be considered by politicians and political leaders.

IV. FORMATION OF THE DEPARTMENTS

At this time the A. F. of L. was also trying to meet the issue of jurisdictional disputes and the challenge of the industrial unionists. Beginning with 1905 the Executive Council became more cautious in issuing charters. This was one of the reasons for the drop in the number of new international unions formed. Only 15 new internationals were chartered between 1905 and 1909. Many of these new unions, for example, the lobster fishermen's, steel-plate transferers', and composition roofers', covered small industrial subdivisions and were too highly specialized to promise much growth. At any rate, fewer unions meant less likelihood of overlapping and consequently a diminution in jurisdictional disputes.

The A. F. of L. also settled in a liberal way the several outstanding jurisdictional quarrels which had dragged on for over a decade.[21] But the greatest innova-

[20] There was only one serious conflict as a result of this policy. Daniel J. Keefe, president of the Longshoremen's Union, refused to stand for re-election on the Executive Council in 1908 because he had been a lifelong Republican. In his place John R. Alpine of the Plumbers' Union was elected. Keefe was soon afterwards appointed Commissioner of Immigration by President Taft.

[21] In 1905 the United Mine Workers were finally granted the right to organize all engine-room employees, and the charter of the Coal Hoisting Engineers, dating from 1899, was revoked. Above all, the bitter feud with the United Brewery Workmen was adjusted, though not without a violent flurry at the end. In June 1907 the Executive Council, exasperated by its failure to discipline the brewery workers, and acting on the authority of a resolution passed at the 1906 convention, revoked the charter of the brewery workers for refusing to relinquish the engineers and firemen. The move provoked a storm of protest; letters and resolutions poured in from the meetings of local unions

tion was the creation of departments. The idea was not new. Gompers himself had suggested it, in a more radical sense, as far back as 1888, when he was casting about for some method of making the A. F. of L. more effective.[22] During the nineties metal and building trades unions had tried joint action, resulting in the formation of local councils and national alliances. The unions in the building trades especially sought some form of more inclusive organization. In 1897 they had set up an International Building Trades Council which the A. F. of L. had refused to recognize because it trespassed upon the authority and rights of the national unions.

To meet the demands of the building trades unions, the A. F. of L. in 1902 created a special committee to handle all building trades disputes. This, however, did not satisfy the unions. In 1903 the largest and strongest of them, with the United Brotherhood of Carpenters and Joiners in the lead, established a Structural Building Trades Alliance to unite all the important unions in the industry for common action. Aside from the desire to aid one another in their struggles against employers, these large unions were hopeful of handling more expeditiously the numerous jurisdictional disputes which kept the unions in a state of turmoil.

For several years the Executive Council refused to

---

and central bodies all over the country. When the convention of 1907 met, Gompers himself and the cigarmakers' delegation of which he was a member had to move the unconditional restoration of the brewery workers' charter, and a new article was added to the A. F. of L. constitution, specifying that charters could only be revoked by the convention on a roll-call vote with a majority of two-thirds. The brewery workers' victory was complete a few years later when their jurisdiction over the engineers and firemen was recognized.

[22] See *Proceedings of the 3d Annual Convention of the A. F. of L.*, 1888, p. 14.

recognize this new-fangled body, but continued activities of the Alliance led Gompers to believe that it was safer to bring this organization within the A. F. of L. than to leave it outside. In 1907 he summoned a conference of building trades unions which evolved a general plan for uniting all the unions in the industry into a Building Trades Department. The latter was to have as its main function the settlement of jurisdictional disputes. It was to occupy a properly subordinate place in the A. F. of L. and work in harmony with the Executive Council. At the 1907 convention of the A. F. of L. the plan was approved. On March 20, 1908 the Building Trades Department was chartered by the A. F. of L. In the course of the same year the Federation chartered the Metal Trades' Department. Early in 1909 two more departments were added—the Railway Employees' Department and the Union Label Department.[23]

[23] For a discussion of departments, see Chap. XIV.

CHAPTER V

SOCIAL JUSTICE AND "MAGNA CHARTA"

From 1909 to 1914 the A. F. of L. experienced a second period of growth though not so marked as that of 1899-1904. It profited by the "quest for social justice" which characterized these years and by the remarkable awakening among new groups of workers which gave it not only more power but a larger social content. For the first time it achieved political success, its legislative efforts culminating in the passage of the Clayton Act—the "Magna Charta of Labor."

I. ECONOMIC DISHARMONIES AND SOCIAL REFORM

The larger trends in the Federation were part of the general expansion of social ideas and programs which produced the Progressive Party, swept Woodrow Wilson into the White House, gave the Socialist Party the record vote of over 900,000 in 1912, and made the I. W. W. a name to conjure with from the Pacific Coast to New England.

The basic causes of these changes lay in the special characteristics of the economic development of these years. In contrast to the period of the seventies and eighties, the economic expansion of the first decade of the twentieth century did not flow so much from new inventions in basic processes, techniques, or methods of business management, as from changes in the size of the market and in price levels. Natural increase in population and unprecedented immigration created an enormous domestic market, and rising standards of living in Europe offered widening markets abroad. This expansion of demand—largely for the necessaries of life—made possible extensive application of the industrial inventions of previous decades, resulting in enlarged industrial operations and in a considerably increased physical volume of goods.

These developments, however, were marked by somewhat contradictory features. Easy markets, rising prices, and the large supply of cheap immigrant labor blunted interest in increasing productivity. While the total output of manufacturing industries showed large gains,[1] the output per worker increased but moderately. The level of efficiency in large sections of industry remained low, as evidenced by conditions in sweat shops, numerous small factories, mines, and on the railroads. Even "trustified" industries, after the first spurt of energy which eliminated excessive competition and risks, settled down to the easier pace made possible by tariff protection and quasi-monopoly.

Total national income increased considerably, but per capita income moved upward slowly.[2] Corporate earnings and savings grew, helping to squeeze out the "water" pumped into the stocks of big industry by the capitalization process of 1899-1902.[3] On the other hand, small and middle-sized businesses had to fight for a place in the sun of prosperity and their returns were neither always large nor certain. Though some groups increased their monetary and real wages, profiting by economic con-

[1] See Frederick C. Mills, *Economic Tendencies in the United States*, 1932, pp. 26, 290-91; Woodlief Thomas, "The Growth of Production and the Rising Standard of Living," *Proceedings of the Academy of Political Science*, July 1927, p. 7.

[2] W. I. King, *Wealth and Income of the People of the United States*, 1915, p. 129.

[3] Henry R. Seager and Charles A. Gulick, *Trust and Corporation Problems*, pp. 66ff.

ditions and union organization, wage earners as a whole increased their purchasing power very slightly. What gains were made in rates and in money earnings were counterbalanced by rising prices and higher living costs.[4] Considered in its totality, there was a growing concentration of income and wealth,[5] and this was accompanied by a growing concentration of industrial and financial power.

With the exception of a brief interval in 1912, the years from 1910 to 1914 were a period of recession and moderate business activity at best,[6] marked by a further accentuation of the features of the previous decade—slow progress in efficiency, rising costs of living, inequalities in distribution, large increase in unearned incomes, relatively slow improvement in the life of the workers, and centralization of wealth and industrial power in the hands of the few.

These economic trends began to affect social relations after the speculative enthusiasm of 1899-1902 collapsed with the "rich man's" panic of 1903.[7] The revelations of industrial and financial malpractices turned the investing public and the middle class generally against the industrialists and financiers. The benefactors of big industry

[4] See W. I. King, *The National Income and Its Purchasing Power*, 1930, p. 80; F. W. Jones, "Real Wages in Recent Years," *American Economic Review*, June 1917, p. 319; Henry Pratt Fairchild, "The Standard of Living," the same, March 1916; Paul H. Douglas, *Real Wages in the United States, 1890-1926*, pp. 581-86.

[5] King, *Wealth and Income of the People of the United States*, Chaps. IV and IX.

[6] See Victor S. Clark, *History of Manufactures in the United States, 1860-1914*, 1928, Vol. II, pp. 546-47; Willard Long Thorp, *Business Annals*, 1926, pp. 141-42.

[7] According to the *Wall Street Journal*, in October 1903 the securities of 100 principal industrial combinations showed a shrinkage from the top prices of 1899 and 1900 of $1,750,000,000, or 47 per cent of their total par value of $3,690,000,000. See Seager and Gulick, *Trust and Corporation Problems*, p. 63.

became the "malefactors of great wealth." President Roosevelt began to swing his "big stick" against the trusts,[8] and a host of "muckrakers" launched a moral attack against "big business" and its political allies.[9]

But it was the panic of 1907 followed by the depression of 1908 which brought matters to a focus. The stringency of credit, the numerous bankruptcies, the severe unemployment, the abrupt fall in the prices of railroad stocks, and the decline in the prices of industrials sharpened the lines of cleavage and created an atmosphere of conscious social antagonisms. What the muckrakers had harped on as individuals became the conviction of large elements of the people. Wall Street became the synonym of financial chicanery and "frenzied finance." The trusts assumed the form of ugly monsters crushing the people in their gigantic hands. The "money power" became an unseen clique playing with the destinies of the people for its own sordid ends. The politician was stamped as the servant of "special privilege" and as the corrupt agent of big business.

The reactions of the major groups of American society were along three main lines. The smaller employers,

[8] The Bureau of Corporations was created in February 1903, and the Department of Justice began dissolution suits against the Standard Oil Company, the American Tobacco Company, and several other combinations. In March 1904 came the decision whereby the Northern Securities Company (organized to combine the Northern Pacific and the Great Northern railroads) was dissolved. The "holding company" was thus put on the defensive.

[9] The campaign of the muckrakers began with the publication in 1902 of Ida Tarbell's articles on Standard Oil. It lasted several years, and among its most important products were Lincoln Steffens' *Shame of the Cities*, 1904; Thomas W. Lawson's "Frenzied Finance," *Everybody's*, Vols. XI and XII, 1904-05; Upton Sinclair's *The Jungle*, 1905; Ray S. Baker's "Railroads on Trial," *McClure's*, Vol. XXVI, 1905-06; and David Graham Phillips' "Treason of the Senate," *Cosmopolitan*, Vols. XL and XLI, 1905-06.

merchants, and their economic allies were reaffirmed in their faith in individual initiative, freedom of contract, and free competition as the safe guides in the helter-skelter of new forces. They remained optimistic about the opportunities of American life provided only the impediments of artificial monopoly were removed. But a growing section of the middle classes, unable to share this optimism, emphasized more and more the elements of scarcity in American life—vanishing frontiers, diminishing material resources, decreasing economic freedom, and limited individual opportunity. Salvation in their opinion could no longer be found in laissez faire, but must be sought in a new program based on concepts of public interest with such specific policies as conservation, governmental aid and regulation, and municipal ownership of public utilities. The third line was that of the socialists, who were breaking through the barriers that had confined them to the foreign settlements in American cities and were making converts among native and Americanized artisans and professional groups.[10]

What was less clear at the time was that in essence the reform forces of the day represented a movement to extend the content and meaning of American nationalism. The nation, cemented politically by the Civil War, aroused patriotically by the Spanish American War, was now to be harmonized socially through the greater equalization of its economic groups. This feature gave the reform movements their evangelical zeal. While deep un-

[10] As early as 1904 the magazines of the country carried articles on "the rising tide of socialism." Between 1904 and 1912 the socialist vote for Debs increased from 408,230 to 901,062. In 1912 there were 5 daily and 262 weekly socialist publications in the English language, and 1,039 socialists were holding municipal and state offices.

der the surface lay the economic contradictions which produced it, the political and social movement itself had its vision fixed on new harmonies, greater equalities, and social opportunities. National regeneration and a new social solidarity were opposed to "special privilege" and class egotism. Unmindful of the problems of productive efficiency,[11] the movement was inspired by faith in the possibilities of distributive justice and looked hopefully forward to a great rise in economic and social standards.

The re-drawing of social lines carried with it a new attitude towards labor. The muckrakers had already dwelt on the dark side of the workers' lot under the rule of big business, and on the human and moral value of the labor struggle. After 1910 the enemies of "special privilege" began visioning the worker as a brother victim of one and the same iniquitous system and lent their help to his cause. They stimulated the movement for labor legislation throughout the country. Workmen's compensation, minimum wage laws, and laws protecting women and children became the field in which they applied their energies and achieved significant results.[12] They also became interested in the immigrant and in his effects on American life. From the growing nationalist point of view, the "unassimilable" immigrant was an all-too-disturbing factor in the building of national consciousness and a new national unity. An anti-immigrant

[11] There were exceptions to this, for it was in 1909-10 that "scientific management" began to attract attention.

[12] By 1912 there were child labor laws in 38 states; laws limiting the hours of women in 28 states; eight-hour laws on public works in over half the states; and laws limiting the work day in hazardous occupations in more than 25 states. Workmen's compensation laws had been enacted in 21 states by 1913, and in that year 7 states passed minimum wage laws for women workers.

attitude developed which helped to strengthen the demand of organized labor for restrictive immigration. Thus wide elements of the middle classes showed a new interest in the life of the wage earners and in the struggles of the labor movement.

II. THE McNAMARA CASE

The value to the Federation of this growing social consciousness was made manifest in the famous McNamara Case in 1911-12. The case grew out of the long and bitter warfare between the American Bridge Company and the Bridge and Structural Iron Workers' Union. The latter was a union of some 10,000 members, highly skilled and "tough-minded," whose work called for much physical strength and involved considerable risk. At one time the union had a collective agreement with the employers.[13] When relations were discontinued, the officials of the union, despairing of their ability to bring the American Bridge Company to terms, resorted to a campaign of dynamiting against the American Bridge Company and other constructors. The campaign was directed from Indianapolis, the headquarters of the union, by John J. McNamara, the secretary of the union, who was assisted in the execution by his brother, James B. McNamara.

In October 1910 J. B. McNamara and his associates "pulled off" a job for someone whose identity has never been determined. They dynamited the Los Angeles Times Building and caused the loss of 21 lives. Los Angeles was at that time the center of a struggle directed by the Central Trades and Labor Council and involving the unions of printers and metal workers. The publisher

[13] See p. 80.

of the *Los Angeles Times*, Harrison G. Otis, had made himself nationally prominent as a leader in the open shop movement. After the explosion William J. Burns was retained by the Los Angeles authorities to solve the Times mystery. In April 1911 he had the McNamara brothers arrested. They were kidnapped by detectives and brought to Los Angeles for trial.

On May 6, 1911 the A. F. of L. issued a circular declaring it the duty of all trade unionists to come to the defense of the kidnapped men. The incident aroused a tremendous amount of excitement. To organized labor it symbolized an attack by corporate interests, backed by great wealth and influence, upon trade unionism. Bitterness engendered by the use of detectives, spies, *agents provocateurs*, and armed guards in many former struggles seemed to concentrate upon the figure of Burns arresting the McNamaras.

The Federation declared the defense of the McNamaras to be its major task. It engaged Clarence J. Darrow as chief counsel for the defense, and an appeal was issued to all organizations to contribute 25 cents per member. A number of union officers attended a conference on June 29 at Indianapolis, the scene of the kidnapping, and made a summary investigation of the facts in the case. As a result the McNamaras were exonerated by the trade union officials.

On July 27, 1911 Gompers wrote a circular letter accusing the National Association of Manufacturers, the Erectors' Association, the Citizens' Alliance, and a hostile press of seeking to fasten the blame upon labor without preliminary investigation. Affirming labor's devotion to lawful methods, he said: "If within the ranks of labor there are those who commit infractions of the law, then they should be punished." But he also asserted that "the organized labor movement believes the McNamaras innocent."

When the McNamaras confessed their guilt,[14] the press and a large part of the public put the blame on the entire trade union movement. Gompers protested and declared that, had he known the men to be guilty, he would not have collected the money for their defense.[15]

The main point, however, was that the question of violence in industrial struggles had been repeatedly presented to the Federation, but without results. While the A. F. of L. publicly opposed violent and terroristic tactics and blamed anti-union employers for whatever violence did occur in labor disputes, it gave no thought to the consequences of terroristic acts by individuals and made no real attempt to evolve methods of action which might make such violence unnecessary. At the time of the McNamara trial, the unions in the garment and other trades were formed to resort to "strong-arm" men to combat police difficulties and violence of gangs hired by employers. The situation called for a frank and courageous policy, not for evasion.

The McNamara case was a blow to the prestige of the Federation, and anti-union employers used it to justify their position.[16] The social spirit described above kept it from being more serious than it was. Also, the National Civic Federation came to the support of Gompers and

[14] For the circumstances under which this took place, see Louis Adamic, *Dynamite*, 1931; Clarence Darrow, *The Story of My Life*, 1932; and *The Autobiography of Lincoln Steffens*, 1931. Vol. II, pp. 658-89.

[15] See Samuel Gompers, *Seventy Years of Life and Labor*, Vol II, pp. 185-88.

[16] General Harrison Gray Otis received an ovation at the 1911 convention of the National Association of Manufacturers.

unanimously re-elected him one of its vice-presidents. Social reformers stressed the fact that the recourse to violence of conservative union officials, who were devout churchmen and respectable citizens, was a clear symptom of unhealthy industrial conditions.[17]

III. CHANGING UNIONS

Other factors which gave the labor movement its amplitude were the changes in the composition and character of the workers in American industry. The newer immigrants, who arrived here between 1904 and 1908, had been imbued with revolutionary and socialist ideas in Austria-Hungary, Italy, Poland, and Russia. After some temporary maladjustments they absorbed the American point of view, which meant to them a desire for higher economic standards and more humane consideration. They turned their eyes to the situation in America, which was becoming home to them, and became interested in making American industry a better place in which to work.

Both in the East and in the West large masses of workers in unorganized or little organized trades pushed forward for a new place in their respective industries. Mass strikes, aggressive in character and often violent in

[17] It was as a result of the conditions revealed by the McNamara case and of the general unrest that Congress in August 1912 authorized the creation of a commission representing employers, organized labor, and the public to make a thorough inquiry into industrial relations. Of the nine commissioners appointed by President Wilson, two—John B. Lennon and James O'Connell—were members of the Executive Council of the A. F. of L. The hearings held by the Industrial Relations Commission during 1913-14 did much to bring to public notice the grievances of the workers and the symptomatic significance of the I. W. W. The reports of the Commission, published in 1914 and 1916, were favorable to the A. F. of L. and its avowed policies, notably the trade agreement.

form, swept the country, led by workers tasting industrial strife for the first time. As no strike statistics were published for these years, the total number of strikes and strikers is unknown. But the scope and intensity of many of them, such as that of the New York "shirt waist girls" in 1909, the cloakmakers in New York, the men's garment workers in Chicago in 1910, the Lawrence textile workers in 1912, the coal miners in West Virginia, the Michigan copper miners in 1913, and the employees of the Colorado Fuel and Iron Company in 1914, bore the imprint of deep social revolts. The unrest spread to the workers already organized in the more skilled trades. Pressed by new immigrants and by employers unable to make economic concessions easily, and realizing the growing difficulties of rising from the wage-earning into the employing class, these skilled workers showed a greater readiness to make common cause with the unskilled and to try new ideas and methods.

The effects of these developments were spectacular. Small unions of a few thousand suddenly became large organizations with considerable funds and influence. The largest increases were registered in the newer unions affected by the industrial upheaval, largely among semi-skilled workers. In order to make room for new members, many of the older trade unions, such as the machinists' and the carpenters', liberalized their admission rules, lowered their initiation fees, and sought to broaden their jurisdictions. A number of unions reorganized on a wider trade and industrial basis.[18] The smaller and narrower craft unions lost heavily.[19]

[18] The International Ladies' Garment Workers' Union, for instance, as a result of the big strikes in 1909-10, became a semi-industrial or amalgamated union combining all the workers within the industry but allowing the separate crafts to retain a certain amount of craft autonomy.

[19] See Appendix A, pp. 476-83.

Concomitant with these changes in structure were efforts to experiment with new forms of collective bargaining, such as the preferential union shop in the garment trades, trade courts in the printing industry,[20] conciliation and arbitration in the building trades, and grievance committees in the anthracite coal mines. Many unions were demanding the formation of new departments,[21] and various proposals for more concerted action in strikes were made in the Metal Trades Department and in the Department of Railway Employees.[22] And owing to the general growth of progressive and socialist ideas, an increasing number of local unions, city centrals, and state federations were showing a keen interest in social legislation.

IV. CONCESSIONS AND RESISTANCES

The A. F. of L. and its leaders played a considerable part in these developments. They helped many groups of workers with advice, organizers, and money, gave guidance in difficult negotiations, and used their good offices to obtain a hearing for workers on strike or with a grievance.

A certain measure of the part played by the A. F. of L. is supplied by its expenditures for organizing work. The Federation spent $46,962 in 1911; $71,060 in 1912; $86,698 in 1913; and $79,713 in 1914. In the five years 1910-14 the total expenditures for organizing were $337,683 as compared with $286,717 for 1905-09

[20] The Printers' League, formed in 1909 by a group of firms which broke away from the Typothetæ, set up a trade court to settle disputes between employers and workers.

[21] In 1911 the Western Federation of Miners affiliated with the A. F. of L. and began negotiations with the United Mine Workers to form a Mining Department. The longshoremen called for the organization of a Transportation Department.

[22] See pp. 387-92.

and $222,854 for 1900-04. The number of organizers rose from 48 in 1910 to 77 in 1913. In 1914 a one-cent assessment, yielding $14,675, was levied to assist in organizing women workers, and $1,800 was appropriated in 1913 and 1914 for the National Women's Trade Union League[23] for the same purpose.

The Federation also made a number of concessions to the forces pressing for new policies. Though continuing to express disapproval of "industrial unionism" and to uphold the Scranton Declaration of 1901, it was more flexible with regard to structural changes. It gave a freer hand to unions seeking to be more inclusive, and granted many extensions in jurisdiction.[24] The term "trade autonomy" was interpreted more broadly so as not to interfere with amalgamations which were enforced more viggorously.[25]

In matters of labor legislation the A. F. of L. took a

[23] The National Women's Trade Union League was organized in November 1903 to assist in organizing women wage earners. Its membership included trade unions with women members and individuals who supported its objectives. The League was especially active in helping to organize the women in the garment trades during 1909-13.

[24] For instance, to the hod-carriers, over common labor employed in street construction; to the carriage and wagon workers over workers in the automobile industry; to teamsters over chauffeurs and stablemen; to the longshoremen over certain types of marine transport workers; to the carpenters over woodworkers in factories; to the Shingle Weavers' Union over all workers, skilled and unskilled, in the lumber industry.

[25] In 1912 the steamfitters were expelled for refusal to merge with the plumbers, while the Amalgamated Woodworkers were forced to join the Brotherhood of Carpenters. That the Federation was none the less dominated by a bias for the craft unions was shown by its handling of the jurisdictional dispute between the carriage and wagon workers and the blacksmiths. In 1912 the Executive Council granted to the Carriage Workers' Union complete jurisdiction over the automobile industry. The blacksmiths claimed the right to workers of their craft in the automobile plants. After some conferences proved futile, the Executive Council upheld the blacksmiths, despite the charter it had granted the carriage workers.

new step. After some hesitation on a curious compromise between employers' liability and workmen's compensation, it fell in line with the general movement for compensation laws.[26] It changed its attitude on the question of old-age pensions. In 1902 the Federation had rejected a resolution introduced by Victor Berger favoring such pensions. In 1909, and again in 1911, it endorsed the idea and likewise demanded a federal retirement law for all government employees. It also went on record in favor of minimum wage legislation and of laws limiting the hours of work of women and minors.

On the other hand, while making these innovations the A. F. of L. leadership was continuously on its guard not to go too far. Gompers talked about the "flexibility of trade unions" and their capacity to adjust themselves to changing conditions. But he was so anxious for the continued life of existing unions, so full of memories of past struggles, and so fearful of radicals and socialists that he put the burden of progress upon the very elements which he resisted. Most of the other leaders, especially the Executive Council, were even less flexible in sizing up new situations and in formulating new ideas and demands.

The resistance of the A. F. of L. to new policies and methods in the industrial field manifested itself especially in connection with issues involving the unskilled worker and strike tactics. Such issues played a prominent part in the events of these years and in the struggle of the Federation to maintain a middle position.

Among the unskilled workers most involved in the

[26] Between 1909 and 1912 commissions were appointed in a number of states to study the question, often with labor representatives. During these years 18 states enacted workmen's compensation laws.

social upheaval of these years were the migratory workers of the West, the unskilled iron and steel workers, and the workers in the textile industry.[27] In 1909 the need for organizing the farm hand and the migratory agricultural worker was urged on the A. F. of L. by several state federations and city centrals. This class of labor, it was claimed, seasonally came into competition "with almost every craftsman in the A. F. of L.," owing to the low degree of labor specialization in the small towns. The Federation, however, showed little disposition to do anything. For a number of years it had allied itself with organizations of farmers and tenant farmers, mainly with an idea of creating a rural market for union-label goods. It was now argued that a union of farm hands would antagonize the farmers. Inconsistently, it was also argued that the farm hands could join the farmers' organizations. Some of the delegates could not see much difference between farm hands and tenant farmers. Others thought the job of organizing them hopeless at the outset because of the isolation in which they lived.

A year later the same problem came up in a different way. A complaint was brought from Texas against the influx of Mexican labor and against inefficient handling of the situation by the A. F. of L. On motion of the Seamen's Union and of the United Laborers of California, the Executive Council was instructed to devise plans for organizing the migratory unskilled workers whose miserable condition in the harvest fields was described at length. Between 1911 and 1913 the Executive Council, urged by the conventions, mapped out a plan of campaign which placed most of the work to be done in the hands of the city centrals and state federations. The

[27] See Paul F. Brissenden, *The I. W. W.*, pp. 155-56.

A. F. of L. was to act as a clearing house for information. Such a plan required not only large funds but close co-operation between separate unions and the A. F. of L. headquarters. Since the workers to be reached were for the most part of a type which had not previously been organized, there were no unions within the A. F. of L. which had an immediate interest in supplying organizers and money. The plan never got beyond the state of discussion. The A. F. of L. thus passed over one of the situations which was fully exploited by the I. W. W.

The A. F. of L. had been called upon for over a decade to help the textile workers build a national union. In 1900 the Federation sponsored the amalgamation of several small unions into a single organization covering the entire industry, which became the United Textile Workers of America. While this union increased its membership from 3,400 in 1900 to 10,000 in 1912 it still had organized but a small fraction of the textile workers of the country. Time and again A. F. of L. organizers were instructed to assist, appeals were issued, and small assessments levied. But the other unions objected to giving one organization more aid than another. They also contended that the United Textile Workers should be able to finance its own strikes, although it was pointed out that high dues were impossible on account of low wages in the trade.

It was for these reasons that the A. F. of L. was crowded out by the I. W. W. in the uprising of the textile workers which began with the strike at Lawrence, Massachusetts in January 1912.[28] Before the strike was

[28] The strike was caused by a decrease in earnings as a result of the state law reducing the hours for women and children from 56 to 54 per week.

over on March 14 some 23,000 workers were involved. The A. F. of L. claimed to have endorsed and supported the strike, but its help was lukewarm and ineffective. The I. W. W. continued in control of the strike and enrolled between 10,000 and 14,000 members. Though this membership soon melted away, it was this strike that gave the I. W. W. an opportunity to play a larger role in the labor movement.

Another issue was the demand of the more radical elements in the unions for more aggressive strike tactics. There were two questions involved, namely, financial assistance and joint action in strikes. In 1909 and again in 1914 the subject of a central defense fund was brought up. At the 1914 convention the committee appointed in 1913 to report upon ways and means for improving co-operation in strikes and lockouts presented a plan empowering the A. F. of L. to levy a per capita tax and to distribute the proceeds to aid national unions in strikes and lockouts. Only a few international unions, however, felt disposed to grant such extensive power to the A. F. of L. Objections were raised that the tax would be difficult to collect, that the per capita tax should be reduced, not raised, and that unions should be able to finance themselves.[29] After hearing this report the convention decided to take no further action in the matter.

V. THE CONTEST FOR CONTROL

The changes and the resistance to them described above were accompanied by an internal struggle in the Federa-

[29] The only unions of any size which supported this plan were the Brewery Workers, the United Mine Workers, the Western Federation of Miners, the Hod-Carriers, Iron and Steel Workers, and the International Ladies' Garment Workers. Gompers at this convention favored endowing the A. F. of L. with more power to obtain better cooperation in strikes.

tion between anti-socialist and socialist groups. The latter supported most of the moves for increased centralized power, for more joint action in industrial struggles, and for social legislation. The Executive Council and the officers of many of the unions consistently opposed them.

The influence of the socialists was considerably enhanced by the changes in the composition of the A. F. of L., and it seemed to them that the time was ripe for another attempt to wrest leadership. In 1911 they introduced into the Atlanta convention a resolution that all officers of the Federation be elected by referendum and initiative, instead of by the convention. The assumption was that the conventions were packed by conservative officials, while the rank and file were alive to new ideas and consequently more socialistic in sentiment. The convention instructed the Executive Council to inquire into the feasibility of such a method of election and the attitude of the trade unionists toward it.[30]

The Executive Council in 1912 circulated a questionnaire among member unions. The replies were filled out by the chief executives and secretaries of the unions. In

[30] The 1911 convention also witnessed an attack by the radical forces on the officers of the Federation for their participation in the National Civic Federation. A resolution of censure introduced by the delegate from the Illinois State Federation of Labor was supported by the delegates of the United Mine Workers. Participation in the Civic Federation was defended, partly on the grounds that each trade union official should be free to act as he pleased in joining associations, and partly on the grounds that it was a service to the labor movement to carry its message into gatherings of employers. After a warm debate the resolution was defeated by a vote of 4,924 to 11,851. As a matter of fact, by 1911 the National Civic Federation had ceased to play an important part in industrial disputes. From 1907 to 1914 it had become more interested in industrial welfare work. It may be noted that John Mitchell, who had left the presidency of the United Mine Workers in 1908 and had become head of the Conciliation Department of the National Civic Federation, resigned from the latter position in 1911 rather than give up his membership in the United Mine Workers.

many cases an expression of opinion from the conventions was not secured. The information thus represented mainly the attitudes of the officials. Thirty-four unions reported electing their own officers by referendum vote, but only 23, representing 508,119 members, favored introducing that system into the A. F. of L. Opposed were 52 unions with 890,240 members. Thirty-seven international unions with 331,787 members did not express any opinion.

On the basis of this report, the Executive Council advised against introducing the referendum and initiative into the Federation. A lengthy debate followed at the convention of 1912. The United Mine Workers and Western Federation of Miners were insistent on the change. William Green made a plea for it. Gompers also supported it, most likely for tactical reasons, for he was accused of secretly working against it. The Committee on Resolutions headed by John P. Frey rejected the proposal on the grounds of expense, difficulty of securing a fair count of ballots, and clumsiness, saying that it would afford the socialists a chance to stir up trouble and that a majority of unions had already decided against it. The report was carried by a vote of 193 to 57. This action was interpreted as a defeat for the socialists.

Undaunted, the socialists for the first time since 1903 put up one of their leaders, Max Hayes, to contest the presidency with Gompers. On the roll-call they obtained 5,073 votes, or 27 per cent of the total votes in the Federation, compared to 11,974 for Gompers. The cleavage was not entirely consistent. Many delegates from socialist unions voted for Gompers, while Hayes obtained some non-socialist votes.

In 1913 another effort to remove Gompers from office was launched Both the part which he played and the part which he failed to play in the events of the day caused irritation. The I. W. W. attacked him bitterly. Radical intellectuals, imbued with the social ferment of the times, denounced him as a hindrance to social progress. Many elements within the A. F. of L. unions were impatient with his policies and leadership.[31]

The plan was to replace Gompers by John Mitchell on condition that Gompers would consent voluntarily to retire to the post of honorary president and editor of the *American Federationist.* But Gompers, in spite of his 63 years, was determined to remain active, and Mitchell refused to oppose him. Mitchell did not feel that important enough issues were at stake. He had fought for industrial unionism for the miners, but did not wish to impose it on other organizations. He had a friendly feeling for the socialists, but, like Gompers, did not wish to see the labor movement made the tail of a political kite.[32] Gompers was re-elected unanimously in 1913.

That the socialists were unable to break through the Executive Council was shown also in connection with the contest of William H. Johnston against James O'Connell. Johnston was a leading socialist and president of the International Association of Machinists. Still, he polled only 6,171 votes against 10,858 for O'Connell in 1912, and about the same number in 1913. The Executive

[31] At the 1913 convention of the United Mine Workers, President Moyer of the Western Federation of Miners charged that the Executive Council of the Federation had been appealed to twice to help in the Michigan strike, and both times had refused to levy even a small assessment to help defray the expenses of $30,000 a week which the union was incurring to maintain the strikers. In the course of his speech Moyer called the Executive Council "reactionary, fossilized, worm-eaten, and dead."

[32] See Elsie Glück, *John Mitchell*, pp. 248-49.

Council continued to represent the group of unionists close to Gompers.[33]

VI. THE CHARTER OF INDUSTRIAL FREEDOM

The desire to steer a course as near as possible to the old paths often made the Federation appear weak when faced with the industrial situations of 1912-14. Social unrest was at its peak. The I. W. W. were experiencing a revival and were carrying on strikes in the East and in the Far West, involving lumber, textile, and cannery workers, farm and dock laborers, and even some skilled groups. The strikes in Lawrence, Paterson, and in the hop fields of California were attracting wide public interest. Intense struggles were being fought in the copper mine regions of Michigan,[34] and in the coal fields of West Virginia. In Colorado pitched battles between striking miners and armed guards of the mining companies created a state of civil war.[35] The indignation of large elements in the labor movement was fanned to white heat and brought conditions in the coal mines of Colorado, including those in the Colorado Iron and Fuel Company, into public view. In a number of unions the rank and file were restless and were breaking down the ma-

[33] From 1905 to 1912 there were two minor changes in the personnel of the Council. In 1913 John Mitchell retired, and the other vice-presidents were advanced in rank. John P. White, president of the radical United Mine Workers, was elected to the eighth, or last, place. White refused it because he wanted Mitchell's place as second vice-president. The deadlock was broken a year later when William Green, then secretary of the United Mine Workers, became eighth vice-president.

[34] The strike against the Calumet and Hecla Mining Company in July 1913.

[35] During one of these battles the tents occupied by the miners evicted from the company houses caught fire. A number of women and children, as well as miners, trapped by the flames and the armed guards, lost their lives. This is known as the "Ludlow Massacre."

chinery of collective bargaining.[36] The disturbances created by increasing unemployment due to the depression of the winter of 1913-14 added to the general discontent.

Despite this unrest the headquarters of the A. F. of L. were slow in acting. In the report of the Executive Council to the 1912 convention the major strikes of the year were not mentioned. In 1913 and 1914, however, the Federation was instrumental in obtaining congressional investigations into conditions in the mines of West Virginia and Michigan. Also, Gompers may have been responsible for President Wilson's intervention in the coal strike in Colorado. But the leaders of the Federation responded only under the pressure of the international unions.

One of the reasons for this lack of vigor in the industrial field was the increasing interest of the Federation in politics and legislation. With the election of Woodrow Wilson and a Democratic Congress in 1912, the Federation began its lobbying activities with new hope. In the House of Representatives, W. B. Wilson, formerly secretary of the United Mine Workers, became chairman of the House Committee on Labor, which included three other trade unionists. In 1913 the Department of Labor was created, and Wilson was made secretary.

The climax of the Federation's legislative victories came in October 1914 with the passage of the Clayton Act. At last Congress had heeded Labor's Bill of Grievances, presented in 1906. The Act was intended to give the Federation what it had demanded since 1895, and

[36] The situation which became of more than local interest was the revolt against the protocol in the cloakmakers' union in New York. See Louis Levine, *The Women's Garment Workers*, Chap. XXVI.

increasingly so since 1906; namely, regulation of the issue of writs of injunction in labor disputes, and freedom of unions from the application of the Sherman Anti-Trust Act.[37]

The Federation had been made to realize the full significance of the situation between 1902 and 1907 in the three famous cases of the Danbury Hatters, the Buck Stove and Range Company, and the Hitchman Coal and Coke Company.[38] As injunctions multiplied and court

[37] Injunctions in labor disputes were then, as now, issued by courts both state and federal under the equity power to protect property against imminent and irreparable injury. The employer in presenting his bill of complaint usually alleges that the defendants have formed a conspiracy to injure him. Federal courts assume jurisdiction in labor cases, either because of diverse residences of the parties, or because of an alleged violation of a federal statute. The statutes which have been made use of are the Interstate Commerce Act, the law regulating the transportation of mails, and the Sherman Anti-Trust Act. Under the Sherman Act the right to sue for an injunction was reserved to the government. But private parties could sue for an injunction, charging a conspiracy to interfere with interstate commerce. This Act, however, had its value to individual employers, for persons sustaining injuries as a result of actions declared unlawful might sue those committing such acts for triple damages. Thus, if a trade union could be proved guilty of a "contract, combination, or conspiracy in restraint of trade or commerce," an employer who was injured by this combination or conspiracy could deplete the union's treasury and even collect from individual members of a union.

[38] For the first two cases see above, pp. 81 and 82. The last case arose when in September 1907 the United Mine Workers sent organizers into West Virginia to organize employees who had been tied to the Hitchman Company by individual contracts, pledging non-membership in the union. A federal court issued an injunction. In the bill of complaint it was alleged that the union was attempting to monopolize labor in violation of the Sherman Act. On Dec. 23, 1912 the circuit court issued an opinion in which it both made the injunction permanent and held that the United Mine Workers was an unlawful organization within the terms of the Sherman Act. It assigned considerable weight to evidence tending to show that the union had entered into a compact with the operators of the Central Competitive Field to unionize West Virginia, not for the benefit of labor in the West Virginia mines, but solely for the purpose of destroying West Virginia's interstate trade for the benefit of the unionized competitive states.

decisions—many of them contradictory—followed one another, the legal status of unions and of collective action became more and more uncertain. Few unions had the resources necessary to put each case to the ultimate test of the Supreme Court of the United States. They were more or less at the mercy of the lower courts. Higher courts might settle the legality of certain actions years later, but that did not prevent strikes from being lost and organization work from being hampered by injunctions which were later to be set aside. The expense of even successful litigation was prohibitive. The Buck Stove and Range case cost the A. F. of L. over $100,000. Also, there was the danger that officials might be sent to jail. The sentences imposed on Gompers, Mitchell, and Morrison hung over their heads for several years. These men did not see any particular glory in going to jail for a cause. They regarded themselves as thoroughly respectable American citizens, and imprisonment to them was "horrible" and morally revolting.

Between 1906 and 1914 a number of bills to which the Federation gave its approval were introduced into Congress for the purpose of limiting the use of injunctions in labor disputes. The fight of the Federation against the injunction and the Sherman Act was premised upon a belief that the courts were usurping powers without legal sanction and were placing a construction upon the Sherman Act which its framers had not intended.[39] The leaders of the Federation maintained that the acts which were enjoined and punished were normally legal and inherent in the Constitution and in the common law.

[39] As to the intent of the framers of the Sherman Act, see A. T. Mason, *Organized Labor and the Law*, 1925; Edward Berman, *Labor and the Sherman Act*, 1930, pp. 3-54.

As a matter of fact, the union activities whose legality was well established included the right to organize (that is, the right of unions to exist and function) and the right of employees to strike against their own employer for objects which would yield direct and immediate advantage to themselves. But the legality of strikes called by a union to unionize unorganized shops, or to force discharge of non-union operatives, was not so well established. The right to withhold patronage, the primary boycott, had only rarely been questioned; but the secondary boycott had been banned by both state and federal courts.[40] The right to picket in strikes and boycotts was widely accepted; but violence, threats, coercion, intimidation, insults, and warnings were all condemned by federal courts in cases arising before 1914.

Many of the acts interfered with contributed indirectly but powerfully to building up union strength and improving the condition of union workers. In fact, prior to 1914, the sympathetic strike, the organizational strike, and the secondary boycott were weapons too necessary to the unions to be relinquished. These were very unpopular among employers and the public. Some of them conflicted with the principle of the sanctity of contracts which the Federation itself cherished. But individual unions insisted on using them, and the A. F. of L. hesitated to take a definite stand. At times it condemned them, at times it defended them in lukewarm and ambiguous terms, but at no time was it prepared to fight for their legalization by statute.

The Clayton Act was the result of a political compromise by which several bills were amalgamated. Its two famous labor clauses were Sections 6 and 20. Section 6

[40] For discussion of boycotts, see pp. 364-66.

contains the introductory declaration that "The labor of a human being is not a commodity or article of commerce."[41]

Those who had been working for the bill were not entirely without misgivings, fearing that its effectiveness had been impaired by certain changes made during its passage through the Senate. However, they were greatly pleased by the addition to Section 6, which stated that the labor of a human being was not a commodity or article of commerce. In this clause, rather than in the bill as a whole, they saw a charter of industrial freedom, a new Magna Charta. Gompers immediately set out to popularize and glorify the declaration. He was partly actuated by the hope that the courts would take notice and base their interpretation of the bill upon the philosophy contained in this declaration. In general, the many extrava-

[41] Section 6 reads further: "Nothing contained in the anti-trust laws shall be construed to forbid the existence and operation of labor or agricultural organizations . . . or to forbid or restrain individual members from lawfully carrying out the legitimate objects thereof; nor shall such organizations be construed to be illegal combinations or conspiracies in restraint of trade under the anti-trust laws."

Section 20 regulates the issuance of injunctions in labor disputes. It provides that they shall not be issued in cases growing out of trade disputes between employers and employees, or between employees, or between employees and persons seeking employment, unless necessary to prevent irreparable injury for which there is no adequate remedy at law. Furthermore, persons may not be enjoined from quitting, either singly or in concert, or from persuading others by peaceful means to do so; or from attempting at any place where they may lawfully be to obtain or communicate information or to persuade persons peacefully to abstain from work (this was in lieu of a straight-out legalization of peaceful picketing); or from refusing patronage, or employment, or peacefully persuading others to do the same; or from paying out money for strike support, etc. Finally, no injunction or restraining order can be issued to prevent persons from assembling in a lawful manner and for lawful purposes, or from doing any act which might be lawfully done in the absence of such dispute by any party thereto. In case of violation of an injunction, trial for contempt of court may be by the court, or, upon demand of the accused, by jury.

gant eulogies which were lavished upon the Clayton Act had reference to this single abstract statement, rather than to the technical sections. It was an intelligible slogan, adaptable to publicity. It summed up a long struggle for status and human dignity.

In one of the earliest pronouncements on the subject, the *Federationist* for November 1914 called attention to certain deficiencies of the newly passed Act. It was pointed out that labor had tried to obtain a more sweeping exemption from the anti-trust laws than that actually bestowed, and that the provisions for legalizing picketing had been considerably whittled down in the Senate. But in the report of the Executive Council to the convention of 1914 nothing was said concerning these deficiencies, and shortly thereafter the campaign for glorifying the bill was in full swing.[42]

Labor's belief in the efficacy of the Clayton Act was strengthened by the outcry raised against it by the National Association of Manufacturers and by the Anti-Boycott League. Their faith was not dampened by the opinion of their legal advisers, who pointed out that the Clayton Act left the common law doctrine of conspiracy essentially unchanged and that the courts were free to find evidence of malicious intent in acts which were motivated by industrial disputes.[43]

The shortcomings of the Clayton Act can be ascribed to the tactics of the Federation, the efforts of employers'

[42] See *American Federationist* for September 1915. The only note of dissent was sounded by Andrew Furuseth, president of the Seamen's Union, who maintained that the Act would not free labor from the injunction.

[43] The British Trades Disputes Act of 1906 was upheld by way of contrast. The British Act recognized that acts done in furtherance of trade disputes might cause damage, and yet still be legitimate acts.

lobbyists to devitalize the bill,[44] and the political and constitutional impossibility of securing sweeping immunities for labor. The leaders of the Federation failed to inform the membership of the fact that the uncertain character of the Act was widely recognized. Many of the speeches in the Senate pointed out that the bill did nothing more than clarify the best judicial practices at the time. The senators were not disposed to do more than make plain what was already lawful. They were not at all inclined to legalize secondary boycotts, which were so unpopular that the Federation itself was afraid to ask directly for their sanction. The leaders of the Federation chose to interpret such statements as the disparagement of enemies. While not entirely easy in mind as to the full meaning of the Act, they honestly believed that some important measure of restraint had been imposed on the judiciary.

The progress of labor-sponsored measures under a Democratic administration was held to justify the nonpartisan policy of the Federation. Gompers now argued that direct popular government through the initiative, referendum, and recall would in time diminish the importance of all parties.[45] He committed the A. F. of L. to the demands for popular government in opposition to revolutionary unionism, socialism, and other programs based on class politics and parties, and led successfully the opposition to all third party movements. The latter were still supported by the United Mine Workers, the West-

[44] Davenport, the lawyer for the Anti-Boycott Association, was responsible for suggesting the insertion of the words "lawful" and "lawfully" in Section 6. The labor lobbyists sensed a danger here, but it would have been awkward to protest in view of the Federation's reiterations that it was not seeking immunity for extra-legal acts.

[45] Sixteen states had the referendum and initiative by 1912.

ern Federation of Miners, the Brewery Workers, and a few other unions. In 1913 George L. Berry of the Printing Pressmen urged that the Executive Council invite the Socialist Party, the Woman's Suffrage League, the farmers, and the Railroad Brotherhoods to a conference for the purpose of drawing up a working agreement for political action. The latter was to be submitted to a referendum vote of the international unions in order to safeguard against outside control. But even this carefully devised plan met with a cold reception from the convention, though a vague promise of a labor party in the future was held out.

VII. A RECORD OF PROGRESS

In 1914 the American Federation of Labor presented the picture of a fairly prosperous federation of well-established national unions. The membership, which had been 1,676,200 in 1904 and dropped to 1,482,872 in 1909, had risen again to 1,770,145 in 1912 and passed the 2 million mark in 1914, reaching 2,020,671. The revenues were also mounting to new heights, being $193,470 in 1910; $207,373 in 1912; $244,292 in 1913; and $263,166 in 1914. The component unions of the Federation were decidedly stronger financially, as is shown by their expenditures for benefits. In 1904, 53 unions reported total benefit payments to their members of $1,734,835; and in 1914, 68 unions reported $3,389,629. The doctrine of high dues and benefits was spreading. A large number of unions had accumulated strike funds and were paying strike benefits.

Between 1904 and 1914 progress was made in extending the recognition of unions and collective bargaining in the garment industry and the anthracite coal industry, and more satisfactory relations were established in New York and Chicago in the building trades. Neither unions nor employers had reached the stage where they could devise ways and means of giving to the workers, in a more scientific and less burdensome fashion, the security which they strove to obtain through working rules. But a vague groping towards such a solution was to be observed in a few industries.

The member unions were not tied to the A. F. of L. by any strong materialistic bonds. The Federation, in spite of its increasing income and a highly skilled relatively well-paid membership, afforded little assistance in strikes. In ten years it raised only $169,553 by assessment and a further $94,822 by appeal. Its usefulness to member unions was chiefly in mediating disputes between unions and between employers and unions. The Federation was not allowed to assume more real power because most of the unions believed that they could stand alone. It could not afford to antagonize the strong unions for the sake of the weak, who would have welcomed more collective power and more joint action.

The A. F. of L. was undoubtedly playing a useful role for the unions in the political field and was becoming more and more a lobbying organization. But its efforts were handicapped because its affiliated unions would not give it entire, enthusiastic, and ungrudging support. The members could not be relied on to vote in accordance with the Federation's endorsement. They formed political ties with the old parties irrespective of decisions by the national body.

Nevertheless, the Federation was becoming more coherent and more representative in character. Its structural forms were becoming more comprehensive.[46] The number of small member unions was decreasing. Largely owing to amalgamations, the total number of affiliated unions decreased from 120 in 1904 to 110 in 1914. While still essentially an organization of skilled workers, the Federation also had a considerable element of semiskilled workers and a growing number of unskilled. The distribution of power among the unions was becoming more even and some of them with a more mixed membership and larger programs were assuming increasing importance.

The leaders of the Federation were beginning to enjoy increased political influence, both nationally and locally. They were becoming prominent and respected citizens. The salaries of the A. F. of L. officials had been increased several times. In 1914 Gompers was receiving $5,000 and Morrison, $4,000. The officials of most of the unions also were compensated with regular and fair salaries.

There were throughout the decade two distinct factions in the Federation, one pressing for independent political action and a program of industrial unionism, the other clinging to non-partisan politics and craft autonomy. The first faction was formed of a socialist core and a near-socialist fringe.[47] It is not possible to draw a straight line

[46] In 1915 it was estimated that of the 133 national unions, most of which were in the A. F. of L., only 28 were strictly craft unions. While only 5 were described as true industrial unions, at least 100 represented intermediate types. See Theodore W. Glocker, "Amalgamation of Related Trades in American Unions," *American Economic Review*, September 1915, pp. 554-75.

[47] The anti-socialist elements in the Federation, according to the socialists, were under the influence of the Catholic Church. See *International Socialist Review*, January 1914.

dividing the unions in the A. F. of L. into these two camps on the basis of their activities. Radical and conservative characteristics were to be found in the same unions. In regard to their contracts, the United Mine Workers, the brewers, the garment workers, the glass workers, the electrical workers, the machinists, and most of the other socialist and industrial unions were very businesslike. The Western Federation of Miners was almost alone in favoring direct action. On the other hand the building trades and a number of other conservative unions used the sympathetic strike and would not allow their contracts to interfere with it.

While there was much animosity between the Gompers group and the socialists, the struggle between the two camps had a constructive influence. It resulted in an enlargement of the policy of the Federation. By 1914 the program of the A. F. of L. had come to embrace a large part of the program for social legislation advocated by socialists and social reformers.

In spite of what appeared to some as overcautious leadership, by virtue of certain phases of its program the Federation was a part of the progressive forces of the country. It supported movements for democratic reform and was an ally of the farmers and liberal middle class. It was affiliated with the International Federation of Trade Unions in token of its declared faith in the brotherhood of the workers of all lands and in the cause of peace between nations. To many observers the Federation seemed on the threshold of a new era of development along industrial and social lines when the World War broke.

PART III

WORLD WAR AND INDUSTRIAL DEMOCRACY, 1914-24

CHAPTER VI

FROM PEACE TO WAR

From the outbreak of the World War in August 1914 to April 1917, the country lived in the shadow of the world conflict, passing from neutrality to active preparations for war. The A. F. of L. passed through a similar transition. During 1915 and part of 1916 the efforts of the workers to take advantage of the situation created by the war and the agitation of reformers for social legislation held the center of the stage. But the increasing interest in the events of the battlefront and the struggle of the peace and pro-war elements steadily pushed social issues into the background. With the re-election of President Wilson in November 1916, the question of America's part in bringing about peace or entering the war became paramount.

The story of the Federation during these years thus falls into two major parts, one dealing with its economic and political activities and the other with its transition from peace to war.

I. INDUSTRIAL PROGRESS AND NATIONAL RECOGNITION

During the winter of 1914-15 the A. F. of L. continued to be affected by unemployment, which was aggravated by the war. There was considerable suffering in the large cities. Municipal lodging houses were full. Soup kitchens were opened. Bread lines became familiar sights. Armies of unemployed were gathering in California and marching from town to town demanding free board and lodging, reviving memories of Coxey's Army of 1894.

But by the summer of 1915 war orders for munitions, raw materials, and foodstuffs began to pour in from the Allies. Unemployment disappeared. Manufacturers soon began to complain of a labor shortage, accentuated by the cutting off of European immigration. Favorable business conditions and rising prices brought numerous strikes for higher wages, shorter hours, extra payment for overtime, and unionization. The workers felt that they were not receiving a fair share of the large profits which employers were making.

In relation to their effects upon the A. F. of L., the strikes of 1915-16 fell into two groups. One included those in which the A. F. of L., through its affiliated unions, took an important part and from which it gained in membership and strength. The most significant of these involved the munition workers led by the International Association of Machinists, the longshoremen in New York, the building trades unions and the street car men in Chicago, and the women's garment workers in Philadelphia and New York.[1]

Indirectly, the Federation was also concerned with the struggle of the Railroad Brotherhoods for the basic eight-hour day and for time and a half for overtime. Over 350,000 men on 52 railroads were involved. Cooperation between the Brotherhoods and the Railway Employees Department of the A. F. of L. was essential. Otherwise, it was feared, the railroad managements

[1] By January 1916 some 60,000 machinists gained the basic eight-hour day; and the 48-hour week, with a Saturday half-holiday, was obtained even more widely. The longshoremen obtained an agreement with several steamship companies providing for payment of double time for handling war munitions and explosives. The strike on the Chicago street-car and elevated lines ended in the recognition of the Amalgamated Association of Electric and Street Railway Employees. The International Ladies' Garment Workers' Union organized the dressmaking industry and won a trade agreement in the cloak trade.

might play some crafts in the department against the strikers.[2] The chiefs of the four Brotherhoods were therefore pleased when the Federation leaders signified their desire to help in every way possible. This they did on March 30, 1916, after demands had been submitted by the Brotherhoods to the general managers of the railroads.

By August 8 the membership of the Brotherhoods had overwhelmingly endorsed a strike. In mid-August President Wilson conferred with both sides, suggesting a compromise: concession of the eight-hour day, and postponement of the granting of time and a half for overtime until after some experience with the eight-hour day. The compromise was accepted by the employees but not by the railroads. As a strike order had been issued for September 4, President Wilson proceeded to force a settlement of the controversy. On August 29 he addressed both houses of Congress on the need for the eight-hour day and for other labor legislation. Congress in record time passed the Adamson Act on September 2, 1916, establishing the basic eight-hour day on the railroads.

The managements of the railroads immediately contested the constitutionality of the Act. The Brotherhoods, apprehensive lest a declaration of war should spoil their chances for a successful strike, issued a strike ultimatum expiring March 15, 1917. Under pressure from the Council of National Defense, a settlement was reached on that date. The strike order was cancelled. A few hours later the United States Supreme Court upheld the Adamson Act.

The second series of strikes in which the A. F. of L.

[2] Machinists in railroad shops and locomotive engineers had antagonized each other at various times. Also, the jurisdictional rivalry between the Brotherhood of Railroad Trainmen and the Switchmen's Union of North America was a source of much friction.

was unable to wrest leadership from the I. W. W. was largely among unskilled workers. The long-sweated foreign-born laborers utilized the economic power which came to them with the war and the suspension of immigration to improve their lot. These conflicts were accompanied by violent clashes between strikers, company guards, and police. Such were the strikes of 5,000 still-cleaners in the Bayonne plants of the Standard Oil Company of New Jersey, Tidewater Oil Company, and Vacuum Oil Company in 1915; of 6,000 unskilled workers in the Republic Iron and Steel Company's plant at Youngstown, Ohio,[3] and of some 15,000 miners on the Mesaba Iron Range in Minnesota.[4]

As a result of these various developments, by 1916 the A. F. of L. had retrieved most of the losses sus-

[3] In the Youngstown strike in December 1915 the grand jury impanelled to deal with damage done during the rioting found that the riot was precipitated by the guards hired by the Youngstown Sheet and Tube Company, and indicted Elbert H. Gary and 113 corporations for violation of a state anti-trust law, charging them with conspiracy to keep down wages of common labor and to raise the price of steel. The indictments were quashed but the company granted a 10 per cent increase in wages, which soon became general through the iron and steel industry.

[4] The miners demanded an eight-hour day, a new minimum wage scale, and abolition of contract labor. After the strike was under way, an I. W. W. organizer, Carlo Tresca, assumed leadership. A thousand mine guards were sworn in as deputies, and many violent outbursts occurred. The strike was lost and ended on September 17, but later the companies conceded a number of improvements in conditions.

By way of contrast, it may be interesting to record the strike for higher wages of copper miners in Arizona, for the most part Mexican laborers, who had for years been receiving wages below those prevalent for other racial groups in the district. No violence occurred in this strike, largely because of the action of Governor Hunt of Arizona. He issued an embargo on strike breakers, enrolled strikers as deputy sheriffs to protect mining property, and caused some mine managers to be arrested for inciting to riot. Federal mediators and investigators secured a settlement which eliminated race differentials, set up a minimum wage equal to that in the best camps, secured a 20 per cent advance for about 80 per cent of the workers, and permitted workers to join the union.

tained during the depression of 1914-15. In 1916 the Bricklayers' Union, which had kept aloof from the Federation, became affiliated. The Federation also made gains among new groups, issuing charters in May 1916 to the Federation of Teachers and to the Actors' Equity Association.[5] The total membership of the Federation in 1916 reached 2,072,702.

The A. F. of L. continued its advance in the field of legislation during these years. Some of the more important gains were the LaFollette Seaman's Act;[6] a new conciliation and arbitration law for railroad employees; an eight-hour law for women and children in the District of Columbia; prohibition of the Taylor system in arsenals, navy yards, and gun stations; extension of the eight-hour law on government contracts; increased appropriations for the Department of Labor and for the Children's Bureau; the passage in 1916 of a federal child labor bill, prohibiting the transportation in interstate commerce of the products of child labor; a compensation law for federal employees; and several measures designed to improve conditions and to raise wages for various classes of government workers. In fact, practically all the industrial demands of the Bill of Grievances of 1906 had been favorably disposed of by 1916.

Though there were some dark clouds on its horizon,

[5] A teachers' union had been in existence in Chicago since 1902. When the grade teachers of Cleveland threatened to organize a union in 1914, in protest against a salary cut, the Board of Education refused to reappoint the union teachers. The Cleveland Central Labor Union took out an injunction against the Board to prevent its dropping teachers from its payrolls. In 1916 teachers' unions were formed in Scranton, New York City, Butte, Oklahoma City, and Missoula, Mont.

[6] This Act, approved in March 1915, provided a nine-hour day for seamen and gave the sailor the right to leave his job while his ship was in port on the forfeiture of one-half of the wages earned and payable to him at the time.

such as the increasing use of injunctions despite the Clayton Act, attempts to limit strikes by legislation,[7] and adverse court decisions,[8] the A. F. of L. continued its forward movement. It continued to benefit by the general interest in social legislation which found expression in demands for minimum wage laws and in advocacy of health insurance. Much of the progress of these years can be attributed to the friendly administration in the White House, which was giving organized labor unprecedented national recognition. This was demonstrated when President Wilson, officiating at the dedication of the A. F. of L. office building in Washington on July 4, 1916, declared that no president of the United States could any longer ignore the organized labor movement of the country.

II. GOMPERS VERSUS THE PACIFISTS

During 1915-16 the interest of the A. F. of L. was being focussed more and more on the problem of America's attitude toward the war. The first reaction of American trade unionists to the war was a horrified recoil from the barbarity of the situation. At first, autocratic governments, reactionary capitalists, and competitive armaments were blamed. The war was regarded as a "tremendous conspiracy" to destroy the labor movement. The news that labor demonstrations for peace and against war had been held on the eve of the outbreak in Germany, France, and England was received with much satisfac-

[7] In 1915 Colorado passed an Industrial Disputes Act modelled after the Canadian law prohibiting strikes without a preliminary investigation by the State Industrial Commission.

[8] In January 1915 the United States Supreme Court confirmed the decision of the lower courts in the Danbury Hatters' Case. In 1916 a federal court in *Dowd* v. *United Mine Workers* handed down a decision that unions could be sued for damages and that assessed damages should be paid from union funds.

tion. But later, when the trade unions and labor parties in almost all belligerent countries unanimously backed their respective governments, their action was accepted as inevitable and as an expression of labor's patriotic loyalty. Only a few local unions and some city centrals condemned the war outright and demanded that the A. F. of L. take action to stop it.

Under the circumstances Gompers became the object of the attentions and solicitations of various elements actively concerned about the outcome of the war. He was approached by pacifists, and later by German agents, who thought that the least he could do would be to mobilize labor opinion for a gigantic protest against war. Gompers' replies to these solicitations indicate a certain bewilderment in the face of the new issues and an effort to play for time while he was making up his mind. To the various appeals he replied that he ardently desired peace, that he had been engaged since the first rumblings of the conflict in strenuous efforts to stop the carnage, and that he would associate himself with any peace movement which promised success. As a matter of fact, he did nothing but give out public statements.

While in this state of mind Gompers received a confidential memorandum from Ralph M. Easley, secretary of the National Civic Federation, dated September 2, 1914, listing a number of problems growing out of the war which deserved study. These included the need for developing a merchant marine and for opening up new export markets; the question of substituting governmental for private enterprise; readjustments in social welfare programs in view of the specter of radical upheavals revived by unemployment; the possible danger of a large foreign-born population only partially assimilated; and finally the question whether the United States should prepare more thoroughly for a possible war. Easley suggested a national committee representing commerce, agriculture, and labor, as well as geographical and racial divisions, to consider these problems from the standpoint of the "general welfare."

In the correspondence which ensued, Easley influenced Gompers by flattery and by playing on the latter's well-known biases. He berated the peace propaganda of the socialists, whom he branded as insincere, since by their own admission they were ready to plunge the world into a class war. Referring to Gompers as "that great statesman, the President of the American Federation of Labor," Easley condemned the "mushy nonsense emanating from the sentimentalists about Peace, with capital 'P'," warned against the "young college men with half-baked ideas imbibed from their socialistic professors," spoke of the need of "peace with honor," and stressed the advisability of leaving all peace moves to President Wilson.[9]

While thus influenced by Easley against the peace movement, Gompers was subjected to a mass of anti-German propaganda. Sir Gilbert Parker, who later became the official secret head of British propaganda in the United States, "ventured" to supply information so as to help to have "the true history of this tragic conflict studied and understood." In October 1914 two British labor emissaries arrived in this country with the official mission "to place before the executive committees and members of the unions affiliated with the A. F. of L. the attitude of the British trade union movement in this grave European crisis." Against this avalanche of "information" the letters from German labor leaders were few and made little impression.

[9] Correspondence is on file in archives of the A. F. of L.

These influences and the growing conviction that he was destined to play a leading part in the settlement of the war determined Gompers' position. Within a few months he ceased to pose as an advocate of peace, began to discourage suggestions that he start action to stop the war, and adopted the attitude that pacifists were impractical and doctrinaire meddlers.[10] He also advanced a plan for an international labor congress at the end of the war to help make terms of peace.[11]

The possibility of a cleavage within the A. F. of L. on war attitudes loomed in 1915. In the spring of that year the American League to Limit Armaments and the American Neutrality League were formed, and German-American societies began to urge neutrality, peace overtures, and embargoes on arms and war supplies. These movements for the most part represented the middle-class: women's organizations, religious groups, social workers, with a sprinkling of journalists, editors, and politicians. But an attempt was made by these societies to reach the wage earners through a series of labor peace councils culminating in Labor's National Peace Council.[12]

When the Lusitania was sunk on May 7, 1915 and German-American relations became strained, a sizable labor opinion against war came to the fore. It was strong-

[10] He declined to nominate trade union delegates to a conference held by the Emergency Federation of Peace Forces in Washington on Jan. 10, 1915, under the chairmanship of Jane Addams.

[11] See Lewis L. Lorwin, *Labor and Internationalism*, pp. 175-78.

[12] Among the star labor adherents were Congressman Frank Buchanan of Illinois, president of the Bridge and Structural Iron Workers' Union from 1900 to 1905; Henry Weissmann, once secretary of the Bakery Workers' International Union, but long disconnected with the labor movement; Joe Cannon, of the Western Federation of Miners; Milton Snellings of the Steam and Operating Engineers; Ernest Bohm of the New York Central Federated Union; John Golden of the Textile Workers; and Homer D. Call of the Amalgamated Meat and Butcher Workmen's Union.

est on the Pacific Coast and in the Middle West. The international unions having headquarters in Indianapolis, a powerful group comprising the Coal Mine Workers, carpenters, barbers, teamsters, bookbinders, stone cutters, bridge and structural iron workers, and typographers, held a meeting of officers on May 27, 1915 to discuss the situation. Daniel J. Tobin, chairman of the meeting, wrote to Gompers that the conference had not adopted any resolution but had decided to suggest that a general trade union conference be called in case the international situation developed to a danger point. Gompers replied that the proposition would receive consideration. He received similar communications from other organizations[13] and replied with the same formula to all—and continued to ignore them.

By this time Gompers had come to insist that peace at any price was undesirable. He set himself to discredit the peace movement in the United States and to retrieve from it "a number of valuable labor men who had been caught in the net." Gompers was now convinced that the various peace societies were avowedly or unwittingly tools of the German government, and he was confirmed in his belief by the disclosures in the late summer of 1915. He also suspected the hand of German agents in some of the strikes which were being called at the time.[14]

[13] Maintenance of Way Employees' Union, Commercial Telegraphers Union, the Chicago Federation of Labor, and the Pennsylvania State Federation of Labor.

[14] In connection with two of these strikes—those of the Bridgeport machinists and the New York longshoremen—Gompers was particularly eager to uncover the work of German-paid agents, who were said to be fomenting the strikes in order to tie up munition shipments to the Allies. In the case of the longshoremen, evidence of attempts to bribe the union heads was disclosed by T. V. O'Connor, president of the Union; in the case of the machinists, Gompers was finally convinced that the strikes were bona fide trade union work. That some strikes were fomented by German agents has been since proved.

Under Gompers' influence, one labor leader after another began severing connections with the National Peace Council, the Friends of Peace, and kindred organizations. At the convention of the A. F. of L. in November 1915 the advocates of peace were decidedly weak, and the convention adopted Gompers' policy against an embargo on arms and in favor of continued neutrality.

III. LABOR'S WAR DECLARATION

As the war continued into its second winter Gompers took a more active part in the movement for preparedness. In December 1915 he helped the National Civic Federation to draft a resolution calling upon Congress to create a Council of National Defense. By this time Gompers had rounded out his ideas on what should be labor's war attitude. Repudiating pacifism and asserting that "human nature" made some wars necessary, he called for a system of national defense which would be based upon co-operation with the organized labor movement, would prohibit the use of the militia for strike duty, guarantee the wage earners an education upon an equality with all other citizens, provide for the democratic organization of the army, and establish a better concept of industrial justice.[15]

Gompers stressed these ideas in all his communications to the "militaristic" organizations which were formed about this time, such as the National Security League and the American Defense Society. Although he consistently refused to associate himself with these organizations, he encouraged them by his support of the "preparedness" movement which gained in strength after

[15] See Gompers' speech to the National Civic Federation on Jan. 18, 1916 and letter to the National Security League, both of which were printed as S. doc. 311 (64 Cong.).

President Wilson's tour of the country in the spring of 1916.[16] In October 1916, the Council of National Defense was created, consisting of the Secretaries of War, Navy, Interior, Agriculture, Commerce, and Labor. The Advisory Commission to the Council, appointed by President Wilson, included Gompers as the representative of labor.

Early in 1917, when it became clear that an emergency was approaching, Gompers began to prepare a nucleus of labor leaders for acceptance of American participation in the war. As a member of the Advisory Commission to the Council of National Defense, he held conferences in Washington in February and in March with officials connected with the metal trades, which were most important for the prosecution of war. At these conferences Gompers pointed out that the European workers had not benefited by peace demonstrations and argued that American labor should profit by this experience and support the government from the start. He also thought it opportune to call a general trade union conference to put the labor movement before the public in a patriotic light.

Such a conference met on March 12, 1917. It was attended by the Executive Council and by 148 officers representing 79 international unions, the A. F. of L. departments, and the Railroad Brotherhoods. The only important international unions not represented were the International Ladies' Garment Workers' Union, the Western Federation of Miners, the Journeymen Barb-

[16] "Preparedness parades" were held during the summer in various cities. It was during the parade held in San Francisco on July 22, 1916 that a bomb exploded, killing eight or ten people. Thomas Mooney and Warren K. Billings were indicted and sentenced to death for the bombing, the sentence later being commuted to life imprisonment.

ers' Union, and the Typographical Union. In addressing the conference, Gompers advised that its purpose was to prove that democracy could be efficiently maintained that it was the duty of the A. F. of L. to help prove the fact that democracies were not deficient or impotent in defense.[17] A declaration prepared by the Executive Council of the A. F. of L. was presented and debated for a whole day behind closed doors. No record of the debate was kept.

The declaration was adopted by the conference, which claimed to "speak for millions of Americans." In the words of the declaration, the situation was one with which all had to reckon whether they approved the war or not. Modern warfare was a contest between all the resources of nations. In no previous war had the organized labor movement taken a directing part. In the past labor's rights and interests had been sacrificed under the guise of national necessity. Nations were thus prevented from benefiting by the voluntary, whole-hearted co-operation of wage earners in war-time, and the workers were made to feel that no matter what the results of a war, they generally lost. These things must not be allowed to recur. It must be realized that war does not put an end to industrial struggle. Wage earners must keep one eye upon exploiters at home and the other upon the enemy, and opportunities for fresh exploitation must be checked. It must be recognized that the corner-stone of national defense is economic justice, and that the organized labor movement is the agency through which the government must co-operate with wage earners. If service is demanded of workers and soldiers, the same demand must be made of property. If workers are asked to give

[17] Memorandum dictated by Gompers, Mar. 13, 1917.

up certain safeguards, employers must also be asked to give up some of their profits. In accordance with these ideas, certain specific guaranties and safeguards were demanded, together with representation of *organized labor* on all agencies determining and administering policies for national defense.

The declaration went on to characterize the war as a struggle between the institutions of democracy and those of autocracy and finally ended in a paragraph which was more widely quoted than any other part of the declaration because it was believed to contain an unconditional pledge to support the government. This paragraph read:

> We, the officers of the National and International Trade Unions of America in national conference assembled in the capital of our nation, hereby pledge ourselves in peace or in war, in stress or in storm, to stand unreservedly by the standards of liberty and the safety and preservation of the institutions and ideals of our Republic. . . . But, despite all our endeavors and hopes, should our country be drawn into the maelstrom of the European conflict, we, with these ideals of liberty and justice herein declared, as the indispensable basis for national policies, offer our services to our country in every field of activity to defend, safeguard, and preserve the Republic of the United States of America against its enemies whomsoever they may be, and call upon our fellow workers and fellow citizens in the holy name of labor, justice, freedom, and humanity devotedly and patriotically to give like service.

After the declaration was published, interpretations, endorsements, and protests began to pour into the headquarters of the A. F. of L. from labor bodies all over the country, as well as from interested outsiders. The *New York Times* declared that the declaration of rights and wrongs and duties was "largely theoretical" and merely a sop to the radicals. Gompers himself, in reporting the action of the conference to the Advisory Commission of the Council of National Defense, omitted all reference to the demands and spoke only of the "comprehensive declaration of loyalty" which the conference had produced.

Within the trade unions the declaration met with lukewarm endorsement or unorganized opposition. Neither the criticisms nor the commendations coming from labor commented upon the economic and social demands set forth. The critics were for uncompromising opposition to war and denounced the conference for helping to stampede America into war.[18] Those who endorsed the declaration did not specifically commend the earlier sections. The opposition to the declaration was in part factional and personal;[19] in part it was inspired by socialist sentiment; in part it came from organizations which had many members of German or Irish extraction such as the Brewery Workers' Union and the Chicago Federation of Labor.

Between March 12, the day of "Labor's declaration," and April 6, when war was declared against Germany, few labor bodies were given an opportunity to express themselves on the declaration. The acceptance of the declaration of March 12 by the labor movement was therefore in a large measure passive. But it was interpreted by the country as an active endorsement of America's participation in the war and as a pledge of labor's loyalty.

[18] John P. White, president of the United Mine Workers, refused to participate in the conference in a letter to Gompers dated Mar. 3, 1917. He wrote: "I see no humanitarian issues in the present war. In my broad travels, I find little sentiment among the working people in favor of this terrible war."

[19] The officers of the Typographical Union stayed away from the conference largely because of a controversy between M. G. Scott, the president of the union, and Gompers. Daniel J. Tobin of the Teamsters' Union protested at the way in which the declaration was rammed down the throats of the delegates, who were "not allowed to change a word."

CHAPTER VII

WAR AIMS AND INDUSTRIAL RIGHTS

For some 20 months after the declaration of war against Germany, all national activities centered around the issue of winning the war. Since the co-operation of labor was essential in meeting successfully the demands of war production, the American Federation of Labor was called upon to play an important role in working out war-time labor policies.

The activities of the Federation during this period appear in clearer perspective when viewed in the light of the reasoning on which they were based. Organized labor shared the general feeling of patriotism aroused by the war. But the A. F. of L. endorsed the war and proffered willing co-operation also because it believed that the interests of labor would be advanced further by such action than by antagonizing the government. The growing power and prestige of labor developed since 1912 by the friendly relations with the Wilson administration also weighed in the decision.

Aside from patriotism, what was uppermost in the minds of trade unionists was the question of protecting existing union standards, rules, and practices. In fighting a world war for democracy, labor's feeling was that, to be consistent, the country must guarantee the hard-won industrial rights which the trade union movement had secured. If enthusiasm for a democratic war was to be aroused among the workers, democracy at home should be extended to include new opportunities in industry.[1]

[1] Official sanction was given to this idea by President Wilson in his speech to the Buffalo convention of the A. F. of L. in 1917. He said:

The Federation met the problems arising out of this complex situation by reassuring the administration and the public of labor's loyalty to war aims and at the same time insisting on labor's rights. A. F. of L. leaders took part in war propaganda and in special loyalty campaigns, while their industrial activities were guided by the desire of allaying friction in order to keep production going.

I. THE LOYALTY CRUSADE

At the time the United States entered the war it was clear that certain labor elements were not ready to rush in with enthusiasm. Many local unions and city centrals leaned toward pacifism. The socialists had considerable influence in some unions in New York and Chicago,[2] and the I. W. W. in the Northwest and on the Pacific Coast. Russian-Jewish workers favored the peace program of the Russian Revolution, while union members of Irish origin showed anti-British sentiment. There was also apprehension in union ranks lest the war weaken union standards in the United States as it had in all belligerent countries. These anti-war elements were not large, but they were sufficient to give some support to the pacifist activities of the Socialist Party and the People's Peace Council and to create an impression that a great loyalty crusade was called for.

A few months after our entrance into the war Gompers was advised that plans were being laid by socialist groups and several unions in New York and by the People's

"While we are fighting for freedom, we must see among other things that labor is free, that the conditions of labor are not rendered more onerous by the war, and . . . that the instrumentalities by which the conditions of labor are improved are not blocked or checked."

[2] The Socialist Party at a special convention in April 1917 condemned the war and America's participation in it.

Peace Council to create anti-war and anti-Federation sentiment and to capture the New York Central Federated Union. Gompers became alarmed and persuaded the Executive Council of the A. F. of L. to start a campaign to "Americanize" the labor movement of New York and its vicinity. During July a special committee of five appointed by the Executive Council conferred on the subject with a number of writers and "intellectuals" who had left the Socialist Party because of its anti-war attitude.

Late in July Gompers laid the New York situation before George Creel, head of the Committee on Public Information financed by the government. Creel agreed to "get behind" Gompers and the Central Federated Union of New York in their efforts to "Americanize" the labor movement. Creel provided funds for renting an office in New York and hiring a staff to carry on a publicity campaign in English, Yiddish, and Italian to put "the meaning of America and the purposes of America" before the foreign born.[3]

As this Americanization campaign got under way, Gompers received a letter from John Spargo, a former socialist, suggesting the creation of an alliance for labor and democracy to resist "aggressive reactionary tendencies" and to make clear to the people that loyalty and democracy went hand in hand. Such work was necessary in his opinion in order to stem the growing influence of the People's Council. Spargo urged the Federation to take the initiative in forming such an organization and to invite the "intellectuals" to lend their aid.

On the basis of this suggestion and with Gompers'

[3] The work was directed by Robert Maisel and Chester M. Wright, who had promoted the enterprise from the start.

help, the American Alliance for Labor and Democracy was organized on August 16, 1917. At first it merely continued the loyalty campaign on the East Side in New York. But the directors of the Alliance sent alarming reports to Gompers and Creel about the growing power and influence of the People's Council, and urged wider activities of the Alliance as a counter-influence. As the People's Council had called a meeting at St. Paul for September 6, it was decided to hold a conference at Minneapolis from September 5 to 7, 1917, to give the American Alliance for Labor and Democracy national scope.

The staff of the American Alliance worked earnestly for three weeks to find delegates to attend the conference. A representative was dispatched to Minneapolis to get either the city labor council or the state federation of labor to extend Gompers an invitation to come. This was no easy matter, since Minneapolis was noted as one of the strongholds of pacifism and socialism. When the invitation was finally tendered by the union central of Minneapolis, it was declined by Gompers because it involved sitting on the same platform and practically engaging in a debate with a representative of the People's Council. In New York local unions were solicited to endorse the Alliance and to send delegates. A special train, the Red, White, and Blue Special,[4] was chartered at a cost of $6,000, half of which was to be paid from government funds. On August 29 Gompers wired to all the organizers of the A. F. of L. to devote their entire efforts to having "representative labor men and unions send

[4] When the Red, White, and Blue Special pulled out of Grand Central on September 2, Maisel wired Gompers: "Great send-off. Two bands music. One Metropolitan Opera singer. Five thousand bid farewell to special. Everyone happy on train."

representatives to National Conference of American Alliance for Labor and Democracy."[5]

Owing to these various efforts the labor representation at the Minneapolis conference was mixed. Out of a total of 170 delegates 89 were trade unionists. The rest were ex-socialist intellectuals and "sympathizers." The trade union contingent was composed of representatives from small federal labor unions and officers of the A. F. of L. itself. There was a conspicuous absence of delegates from the industries especially connected with the war.

President Wilson had been invited to deliver an address. He sent a letter expressing his appreciation and approval. All the delegates signed a loyalty pledge to support the government and the A. F. of L. A declaration was adopted, stressing unswerving adherence to the cause of democracy, denouncing the enemies of the Republic who were obstructing the government, affirming that "a sturdy defense of the interests of labor is wholly compatible with supreme loyalty to the government," and demanding in exchange for the conscription of men the conscription of wealth. While defending the freedom of speech, of the press, and of assemblage, the conference demanded that all those whose expressions were obstructive to the government in its conduct of war, or who were capable of giving aid or comfort to the nation's foes, should be repressed by the authorities. Pledges of support were extended to the Russian Democracy, interwoven with prayers for Russian victory.

About a half-dozen labor bodies wrote in after the Minneapolis conference to endorse its declarations. A few

[5] Part of the cost of the Minneapolis conference was defrayed by the Committee on Public Information; the telegrams sent by Gompers concerning its launching were charged to the Council of National Defense; certain unnamed sums were donated by the National Civic Federation. The Committee on Public Information handled all the press releases of the conference.

denounced it, on the grounds that it merely advertised a few individuals, or that it used patriotism to cover up undemocratic action. However, Gompers persuaded the A. F. of L. convention in November 1917 to endorse the Alliance and its work, though many labor leaders regarded the performance as an unnecessary display of super-patriotism and as a doubtful diversion from the real problems of labor.

The Alliance was soon weakened by a falling out with the intellectuals who had helped to form it. While willing to "serve" the labor movement, the intellectuals were unwilling to let the A. F. of L. or the Alliance monopolize the representation of all the liberal elements in the United States. Some of them took a leading part in summoning a conference of single-taxers, prohibitionists, farmers, socialists, and laborites which met in Chicago early in October and launched the New National Party. Gompers was annoyed and alarmed. He did not want a new political party. He argued that such a party must either oppose the administration—which was clearly undesirable in the midst of a war—or support it, in which case the party was superfluous. He accused those taking part in the movement of violating the purpose and spirit of the American Alliance, which wished to establish unity. He and Creel sent representatives to Chicago to observe, discountenance, and even disrupt the new party. The "intellectuals" resented Gompers' accusations of bad faith, asserted their right to join political parties outside the Alliance, and warned against making the Alliance "the tail of the Democratic Party."

The Alliance, split by dissensions and hampered financially,[6] had an uphill struggle. It did a few spectacular

[6] Schemes were conceived for raising $100,000 from exporters who wanted a market in Russia and from large firms working on war contracts, but they accomplished little. Between Aug. 25, 1917 and Mar. 8,

things in New York, such as staging a mass meeting of 7,000 persons in Madison Square Garden on September 15, 1917. It supplied some 450 weeklies and dailies with "loyalty material." Secretary of Labor Wilson co-operated with Gompers in sending out men to urge workers in shipbuilding and other war plants to join the Alliance, but few meetings were arranged.[7] Labor's Loyalty Week in February 1918 brought the number of branches to 65, with 71 in process of formation, and in March 8,000 new members came in.

By March 1918 dissatisfaction with the work of the Alliance became general. Spargo wrote Gompers suggesting that its failure might be connected with "failure to push a domestic program similar to that of the British Labor Party," but Gompers was unwilling to talk reconstruction while the war was in progress. On July 17, 1918 Creel notified Gompers that the Committee on Public Information would no longer be able to extend financial aid to the Alliance. The reason given was that Congress had appropriated the meager sum of $1,250,000 for the committee's use. Gompers protested and pleaded for continued support, asserting that the total cost of the Alliance was about $5,000 a month, or $60,000 a year, which could not be raised through volun-

---

1918 contributions received from unspecified outside sources totalled $11,834. Rent and salaries continued to be paid by the Committee on Public Information until July 1918, at the rate of about $2,500 a month. But Creel was impatient with the Alliance, continually threatened to withdraw his support, and restricted financial aid to an amount regarded as insufficient for extensive campaigns.

[7] An organizer for the Brotherhood of Carpenters and Joiners in the Detroit shipyards, who was asked to join the force of speakers, replied that "if organized labor is given the opportunity to make things necessary for carrying on the war, under fair living conditions, they need but little talking to about their loyalty."

tary contributions. Creel agreed to continue to pay some of the expenses of the Alliance[8] for a while longer. In December 1918 the Committee on Public Information appropriated $10,000 for the Alliance, which was now engaged in promoting "one hundred per cent citizenship" among wage earners and in combating Bolshevism and profiteering. The Alliance was discontinued early in 1919.[9]

II. LABOR MISSIONS ABROAD

In the campaign for maintaining war morale the A. F. of L. was also given an opportunity to play a prominent part on the international stage. Spokesmen of the A. F. of L. were sent, at government expense, on foreign missions to win the trade union and socialist organizations of Europe to President Wilson's war aims. The A. F. of L. was following the precedent of British and French trade unionists who had been sent on missions to America.

The first mission in which the A. F. of L. participated was sent to Russia in May 1917, under the chairmanship of Elihu Root, to stave off a separate peace by Russia. President Wilson wanted Gompers to go, but as the latter did not wish to lose touch with the situation at home, James Duncan, first vice-president of the A. F. of L., a man who saw eye to eye with Gompers on all important issues, was sent in his place. Though the mission failed to help Kerensky in his efforts to keep Russia in line, Duncan's report on its work to the Buffalo convention of the A. F. of L. in November 1917 helped to give the leaders

[8] According to the arrangement, Chester M. Wright was to divide his time between the A. F. of L. and the Alliance.

[9] Gompers also co-operated with Easley in supplying the Department of Justice with information against alleged spies and pro-Germans.

of the Federation their first inkling of the new powers for international action which the war opened up to them and to enhance their sense of importance.[10]

In the spring of 1918 a special labor mission was sent to Great Britain and France for the purpose of clearing up "considerable misunderstanding as to the policy which the A. F. of L. had pursued" and to afford the members an opportunity for observation. This mission did something to combat the demand for a general international labor and socialist congress which was then being made.[11]

Upon its return the mission reported that there was a demand in Europe for a visit from Gompers. Accordingly the 1918 convention of the Federation approved his going, and he visited England, France, and Italy. Gompers and the other trade union delegates were showered with attentions, tributes, and honors.[12]

[10] Duncan was tremendously impressed by the fact that he, a worker and trade union official, was traveling such vast distances in company with distinguished public personages on a mission for the United States government. He traveled upon what had been the personal train of the Czar; made a speech in the hall of the Duma; conferred with the Russian Cabinet and with delegates of the Moscow Workmen's and Soldier's Council. Duncan made naïve speeches in Russia on the methods and achievements of the A. F. of L., unaware of the effects of these speeches upon the revolutionary minds of his audiences.

[11] Lewis L. Lorwin, *Labor and Internationalism*, pp. 185-91.

[12] The British government, the American Embassy, and British labor groups joined in welcoming the mission on its arrival in London. An official luncheon was tendered to the party by the government at the Carleton Hotel, at which Gompers sat next to Lloyd George. In France much the same round continued. Appearing in the gallery of the Chamber of Deputies, Gompers was recognized by Paul Deschanel, the presiding officer, who immediately adjourned the Chamber in order to give the representatives a chance to meet the distinguished visitor. Gompers and his colleagues were received by the King of Belgium, met General Haig, and were escorted by André Tardieu through the Citroen Munition Works. In Italy a reception was held for them in the Capitol by the government and they were invited to dine with the King. They were received by generals at the front. D'Annunzio staged special aircraft displays for their benefit.

These experiences were startlingly new for labor leaders, even for Gompers who had associated with industrial and financial magnates in the Civic Federation and who had had the ear of American presidents. These honors were dazzling proof of the long way the A. F. of L. had come since its first struggles for recognition and were an exhilarating stimulus to seek further opportunities of the same character.

III. THE COUNCIL OF NATIONAL DEFENSE

Far more complex than the promotion of loyalty campaigns was the task of the A. F. of L. to help maintain uninterrupted and efficient war production. In so far as the Federation wished, or was forced by pressure from local unions, to solve this problem without jeopardizing union standards, it came up against its greatest difficulties.

It seemed at the outset that the A. F. of L. would have little opposition to its aims and purposes. Both capital and the government were seemingly ready to take labor into partnership. Gompers was chairman of the Committee on Labor of the Advisory Commission of the Council of National Defense to advise the government upon its labor policies.

But difficulties soon developed. On April 7, 1917 the Council of National Defense issued a declaration appealing to employers and workers not to change existing standards for the duration of the war. This was construed to mean that labor should waive all claims for improvements. The trade unions throughout the country protested. On April 16 the Council of National Defense was forced to interpret its declaration of April 7 to mean that the principal standard to be maintained was the standard of living, and that the Council was not averse to having unduly low standards of living raised, even during the war emergency. The next day the Advisory Commission of the Council requested Gompers to submit recommendations for setting up machinery to deal with labor disputes.

A week later Gompers submitted a comprehensive scheme to set up a board of nine, including two trade unionists, to fix minimum standards for government contracts and government operated plants and to establish joint committees of employers and employees to settle grievances locally, with the right of appeal to the national board. The Council of National Defense, however, favored a plan offered by Secretary of Labor Wilson for a board which was to include three employers, three workers (not necessarily trade unionists), and three representatives of the public and which was to fix as its minimum standards the eight-hour day and time and a half pay for overtime.

When Secretary Wilson's plan was made public it aroused a storm of protest both among trade unionists and employers. The former were afraid of a board which had three labor to six non-labor members. The employers were opposed to the eight-hour day.

While this wrangling was proceeding the trade unions in the coal and building industries showed a determination to press their claims for recognition from the war authorities. On May 14 the newly appointed committee on coal production made public its plans for stimulating output, which among other things proposed to reduce labor turnover. The United Mine Workers at once issued a protest against limiting the laborer's right to change jobs in search of higher wages. Some weeks before, a joint committee of miners and operators had offered the Council of National Defense co-operation in maintaining maximum production. This offer had been ignored. Now came the announcement of the coal production committee on which there were no labor representatives, and on which the Western and Southern coal fields were represented by anti-union operators. On receiving the miners' protest, Secretaries Wilson and Baker and the chairman of the committee hastened to explain that it had been intended to have labor representatives on the committee, but that in their haste they had gone ahead before the nominations of labor members, to be made by Gompers, were ready. The affair ended with the addition of seven labor members to the coal committee on June 15. This was the first clear victory scored by labor in securing a voice upon a committee which was directly concerned with war production.[13]

At the same time the unions in the building trades took issue with the government over the question of wages and union rules in the building of 16 new cantonments. Many of the government contractors refused to exclude non-union workers. The government, intent upon hastening construction, was unwilling to tolerate any limitation of the labor supply. Gompers protested to the Council of National Defense that the government was favoring "unfair" employers and that serious consequences might follow. The War Department felt impelled to make some concession. On June 19 Secretary of War Baker and Gompers signed an agreement which provided that on the construction of cantonments union

[13] Gompers' opponents took pleasure in pointing out that it was won by President White of the United Mine Workers, and not by the president of the A. F. of L.

scales of wages and hours and working conditions, as of June 1, 1917, should be adopted as basic standards. There was a private understanding that the term "union working conditions" would *not* include the closed shop, but would mean only rules as to overtime and holidays. For the adjustment of disputes, on the basis of these standards, Secretary Baker later appointed an Emergency Construction Wage Commission, consisting of one representative of the Army, one of the public, and one of labor.[14]

Thus came into existence the first of a series of special adjustment bodies to meet a special emergency in a single industry. The Council of National Defense was not yet ready to go further. Throughout June and July of 1917 it continued to debate various plans for a national adjustment board. Gompers insisted that the labor members of such a board must represent organized labor. The objectors were willing to let Gompers nominate the labor representatives, but did not want "representatives of organized labor" written into the constitution of the new body. On August 1 the Council adopted Secretary Wilson's plan, but it was never put into effect because of the opposition it aroused.

Neither was the Council of National Defense ready to accord organized labor representation on committees handling war contracts. Toward the end of June the Executive Council of the A. F. of L. voiced its disappointment in a letter to the Council of National Defense demanding for the workers "democracy in all things concerned in a world war for democracy, . . . direct repre-

[14] Gompers selected John R. Alpine of the plumbers union and a vice-president of the A. F. of L. for the post.

sentation by workers, co-equal with all other interests, upon all agencies, boards, committees, and commissions entrusted with war work."

This protest may have had something to do with the appointment of Hugh Frayne to the War Industries Board which was organized in July 1917 as a successor to the Committee on Munitions, Supply, and Raw Materials of the Council of National Defense. However, except for Frayne and Gompers, who occupied special positions, labor during the war gained only representation on boards or committees handling labor disputes, not on those concerned with the letting of contracts.

IV. THE WAR LABOR BOARD

While the Council of National Defense was struggling with the issue of labor policy, industrial conditions were growing tense. By midsummer of 1917 labor unrest had become acute in many sections of the country. The areas of disaffection included New York, the Atlantic Coast, Chicago, and Wisconsin, but the areas in which disturbance threatened to interfere seriously with war production lay in the Northwest and Southwest. In these sections the war had intensified the unwholesome situation created by absentee control of large corporations, migratory labor, wretched living conditions in isolated camps, autocratic attitudes of employers or managers, and radical unionism, especially in metalliferous mines and in lumber camps. During the summer of 1917 the I. W. W. had been conducting a strike for the eight-hour day in the lumber camps of Idaho and the Pacific Coast. The employers refused all concessions and through their association presented a united front. The I. W. W. transformed the fight into a "strike on the job." As a result the government's program for airplane and shipbuilding production was crippled.

At the same time strikes were in progress on the street-car lines of Seattle and on the water fronts of some of the Puget Sound ports. A tie-up for a general wage increase, involving 100,000 men in Pacific Coast shipyards, was threatened in August, which was especially serious since 15,000 men had already laid down their tools in the shipyards on the Atlantic Coast. In Arizona, which produced 28 per cent of the total copper of the country, output had fallen short of expectations by a hundred million pounds during the summer of 1917, on account of strikes among Mexican copper miners, whose chief demand was for union recognition. Local loyalty leagues which had taken a hand in suppressing strikes and unions had made relations more bitter by deporting a thousand people from Bisbee, Arizona. While these were the most serious situations, there were also strikes and threats of strikes in the oil fields of southern California, on the Pacific Coast telephone system, in the Chicago packing plants, on the iron ore ranges of the Lake Superior district, and in California canneries.[15]

The unrest in the summer of 1917 was due primarily to the industrial confusion and strain created by the war. At a tremendous speed new industries were organized from the ground up and old ones expanded from insignificant to gigantic proportions. Geographical shifts of workers and factories were taking place on a large

[15] The number of strikes in 1917—a total of 4,233—exceeded those of any preceding year, and the number of lockouts—126—was near a maximum. In 1918 there were 3,181 strikes and 104 lockouts. The building trades, the metal trades, and the clothing industry account for the highest proportions of strikes in both years.

scale, orders were speeded up, and price was becoming a minor consideration. Living costs rose rapidly in spite of government efforts to control prices and profits. The workers felt that they alone as a group were being unjustly prevented from taking full advantage of the situation. Local union officials, regardless of their "loyalty," felt that A. F. of L. leaders in Washington had not guarded sufficiently the interests of the workers.

Some of the unrest, however, was caused by efforts either to maintain or expand unionism in old and new industries. Despite the understanding at Washington that the status quo in industrial relations should not be disturbed, a number of unions were engaged in active organizing campaigns. Only to a small extent was this unrest heightened by antagonism to the war or by a desire to take advantage of a national emergency to carry on revolutionary struggles. The Socialist Party played no part in these industrial movements and even the I. W. W., which reached the peak of its industrial power in 1917, was concerned primarily with economic purposes.

Faced with these struggles in one vital industry after another, Secretary Baker wrote to Gompers on August 16 asking advice. Gompers in reply made one more plea, in somewhat ambiguous terms, for the complete recognition of organized labor and of union standards. But the Council of National Defense opposed this. Secretary Baker then suggested appointing a commission to investigate conditions in Washington and Arizona.[16]

[16] It was decided in making the plan public to give credit for it to Gompers. The Commission appointed by the President was headed by Secretary of Labor Wilson. It included E. P. Marsh, president of the Washington State Federation of Labor; John H. Walker of the Illinois State Federation; two employers; and Felix Frankfurter as secretary and counsel.

The Commission, which became known as the President's Mediation Commission, set up adjustment machinery in the Arizona copper mining industry, in the California oil fields, in the telephone system of the Northwest, and in the packing industry.[17] It endeavored to assure union recognition wherever possible. Where this was not possible because of the newness or weakness of unionism, it guaranteed the workers the right to form a union, free from discrimination. United States administrators were to see that this right was respected and to adjust disputes. The Commission thus gave great impetus to union organization in many industries.[18]

Following close upon the appointment of the President's Mediation Commission, the Shipbuilding Labor Adjustment Board and similar bodies for other industries were set up, based on the tri-partite representation of workers, employers, and the government. The task of these boards was far from easy. Against the workers' demands for higher wages were the employers' insistence that the government foot the bill for increased costs. Union efforts to push organization were opposed by employers. Changes in living costs called for wage adjustments, but the question of what should be the basic standard gave rise to dissension. Local and craft differentials complicated matters. Gains made in one industry, notably shipbuilding, stirred up discontent in other industries. Labor troubles and local strikes continued. But the boards did succeed in bringing some order out of chaos by

[17] The Commission also submitted a confidential report to President Wilson, recommending a new trial for Mooney and Billings.

[18] In addition to these administrators the government appointed labor adjusters on the Navy Yard and Arsenal Wage Commission, on the Board of Control for Labor Standards in Army Clothing, and in other government war production bodies.

establishing basic standards, by bringing wage levels in different parts of the same industry, in related occupations, and in neighboring or similar districts, into closer relationship with each other and with the cost of living. They were instrumental in securing overtime pay for those employed in excess of eight hours, and they extended some aid to unionism by protecting workers against discharge for union activities.

By January 1918 it was apparent that, successful as the various boards, commissions, and administrators so far created had been in their respective industries, there still remained a large field which was not covered by any agency and in which strikes could interrupt war production. Furthermore, it was realized that there was more to a successful war labor policy than the adjustment of wage rates and the prevention of strikes. More than hasty and sporadic attention was required to settle problems of supplying different grades of labor, priority of demands for labor, distribution of workers to places where they were needed, and training the unskilled. The Committee on Labor of the Council of National Defense had tried to formulate certain policies. The War Industries Board had advised the executive branches of the government, but had no authority to see that its advice was carried out. The Department of Labor had offered its services to the extent to which its budget would permit. There was duplication and conflict, and none of the problems was adequately handled. Lacking an efficient system of information and labor exchanges, employers relied upon their competitive bids to attract labor. But where machinery for fixing wage scales had been set up they were prevented from doing so. As a result, either labor was drawn from localities and industries where most needed, or the government agencies were forced to raise wage scales over which they had control in order to retain adequate labor forces. Wages consequently could not be regulated solely with reference to cost of living in accordance with agreements.

Thus the problem of preserving industrial peace broadened out into the problem of adjusting labor to war needs. It was seen that the lack of a labor policy, as well as the decentralized methods of handling war contracts, made the War Industries Board ineffective as a co-ordinating agency. A strong central control over production as well as a centralized labor policy were called for.

It was for the purpose of working out such a policy that the War Labor Conference Board was set up in March 1918. On its recommendations, a month later, the War Labor Board was established. The latter was composed of five representatives of employers; five members nominated by the A. F. of L.; and two representatives of the public, one selected by the employers—William H. Taft—and one selected by the workers—Frank P. Walsh. The function of the Board was to settle by mediation and conciliation controversies arising between employers and workers in fields of production necessary for the effective conduct of the war, or in other fields of national activity in which delays and obstructions might, in the opinion of the National Board, detrimentally affect such production. The agencies which had been set up the preceding summer were to continue, but the War Labor Board was to act as a court of appeal for cases under their jurisdiction, as well as a court of first instance for other cases involving war production.

The War Labor Board adopted the principle that

there should be no strikes or lockouts during the war, though no penalties were provided for a breach. The right of workers to organize in trade unions and to bargain collectively through chosen representatives was recognized. Workers were not to be discharged for membership in trade unions, or for legitimate trade union activities. The workers, however, were forbidden to use coercive measures to induce persons to join unions or employers to deal with them. The concession of the right to bargain collectively was further modified by the provision that in establishments where both union and non-union workers were employed, and where the employer met only with union representatives engaged in his own establishment, the continuance of such a condition was not to be deemed a grievance, though the War Labor Board recognized the right of workers to form unions even in such plants. The principles of the War Labor Board provided for a basic eight-hour day in all cases in which the existing law required it. In other cases the question was to be settled with due regard to governmental necessities and to the welfare, health, and proper comfort of the workers. The union rate of wages was guaranteed where it had been customary in the past, and the principle of a living wage was made to apply to all workers, including common laborers. It was specifically declared that minimum rates of pay should be established to insure the subsistence of the worker and his family in health and reasonable comfort.

These principles marked a great gain for unionism. Organized labor relinquished its right to strike, but in such general terms that no penalties were involved. That was its only concession. On the other hand, labor gained protection against lockouts and against discharge for union activity and thereby an opportunity to push peaceful organization work with government sanction. The lowest paid and least skilled workers obtained a means of securing higher rates of pay which stimulated their interest in unionism.

That the Board was instrumental in promoting unionism was evidenced in the 490 awards which it made during its existence. In all cases where the issue of organization was involved, the Board insisted upon reinstatement of workers discharged for union activity and forbade blacklisting and individual contracts. Where the Board could not secure for employees the right to bargain collectively through trade unions, it provided some form of joint dealing if the employees demanded it. Frequently the Board took the initiative in setting up shop committees for handling local grievances, and sometimes local mediation boards were added. It looked upon such arrangements as preparatory steps towards trade unionism. That was the reason employers feared these committees and boards.

While the War Labor Board was successful to a considerable extent, its principles never gained general acquiescence. This was illustrated in its clashes with the Western Union and Postal Telegraph companies and with munition manufacturers in Bridgeport, dominated by the Remington Arms Company.[19]

V. THE WAR LABOR POLICIES BOARD

Although no field of war production was now without access to some specially devised war-time adjustment agency, the need for an agency which would co-

[19] See Richard B. Gregg, "The National War Labor Board," *Harvard Law Review*, November 1919, p. 39.

ordinate all parts of the government labor policy was still felt. To serve this purpose the War Labor Policies Board was created on May 7, 1918.[20]

Unlike the War Labor Board, the War Labor Policies Board was little concerned with questions of unionism and collective bargaining. Its main task was to secure the adoption of common labor policies by the government departments. It set out to standardize wages and hours in all branches of war production, to study the needs of industry with reference to the housing and transportation of workers, and to devise machinery for securing more directly and economically a proper labor supply for essential industries.

In this comprehensive program the War Labor Policies Board was far from successful. Its attempt to prevent wage changes until it had studied conditions in the different industries caused discontent and strikes among workers, and had to be abandoned. Also its efforts to standardize wages and working conditions in the metal and building trades through the creation of national boards composed of employers and union delegates were defeated by the inability of capital and labor in these industries to co-operate. The main achievement of the War Labor Policies Board was to formulate standard labor clauses for contracts let by the War Department, the Navy Department, the Emergency Fleet Corporation, and the United States Housing Corporation, which expressly required compliance with existing labor laws

[20] Those represented were the Departments of Labor, War, Navy, and Agriculture, the War Industries Board, Fuel Administration, Shipping Board, Emergency Fleet Corporation, Food Administration, Railroad Administration, and the Committee on Public Information. The chairman of the Board was Felix Frankfurter.

most favorable to the workers. But by various modifying provisions the Board tended to limit the upward trend of some wage rates and to stimulate others, stopping the soaring of wages among the groups of skilled wage earners whose scarcity was especially felt.

Despite all the agencies created during 1917-18, the problem of labor policy continued to vex those responsible for it. The shipbuilding industry was suffering from labor shortage and so was the anthracite coal industry. Wage increases in one industry or district, for whatever reason, created labor unrest in other occupations, either by increasing turnover or stimulating dissatisfaction. All efforts to keep wages in the same crafts uniform (allowing for local variations in costs of living), to reduce turnover to a reasonable figure, and to produce a satisfied state of mind among the laboring force—the ostensible aim of the war labor adjustment agencies—were continually obstructed by employers and government departments eager to obtain labor at any cost, or by the conflicts between employers and employees which made special bargains and arrangements inevitable.

To meet these problems the War Labor Policies Board in September 1918 organized the Conference Committee of Labor Adjusting Agencies. This new co-ordinating agency included representatives from the same bodies as the War Labor Policies Board, excepting the Department of Agriculture and the Food Administration. Its purpose was twofold: to make another attempt at standardizing wages, hours, and working conditions, not only in government work, but throughout all industry; and to formulate a new statement of national labor policy to be proclaimed by the President of the United States, as a new basis for American industry.

The Conference Committee struggled with its first task with no more success than the other agencies. Its failure was due partly to the fact that its supervisory powers began after the wage boards had reached a settlement, when it was usually inexpedient to put off and disappoint parties to the dispute still further; partly to the fact that, in spite of elaborate employment machinery and priority regulations, a wage differential remained the best way of attracting labor supplies to essential industries. In the performance of its second task it prepared an elaborate statement of policy providing for adjustments to meet changes in the cost of living, adequate wage differentials, continuity of employment, the maintenance of a "proper" standard of living for all workers, an eight-hour day, the limitation of night work, seven legal holidays with pay a year, and agencies of enforcement. While designed especially to guide the activities of governmental wage boards, these principles were regarded as capable of being developed in time into a general industrial code. But the principles failed to obtain the approval of the most important body in the Conference Committee, the War Labor Board, whose chairman, William Howard Taft, objected to the promulgation of a general eight-hour day. President Wilson kept delaying its promulgation, and after the Armistice the subject was altogether dropped.

VI. THE WAR BALANCE SHEET

Opinions differ as to the benefits derived by the A. F. of L. and its unions during the war period. Some claim that the government bestowed numerous favors and advantages upon labor; others that labor leaders bound the workers so completely that they got nothing out of the war. Organized labor has been praised for its loyalty, self-sacrifice, and devotion; and condemned for its failure to put group interests aside.

The facts bear out neither of these extreme views. The A. F. of L. urged individual workers to buy war savings stamps and liberty bonds and many unions invested considerable sums in the latter. It lent its influence to the campaigns for sustaining morale at home and abroad, and it did much to preserve industrial peace. The officers of the A. F. of L. and of many of the international unions, as the war went on, put aside their roles of organizers and strike leaders to become conciliators and mediators.

If union leaders were not always successful, it was because of conditions beyond their control. Patriotic appeals could not overcome the many causes of discontent released by the war. The devices for minimizing friction were only gradually and haltingly created. Solutions reached at the top were not always acceptable to local labor groups or local employers. Workers and employers were unwilling to make what they regarded as unreasonable concessions which might strengthen the other side in the future. The government's personnel, consisting of men drawn from the universities and professions, who were impressed with the possibility of utilizing a "war for democracy" to democratize American industry, were slow in hammering out a new labor policy, and not always able to enforce it. On the other hand, the government's concessions to organized labor came piecemeal and gradually, only as serious difficulties arose in an industry. And, as a rule, the government machinery worked best in plants and industries in which strong unions had existed before the outbreak of the war.

What organized labor did gain, however, was the opportunity to extend its numbers and influence to fields in which there was determined opposition, though in many munition plants and in the iron and steel industry, the employers warded off all government boards. The demands of the workers were never granted fully, and the government policy was not favorable to all groups of labor. The workers who profited most were those who had not been organized at the beginning of the war. The wage rates of unskilled workers rose, while the wages of the skilled remained about stationary.[21] Earnings, however, were much influenced by overtime and bonuses. Hours were shortened, especially in unionized plants, but the reduction in normal hours was obscured by the large amount of overtime. The government did not prohibit strikes, although it enforced awards by drastic measures when suasion failed.

These gains were considerable, but they do not indictate that labor exploited its unusual war opportunities to the full. They show that organized labor was prevented to some extent from making as good a bargain as it might have through unregulated action. The restraining influence was exercised by leadership, public opinion, and government pressure.

In brief, labor both paid for and profited by its war policy, and the A. F. of L. tried to strike as favorable a balance as possible. Gompers and his associates, subjected to pressure and flattery from high sources, were

[21] See Paul H. Douglas, *Real Wages in the United States, 1890-1926*, Chap. XXVI. See also Hugh S. Hanna and W. Jett Lauck, *Wage Movements and the War*, p. 3.

tempted to relax their vigilance for labor's interests, and were ready to make what they regarded as necessary compromises. But they had to be watchful, for they could pacify the men on the job only by regard for their grievances. The presence of a closely knit corps of A. F. of L. officials at Washington, in contact with the President, the Cabinet, and the government departments, was invaluable in securing a hearing for labor groups on specific complaints, as well as on large issues. The Federation representatives on the boards were kept busy with endless conferences between workers' delegations, contractors, and government purchasing agents. They became union business agents on a scale never before dreamed of and in a new spirit of co-operation with the government.

The A. F. of L. and labor organizations generally took much credit to themselves for their patriotic behavior. They received commendations for their cooperation from the President, the government officials, the National Civic Federation, and some of the defense societies. But groups which before the war had been antiunion were not conciliated by the unions' activities during the war. Some of these groups and the A. F. of L. emerged from the war still more embittered against each other. The public too was divided as to the value of labor's contribution during the war. These rifts in public opinion were an important factor in shaping industrial relations immediately after the war.

CHAPTER VIII

RECONSTRUCTION AND RADICALISM

By November 1918 considerable progress had been made toward a national labor policy based on large principles. There was reason to expect that the experience of the war would be utilized for the period of reconstruction, and that the government machinery devised during 1917-18 would serve as a lever for placing industrial relations on a higher plane.

Contrary to expectations, this did not happen. Almost immediately after the Armistice, the elaborate machinery set up for dealing with industrial relations began to be scrapped. In vain did the War Labor Policies Board and other government bodies call attention to the need for stabilizing employment, prices, and wages. Business men were keen to resume laissez faire, and organized labor, impatient with the tendency of the government boards during the last months of the war to check the rise of wages, also clamored for freedom of action.

In consequence, labor and capital were soon clashing along the entire front of American industry. For nearly two years the country witnessed an industrial upheaval which, owing to the issues of reconstruction and "industrial democracy" and to the great advance of unionism, reached an intensity and scope far beyond all previous manifestations of unrest.

I. FAILURE OF A NATIONAL LABOR POLICY

After the Armistice an enormous volume of talk concerning reconstruction was let loose in the United States.

During December 1918 many "reconstruction" conferences were held which put forth programs ranging from demands for a return to the pre-war order to radical and socialist proposals of comprehensive reform. The Conference of American Industries endorsed John D. Rockefeller, Jr.'s credo for collective relations through shop committees. Social workers and the churches expatiated on the need for a new spirit of social justice. Radical elements in the labor movement drew their inspiration from the reconstruction program of the British Labor Party.[1]

The leaders of the A. F. of L. were anxious to offset the programs emanating from non-labor organizations, as well as those of radical labor groups. The special reconstruction committee appointed by the A. F. of L. convention in June 1918 now produced a report with this purpose in view. The basic principle of the program was democracy in industry, interpreted as the right of the workers to be represented through trade unions. Employers interfering with the workers' right to organize were to be guilty of a criminal offense. A living wage was demanded for all workers, and trade union activity was declared to be the only method for obtaining and maintaining such a wage. No connection between wages and productivity was pointed out. An eight-hour day and a five and a half day week were called for, with prohibition of overtime. Protection for women and chil-

[1] Shortly after the Armistice the Chicago Federation of Labor published a program of 14 points including demands for a league of workers as opposed to the League of Nations; for the abolition of unemployment through the stabilization of industry; for public works during depressions; for the public ownership of railways, telegraphs, telephones, steamships, stockyards, grain elevators, and public utilities; and for a complete amnesty of war political prisoners.

dren in industry and the right of organization for public employees were demanded.

The program further endorsed consumers' co-operation to curb profiteering; government ownership of "public and semi-public utilities";[2] and federal and state development of water power, the power generated to be supplied to all citizens at rates based on cost. Federal regulation of corporations, tax reforms, government housing schemes, and public employment agencies were also endorsed. Other significant planks were those calling for a two-year suspension of immigration, limiting the power of the Supreme Court, and abolishing restrictions on freedom of speech, though nothing was said about an amnesty for war political prisoners. This program was approved by the Executive Council of the A. F. of L. on December 28, 1918.[3]

While reconstruction talk was proceeding, the wartime industrial machinery was being dismantled piecemeal. At the end of November William G. McAdoo resigned from the Railroad Administration. By January 1, 1919 the War Industries Board dispersed. On February 1 the Fuel Administration ceased to regulate the price of coal, although it continued in existence until its funds ran out in June. In March the Shipbuilding Labor Adjustment Board ceased to function. In May the National War Labor Board became defunct. The

[2] The report, however, was not specific about the railroads, the only industry in which the issue was at all prominent. It was also ambiguous on the development of an American merchant marine "under governmental control" though the government was urged to operate all wharves and docks connected with public harbors.

[3] There was disagreement in the Council on the questions of compulsory social insurance and political action. But Gompers' pleading was effective in having the Executive Council reaffirm its non-partisan political policy and opposition to social insurance.

United States Employment Service was forced to curtail its work for lack of appropriations. A similar fate overtook most of the other boards.

The dissolution of the government adjustment agencies was generally accepted by labor and employers as the end of the industrial truce. Strikes became the order of the day. The situation began to grow tense during the summer of 1919 when business stagnation gave way to the hectic post-Armistice boom. The unprecedented increase in the cost of living provoked charges of profiteering, while competitive bidding for labor started a general scramble among workers to recoup themselves for lags in wages. Organized groups, working under agreements which still had some months to run, or in industries where government regulation still continued, as in coal mining and on the railroads, attracted a great deal of public attention by their demands for the abrogation of agreements, or for special consideration. Employers endeavored to throw the onus of increasing prices on the restrictive policies of unions and on labor inefficiency. The A. F. of L. blamed the profiteers, and demanded congressional investigation of those who were conspiring to increase the price of the necessaries of life.

President Wilson and Congress were too absorbed during these months with the question of the ratification of the Versailles Treaty to consider domestic issues. But by September 1919 it was no longer possible to ignore the industrial situation. In August the railway shop crafts, impatient with the slowness in the adjustment of their wages, walked out against the orders of their officers. The United Mine Workers were calling for the nationalization of the mines, and negotiating for an alliance with the railroad unions in case of a strike. A special committee in the steel industry was ready to issue an order for a general strike. The imminence of simultaneous struggles in the three basic industries of the country created serious apprehension. As a climax came the strike of the Boston policemen in September 1919.

On September 3, 1919 President Wilson, aroused by these developments, issued invitations to representatives of employers, labor, and the public to a National Industrial Conference to be held in Washington, commencing October 6, to formulate principles for a "genuine and lasting co-operation between capital and labor." In accordance with this invitation, an employers' group was constituted of five nominees from the United States Chamber of Commerce, five from the National Industrial Conference Board,[4] three from farmers' organizations, and two each from investment bankers and railroad managements, making a total of 17. The public group selected by President Wilson comprised 21 individuals, some of whom were associated with large corporations as directors or executives.[5] The labor group consisted of 15 representatives of the A. F. of L. named by Gompers and four representatives of the Railroad Brotherhoods.[6]

When the Industrial Conference met, it was confronted with a tense situation. Some 300,000 steel

[4] The National Industrial Conference Board was formed in 1916 by 16 employers' associations for the purpose of studying changes in the cost of living as a basis for wage adjustments.

[5] The public group included John D. Rockefeller, Jr., Thomas L. Chadbourne, Bernard M. Baruch, Robert S. Brookings, Elbert H. Gary, Charles W. Eliot, and Lillian D. Wald.

[6] The labor group included the Executive Council of the A. F. of L., excepting Duncan and William Green, and John L. Lewis, Sara Conboy, William H. Johnston, Paul Scharrenberg, John Donlin, and F. Tighe. Lewis resigned on September 25, expressing lack of confidence in the outcome on account of the composition of the public group.

workers were on strike.[7] The miners were on the verge of a strike. Local groups of workers were defying their union officers and calling strikes in violation of contracts. Many of the representatives of large corporations, banks, and employing interests attending the conference ascribed the turmoil in large measure to the favored treatment which they believed labor had enjoyed during the war, and were convinced that a halt must be called.

The conference appointed committees to deal with the cost of living, production and vocational training, unemployment and unemployment insurance, wages, and immigration. However, before it could consider these matters, it deadlocked upon two questions—the steel strike and collective bargaining. As soon as the conference opened, the labor representatives introduced a resolution that the dispute in the steel industry be submitted to arbitration. The acceptance of arbitration would have implied that the heads of the United States Steel Corporation recognized the right of trade unions to organize its employees. The conference voted to postpone this resolution until the question of collective bargaining could be disposed of and proceeded at once to try to formulate a principle. The labor group presented a program which emphasized the right of workers to organize into unions and to be represented by delegates of their own choosing in collective negotiations with employers. The employers' group rejected this formula as "ambiguous." They insisted that workmen should be free to join lawful associations, other than trade unions; that collective bargaining be defined in such a way as to recognize shop committees and employee representation plans, which a number of corporations had begun

[7] See below, p. 180.

to establish in 1919 as an alternative to trade unions.[8]

President Wilson made a last minute appeal to save the conference. On October 22 he asked the groups to consider other items of the agenda which might lead to some agreement upon the program as a whole. But when it became clear that no agreement upon collective bargaining could be reached, the labor group on October 23 walked out. The next day the public group issued a statement deploring the collapse of the conference and suggesting that a small committee, representative of various points of view, be selected by the President to continue working upon machinery for the settlement of industrial disputes.

President Wilson accordingly nominated a commission on November 16. No labor men were appointed to the new body, which was supposed to represent the public only. On December 29, 1919 the commission issued a report, proposing an elaborate system of tribunals for the investigation and adjustment of disputes, and recommending the prohibition of strikes in all industries of a public character. The attitude of the commission was reflected in the statement of its report, which read: "The plain fact is that the public has long been uneasy about the power of great employers. It is becoming uneasy about the power of great labor organizations. The community must be assured against domination by either." This report had little effect. The attempt to formulate a national industrial policy had failed.

[8] Early in 1919 the International Harvester Company installed an employee representation plan in 17 of its 20 plants, by vote of the employees. By September 1919 there were 44 firms in this country which had inaugurated some form of employee representation or works council, among them the Bethlehem Steel Company, Standard Oil Company of New Jersey, the General Electric Company, and Procter and Gamble. For a further discussion of these plans, see pp. 236-37.

II. THE STEEL STRIKE

While the Industrial Conference was wrangling over a definition of collective bargaining, the powers of unionism were being tested in the two greatest industrial struggles of the period—the steel strike and the strike of soft coal miners. The former was by far the greater of the two. Since 1901 the Amalgamated Association of Iron and Steel Workers had continued to sign wage agreements with a number of steel mills; but its membership, confined to the skilled men, had been declining. The Amalgamated Association made some efforts to organize the unskilled, but failed because of two major obstacles. The skilled men were unwilling to sacrifice the loss of their high wages in prolonged strikes essential for organizing the unskilled; and the union mill employers opposed collective bargaining with the unskilled and made their contracts with the union contingent on the Amalgamated Association's not pressing the issue.

The war seemed to offer a new opportunity. The A. F. of L. convention in 1918 adopted a resolution introduced by William Z. Foster to begin an organizing campaign in the iron and steel industry. A national organizing committee was appointed consisting of the presidents of 24 international unions which had jurisdiction in the industry and were to finance the enterprise.[9]

In September 1918 organization was started in the

[9] The unions were those of the blacksmiths; boilermakers; brick and clay workers; bricklayers; structural iron workers; coopers; electrical workers; foundry employees; hod-carriers; iron and steel workers; machinists; mine, mill, and smelter workers; the coal mine workers; molders; pattern makers; plumbers; quarry workers; railway carmen; seamen; sheet metal workers; stationary firemen; steam and operating engineers; steamshovel and dredgemen; and switchmen. The headquarters were in Pittsburgh, and the committee was directed by John Fitzpatrick and W. Z. Foster.

Chicago district. Owing to the aid of the War Labor Board, which prevented the steel companies from discharging employees who joined the unions, considerable success was achieved. The steel companies endeavored to cut the ground from under the unions by promising the basic eight-hour day. But organizing continued, and by the spring of 1919 there were nuclei of organization in most of the steel centers of the country.

On July 20, 1919 the national committee met and drew up a list of demands, the more important of which were the abolition of the 24-hour shift, one day's rest in seven, wage increases to guarantee an American standard of living, the right of collective bargaining, the check-off system for collecting dues, and the abolition of "company unions." Of the 14 unions represented at this meeting, 12 voted in favor of taking a strike vote.[10] Within a month the vote had been taken and it was overwhelmingly in favor of a strike.

As the heads of the United States Steel Corporation refused to negotiate, Gompers asked President Wilson to intercede. But the President of the United States could not induce the corporation to give the unions a hearing. On September 9 the presidents of the international unions concerned met to consider issuing a strike call. Gompers was present and tried to ward it off, claiming that the open shop interests in New York had picked the United States Steel Corporation to start an attack against unionism. However, those favoring a strike urged that the boom in the industry and the labor shortage promised success while further delay might jeopardize the movement.

[10] Those voting against it were the Amalgamated Association of Iron, Steel, and Tin Workers and the United Mine Workers.

The strike call was issued for September 22. On September 10 President Wilson wired the committee to put off the strike until after the opening of the Industrial Conference. Gompers and the officers of several other international unions supported this request. But the national committee reaffirmed the strike order.

On September 22 the strike began. The unions estimated that 279,000 workers were idle on that day, and 367,000 by October 9. The steel companies maintained that there were never more than 200,000 workers out at one time. The companies enrolled a large number of deputy sheriffs and barricaded some of the mills. The Pittsburgh district impressed outside observers as preparing for civil war. Some clashes did occur, resulting in a number of deaths on both sides. In spite of these incidents, the strike, considering its magnitude, was remarkable for its peaceable character.[11]

The strike attracted wide public attention. In October a Senate committee conducted an investigation of the strike regions. Leaders of the Inter-Church World Movement[12] made efforts to bring both sides into con-

[11] Excepting the molders and coopers, who paid strike benefits to their members, the strikers were sustained by a commissariat which operated from October 26, 1919 to January 31, 1920 through 45 local commissaries. Standard packages of food were distributed bi-weekly to strikers' families, at a total cost of $348,509. Excluding local contributions, over a million dollars was raised. Of this amount, the co-operating international unions contributed $101,047 direct to the national committee; they, together with the A. F. of L., spent $479,375 in financing organizers. As a result of appeals issued by the A. F. of L. $426,832 was received. Among large outside donations were those of the Amalgamated Clothing Workers of $100,000, the International Ladies' Garment Workers of $60,000, the Furriers of $10,000, and the Marine Engineers of New York of $10,000. The sums contributed by locals of the Brotherhood of Carpenters and Joiners came to a very considerable sum.

[12] The Inter-Church World Movement of North America grew out of a conference called in 1918 by the executive committee of the Board of Foreign Missions of the Presbyterian Church in the United States (South)

ference. On November 9 the Senate committee reported, confirming the justice of the workers' complaints as to long hours, censuring the companies for not permitting the workers to select their own representatives to present grievances, but also affirming that there was a "red" element behind the strike. The anti-union press featured stories of violence and depicted the steel workers as uncouth aliens, unassimilated, and a menace to American institutions. The liberal press vehemently denounced "Garyism."

Early in November the strike showed signs of weakening. Members of the Amalgamated Association of Iron and Steel Workers began returning to work. Tighe, president of the Amalgamated Association, insisted that in the mills in which members of his organization were under contract they should be allowed to continue at work. This stand provoked much bitterness and recrimination. The introduction of colored strike-breakers, estimated at some 30,000, further undermined morale. During December several attempts were made to reinvigorate the strike, but without result. On January 8, 1920 it was called off.

The major cause of the loss of the steel strike was the determined attitude of the steel corporations to prevent unionization regardless of cost. The refusal of Gary to confer with strike leaders reflected the determination with which industrial and financial leaders had set themselves against unionism as a result of the war. The dis-

---

to discuss co-operation among the Protestant churches of the United States. The movement was endorsed by more than 70 denominational and interdenominational boards and agencies. It established an Industrial Relations Department which undertook the study of the steel industry. The Inter-Church World Movement Report on the strike was published in 1922. The Movement disbanded the same year because of lack of financial support.

trustful attitude of Gompers and of the Executive Council towards Foster, the jealousies of the 24 unions, the lack of co-ordination among their organizers, the jurisdictional fights between several of the unions involved, were serious contributory causes. Also Foster's radical record was used against the strike during its later stage.

The collapse of the strike ended the organizing campaign in the steel industry for the time being. The national committee was crippled by the withdrawal of the Amalgamated Association of Iron and Steel Workers, who refused to be further "subject to outside interference." Of the workers organized during the campaign, estimated at 250,000, few remained in the unions.

III. THE SOFT COAL STRIKE

While the steel strike proved the superior strength of the United States Steel Corporation, the coal miners' strike showed the changing attitude of the Wilson administration. The United Mine Workers had entered into a wage contract with the United States Fuel Administration in October 1917, which was to run for the duration of the war but in no case later than April 1, 1920. In February 1919 the Fuel Administration ceased to regulate coal prices and by the end of June 1919 it ceased to function. Coal prices to consumers soared with the general rise in the cost of living. The miners contended that for practical purposes the war was over and declined to consider themselves bound by war-time arrangements which no longer bound the operators. At the miners' convention in September 1919 a number of drastic demands, necessitated by the overgrown condition of the industry which was causing under-employment, were endorsed, including a 60 per cent wage increase, a six-hour day, and a five-day week. The officers of the union were authorized to call a strike in case no satisfactory agreement with the employers was reached. The mine operators refused to negotiate unless the strike order was cancelled. On October 15 the strike order, effective October 31, was issued to all districts, although the negotiations had included, as was habitual, only the operators of the central competitive field. Several efforts at settlement were made by the Secretary of Labor, but without success. On October 24, 1919 President Wilson issued a proclamation that the country was still at war and that a strike of miners which would prevent aid from going to the Allies was unjustifiable and unlawful. He appealed to the United Mine Workers to prevent a stoppage of work, offering to appoint a tribunal to investigate the facts.

On October 29 Gompers, after conferring with several members of the President's Cabinet, wired Lewis that if the strike were postponed a conference with the operators could be arranged. Gompers urged Lewis to "face the situation courageously and endeavor by all means to avert the strike or at least postpone it," the instructions of his convention notwithstanding. On the same day Attorney General A. Mitchell Palmer issued a statement that the strike was illegal because the Lever Act creating the Fuel Administration was still in force. He quoted sections of the Act which were aimed against combinations to limit facilities for production and transportation. Although the A. F. of L. had received assurance from Congress in August 1917 that these sections were not aimed against labor, Palmer warned that "every resource of the government would be brought to bear to prevent the national disaster which would inevitably result from the cessation of mining operations." On October 29 the miners' officials decided to go ahead on the ground that a great principle was at stake which could not be compromised.

On October 30 President Wilson restored the war-time regulations concerning coal prices. Nevertheless, on October 31, about 425,000 miners quit work, of whom 250,000 were in the Central Competitive Field. The same day the Attorney General, basing his action on the Lever Act, obtained from Judge Anderson of the Federal District Court of Indiana a restraining order which prevented the officers of the United Mine Workers and "all other persons whomsoever" from doing anything in any way connected with the strike.

The A. F. of L. leaders—Gompers, Morrison, and Woll—protested to the Attorney General and continued to strive for some basis of settlement. The government and the operators would assure nothing until the strike order was recalled. The miners would not take the first step, demanding that the restraining order be rescinded first.

On November 8 the court granted the government a permanent injunction and ordered the United Mine Workers to cancel the strike order by 6:00 p.m. on November 11. On November 10, in response to urgent appeals from the miners' leaders, the A. F. of L. Executive Council met and gave out a statement justifying the miners' strike, accusing the government of breaking faith with the miners in the matter of the Lever Act, and calling upon all affiliated organizations to support the United Mine Workers. The same day, however, a conference of the officials of the United Mine Workers was held in Indianapolis at which leaders from 16 districts insisted that the mine workers must show again that they were law-abiding citizens and refused to support a strike which implied defiance of the government. Lewis then called the strike off.

The rank and file of the miners failed to return to work when the strike order was rescinded. In many places the strike continued into December. On December 9 the union agreed to the Fuel Administration's proposal for a 14 per cent increase in wages to go into effect immediately and to President Wilson's proposal to appoint a tri-partite coal commission to pass on further demands.

IV. THE FEDERATION AT ITS HEIGHT

Despite the failure of reconstruction and of the steel and coal strikes, the A. F. of L. was carried to new heights during 1918-20, stimulated by the shortage of labor, the industrial boom, the rising cost of living, and the post-Armistice restlessness. The gain in membership of its unions was 1,375,000 members, and the total average membership for 1920 was 4,078,740, or twice that of 1914.

Excepting unions which had become stationary before 1914 or such as were troubled by internal divisions, all the international unions affiliated with the A. F. of L. shared this advance. But the most spectacular gains were made by unions in trades affected by the war—munitions, shipbuilding, car repairs, railroads, textiles, and clothing.[13] Notable advances were made also by longshoremen, teamsters, seamen, street and electric railway em-

[13] The Machinists' Union reached a membership of over 300,000; the Boilermakers' Union jumped to over 100,000; the membership of the Railway Carmen went to 182,000; and that of the Railway Clerks to 186,000. The latter two unions built themselves up from insignificant beginnings. See Appendix B, pp. 502-03 and 538-40.

ployees, and by painters, carpenters, and electrical workers. The effect of the work of the War Labor Board and other governmental adjustment agencies was seen especially in the growth of unionism in the oil fields, the packing industry, shipbuilding, and transportation.[14]

The financial resources of the unions were augmented by the increase in membership and were further strengthened by the general tendency to raise union dues and other payments. The budgets of the larger international unions began to run into hundreds of thousands and millions of dollars. These larger funds gave impetus to organization drives on a new scale. Big, costly strikes were carried on. Also, the unions used their newly acquired means to strengthen permanent benefit funds to establish reserves and to acquire office buildings.

Relying on their economic and financial strength, the various international unions made the largest drive in the history of American trade unionism for the extension of collective bargaining[15] and for higher wages and shorter hours. The eight-hour day was introduced into unionized sections of many industries while the 44-hour week became a reality in the clothing and building trades.

[14] See Appendix A, pp. 476-83.

[15] In a number of industries collective bargaining was extended by the continuation of the government agencies inaugurated during the war. Several shipbuilding companies, for instance, negotiated agreements with the Metal Trades Department of the A. F. of L. after the Shipbuilding Labor Adjustment Board was dissolved in March 1919. The Bethlehem Shipbuilding Company made an agreement covering 75,000 workers and providing for the adjustment of all matters relating to hours, wages, and working conditions by a committee representing management at the various plants of the company and a committee representing the international unions in the Metal Trades Department. A few months later a similar agreement was signed with the American Shipbuilding Co. for 22,000 workers in shipyards on the Great Lakes. In the packing industry, in the California oil fields, and in copper mining, labor adjusters who had been set up as arbitrators in 1917-18 continued to function through 1919-20.

The standard working week for industry as a whole was reduced from 53.3 hours in 1916 to 50.4 in 1920, and for unskilled labor from 55.2 hours in 1916 to 53.7 in 1920. While some of the largest gains were made in unorganized trades, and while some trades with long established unions fell behind, trade union activity raised wage rates and real earnings in a considerable number of industries.[16]

The outlook and programs of most unions were much enlarged as a result of the new feeling of power. Demands for a living wage on a basis of comfort became general. The traditional demands for a voice in determining working conditions were interpreted to mean industrial citizenship and constitutional government in industry. Many of the international unions also felt the need for wider social activities and provided health services, education, and recreational opportunities for their members.

Also, the receipts of the A. F. of L. rose to $780,008 for the year ending May 1, 1919 and to $1,121,746 in 1920.[17] Though rising prices increased operating costs,[18] the Federation was able to use more money for organizing purposes. In 1919, $165,609 was spent for such work, and in 1920, $285,584.[19] The organizers of the

[16] See Paul H. Douglas, *Real Wages in the United States, 1890-1926*, pp. 256-57; "Union Scales of Wages and Hours of Labor," *U. S. Bureau of Labor Statistics Bulletin No. 540*, 1931, p. 14.

[17] This increase was in part accounted for by raising the per capita tax in 1919 from seven-eighths of a cent to one cent per member per month or to twelve cents per member per year.

[18] The salaries of organizers were raised from $7.00 to $8.00 per day, and their expense allowances from $4.00 to $6.00. The salary of the president of the A. F. of L. was raised in 1919 from $7,500, over the protest of Gompers, to $10,000, and that of the secretary from $5,000 to $7,500. In 1921 they were raised to $12,000 and $10,000 respectively.

[19] See pp. 360-64.

A. F. of L. were active over a wide expanse of territory, especially in Pennsylvania, New York, and Ohio.

The rapid advance was in itself sufficient to cause widespread ferment in the unions. The new members, unfamiliar with established traditions and methods, placed large expectations in labor organization, and were ready for aggressive action. In many locals and in some of the international unions, there was a turnover in leadership which brought to the fore new men. The war phrase "industrial democracy" and the post-Armistice talk about reconstruction helped to swell the wave of economic and social radicalism.

In some ways the developments of these years followed the trends of 1910-14. But they were also influenced by many new ideas evolved in Europe and dramatized to the world by the British labor unions and Soviet Russia. Such were the demands for shop councils and shop stewards, for new methods of organizing, for mass tactics against employers, for democracy in union administration, and for larger political and social goals. There was, therefore, considerable agitation in many international unions and in the A. F. of L. as a whole, but the city central unions formed the rallying point for the radical forces.

Through 1919 A. F. of L. leaders watched with concern the manifestations of the rising tide of radicalism—the Seattle general strike,[20] the agitation over the

[20] In January 1919, 32,000 shipyard workers in Seattle went on a strike which continued for six weeks and became a general sympathetic strike of all organized labor in Seattle. The mayor of Seattle, Ole Hanson, called out the state militia, and afterwards claimed credit for suppressing the strike. The officers of the international unions in most instances failed to countenance the strike of their locals and ordered the men back to work; and the A. F. of L. severely censured the central labor union of Seattle for its action in calling the strike for alleged "un-American" motives.

Mooney-Billings Case,[21] the "One Big Union" movement,[22] the "illegal" strikes of printers, longshoremen, and miners, and the new moves for an independent labor party.[23] In the fall of 1919 there were rumors that the success of the steel strike would be the entering wedge for a concerted attack upon the old leadership of the A. F. of L. and for a revision of policy.[24]

The first skirmish between radicals and conservatives took place at the Atlantic City convention in June 1919. Of the several issues which served as points of contest between the opposing forces, most important were the Plumb Plan for the nationalization of railroads,[25] politi-

[21] In January 1919 a labor congress was called in Chicago by the International Workers' Defense League to protest against the continued imprisonment of Mooney. It was endorsed by the Chicago Federation of Labor and the central labor unions of Seattle and Oakland. A thousand delegates attended, and voted to submit to the local unions a referendum for a nation-wide strike for four days beginning July 4, if Mooney were not granted a new trial before then.

[22] In March 1919 a western labor conference composed of 237 delegates from four Canadian provinces met at Calgary and adopted resolutions calling upon organized labor to sever connections with the old-line unions and to form an industrial organization of all workers, with the ultimate end in view of abolishing the profit-making system of production. Thus was launched the "One Big Union" movement which reached its climax in the general strike in Winnipeg in May 1919.

[23] Beginning with the formation of the Labor Party of Greater New York in January 1919 and with the campaign of John Fitzpatrick for mayor of Chicago in April 1919, the movement gained strength. It culminated in the formation of the National Labor Party in November 1919.

[24] The leaders of the A. F. of L. in 1919-20 tried to explain the radical elements as a phase of Bolshevism. As a matter of fact, the "Bolshevist" element in the trade union radicalism was slight. The quarrels between right and left socialists and the various communist groups were carried on outside the trade unions. The Third International was still in the process of finding itself, and its activities in the trade unions had not yet begun. See Lewis L. Lorwin, *Labor and Internationalism*, pp. 229-31.

[25] The Plumb Plan was advocated in 1919 by Glenn E. Plumb, counsel for some of the Railroad Brotherhoods. The basic idea advanced by the plan was to make the national government trustee for the entire railroad system. The management was to be in the hands of a board of directors,

cal action, political amnesty, the Mooney case, and Soviet Russia. The radicals won in having the convention demand a pardon for Mooney, the commutation of sentences of war political prisoners, and in obtaining approval of the Plumb Plan. But the leaders in control of the Federation won out on most other points by a safe majority vote. The convention approved the reconstruction program of the Executive Council, condemned the Soviet government of Russia, curtailed the rights of city centrals to conduct strikes,[26] and rejected proposals for such changes in the constitution of the A. F. of L. as the election of officers by referendum vote.

The radical tide continued to rise in the fall of 1919, accentuated by the experience of the steel and coal strikes and by the breakdown of President Wilson's industrial conference. On the other hand, the "anti-red" hysteria and the campaign for 100 per cent Americanism being at their height, public opinion was agitated over the growing power of labor and "Bolshevism."[27] The leaders of

consisting of 15 members—5 appointed by the President of the United States to represent the public, 5 elected by the classified railroad employees to represent labor, and 5 elected by the railroad officials to represent the management. Government bonds were to be issued to purchase the railroads at valuations determined by the courts. A gradual amortization was to take place through the reduction of the outstanding indebtedness by 1 per cent each year. Profits resulting from efficient operation, after fixed charges were met, were to be divided equally between the government and the operating force. Whenever the government's share of profits exceeded a fixed percentage of the gross operating revenue, the freight and passenger rates were to be reduced to absorb the government's surplus.

[26] See pp. 346-49.

[27] The high spots of this period were the conviction of Debs and four other officials of the Socialist Party under the Espionage Act in January 1919; the conviction of 44 I.W.W.s in Sacramento, Calif.; the activities of the Lusk Committee in New York in the summer of 1919; the Centralia Case; the raids of the Department of Justice in August 1919 and January 1920; the deportation of 249 radicals to Soviet Russia on the steamer *Buford;* and the refusal to seat Victor Berger, elected to Congress from Milwaukee.

the A. F. of L. were between the devil and the deep sea. They were disappointed and hurt by the attitude of employers and of the government, which seemed to them to show a lack of recognition of labor's war services. At the same time, they were anxious to restrain the radical forces in the labor movement which threatened to make a sweep of established methods and policies. The majority of officers in the unions of the Federation shared the antagonism of the public toward radicalism and were unable to shake off the psychology of war emotions.

To ward off the radicals and to placate public opinion, the Executive Council of the A. F. of L. called a conference for December 13, 1919 in Washington. The chiefs of the Railroad Brotherhoods who were asked to this conference urged Gompers and his associates to invite the Non-Partisan League[28] in order to unite farmers and workers on a general legislative program. But the Executive Council objected that this might be an entering wedge for a new party. The report which they prepared and which was adopted by the conference under the title "Labor's Bill of Rights," besides reiterating the main ideas of the reconstruction program of 1918, censured the United States Steel Corporation, called for the deflation of the currency and for disclosure of costs and profits by corporations, expressed the willingness of labor to co-operate with scientific management in lowering costs of production, and endorsed the League of Nations and the International Labor Organization. The conference offered no immediate measures for general and concerted action by labor.[29]

[28] The Non-Partisan League, the radical farmers' organization in the Northwest, was at the height of its power at this time.

[29] The conference rejected a suggestion made by some members to

During 1920 the struggle of the Executive Council against radicalism centered around the presidential campaign and the National Labor Party. The latter had been formed in November 1919 by various local and state labor parties which came into existence after the Armistice. Under the leadership of the Chicago Federation of Labor, it had adopted a collectivist program, attracted some socialist groups, and had become the rallying point of the politically radical trade unionists.

To counteract the National Labor Party, Gompers[30] threw himself energetically into the political campaign. He appointed a committee consisting of the entire Executive Council and of the officers of the departments to consider ways and means of combating the growing sentiment in favor of a labor party. A special bureau of publicity and a speakers' bureau were set up for campaign purposes. An appeal for funds was issued which brought in nearly $30,000 within two months. Altogether $53,934 was raised and expended. At first the campaign of the A. F. of L. attracted attention in the press. The fact that the A. F. of L. was a great deal stronger in 1920 than before the war lent a new interest to its political activities.

The campaign, begun with much advertising, amounted to little. The A. F. of L. submitted its demands to both the Republican and Democratic conven-

---

censure the government for having aided the steel corporations. Hutcheson, president of the Carpenters' Union, protested that there was enough I.W.W.ism in the labor movement, and that he, as an American citizen, would not go on record as saying that the government agencies were autocratic and oppressive.

[30] Aside from his opposition to radicalism and independent politics, Gompers was moved by his commitment to support President Wilson, especially on issues of foreign policy.

tions in 1920, but neither gave them much consideration. The Executive Council of the A. F. of L. condemned the Republican Party as the "unqualified defender of the enemies of labor," but refrained from approving the Democratic candidates for the presidency and the vice-presidency.

The activities of the A. F. of L. did help to frustrate the forces of independent labor politics. Many city centrals and state federations, fearing the displeasure of A. F. of L. headquarters, dissociated themselves from the movement. The Farmer-Labor Party[31] polled a small vote in the elections. The A. F. of L. reasserted once more its non-partisan policy.

In the industrial field the leaders of the A. F. of L. during 1919-20 squelched not only the movements for "One Big Union" and for the "Seattle Amalgamation Plan,"[32] but also all demands for additional departments.[33] Though a great part of the organizing activities of the Federation during these years were among relatively unskilled workers, the A. F. of L. continued to favor the skilled trades in the numerous jurisdictional disputes caused by the growth of unions and by industrial changes. Despite many demands to reconsider the entire question of internal structure, the Executive Council clung to its traditional policy of trade autonomy and narrow interpretation of the Scranton Declaration.[34]

[31] The National Labor Party in July 1920 joined forces with the radical wing of the Committee of Forty-Eight to form the Farmer-Labor Party which nominated P. P. Christensen and Max Hayes for the presidency and vice-presidency.

[32] This plan provided for the reorganization of the unions of the A. F. of L. into twelve departments.

[33] See pp. 339-40.

[34] See pp. 68-69.

V. THE AFFILIATION OF THE RAILROAD BROTHERHOODS

One of the most important results of the policy of the A. F. of L. during these years was the failure to secure the affiliation of the Railroad Brotherhoods. Since 1889 the A. F. of L. had repeatedly urged the Brotherhoods to affiliate. During the decade preceding the World War, relations were uncertain. There were friendliness and co-operation at the top, particularly in legislative activities, but in the ranks sometimes acute friction and sometimes co-operation went further than the chiefs approved. In 1914-15 relations were again strained, largely because the Railroad Brotherhoods would not co-operate with the shop crafts in their wage demands. There were many outbursts of impatience in the ranks of the A. F. of L. and even threats of starting dual unions, to which the Brotherhoods retorted that they would withdraw their patronage of union-label goods. One of the greatest stumbling blocks in the path of unity was the Switchmen's Union of North America, a small organization of about 9,000 members. The A. F. of L. recognized it as the only bona fide organization of railroad yard employees, thus treading on the toes of the Brotherhood of Railroad Trainmen, which claimed about 34,000 of this class of the service. To enter the A. F. of L. implied for the trainmen the necessity of accepting rulings by the Executive Council and the convention concerning jurisdictional rights.

In 1916-17 the campaign for the eight-hour day which resulted in the Adamson Law brought the Brotherhoods closer to the A. F. of L. But when Gompers, on October 13, 1917, wrote to the four chiefs urging affiliation, reinforcing his appeal with the argument that "a united labor movement would be the strongest answer to the enemies of our country and our cause," three of the chiefs replied, stating the obstacles at some length. Warren S. Stone, the grand chief of the Locomotive Engineers, gave the most comprehensive statement. He mentioned three fields in which jurisdictional disputes were particularly feared—between the switchmen and the railway trainmen; between the locomotive engineers and the Amalgamated Association of Electric and Street Railway Employees, who were laying claim to all electric lines; and between the Brotherhood of Locomotive Engineers and the Brotherhood of Locomotive Firemen and Enginemen. The dispute between the two latter organizations had long been quiescent, because of the personal influence of the officers, but it was feared that in an A. F. of L. convention some member of the "candlestick makers'" union might get up and offer a resolution that only one organization of engineers be recognized. Then war would break out.

Other objections concerned the A. F. of L. policy of the closed shop and the method in vogue in the building trades of settling disputes by calling strikes in defiance of agreements. Just how these practices affected the Brotherhoods was not very clear, but they contributed to a feeling of uneasiness over possible consequences of affiliation. The Brotherhoods did not advocate the closed union shop, insisted upon regular and peaceable negotiations concerning working conditions, and felt that some of the A. F. of L. unions acted differently and might not tolerate these practices. In addition, the Brotherhood of Firemen and Enginemen feared that the A. F. of L. would force it to admit negro workers to membership. Gompers personally assured them that this would not happen, but his assurance was not enough.

In spite of these arguments, the Brotherhood of Locomotive Engineers at its May 1918 convention voted to affiliate with the A. F. of L. During 1919 all four of the Railroad Brotherhoods applied to the Federation for charters. The new factor in the situation was the desire of the Brotherhoods to have the support of the A. F. of L. in their fight for the Plumb Plan and against such legislation as later resulted in the Esch-Cummins bill. But as negotiations proceeded the leaders of the A. F. of L. became more and more indifferent to the proposal of affiliation. Most of them had no use for the Plumb Plan[35] and were afraid that by endorsing it they would place themselves under the orders and leadership of the Brotherhoods, which might lead them into an independent labor party.

Technically, the negotiations for the admission of the Brotherhoods were blocked by the attitude of the Amalgamated Association of Street and Electric Railway Employees. During the fall of 1919 Grand Chief Stone and President W. D. Mahon of the Street and Electric Railway Employees negotiated about the claim of both organizations to electric railway motormen. No adjustment was reached as Mahon opposed admitting the locomotive engineers first and arbitrating afterwards. The applications of the Brotherhoods were laid over until the meeting of the Executive Council in May 1920, but were not considered.

At the 1920 convention of the A. F. of L. the railway

[35] In a report on the subject to the Executive Council, Matthew Woll argued that the Plumb Plan was financially unsound and would deprive widows and orphans of their savings, that it would set a dangerous precedent and be followed by plans to nationalize other industries, and that it would deprive the Brotherhoods of the right to strike.

unions fought for the endorsement of the Plumb Plan.[36] Despite the arguments of Gompers, Frey, and Woll, the convention went on record in favor of the plan by a vote of 29,159 to 8,349. However, nothing came of this spectacular victory of the progressive forces. The Railroad Brotherhoods were already losing interest in the Plumb Plan, having decided in favor of a compromise with the railroad managements on condition that their war-time gains be safeguarded. The Executive Council of the A. F. of L. was advised to let the plan alone. With the shelving of the Plumb Plan, the matter of the affiliation of the Railroad Brotherhoods was dropped.

VI. SUMMARY

In brief, the A. F. of L. came through the unrest of reconstruction essentially unchanged though much enlarged in scope and influence. At its peak, in midsummer of 1920, it represented an alliance of 110 unions with over four million members out of an estimated total of 5,136,000 organized workers in the country.[37] It was showing an interest in the larger problems of economic life and world politics. Against the will of its leaders it had endorsed the Plumb Plan and had approved and endorsed the demand of the United Mine Workers for the nationalization of mines. It was demanding government control of credit. It gave its support to many of the newer enterprises of its unions, especially to that of workers' education.[38] But in all these respects it was

[36] Their case was argued by William H. Johnston, president of the Machinists' Union, and William Green, then secretary of the United Mine Workers.

[37] Leo Wolman, *Trade Union Growth in the United States*, p. 136.

[38] See pp. 439-43.

often acting under the stress of unrest, and its leaders took no steps to devise methods for putting these policies into effect.[39]

[39] Between 1917 and 1920 the Executive Council underwent some changes. Daniel J. Tobin, of the Teamsters' Union, became treasurer of the Federation in 1917. James O'Connell resigned in 1918 and his place was taken by Jacob Fischer, president of the Barbers' Union. In the same year T. A. Rickert, president of the United Garment Workers, was elected a member of the Council. In 1919 Matthew Woll became eighth vice-president. These changes broke up the old nucleus which Gompers had on the Council; but he formed a new one, including Rickert and Woll.

CHAPTER IX

NORMALCY AND RETREAT

With the election in November 1920 of Warren G. Harding as President of the United States, America turned from "reconstruction" to "normalcy." The next four years, characterized by reaction against pre-war social idealism and war-time Wilsonian internationalism, strengthened the economic and political position of the business elements, while organized labor lost ground.

I. THE OPEN SHOP DRIVE

During 1921-22 the unions in the A. F. of L. were occupied primarily with the problems of resisting the recoil from the post-Armistice boom and the anti-union drive. Business men generally took the position that wages had to be "deflated" and many employers, restive under labor domination since 1917, began to seek freedom from unionism. Profiting by the industrial depression,[1] they inaugurated an open shop campaign which in vigor, extent, and results exceeded all previous experience.

The same organizations that had been active before 1914 took the leading part in this open shop drive. The National Association of Manufacturers and the National Metal Trades Association, after the war and post-war experience, were now interested in eliminating the causes of labor unrest, their premise being that unionism would

[1] Labor was hard hit by the depression. In December 1920 the number of idle was estimated at 2,000,000, and in August 1921 at 5,735,000. About 209 cities with a population of over 20,000 organized emergency unemployment committees during the winter of 1921 to give urgently needed relief.

not flourish among contented workers. They turned to scientific management and to efficiency engineers, whose work had received an enormous impetus during the war and who were now beginning to "sell" employers the idea of "personnel management" as a means of solving the "labor problem." Employee representation plans were approved by the National Association of Manufacturers as a basis of industrial relations which made unionism unnecessary. The American Anti-Boycott Association, having changed its name to League for Industrial Rights, opened an Industrial Relations Department for the purpose of giving advice to members upon the latest developments in personnel welfare work and "industrial democracy." It further stressed the idea of making unions responsible for the acts of their agents, and of establishing the legal principle that where an employee has contracted with an employer not to enter a union it should be illegal for the union, having knowledge of the contract, to induce the employee to violate it.[2]

Early in 1920, after the failure of the steel strike, several associations of employers in the metal trades entered into an agreement to support the open shop. In June 1920 the United States Chamber of Commerce, in a referendum adopted by its members, stressed "the right of open shop operations" by employers. In the fall of 1920 the National Association of Manufacturers established an open shop department which started issuing special bulletins.[3] Within a short time these efforts were

[2] This is the essence of what the unions call "Yellow Dog Contracts"—a variation of the old "Iron Clad."

[3] In 1923 the convention of the National Association of Manufacturers defined an open shop as "an establishment where employment relations are determined by individual right of contract, without arbitrary discrimina-

seconded by old and newly formed local and state employers' associations and citizens' committees under a variety of names, such as the Southwest Open Shop Association, the American Plan League (formed by the Associated Employers of Indianapolis), the American Plan Open Shop Conference.[4] In some localities the chambers of commerce took a leading part in this drive.

The open shop move was directed primarily against the unions in the building and metal trades. The acute housing shortage was attributed to the high wages and union rules of these trades. Public opinion was inflamed against labor because of graft in some unions and collusion between employers and some workers' organizations. The public seemed to hear less about illegal combinations of dealers and supply men. The tactics of some of the unions in minimizing the charges brought against them and in refusing to abide by arbitration awards strengthened the employers' organizations in their fight. In the end, the associations succeeded in breaking union control in a number of cities. Even San Francisco—at one time the union stronghold of America—was temporarily turned into an open shop city by the activities of the Industrial Association formed by the Chamber of Commerce.[5]

The National Metal Trades Association was aroused

---

tion based on membership or non-membership in any lawful labor organization."

[4] Robert W. Dunn in *The Americanization of Labor* lists over 300 such associations in New York, Illinois, Ohio, Pennsylvania, Michigan, California, Texas, and Iowa. Many of these, however, were paper organizations. See also Magnus W. Alexander, "Employers' Associations in the United States," *International Labor Review*, May 1932, pp. 605-20.

[5] There were efforts of an opposite character to promote industrial co-operation, as exemplified in the National Board of Industrial Awards in the building industry and in the National Council of Industrial Relations in the electrical construction industry. See pp. 515-19.

by the enormous strides made by the Machinists' Union during 1919-20 as a result of vigorous strikes. As the latter organization and other unions in the metal trades operated in both railroad shops and private foundries and machine shops, the National Metal Trades Association became interested in establishing an open shop policy on the railroads. Its efforts in this direction met with increasing success.

While the open shop campaign was achieving results, union control was being further broken down as a result of union efforts to maintain their gains of previous years in spite of the depression. Only a few unions adopted the policy of trying to keep employers in line by granting concessions. In the clothing, printing, coal mining, and textile industries, strikes and lockouts resulted from the inability of employers and workers to readjust wages downward by mutual agreement.

Early in 1921, as unemployment and the open shop drive were threatening the union gains made in 1919-20, there was a demand for a plan of co-ordinated action. In response the Executive Council of the A. F. of L. convened a conference of trade union officials which met at headquarters on February 23 and 24, 1921 to consider the problems arising from "unemployment, reaction, and Bolshevism." The conference decided to organize a publicity bureau to win public opinion for the workers, but could offer little tangible aid to the unions. Each international union had to face its own problems and try to maintain its position in the face of depression and deflation. Some of the unions proved more than able to hold their own.[6] But generally the unions were on the losing side.[7]

[6] The major strike of 1922 which ended in favor of the workers was that of the soft coal miners. Some unions in the building trades made

II. THE RAILWAY SHOP CRAFTS

The climax of the unsuccessful struggles of 1921-22 was the strike of the railway shopmen. The shop craft unions[8] had benefited from the operation of the railroads by the government. The Board of Railroad Wages and Working Conditions set up in 1918 eliminated many of the inequalities and discriminations in wage rates, thus creating a fairly balanced wage structure for certain branches of the service. About 1,500,000 employees, or over 80 per cent of those in the entire service, were affected. Piece work was abolished in all organized railroad repair shops by a vote of the system federations in January 1919.[9] During 1919 the shop craft unions bent their efforts to secure a national agreement covering all the roads, which would introduce uniformity in hours, in overtime rates of pay, seniority, and other working rules. Demands for wage increases were also raised by various branches of the service. As negotiations dragged along,

---

gains in wages and obtained the 44-hour week. The International Ladies' Garment Workers' Union won a large strike in New York in 1922 by obtaining a writ of injunction against the employers. The Typographical Union ordered a nation-wide strike on May 1, 1921 for the 44-hour week. It continued for over two years, involving 20,000 members and costing the union over $15,000,000, but was only partly successful. The union won the 44-hour week where it retained control, but the open shop elements gained control over a larger section of the industry.

[7] In the oil fields and packing plants in which unionism had been established by war adjustment boards, wages were cut and the machinery for collective bargaining scrapped. The agreements signed in the spring of 1919 between the Metal Trades Department of the A. F. of L. and the Bethlehem Shipbuilding Company and the American Shipbuilding Company, covering 100,000 workers, were abrogated in July 1921 after successive wage cuts. In May 1921 the seamen and marine engineers went on strike against a wage cut which resulted in the lapsing of the collective agreements with the American Steamship Owners' Association. Serious losses were experienced by the building trades unions in a number of the large cities of the country. See Appendix B.

[8] For organization of these unions and their relation to the Department of Railway Employees of the A. F. of L., see pp. 390-91.

[9] For the system federations, see pp. 391-92.

unauthorized strikes, involving some 250,000 men, broke out in August 1919, the rank and file being anxious to force a decision. The government granted a flat wage increase of four cents an hour but refused further increases, holding out the promise of reducing the cost of living. In September the government signed national agreements with the six shop crafts and with ten railroad unions including the maintenance of way employees, stationary firemen and oilers, railway clerks, and signalmen.

When the railroads were returned to private ownership in March 1920 under the Esch-Cummins Act, the United States Railroad Labor Board was set up. It represented management, organized employees, and the public in the settlement of disputes which could not be disposed of by direct negotiations. On July 20, 1920 the Railroad Labor Board granted wage increases of 22 per cent, bringing the rate for shop mechanics, excepting carmen, up to 85 cents an hour, the highest ever paid.

Throughout 1921 and 1922 friction between the unions and the Board increased. Early in 1921 the railroad managements inaugurated demands for the abrogation of the national agreements, followed by demands for wage reductions. In April the Board abrogated the much prized agreements, and instructed carriers and unions to negotiate new agreements by systems, under conditions which, to make matters worse, opened the door to company unions. As a direct result the shop crafts organization on the Pennsylvania Railroad disintegrated in the face of determined managerial opposition. In July a general 12 per cent wage reduction was ordered for all railroad workers, which very nearly precipitated a strike. It did not materialize at this time, however, chiefly because the four Railroad Brotherhoods at the last minute gained their demands and did not strike.

When the Railway Employees Department assembled in convention in April 1922, there was much excitement and indignation among the delegates over the abrogation of the national agreements, the practice of contracting out repair work, and the proposal of the railroad managements to restore piece work. Against the advice of some of the officers, who thought a nationwide strike inopportune and inexpedient, a strike ballot was authorized on the last two points. On June 5, 1922 the Railroad Labor Board ordered another wage cut. This award was likewise submitted to the membership when the ballots were sent out on June 8. On all three questions about 95 per cent of the men voted to strike. On July 1 and the following days about 400,000 shopmen walked out. The convention had previously directed that in case a strike was ordered, it should cover all the railroads and that no separate settlements with single roads be made.

The Railroad Labor Board made a final attempt to prevent the strike. But the shop craft union heads refused to appear when summoned, for fear they would thus disorganize the walkout. However, the officials of the Maintenance of Way Employees' Union, whose members had voted to walk out, were persuaded by the Board to abandon the strike, with the result that members of this union joined in the strike in a few places only. The train service men continued at work during the entire strike. By October 1922 virtually all the roads had renewed agreements with the four Brotherhoods, continuing working rules and the same rates of pay. The shop crafts maintained that the Brotherhoods thus realized benefits from the strike by refusing to participate in it.

A. F. of L. headquarters played a more active part in the shopmen's strike than in any other strike or lockout of these years. On August 29 the Executive Council of the A. F. of L. issued an appeal for funds.[10] Gompers repeatedly tried to bring the Brotherhoods and the Railway Employees Department into closer contact with the Executive Council of the A. F. of L. by organizing a national policy committee, but without success. The principal contribution of the A. F. of L. lay in its efforts to influence public opinion. From the beginning the strike was put in an unpopular light by President Harding's proclamation warning strikers against interfering with the movement of interstate commerce—particularly the United States mails. B. M. Jewell, the president of the Railway Employees Department, replied that the organized employees were not combating the Labor Board or the government but were engaged in a dispute with their employers concerning wages and working conditions. Their action, it was maintained, at no point violated the Transportation Act. The minimum wage set by the Board at 23 cents an hour, making an average for all section men of 32.7 cents, was declared to be insufficient for a decent standard of living, and the Board was accused of having failed to take into account wages paid for similar work in other industries, or the relation between wages and the cost of living.

On July 27 the Executive Council of the Railway Employees Department and President Harding reached an agreement concerning terms of settlement. This was to be submitted to the railway managements and to the General Conference Committee of the workers, which alone had power to settle the strike.[11]

[10] It brought in only $16,178, but its purpose was to give the strikers moral support.

[11] This conference committee was composed of delegates from system federations. See pp. 390-91.

On August 1 the railway managements agreed to most of the terms, but refused to guarantee strikers returning to work their seniority rights. On August 2 the General Conference Committee accepted the agreement, provided all terms were enforced. President Harding on August 7 appealed to the shopmen to return to work and to bring the seniority question before the Railroad Labor Board. This they refused to do. The railroad managements, on the other hand, would make no concession on this issue.[12]

Negotiations were continued with the Railway Executives until August 25, but without success. With the failure of the general negotiations, the strike entered a critical phase. Funds were low. The strategic position of the shopmen had already been weakened by the failure of the maintenance of way employees, clerks, station men, and the Brotherhoods to walk out with them, by the procedure of the Railroad Labor Board, and by the action of the railroads in procuring numerous restraining orders against the strikers. But now Attorney General Daugherty swung into action. On September 1 he obtained from Judge Wilkerson in the Chicago Federal Court an order restraining the Railway Employees Department from using funds or doing anything in support of the strike. The order was based upon alleged conspiracy to violate the Sherman Act and the Transportation Act of 1920. Acts of violence and interference with the mails and interstate commerce gave grounds for the former charge, disobedience to the decision of the Railroad Labor Board for the latter.[13] The unions disregarded the injunction,

[12] Letter of Association of Railway Executives to President Harding, Aug. 11, 1922.

[13] It is widely conceded that in this injunction the use of the Sherman Act to interfere with trade union activities was pushed to its

but the strike had already begun to slacken. When three railroad presidents offered to continue negotiations, even the General Conference Committee was willing to settle, leaving the troublesome seniority question to be disposed of by a joint commission. On September 15 an agreement was signed with the Seaboard Air Line, New York Central, and Baltimore and Ohio railroads, which became known as the Baltimore Agreement. It was eventually adopted by eight more railroad systems. On the other railroads the strike was not called off until 1923 although it disintegrated long before.

III. ADVERSE COURT DECISIONS AND LEGISLATION

While meeting reverses in the industrial field, the A. F. of L. was also experiencing setbacks in the courts and state legislatures. Even during 1917-18, while organized labor was receiving favorable consideration from the Wilson administration, the courts rendered several decisions which imperiled the rights of unions. In December 1917 the Supreme Court of the United States upheld the decree of the lower court in *Hitchman Coal Company* v. *United Mine Workers of America* that a union must not interfere with employees having individual contracts with a company in which they promised not to join labor organizations. In April 1919 a federal

furthest logical limit. The strike was neither a sympathetic strike nor a boycott, nor was it conducted for purposes such as organization of non-union workers which might be construed as only remotely affecting the welfare of the strikers. It was a strike over a wage dispute, and was conducted by employees against their immediate employers. The attorneys of the unions pointed this out at court hearings and moved to dismiss the government's bill on the grounds that the strike was a lawful strike. They contended that the Attorney General was himself unlawfully aiding the railway executives in a conspiracy to destroy the railway unions, as part of a national open shop campaign. Nevertheless, the order was granted and was made permanent on May 1, 1923.

court of appeals, in *United Mine Workers* v. *Coronado Coal Company*, upheld a judgment against the union for triple damages under the Sherman Act for calling a strike in Arkansas.

After 1919 courts became an even greater factor in blocking union efforts. On May 2, 1919 a North Carolina judge—the same one who had challenged the constitutionality of the 1916 federal child labor law—declared the second child labor law, enacted February 24, 1919, invalid on the grounds that Congress had attempted to use its power of taxation to accomplish indirectly a purpose which it could not legally accomplish directly.[14] On January 3, 1921 the United States Supreme Court handed down a decision against the unions in *Duplex* v. *Deering*. It held that, notwithstanding the Clayton Act, the boycott conducted by the International Association of Machinists against the non-union Duplex Company, a manufacturer of printing presses, to force unionization of its plant was illegal under the Sherman Act. The court held that this was not a dispute between an employer and his employees; that the Clayton Act did not apply because only Section 6 applied to labor as a class, while Section 20 applied to employers and their own employees only. The majority opinion held that Congress had not intended to "confer a general immunity for conduct violative of the anti-trust laws or otherwise unlawful," because it had emphatically used the words "lawful" and "lawfully," "peaceful" and "peacefully" in speaking of labor activities.[15] In the same year, in *American Steel Foundries* v. *Tri-City Trades*

[14] See pp. 406-07.

[15] Justice Brandeis rendered a dissenting opinion in which Justice Holmes and Justice Clarke concurred.

and Labor Council, picketing was limited to "peaceful" picketing, and to the stationing of a single picket at each entrance of a factory.

The year 1922 brought new disasters to labor in the courts. In June the Coronado case was decided by the United States Supreme Court. Although the Supreme Court rescinded the verdict against the United Mine Workers for damages, its decision was regarded as distinctly unfavorable to labor, for it held that a trade union was suable and that its funds were "subject to execution in suits for torts committed in strikes." In September Attorney General Daugherty had obtained the injunction from Judge Wilkerson against the striking shopmen. During the year the United Mine Workers and other international unions were also hampered in their activities by numerous injunctions.

These court actions indicated that the menace of the injunction to the A. F. of L. had not been lessened if not increased by the Clayton Act. The provision responsible for this was Section 16 whereby private parties were given the right to sue for injunctions in the federal courts. Until then only the government had exercised this prerogative. The private injunction suit was the form of prosecution under the anti-trust acts which proved to be the most dangerous. In spite of the precedents for depleting unions of their funds in damage suits set by *Loewe* v. *Lawler*, comparatively few suits for damages had been instituted against unions, because of the long and costly proceedings involved and the uncertainty of obtaining not only judgments, but collections. The injunction was far more effective than the damage suit in defeating a strike or boycott. Regardless of the ultimate outcome a suit could badly cripple a union during the crucial period of an industrial dispute. Lower courts were not prevented by any number of Supreme Court decisions from issuing temporary restraining orders and injunctions, the annulment of which involved costly litigation and much delay.

Public opinion evidenced its unfriendly attitude towards unionism also in state legislation designed to destroy the more radical types of unions and in general to curb the power to strike. Most of the criminal syndicalism laws were passed in 1919-20,[16] but their full effects were felt between 1921 and 1923. The A. F. of L. did not show much concern over these laws, because they were used chiefly against the I. W. W. and communists. It was aroused, however, by the laws regarding compulsory arbitration. Such was the Kansas Industrial Court Law passed in January 1920. This forbade picketing and strikes in a number of important industries declared affected with a public interest, and gave the courts power to regulate employment, hours, and practices in those industries and to prescribe minimum wages. Similar laws were being considered in other states, while a number of anti-strike bills were introduced in Congress during 1921-22.

IV. OLD IDEAS AND NEW FORMULAS

Depression, loss of strikes, the open shop drive, the unfriendly attitude of the government and the courts, coupled with the inability of union officials to improve the situation, created in union ranks a condition of dissatisfaction more acute than that of 1919-20. During the earlier years workers were restless and eager to

[16] See Lewis L. Lorwin, "Criminal Syndicalism," *Encyclopædia of the Social Sciences*, Vol. IV, pp. 582-84.

reach out for new rights and powers. But in 1921-22 many of them were exasperated. This led to "rebellion" in many unions and intensified efforts for a change in the methods and leadership of the A. F. of L.[17]

This unrest found expression at the Denver convention of the A. F. of L. in 1921. Several unions which were experimenting with new ideas and methods, and which were eager to have these endorsed by other unions, sought to make serious changes in the structure and program of the Federation. The railway unions introduced a resolution for the nationalization of railroads and all other corporate enterprises. The electrical workers demanded measures to prevent the Federal Reserve system from lending money for speculative and non-productive purposes. The machinists and the delegates of the United Mine Workers called for old-age pensions. The International Ladies' Garment Workers' Union urged the promotion of workers' education.

A phase of this wide unrest was the first contest since 1912 for the presidency of the A. F. of L. Gompers' candidacy was opposed by John L. Lewis of the United Mine Workers. Lewis was selected by the "progressive" delegates, not because of his personal popularity or progressivism, but because he was president of the largest union in the A. F. of L. and there seemed a chance of uniting a majority of votes on his candidacy. As a matter of fact he polled one-half as many votes as Gompers, or 12,324 against 25,022. The contest was engineered by a few radicals and socialists attending the convention who thought the situation opportune for displacing Gompers. The vote was influenced by personal considerations. Lewis was not the person to rally the

[17] See Sylvia M. Kopald, *Rebellion in Labor Unions*, 1924.

progressive opposition. Most of the delegates from the railway unions lined up behind Gompers, as did those from the Ladies' Garment Workers' Union and other socialist unions. Lewis obtained only five of the eight votes of his own union.

In 1922 the main issue raised by the "progressives" in the unions was amalgamation, which was brought to the fore by the large strikes of the day. The principle was endorsed by at least a dozen international unions and by many state federations of labor.[18]

During 1922-23 the work of these "progressives" began to be used for their own purposes by the communists, who were then beginning their activities in the unions in accordance with the newly adopted tactics of the Third International and the Red Trade Union International.[19] In the unions of the ladies' garment workers, the machinists, longshoremen, maintenance of way workers, and mine workers the communists stirred up agitation for amalgamating existing craft unions into industrial unions, for "class struggle against capitalism," and for supplanting the "reactionary official bureaucracy" by shop delegates.

The injection of communism into the situation gave the leaders of the A. F. of L. the opportunity of ascribing the unrest in the unions to communist fomentation.

[18] See E. B. Mittelman, "Basis for American Federation of Labor Opposition to Amalgamation and Politics at Portland," *Journal of Political Economy*, February, 1924, pp. 86-100. The idea was gaining ground among the railway workers. At the 1922 convention of the locomotive firemen, Warren S. Stone appeared to propose a discussion of their amalgamating with the engineers. A committee was appointed to negotiate and to consider the insurance funds of the two Brotherhoods which presented the greatest difficulty. The Brotherhood of Railroad Trainmen voted in favor of consolidation with the Switchmen's Union belonging to the A. F. of L.

[19] See Lewis L. Lorwin, *Labor and Internationalism*, pp. 271-73.

They proceeded to attack the communists as an alien and destructive element. With the approval of the A. F. of L. one union after another declared that communist "cells" and "nuclei" would not be permitted and that membership in the Trade Union Educational League would make members liable to expulsion.[20] At the Portland convention in 1923 the anti-communist campaign was given official sanction by unseating William F. Dunne, a delegate from the Silver Bow Trades and Labor Council of Butte, Montana, on grounds of disloyalty and communist affiliations.

In the fight against the radical element during 1919-22 the A. F. of L. was forced to make a number of concessions. By the declarations of the Montreal convention of 1920 and the Denver convention of 1921, the Federation stood committed to the nationalization of railroads, mines, and public utilities. It had given its support to such social legislation as the Sheppard-Towner bill and had endorsed once more the demand for old-age pensions.[21] It had carried out a number of amalgamations of unions.

As in 1912-14, the Federation seemed in the process of transformation. This worried the upholders of tradition who were anxious to call a halt to further changes and to re-state the original philosophy of the Federation, modified only by such changes as seemed acceptable to them.

This was attempted in the opening section of the report of the Executive Council to the Portland conven-

[20] In 1922 the Trade Union Educational League, founded by William Z. Foster in 1920, became a subsidiary organization of the Communist Party and began organizing secret "nuclei" within the unions to contest offices in trade union elections and to influence union policies.

[21] See pp. 409-10.

tion of 1923 entitled *Industry's Manifest Duty* and designated as the Portland Manifesto. The main theme of this Manifesto was the danger of state intervention. The Manifesto declared that "the continuing clamor for extension of state regulatory powers under the guise of reform and deliverance from evil can but lead into greater confusion and more hopeless entanglements." Taking cognizance of the emerging idea of the value of functional relations in industry, the Manifesto urged that the various functional groups organize for purposes of co-operation in solving industrial problems with which politicians were futilely meddling. The trade unions, according to the Manifesto, were ready to lead the way. A new era of industrial democracy was predicted when employers, managers, workers, and technicians would legislate for industry and would work out an orderly economic system, comparable to our orderly political system, with an "industrial franchise" comparable to the political franchise.

In contrast to the reconstruction program of 1918, the Portland Manifesto showed concern with the processes and purposes of efficiency. Of special interest is the appeal to management for closer contacts between "the scientists of industry and representatives of organized workers" to insure order, discipline, and productivity in industry.[22] In fact Gompers and his associates now saw a deep antagonism between management and finance and called for an alliance with the former against the latter. They stressed the undemocratic character of banking and the sinister influence of private finance on industrial relations. The Portland Manifesto, however, offered no

[22] In the winter of 1920-21 the A. F. of L. took part in the formation of the Personnel Research Foundation.

program for dealing with this problem. The Executive Council of the A. F. of L. had no faith in the banking schemes which were attracting organized labor. In 1922 the Council refused to endorse government banks or to encourage trade unions in founding labor banks. The Executive Council feared that through their banks the unions would become involved in money-making and would tie up their funds. The suggestion that a central labor bank to co-ordinate the activities of all labor banks be established by the Federation at Washington was disapproved by the Council.

During 1923-24 the Federation rounded out the revision of its program. It endorsed workers' insurance.[23] It made arrangements with the Workers' Education Bureau for carrying on educational work.[24] The A. F. of L. *News Service*, a weekly clipsheet to inform daily and weekly newspapers on labor matters, was started and a beginning was made in collecting data for research purposes. A legal information bureau was established in 1923 to collect court decisions affecting labor and to act in an advisory capacity to individual unions. Regular conferences between the Federation's legislative agents and those of the international and local unions stationed in Washington were arranged to improve labor's lobbying technique.

V. ORGANIZATION WORK

During 1922-23 many requests for assistance in organizing were presented to the Executive Council of the A. F. of L. The Council decided to lend its support to

[23] The Union Co-operative Insurance Association was formed in 1924 by the Electrical Workers' Union. The Union Labor Life Insurance Co. was formed in 1925.

[24] See pp. 439-43.

organizing only the iron and steel industry and the women workers—on the assumption that such concentration of effort would yield better results.

The campaign to organize the steel industry started out in the summer of 1923 with 14 international unions co-operating. A fund of $70,000 had already been collected by these unions before the drive started. Initial efforts appeared promising, but the campaign collapsed within a few months. Co-ordinating direction was lacking and the paid organizers did not show the necessary devotion to the task.[25] Some of the organizers collected initiation fees and left town without turning the money over to the national organizing committee. The meetings of the latter were concerned largely with complaints regarding the quality of the organizing and the size of the expense accounts. The campaign avoided the Pittsburgh district where the communists were staging free speech fights. The meetings in Gary, Indiana, were heckled by I.W.W.s and broken up. Neither did the steel workers respond. The recent depression had left them fearful of losing their jobs. Furthermore, the companies had again stolen some of the unions' thunder by promulgating the eight-hour day almost as soon as the campaign started.

The president of the Amalgamated Association of Iron and Steel Workers on September 10, 1923 advised abandoning the campaign. Nevertheless, it was carried on in a half-hearted fashion for a year, costing about $3,000 a month and bringing in practically no new union members. Co-operation was proffered by the Negro As-

[25] Organizers were employed at salaries of $250 a month and were allowed expense accounts of $7.00 a day when away from home and $3.50 when at home.

sociated Press but not accepted in spite of the lesson of the 1919 strike. In 1924 the Amalgamated Association of Iron, Steel, and Tin Workers asked the A. F. of L. to request all other organizations to relinquish jurisdiction over workers in the steel mills and to lend support to it in organizing the steel industry. After holding hearings, the national organizing committee rejected the first request and endorsed the second. The Amalgamated Association would not undertake the job on such conditions, and the campaign came to an end.

The idea of an organizing drive among women workers had its impulse in the invalidation of the Minimum Wage Law for the District of Columbia by the Supreme Court in 1923. When a number of women's organizations met to discuss means for overcoming this legislative set-back, the A. F. of L. suggested that the problem should be met through industrial organization. At the request of the Executive Council, the Portland convention authorized Gompers to prepare a plan for an organizing campaign.

On February 14, 1924 President Gompers invited the presidents of 45 international unions to a conference. Thirteen came or sent representatives. The Executive Council, a representative of the Women's Trade Union League, the director of the Women's Bureau of the United States Department of Labor, and a few others attended. Gompers suggested setting up a woman's department in the A. F. of L. A committee was named which agreed that an executive officer, preferably a woman, be appointed by the Federation to work under the supervision of the president of the A. F. of L., and to be assisted by an organizing council composed of representatives from the national unions concerned with the problem. A joint organizing campaign was to be launched, but each union was to designate and pay its own organizers. The president of the A. F. of L. was to call another conference to prepare for an immediate campaign. It was estimated that the budget for the executive secretary and her office staff would amount to about $12,240 a year.

During the summer of 1924 a few organizers were assigned to selected places in New York, New Jersey, and elsewhere. Gompers also consulted officers of several international unions on the selection of a person to head a woman's department in the A. F. of L. But these preliminary steps had no further results. At its meeting in August 1924 the Executive Council abruptly decided to terminate the effort for the reason that the work did not meet with the approval of a sufficient number of unions. The real difficulties were the opposition of many union men to the organization of women on the grounds that women undermined working standards or that woman's place was in the home, and the fear of international unions that a woman's department in the A. F. of L. would encroach upon their prerogatives.[26] The Executive Council promised to hold itself in readiness to co-operate with interested organizations just as soon as a propitious time should arrive, which signified the collapse of the effort.[27]

VI. INDEPENDENT POLITICS

During 1922-24 the Executive Council of the Federation was watching developments in the political field. A new effort at realignment of the political forces of the

[26] The discussion of the problems of the woman worker received a great impetus as a result of the large influx of women into industry during the war. At the 1921 convention of the A. F. of L., the prohibition of some unions against the admission of women was made an issue.

[27] Compare pp. 304-05.

country was coming to a head. The railroad unions initiated the movement by calling a conference on progressive political action to be held in Chicago February 21 and 22, 1922. Their political interest was prompted by opposition to the Esch-Cummins Act and to the Railroad Labor Board.

The conference call was welcomed by many city labor centrals and state federations of labor which had been promoting political movements since 1919, and by several international unions which had grown discouraged by the industrial developments of 1920-21. The Socialist Party too, broken up by left-wing and communist secessions, turned expectantly to possible allies.[28] As a result 28 international unions, eight state federations, the Chicago Federation of Labor, the Socialist Party, the Farmer-Labor Party, a number of farmer organizations, and two religious bodies (Catholics and Methodists) sent a total of 124 delegates. They organized the Conference for Progressive Political Action for the purpose of electing to state and federal offices candidates pledged to the interests of the producing classes.

In the congressional campaign of 1922 both the Conference for Progressive Political Action and the A. F. of L. waged an active campaign. Conferences were held with farmers' organizations and agreement reached upon the candidates to be supported. After the elections of

[28] In April 1917, at an emergency convention held in St. Louis, the Socialist Party of America adopted the "St. Louis Platform" in opposition to American participation in the war and to conscription. A number of pro-war members then withdrew and formed the American Social Democratic League. In 1919 the more radical groups within the party seceded and organized the American Communist Party and the Communist Labor Party of North America. The Socialist Party polled 919,799 votes in the presidential election of 1920. Its membership, however, declined from 104,822 in 1919 to 26,766 in 1920 and decreased to 12,000 in 1923 as a result of internal splits.

1922 the issue of an independent labor party was again raised. John Fitzpatrick, acting for the Farmer-Labor Party, called a conference for July 3, 1923 in Chicago to which he invited the Workers' Party,[29] which was the legally existing communist political organization.[30] The Socialist Party and the Socialist Labor Party, as well as the international unions affiliated with the A. F. of L. and the Railroad Brotherhoods, refused to participate because of the communists. The Workers' Party captured the conference, changed the name from Farmer-Labor Party to Federated Farmer-Labor Party, and put through a radical program with communists in control. This, however, merely helped to weaken the advocates of a labor party within the A. F. of L.

On July 4, 1924 the Conference for Progressive Political Action assembled in Cleveland about 600 delegates from international unions, state and city federations, co-operative societies, the Socialist Party, the Committee of Forty-Eight, the Progressive Party, the Women's Committee on Political Action, and "miscellaneous university, educational, and third party groups," together with "a sprinkling of farmers."[31] The convention nominated Senator Robert M. LaFollette for the presidency. He accepted on condition that no attempt be made to run candidates for offices other than the presidency and vice-presidency. He did not want to interfere

[29] The Workers' Party was formed in December 1921 to unite the various communist factions. In 1922 it numbered 12,394 members and in 1923, 15,233. Its membership was mostly in New York, Boston, Minneapolis, Chicago, Cleveland, Pittsburgh, and Detroit, in the order named. More than half of its membership was composed of foreign born.

[30] Fitzpatrick and Nockels were on good terms with William Z. Foster. But the question was also raised whether Fitzpatrick had not invited the communists in order to "queer the show."

[31] William H. Johnston, president of the International Association of Machinists, presided.

with the chances of electing any of the progressive senators and representatives. No steps were taken towards the immediate formation of a third party. The nominees for the campaign were to run as independents.

The program adopted at Cleveland demanded the crushing of private monopoly and the unqualified enforcement of constitutional guaranties of freedom of speech, press, and assemblage. It called for a publicly owned super-power system, public control of all natural resources, high progressive taxation, repeal of excessive tariff duties, more direct public control of money and credit, creation of a government marketing corporation for farm produce, assurance of the right to organize and to bargain collectively, abolition of "the tyranny" of the courts, and abolition of the use of injunctions in labor disputes. The program was silent upon social legislation, except on child labor, and on nationalization, except for railroads and power. It denounced imperialistic foreign policies and called for revision of the Versailles Treaty. After the adjournment of the convention, Senator Burton K. Wheeler of Montana, a Democrat, accepted the vice-presidential nomination.

During these developments the Executive Council of the A. F. of L. continued to insist on its non-partisan policy.[32] In the summer of 1924 it presented demands to both the Democratic and Republican conventions. The

[32] It pointed to the results achieved in Congress during 1921-23 in which the "Farm Bloc" and the progressives put through a number of measures supported by the A. F. of L., such as the repeal of the Lever Food Control Law; the Industrial Rehabilitation Act, offering federal funds to states to assist in vocational training of persons injured in industrial accidents; the Johnson bill, limiting immigration to fixed quotas of 3 per cent of the number of different nationalities resident in the United States in 1910; the Sheppard-Towner bill, extending federal aid to states for maternity and infant care; increased appropriations for the United States Employment Service; and the extension of the Federal Workmen's Compensation Act to longshoremen.

latter accorded labor's spokesmen a scant hearing. The Democrats, while more courteous, "ignored the hopes and ideals and demands of labor" in their platform. Because of this, the Executive Council of the Federation, in August 1924, decided to support Robert M. LaFollette and Burton K. Wheeler as long-standing friends of organized labor running as independent candidates on a platform which was acceptable, except for its plank on international relations. However, in endorsing them, the Council added: "Co-operation hereby urged is not a pledge of identification with an independent party movement or a third party, nor can it be construed as support for such a party, group, or movement, except as such action accords with our non-partisan political policy. We do not accept government as the solution of the problems of life. . . . Neither can this co-operation imply our support, acceptance, or endorsement of policies or principles advocated by any minority groups or organizations that may see fit to support [these candidates]."[33]

The campaign did not bring about the united action of labor.[34] The money collected by the A. F. of L. for campaign purposes amounted to $25,013, about half of the sum spent in 1920.

In the elections the Progressive Independents polled 4,826,382 votes, or 16.5 per cent of the popular vote, but carried only 13 electoral votes—those of Wisconsin. The

[33] This was evidently intended to minimize the fact that the A. F. of L. was for once allied with the Socialist Party in a political campaign.

[34] The greater New York Central Trades and Labor Council at first endorsed the progressive candidates, but on the eve of the elections retracted the endorsement and supported the Democratic Party. George L. Berry of the Printing Pressmen, who had been mentioned as vice-presidential candidate, supported the Democratic Party; John L. Lewis of the United Mine Workers, William Hutcheson of the Brotherhood of Carpenters, and Terrence V. O'Connor of the longshoremen supported the Republican Party.

unsatisfactoriness of this result was alleged by the railroad unions in declining to interest themselves further in a third party. This reinforced the position of the Executive Council of the A. F. of L. At the 1924 convention of the Federation a few resolutions urging the formation of a Labor Party were presented, but the convention, with only one negative vote, endorsed the continuation of the non-partisan policy of the A. F. of L.

VII. A DECADE OF GAINS AND LOSSES

The Federation went to its greatest heights in numbers and economic power between 1915 and 1920, as a result of the war. During this period it achieved one of its main objectives—that of becoming a recognized element of the nation and of national life. The statement often made that the Federation did not make the greatest use of its opportunities and did not insist upon obtaining a major control in industry does not take account of the fact that the Federation was not prepared for such a task in 1917 or 1920, its pre-war history having centered around the struggle for mere recognition by employers. The idea of control was foreign to the labor movements of most countries, emerging only during the war years. In this respect the Federation did not differ materially from the national labor organizations of Western Europe.

Whether the Federation might not have gained national recognition of collective bargaining, which was its major aim in 1919-20, is a more pertinent question. The labor organizations of England, France, Germany, Belgium, and other European countries did achieve during these years legal and political recognition for the principles and methods of collective bargaining. The evidence points to the conclusion that the Federation did not pursue a vigorous policy and that its efforts at reconstruction were thwarted by its fear of change and radicals.

Also, the decline of the Federation in national influence during 1920-21 was in large measure the result of its own policies. The impatience of the Federation with the government war boards, as a result of the special interests of the skilled crafts, hastened the dismantlement of the agencies established during 1918-19 and accelerated the process of disintegration of the new unions formed during the war. The traditional opposition in the Federation to legislative fixing of wages swung the Federation even further than before the war into an abstract anti-state position which was out of harmony with the needs of the new unions stimulated by the war. The campaign of the Federation against profiteering in 1919-20 was carried on in such a way as to create a cleavage between labor and the middle classes which was not bridged by the Federation's participation in the outcry against radicalism. The Federation thus came out of the post-Armistice period socially isolated. Its foreign policies, dominated by a hang-over of war emotions, alienated it from the labor movements of Europe with which it had established co-operative contacts before 1914.

The deflation of the Federation in numbers between 1921 and 1923 was to be expected. The depression alone did not at first materially reduce membership.[35] But in

[35] For the most part, only the smaller unions were as yet seriously affected. A number of the principal unions, such as those of the carpenters, railway carmen, electrical workers, miners, painters, plasterers, printing pressmen, street railwaymen, seamen, teamsters, and typographers, were still expanding. The Federation's income was only slightly curtailed and still exceeded a million dollars.

1921-22 the depression and the open shop drive combined took a heavy toll.[36] Membership continued to decline during 1923 and 1924. The capacity of the unions in the A. F. of L. to hold their gains was now weakened by new employers' policies, internal dissension, communist agitation, and by the general change in the industrial situation, which reached its highest development in the following five years.[37]

Altogether, the A. F. of L. between 1920 and 1924 lost 1,212,941 members or about 30 per cent.[38] This was accounted for by a loss of 172,212 in 1921; 710,893 in 1922; 269,167 in 1923; and 60,669 in 1924. These losses were distributed over most of the international unions in the A. F. of L., only 23 of them showing no losses. But the largest part of the losses was sustained by a few unions which had made extraordinary gains between 1918 and 1920.[39] Also, some of the older unions which had begun to decline before 1914, but had been helped by the war, such as those of the brewers, cigarmakers, boot and shoe makers, granite cutters, and molders, resumed their downward trend.

Still, in 1924 the membership of the A. F. of L. was larger by nearly 800,000 than in 1914. This gain was

[36] Only a few unions, such as those of the electrical workers, plasterers, plumbers, and street railway employees, held their own or made small gains in 1922. Some of these chose to conceal losses by continuing to pay a per capita tax on their former membership rolls. See Appendix A, pp. 476-83.

[37] See Chap. X.

[38] This loss was not greater than that experienced by labor organizations in other countries. Membership of the free trade unions in Germany, for instance, declined from 7,890,102 in 1920 to 4,618,353 in 1924, or 41.4 per cent.

[39] Such were the Machinists' Union, which lost over 250,000 members and fell below its membership of 1914; the Boilermakers' Union, which lost 85,500 members; the railway clerks, who lost 97,600; the textile workers, seamen, longshoremen, and railway carmen. See Appendix A.

concentrated in a few unions such as the railway carmen, the electrical workers, the miners, and the unions in the building trades.[40] The increase of union membership in "service" occupations and among government employees was striking. The Federation had gained during the decade some 200,000 "white collar" members. The activities of the Federation were on a larger scale, having extended into several new fields.

In its internal structure the Federation during these years underwent several changes which were designed to strengthen the international unions and to check opposition movements.[41] As a result of these changes, of the policy of expulsions, and of the widespread social reaction, the Federation became more homogeneous in spirit than it had ever been before. Conservatives, progressives, and socialists within the Federation were drawn more closely together to combat the communists and "left-wingers." At the conventions of 1923-24 there were no contests for office. In other ways, too, the 1924 convention showed a harmony which appeared to many as listlessness. There were no extended debates and not a single roll-call. The turbulent era which began with the World War was coming to an end. So also was the rule of the man who had been the largest personal factor in the life of the Federation. On December 13, 1924, on his way back from the convention at San Antonio, Texas, Gompers died, at the age of 72. During his last years he had been far from equal physically or mentally to the tasks of his office. The question now was whether an effective new leadership would come to the fore to face the new problems that were on the horizon.

[40] See Appendix A, pp. 476-83.

[41] These are discussed in Part V, in connection with the analysis of the functions of the Federation.

PART IV

PROSPERITY AND DEPRESSION, 1925-33

CHAPTER X

THE "NEW ERA" AND ITS AFTERMATH

At the time William Green succeeded Gompers in the office of president of the American Federation of Labor,[1] the United States was entering what was heralded as a "new era" of unprecedented prosperity. Organized labor looked forward to a new period of growth. The process of post-war liquidation was over, the drop in union membership seemed to have reached an end, and above all the upward course of business in accordance with the accepted theory was expected to bring in its wake a corresponding expansion of unionism.[2] As a matter of fact, the theory did not work. The conditions created by the prosperity of 1925-29 and by the depression which followed were not favorable to unionism and brought the Federation complex and difficult problems, with some of which it has been unable to cope successfully.

I. LABOR IN THE "NEW ERA"

Though the prosperity of 1925-29 was uneven in its effects on the American wage earner, it did bring considerable economic benefits to large groups of labor. Wage rates were raised in many industries, especially in

[1] Green was appointed by the Executive Council on Dec. 19, 1924.

[2] Gompers formulated the "law of the growth of labor" in 1904 as follows: "From the formation of the first bona fide trade union movement in modern times, it has grown with each era of industrial activity and receded to some degree with each industrial depression, but with each recurring revival in industry the degree of growth has been greater, and with each recurring period of depression it has receded to a lesser degree than its immediate predecessors." *Report of the Proceedings of the Twenty-Fourth Annual Convention of the American Federation of Labor*, 1904, p. 15.

unionized plants.[3] Increased productivity, industrial expansion, a relatively stable price level, and increasing employment per family resulted in increased purchasing power and in a general rise in the standard of living.[4]

However, as the other side of the picture, large numbers of workers, especially in transportation, coal and metal mining, oil production, and the textile industries were still earning a wage below a minimum standard of health and efficiency.[5]

Of special importance among the industrial and economic changes which affected labor was the increasing mechanization of industry. The development of mechanical appliances, the introduction of new machines, and the application of power, while not new in character, were intensified to such a degree as to constitute a "second industrial revolution." Industrial managers concentrated on process analysis, and the greater specialization and serialization of machines became the basis of the economy of mass production. Mechanization, mass production, and increased productivity cut seriously into the demand for labor in many industries, giving rise to vexing questions of "technological unemployment."[6] Undoubtedly the new service industries absorbed considerable numbers of those displaced in the older indus-

[3] The index number of union wage rates per hour increased from 237.9 in 1925 to 262.1 in 1929. See "Union Scales of Wages and Hours of Labor," *U. S. Bureau of Labor Statistics Bulletin No. 540*, October 1931, p. 14. For wages in separate industries, see Paul H. Douglas and Florence T. Jennison, *The Movement of Money and Real Earnings in the United States, 1926-1928.*

[4] See *Recent Social Trends in the United States* (Report of the President's Research Committee on Social Trends), 1933, Vol. II, pp. 824-28.

[5] The same.

[6] See Paul H. Douglas and Aaron Director, *The Problem of Unemployment*, 1931, Chaps. IX-X.

tries. But the process of readjustment involved considerable loss of time and income.[7]

Workers were similarly affected by changes in the geographic location of industries. Illustrations of this process were the growth of the textile industry in the South and the movement of plants in clothing and printing industries from the large cities to the smaller towns. The process caused deep dislocations in long established industrial communities and stimulated the tapping of new sources of cheap native and foreign labor in competition with the older labor forces. Similarly, changing habits of consumption and new trends in world economy upset the labor market in such industries as textile and clothing manufacture, fuel production, metal mining, and lumbering.

Changes in industrial structure and control also had important consequences for labor. By 1923 nearly one-fourth of the wage earners in factories were employed in establishments having 1,000 or more workers, while less than one worker in five was employed in factories having 50 or less. In 1929, 85 per cent of the factories supported less than 20 per cent of the workers, while between 8 and 9 per cent employed more than 71 per cent of the wage earners. Large-scale enterprise and consolidation of control spread from industry to banking and distribution, resulting in the formation of mergers, chain systems, and combinations on a large scale, bringing the giant corporation to a new position of power and importance, especially in the field of public utilities, banking, iron and steel, machinery, textiles, and food-

[7] See *Recent Social Trends in the United States*, Vol. I, Chap. VI; also Isador Lubin, *The Absorption of the Unemployed by American Industry*, 1929.

stuffs.[8] As this consolidation movement was prompted by motives of speculation as well as of economy, both the public and managements became increasingly impatient with labor demands and with unionism.

These industrial changes assumed special significance because they facilitated plant and personnel policies which deeply affected industrial relations. These policies, which may be traced back as far as 1915 and which attracted considerable attention in 1919-20 and in 1922-23, were now furthered systematically on the assumption that they were an essential part of the new industrialism based on scientific method and mass production and were considered a successful antidote to organized labor. While there was considerable variation in the programs of different employers, they were alike in character. Employee representation plans were set up to promote amicable industrial relations.[9] Financial incentives were offered for the increase of productivity. Bonuses in cash or in stock and savings certificates, schemes of profit-sharing, offerings of corporate stock below market price, and arrangements to enable em-

[8] See *Recent Economic Changes in the United States*, National Bureau of Economic Research, Inc., 1929, Vol. I, pp. 167-218; also Gardiner C. Means, "The Large Corporation in American Life," *American Economic Review*, March 1931, Vol. 21, pp. 10-42.

[9] In all such plans elected representatives of the employees of an industrial plant meet with the management for collective discussion of working conditions and grievances. In some cases the method of "block representation" is followed, in which the plant is divided into "blocks" or divisions of from 50 to 200 employees each, irrespective of crafts, and each "block" elects one or more representatives. In other cases the various crafts elect representatives on a proportional basis. Still another method is the "Federal Plan," which involves a "cabinet" of management officials, an "upper house" of foremen and other supervisory staff, and a "lower house" of the rank and file. These schemes for collective discussion differ from collective bargaining in that the ultimate decision on disputed issues usually rests with the employer and the existence of the plan itself is at the will of the management.

ployees to pay for stock through deductions from wages were introduced on a large scale.

Another set of activities was devised to protect the workers in emergencies. Benefits in case of sickness, accident, and death were provided by company funds into which the workers paid small sums regularly and to which the companies contributed. Social and recreational activities, such as dances, outings, orchestras, and baseball and football were encouraged. Group insurance, either non-contributory, in which premiums were paid entirely by the employer, or contributory, where the cost was divided between employers and employees, was established. Pension plans providing financial assistance to superannuated employees both on a non-contributory and contributory basis were introduced. Vacations either with full or part pay were granted by an increasing number of companies to wage earners who had satisfied certain requirements as to length of service.

Efforts were made to increase the conveniences of plant facilities for the employee. Lunch rooms or other means for employees to obtain wholesome food at prices below those charged in commercial restaurants were provided. Low-cost lodging for employees was supplied. Sometimes aid was given in the financing of homes. Company operated buses supplied transportation at reduced rates or even free of charge. Some companies stimulated saving among their employees by contributing a specified portion of the amount saved. Facilities for loans at low rates of interest to meet emergencies were extended.

Health and safety work became a feature of many industrial establishments. The safety committee, the company dispensary, the company hospital, and the plant physician and nurse were introduced for the purpose of reducing accidents and facilitating medical care of the employees. Dental and optical clinics were established, and provisions were made for home nursing and for the physical examination of the families of employees.

The actual number of workers affected by these various activities is unknown. In 1926 it was estimated that 4,700,000 workers were covered by company group insurance schemes for a total value of 5.5 billion dollars, and the total exceeded 10 billion dollars in 1931.[10] Group, health, and accident protection were extended to several hundred thousand employees with an average benefit between $25 and $30 a week during the period of disability. Some 400 companies employing about 4 million persons established pension schemes for about 90,000 persons. In 1924 it was computed that 447 establishments with over a million workers supplied their employees with medical service, spending over 5 million dollars for that service. A small number of workers were affected by the provisions for vacations with pay, profit-sharing, and supplemental bonuses. Generally, these activities were developed by establishments employing 500 or more workers.[11]

The companies having employee representation plans increased from 385 in 1922 to 432 in 1926; the number of workers participating in these plans from 690,000 to 1,369,078. Railroads and public utilities had the largest number of such plans. Next in order came iron and steel mills, plants making electrical supplies, and street railways. As a rule these schemes were developed by large

[10] See E. E. Cummins, *The Labor Problem in the United States*, 1932, p. 528, and *Recent Social Trends in the United States*, Vol. II, p. 846.

[11] See *The Economic Status of Wage Earners in New York and Other States*, National Industrial Conference Board, 1928.

concerns. Some 30 companies had nearly 1 million workers of the total 1,369,078 included in these plans. In small plants, employee representation schemes tended to be short lived.

II. NEW PATTERNS OF LABOR BEHAVIOR

The sociological and psychological effects of the changes described above on the working population were complex. The shifting of industry created friction between the older experienced workers and the newer strata brought into factory and workshop. Increasing mechanization tended to make employment less stable, especially for those over the age of 40 who were impelled to seek employment in the new subsidiary trades or in the expanding service industries. On the other hand, the personnel policies in large-scale industries tended to immobilize their workers because of the purchase of homes, pension arrangements, ownership of stock, and hope of preferment through longer years of service.

The more highly paid workers were brought nearer than ever to the middle-class standard of living. The increasing opportunities offered their children in clerical and supervisory positions created new connecting links between the two classes. These links were strengthened as a result of the new devices which enabled people of small means to participate in the general speculative movement. Thus sections of workers shared in the get-rich-quick psychology which characterized the period. The desire for steady employment and higher earnings became more dominant in the minds of the workers than the feeling for industrial freedom and independence.

This attitude of the worker was reinforced by new opportunities for gratifying the desire for comfort and recreation. The automobile supplied a relative mobility which compensated for the former habit of moving from job to job. The motion picture and the radio supplied new ways of spending leisure which displaced the older forms of recreation based upon shop associations and collective action with fellow workers. In brief, the increasing use of social inventions made the worker more individualistic in his ways of life.[12]

The outstanding feature of industrial relations during these years was the comparative peace and freedom from

AVERAGE NUMBER OF INDUSTRIAL DISPUTES AND WORKERS INVOLVED, 1916–30[a]

Period	Disputes per Year		Workers Involved per Year	
	Average Number	As Percentage of 1916–21 Figures	Average Number	As Percentage of 1916–21 Figures
1916–21.........	3,503	100	1,798,809	100
1922–25.........	1,304	37	863,051	48
1926–30.........	791	23	244,949	13

[a] Computed from "Statistics of Strikes and Lockouts," *Monthly Labor Review*, June 1931.

strikes. With the exception of a few large strikes, chiefly in the "sick" industries, the five years 1925-29 showed a marked decline in the frequency and intensity of industrial struggles.

III. THE SEARCH FOR NEW IDEAS

Beginning with 1925 the A. F. of L. showed increasing awareness of the changes described above. In its report to the 1925 convention the Executive Council included a section entitled "New Economic Develop-

[12] See Robert S. and Helen M. Lynd, *Middletown*, 1929, Chap. XIX

ments," in which the new labor policies of employers, company unions, stock ownership, group insurance, and welfare work were discussed. At the 1927 convention the Council grouped the important problems of the unions under three heads: legal status, organizing the mechanized industries, and making unionism attractive to workers. Repeated reference was made by the Council to the futility of applying past methods to new conditions and to the need of developing new policies and methods.

The new ideas offered by the Federation to the unions as a possible guide through the maze of "the new era" included union management co-operation, the "social wage," the five-day week, union labor insurance, and research. In advocating union management co-operation the Federation based its action on the assumption that industrial relations were shifting from a basis of conflict to one of continuous co-operation. Management was presumably becoming conscious of the value of the human agent and of morale in production, and was willing to direct workers in a large spirit and to share with them responsibility in production. Employers and managers who were still antagonistic to trade unions were bound to realize that this would prove detrimental to both the workers and industry, and that only the trade unions, as the "custodians of skill and craft," were capable of helping management to achieve the main tasks of industry —efficiency, high quality of work, low labor turnover, and regularity of employment. The special value of union management co-operation was that it enabled workers not only to establish bargaining equality in order to fix wage rates and working rules, but also to participate with management in finding better methods of production and in reducing wastes in industry. It was thus a step in advance in the development of collective bargaining, and the Federation urged all unions and employers to adopt it.[13]

The principle of the social wage as stated at the conventions of 1925 and 1926 asserted that social inequality and industrial instability must increase unless the workers' real wages progressed in proportion to man's increasing power of production. The conclusion drawn from this was that wages should be adjusted to the rate of increase in per capita output.

A new departure was also made in the formulation of the theory of shorter working hours. According to the Federation progress in productive capacity, technological unemployment, and the tendency of industry to make a machine of man made it imperative for economic and humanitarian reasons that not only the shorter work day but also the shorter work week be demanded. In 1926 the Federation declared for the five-day week in industry.

Labor group insurance by unions was now urged to counteract group insurance inaugurated by employers and to modernize on an actuarial basis the traditional benefits of unions.

To promote greater interest in research, the Federation urged its unions to collect information on membership, on the condition of their respective industries by cities and geographic districts, and to improve accounting records. The Federation itself promised to investigate company unions, to study the problem of old-age pensions, and to make other studies necessary for the formulation of new policies.

[13] For the technique of union management co-operation, see pp. 394-95.

IV. ORGANIZING CAMPAIGNS

The Federation during these years also tried new methods for increasing membership. During 1925-27 these were applied in the union-label campaign and in the automobile industry, and after 1928 in the South.

A. The Label Campaign

The union-label campaign was started in 1925 at the suggestion of the Label Trades Department.[14] It was planned to extend the campaign over 40 weeks and to cover the entire country. Meetings were to be held in some 817 cities and towns in the United States and Canada in which a central labor body existed. A budget of $125,000 was voted by representatives from 62 national unions interested in the label. Lecturers were to be sent out with a motion picture, entitled "Labor's Reward," and were to collect information concerning the state of union organization, the demand for union-label goods, and the possibilities of organization.

The campaign actually lasted seven months; 591 meetings were held in 30 states, and the total attendance was estimated at 479,500. The whole of the promised budget failed to materialize and activities had to be curtailed. The campaign disclosed the need for intensive organization work; but not much information was secured on the sale of union goods. The motion picture was well received and was hailed as a new and effective method of publicity. The Label Trades Department reported an increase in membership of 10,000 in 1927, but this was not attributed directly to the campaign. No further efforts to continue agitation for the use of the label were made after that year.

[14] For a description of this department and for the importance of labels, see pp. 367-74.

B. Automobile Workers

In 1925 the question of organizing the workers in the automobile industry was raised again. The industry, one of the largest in the country, with over half a million workers, was completely unorganized. In 1925 James O'Connell, the president of the Metal Trades Department, brought the question to the convention of his department. Added interest in the issue had been aroused by the effort of the Machinists' Union to organize garage mechanics. In some cities, dealers and service stations were forced by automobile manufacturers to oppose unions. It was felt that only organization of the automobile plants could hold the gains made in the service stations. Furthermore, the communists utilized the unorganized condition of the industry in their attacks on the Federation.[15]

How to draw jurisdictional lines among the highly mechanized, repetitive operations in plants where mass production methods prevailed was the first difficult question which had to be faced. The committee of the 1925 convention of the Metal Trades Department appointed to consider the subject recommended that the automobile workers be organized along industrial lines. This provoked opposition from the craft unions. The committee then suggested that the workers be organized into federal labor unions, with the idea that they would later be parceled out to the appropriate international unions. This recommendation also seemed too drastic for the convention.

In 1926 the Metal Trades Department decided to

[15] The Federation during 1925-29 was directly and indirectly affected by the activities of the communists and other opposition groups which are described on pp. 258-71.

ask the A. F. of L. to undertake the campaign, partly because other organizations not affiliated with the department had claims in the industry. A resolution calling for a general organizing campaign among automobile workers was introduced at the convention of the A. F. of L. held in Detroit in 1926. The Committee on Organization recommended that the question of trade jurisdiction be waived during the campaign. A resolution to that effect was adopted by the A. F. of L. convention.

On December 2, 1926, 17 international unions with jurisdictional claims in the automobile industry met in conference at A. F. of L. headquarters in Washington. William Green declared in his opening speech that "the real question to be considered by this conference is the question of suspension of jurisdiction." The character of the automobile industry based upon mass production and on fine subdivided repetitive processes made it nearly impossible, he said, to draw jurisdictional lines. It was imperative to disregard them, at least in approaching the workers. Later, he thought, transfers to the proper unions might be effected. If the international unions would agree to a waiver of jurisdictional claims, the A. F. of L. would take the lead, and the Executive Council would work out a plan. Green suggested that the workers might be best organized by shops and factories. Joint committees could then be set up to deal with wages and working conditions.

The international unions showed no enthusiasm for the plan. One of the difficulties in getting these unions to agree to a waiver of their jurisdictional rights was the existence in the automobile plants of small groups of organized skilled workers, such as pattern makers and painters. Only the machinists and the upholstery workers favored the plan. Green intimated that some automobile manufacturers were in a receptive mood and might consider allowing their plants to be organized if they were safeguarded against jurisdictional disputes. When the meeting proved unable to agree, he suggested calling a second conference later to consider a plan to be worked out by the Executive Council.

When the Executive Council met January 11 to 19, 1927, Green reported that the General Motors Company was prepared to agree to the organization of some of its big plants as an experiment in union management co-operation, provided that there would be no jurisdictional fights. On March 24, 1927 another conference was held. This time only nine unions were represented: those of the machinists, molders, draftsmen, plumbers, pattern makers, upholsterers, painters, operating engineers, and electrical workers. The sheet metal workers wrote that they thought it a mistake and a waste of money to try to organize the automobile workers, as, in their opinion, the men in the industry did not care for organization.

A plan submitted by Green was adopted with a few minor changes. It provided for the waiving of jurisdiction by the international unions over the workers in all plants where methods of mass production were used. The A. F. of L. was to direct the campaign. The international unions, as well as the Metal Trades Department, were to designate organizers and to contribute toward expenses. Workers were to be organized into federal labor unions affiliated directly with the A. F. of L. But the Federation also pledged itself to bring about the transfer of those thus organized to the several international unions as speedily as possible. In the meantime, local unions were to be made co-extensive with the plant as far as possible. Members of these locals were to receive exchange privileges from all co-operating international unions. Organizers in the campaign were to stress the inter-dependent interests of unions and management, the duties and obligations of both sides with regard to collective agreements, and the need not only for regulating wages and hours, but also for improving work and for stabilizing employment. At the same time it was agreed that where skilled workers were already organized by crafts, their locals should not be disturbed. It was decided to prosecute the campaign cautiously and quietly at first, to fix initiation fees at $5.00 per member and dues at $2.00, of which 50 cents was to be set aside in an organizing fund.

On June 24, 1927 a still smaller conference convened to decide upon immediate steps. An A. F. of L. organizer[16] was appointed head of the campaign, with five other organizers assigned to work under him. It was decided to start work in Detroit. The organizers were warned to avoid premature strikes, since there was no money for strike benefits. They were instructed to impress upon the employers the concern of the A. F. of L. for the welfare of industry, and its desire to be constructive and helpful through collective bargaining.

The campaign encountered discouragements from the start. The support of the international unions was lukewarm. The organizers sent by them were tied up with local union politics in an undesirable way. Detroit was filled with a surplus of workers estimated at 125,000. The Ford works were closed, pending alterations for producing the new Model A. The large labor turnover made it almost impossible to keep track of key men in different

[16] Paul Smith, formerly an organizer of the United Mine Workers.

shops—a method much relied on by the unions. In short, conditions looked so unfavorable for a mass campaign that the only angle from which the organizers thought the problem could be approached was to attempt to arrange for a conference between Green and Henry Ford. Feelers were also put out in the direction of other large motor companies.

However, none of these attempts materialized, and the campaign was given up without further effort to reach the workers.[17] Thus failed the first large campaign in which the Federation tried to apply its new tactics of conciliating the employer while sending organizers among his employees. The Federation possessed neither the financial resources necessary for an active drive among the workers nor agents capable of winning the confidence of the managements. The conclusion is also inescapable that the international unions, except possibly those of the machinists and the upholsterers, were not eager to organize the industry, especially if it had to be done through federal labor unions.

C. The Southern Campaign

During 1928-29 the Federation was perforce drawn into the struggles of the Southern textile workers. The question of organizing the South had been before the

[17] There was in Detroit in 1926 a local union of the United Automobile, Aircraft, and Vehicle Workers of America, which seemed willing to co-operate. This union had once belonged to the A. F. of L. and had been granted jurisdiction over the automobile industry; but it was expelled in 1918 for refusal to surrender some of the skilled workers whom the craft unions claimed. In 1926 it had only a few members in the automobile plants of Detroit. It was under suspicion of having communistic leanings. Paul Smith, after conferring with the president of the local, wrote of him as "a miniature Foster" who talked "united front." Neither was Smith much impressed with the union's headquarters, in a frame shack with a negro family living upstairs.

Federation many times, but all attempts at organization there had been without success. Between 1924 and 1928 several state federations of labor in the South called the attention of the A. F. of L. to the growing industrialization of the area and asked for organizers. But no action was taken.

The A. F. of L. was thus taken by surprise when, in the spring of 1929, a wave of strikes swept through the mill villages of the South. The grievances of the workers were low pay, long hours, and especially the "stretch-out" system, which required each worker to tend an increased number of machines. That these grievances came to a head in the spring of 1929 was due to the economic position of the industry. For five or six years the cotton textile industry, both in the North and the South, had been experiencing declining profits, shrinking markets, and increasingly keen competition due to over-expansion. Because of the large supply of cheap labor and other advantages such as tax exemptions, the migration of spindles and looms from New England to the Piedmont became marked. But in spite of these advantages, the Southern mills too began to feel the pinch and started cutting costs by means of the stretch-out and other efficiency devices.[18] When the textile business picked up early in 1929, it gave the workers the stimulus for trying to retrieve ground.

Once organization started in a given mill territory, another cause for strikes quickly appeared. The management would discharge or lay off the workers most actively associated with the union. After organization had

[18] In some well-managed mills increased efficiency did not mean greater hardship for the workers. See Tom Tippett, *When Southern Labor Stirs*, p. 314.

reached a degree which seemed to promise success, union committees would wait upon the management, submit grievances, and ask for the reinstatement of discharged members. They were invariably rebuffed; the management would not treat with outsiders, blaming "foreign" agitators from the North for the trouble.

The Southern strikes varied in magnitude. Some, especially in South Carolina, were small local walk-outs which ended quickly after a few adjustments. Others included a large number of workers and were serious struggles. The most important of these were the strikes in Gastonia and Marion, North Carolina,[19] in Elizabethton, Tennessee, and in Danville, Virginia.

The A. F. of L. entered the scene with the strike at the Bemberg-Glanzstoff mills in Elizabethton, Tennessee. There had been a number of small strikes at these mills in 1927. On March 12, 1929 a number of girls in the inspection department of one of the two mills walked out again, demanding an increase in wages. They had been working 56 hours a week for 16 to 18 cents an hour. In less than a week both mills were shut down completely. The strikers turned to the American Federation of Labor for aid. The president of the Tennessee Federation of Labor and Alfred Hoffman, organizer for the Full-Fashioned Hosiery Workers' Union, with the aid of a conciliator from the State Department of Labor, patched up a verbal agreement which provided that there was to be no discrimination against union members, but it did not include union recognition. Instead, shop committees were set up. A uniform wage scale, the higher of the two scales formerly applying in the two mills, was

[19] The Gastonia strike was conducted by the communists who had started organizing work there in March 1929.

to be maintained. But the company violated the agreement. President Green sent a representative of the A. F. of L., Edward F. McGrady, to straighten matters out. The night of April 3 he and Hoffman were "taken for a ride" by a committee of business men, bankers, and politicians of the town, deposited at the state line, and warned never to return. This incident provided much publicity and brought President Green to Elizabethton to address the workers. A week later the mills closed again. The A. F. of L. then issued a general appeal for financial support for the Southern textile workers.

The fact that injunctions and the state militia were used freely during both strikes, and lack of funds,[20] made it impossible for the workers to hold out for victory. On May 25, 1929 the strikers accepted a settlement which was no improvement over the first agreement. Discrimination against strikers continued. Another strike was being agitated by workers outside the mills and by the remnant of the union. Green and the United Textile Workers advised against it and warned the workers that if they struck the national organization would assume no responsibility. However, in March 1930 the Elizabethton local voted another strike. Only about 250 workers responded. About 3,000 stayed at work. The numbers "on strike" were swelled by those who had been laid off or not re-employed after the last strike. The company termed this an "unemployment demonstration" and ignored it. There was no money for the strikers, and neither the United Textile Workers nor the A. F. of L. would promise aid. Presently the mills began reducing their working force as a result of the depression, and the strike was ended.

[20] Between May and Aug. 31, 1929, $19,000 was raised and another $21,000 during the following year.

The disturbances at Marion, North Carolina began when operatives in the Baldwin mills invited organizers from Elizabethton to help them form a union. Their grievances were the stretch-out system, shifts of 11 and 12 hours, and wages ranging from $5.20 to $19.20 a week. To these was added discharge for joining the newly organized union. Representatives of the United Textile Workers advised against a strike. Nevertheless on July 11, 1929 the East Marion operatives struck, and the employees of a neighboring mill under the same ownership joined them. The company began evicting union members from the mill village and so food and shelter had to be provided at once. As in Elizabethton, the state sent troops to the scene, and the mills resumed operation with new recruits. The strike was nominally settled on September 11, 1929 by another "gentlemen's agreemen," reducing hours to 55 a week, reinstating all but twelve strikers, and providing for a grievance committee. However, strikers were blacklisted and evictions continued. Another strike was brewing. On the morning of October 2, while the leaders were absent attending a conference called by the Southern state federations of labor, the "Marion massacre" occurred. The sheriff and his deputies attempted with tear-gas bombs to disperse workers who had collected at the mill gates to notify the day shift that the night shift had gone on strike. In the confusion which resulted shots were fired; six strikers were killed and 25 wounded. A trial took place which resulted in the acquittal of officers of the law and in a prison sentence for union leaders. The strike was lost.

The A. F. of L. convention of 1929 discussed the Southern industrial situation and instructed President Green to summon a conference of international unions to devise a plan for a general organizing campaign. The conference met in Washington on November 14, 1929. It urged the United States Senate to make an investigation of the Southern textile industry; called upon each international union to assign at least one organizer to the Southern states; instructed the Executive Council to issue a second appeal for financial assistance for the United Textile Workers; and admonished the legal authorities in North Carolina to bring to justice those responsible for the loss of life during the labor struggles in the state.

Shortly after, Green appointed a committee to take charge of the campaign and Birmingham was selected as headquarters. In addition to the organizers, a publicity man, a consulting engineer, and an educational director were attached to the Southern office. After the campaign got under way, the United Textile Workers had five men in the field, the A. F. of L. had several, and approximately 30 international unions assigned men to work there. Still the response of most international unions to the appeals for money and organizers was meager.[21]

In accordance with the adopted plan, Green toured the South addressing meetings. He was received nearly everywhere by mayors of cities who extended official welcomes. His meetings were attended not only by wage earners, but by the substantial business and professional classes, and occasionally by manufacturers as well. He addressed the joint sessions of three state legislatures,

[21] Only $14,000 came in. The largest donations—$1,000 and over—came from the bridge and structural iron workers, musicians, pulp and sulphite workers, theatrical stage employees, and commercial telegraphers. The actors and artists, brewers, post office clerks, railway clerks, electrical workers, federal employees, hatters, molders, painters, plumbers, and street railway employees gave $500 each.

meetings of Rotary and Kiwanis Clubs, students of universities and high schools; conferred with governors of four states; and reported to the Executive Council "a very fine spirit of deep and sympathetic interest manifested by many influential, outstanding people in the South."

In his speeches Green censored industry for going to the South to exploit the workers, and assured his audiences that the A. F. of L. had come not to stir up hate and class war but in response to the appeal of the Southern workers for assistance in raising their standard of living. He declared that the A. F. of L. would help the manufacturer not only to produce more efficiently but also to dispose of his products by stimulating consumption, and that it was a bulwark against communism.

His conciliatory speeches reflected not only the newer philosophy of the A. F. of L. but also the cold fact that the Federation had no money for a more dashing campaign. However, they foreshortened the picture by putting the union's function of co-operation ahead of its function of raising wages, reducing hours, redressing grievances, and protecting workers against discrimination. As a matter of fact, union organizers in the field were not consulting engineers. They were organizers and fighters used to the old union ways. Inevitably, the campaign ran along two divergent paths—old-fashioned organizing work including strikes, and conciliatory overtures to friendly employers. The A. F. of L. sponsored both lines of attack without quite reconciling them either in practice or in public opinion.

Some of the difficulties involved in these tactics were illustrated in the Danville strike. Workers in the Danville mills became discontented with the company's "industrial democracy" plan when the company proposed an unexpected wage cut of 10 per cent. They appointed a committee to request the A. F. of L. for help. On February 9, 1930 the United Textile Workers held a mass meeting in Danville and 1,000 out of some 4,000 mill operatives joined the union. A union committee attempted to interview Fitzgerald, the president of the company. Great emphasis was laid upon the constructive features of union management co-operation, but Fitzgerald was not impressed by the idea. He proceeded to discharge a large number of workers who had joined the union. Agitation for a strike began.

Both the United Textile Workers and the A. F. of L. did their best to prevent a strike. But during the summer the situation continued tense and the local union grew stronger. By September 1930 local impatience had reached such a point that a strike was called after every effort to negotiate with the company concerning grievances failed. The union was willing to accept arbitration or mediation, but the president of the company flatly rejected all proposals, including an offer from the Governor of Virginia.

Although the workers had a great deal of favorable local public opinion, the A. F. of L. officials were gloomy about the prospect of winning. Green regarded the economic situation as inopportune because of the great reservoir of cheap labor. In spite of the splendid condition of the Danville local, he thought the workers indifferent. Also the outlook for financing the strike was bad. The Executive Council agreed with Green and thought that it would be better to care for the families of those discharged than to risk a strike. But no one could stop the local from embarking upon its hopeless struggle. The A. F. of L. 1930 convention, willy-nilly, endorsed the strike and urged its members to contribute relief, but did not adopt any special measures for financing it. The Danville union, handicapped by injunctions, by the militia, and still more by lack of money, carried on the fight for four months. The strike was called off on January 29, 1931 when it became apparent that the mills were operating normally with a force made up partly of former employees and partly of new recruits.

The results of the campaign in the South were meager. Few of the concessions gained were maintained. The gains in membership[22] were soon lost. Also, the efforts of the A. F. of L. to interest employers in union management co-operation were far from successful. During 1930-31 a few employers seemed responsive, but agreements were signed with only three small companies, a candy and syrup factory, a hosiery mill, and a coffee blending and roasting establishment, the latter employing only ten workers. The agreements which these firms signed embodied some of the new devices of union management co-operation, such as joint research committees, but lacked definite provisions for protecting workers in settling grievances.

The main factors in accounting for the poor results of the Southern campaign were the lack of funds needed to

[22] The United Textile Workers submitted reports in May 1930 showing that 29 locals had been organized with 10,340 members, of whom about 2,175 paid dues. The Birmingham office in 1930 reported a total of 112 locals organized in different crafts in the South, including textile locals, and five new central labor unions. The centers of greatest activity were Birmingham, Ala. and North and South Carolina. Two colored organizers were on the staff of the Birmingham office, and in one report Smith wrote: "The colored labor of the South apparently will be easier to organize than the white, but as a matter of policy we are trying to be careful and not shove the organization work among the colored people out in the spotlight of notoriety ahead of the organization of white labor."

take care of the strikers and the general industrial depression after November 1929. It was impossible to win strikes with the entire industry forced on short time. The attitude of the Southern community towards incoming unionism has been stressed as peculiar, but in reality it did not differ much from that which had prevailed elsewhere at a corresponding stage of industrial development. Many Southerners, especially among the professional classes, in the colleges, and in some of the churches, were sympathetic with unionism. Community pride was stirred to protest over the exploitation of the South's labor resources, particularly by Northern and foreign capital. But employers in whose mills walkouts occurred did not show themselves any more tractable to union reasoning than employers correspondingly situated in the North. The employers' associations, tightly organized and powerful, were adamant, and are said to have brought pressure to bear on employers who might have yielded.

The workers proved themselves good fighters and impatient for action when aroused by the union's appeals. Union meetings often took on the aspect of revivalism. But there were many hindrances to organization, such as the high mobility of labor in the mill villages, the incoming from the mountains of new families with low standards of living, the isolation of many of the company controlled mill villages, and low earnings—particularly during the time of curtailment of output—which made the collection of dues difficult and immediate strike relief imperative.

Other factors in the failure of the Southern campaign were the vacillating policy of the Federation and the inadequate financial response by the unions, though many of them had large incomes and reserves. The A. F. of L. was extremely cautious in endorsing strikes and consistently discouraged them because of shortage of funds for adequate strike relief and the depressed state of the industry. A. F. of L. leaders deprecated the strikes and class warfare and stressed the possibility of persuading Southern employers to admit the unions to their plants peacefully. The officials of the United Textile Workers were convinced that the time was inopportune for winning strikes in the South and placed their hope upon building up union organization inside the mills, carrying on educational work quietly, and avoiding strikes. This policy was pursued throughout 1930, mostly in localities far removed from the scenes of the first strikes. While this may have been a realistic approach it produced a bad impression and played into the hands of the radicals. It cast doubt upon the sincerity of the whole campaign, and seemed to amount to an acknowledgment of failure at the outset. The workers asked why they should join a union that had shown itself incapable of supporting the promising beginnings made by the mill workers themselves. They had expected real aid from the A. F. of L. and attributed its failure to extend such aid to weakness and timidity.

V. NEW AND OLD OPPOSITION

While the A. F. of L. was struggling with the complex issues of the "new era," its problems became further complicated by the activities of the communists and of new groups of critics. The efforts of the Federation to combat the influence of these opposition groups figured importantly in determining its course during these years.

A. Communist Groups

More than any other group the communists brought the Federation trouble and disunion. From 1925 to 1927, under the guidance of William Z. Foster and the Trade Union Educational League, they "bored from within" in several unions, hoping thus to gain control over organized labor. They were particularly successful in the needle trades unions where they "captured" for a while the offices in several local unions in New York City. They were defeated only after several years of bitter struggle in which the A. F. of L. lent its active aid to the local union officials. The two most devastating fights occurred in the Furriers' Union and the International Ladies' Garment Workers' Union.[23]

During 1928 there was a lull in communist union activities because of internal dissensions which resulted in three contending communist "factions," not to mention the smaller groups which split off from the main factions.[24] The most important and numerous faction,

[23] See Appendix B, pp. 521-23.

[24] In 1924 the Workers' Party was already divided into two factions—a majority headed by William Z. Foster and a minority under Charles E. Ruthenberg. The chief difference concerned the attitude towards a "mass Farmer-Labor Party." The majority, under Foster, wanted to concentrate efforts upon building up the Workers' Party. The minority wanted to bring the masses who were not yet ready for straight communism into the fold of such a party. The Third International, to whom the quarrel was referred, decided that work in the trade unions was more important than work in the political field, and that a labor party should not be launched until 500,000 workers were ready to join it. The factions were ordered to unite. During the Workers' Party's next congress, however, the Third International further muddied the waters by reversing itself and cabling an endorsement of the minority Ruthenberg group. Foster's tactics in securing a majority of the delegates were condemned as "ultra-factional and mechanical." In accordance with the orders of the Third International, 40 per cent of the seats on the executive committee of the Workers' Party now went to the Ruthen-

headed by William Z. Foster, attacked the A. F. of L. and its constituent unions as tools and allies of employers and financiers, and began building up dual unions in various industries in opposition to those of the A. F. of L. In August 1929 this faction formed the Trade Union Unity League to take the place of the former Trade Union Educational League as a center for communist unions. The second faction, known as the Communist League or Left Opposition spent most of its time denouncing the Foster group. It pursued largely a negative policy of criticizing all other communist groups and of supporting movements directed against the A. F. of L. and the Trade Union Unity League. Between these two groups the third faction, the so-called "Lovestoneites," held a middle position. In view of the absence of a revolutionary situation in the United States, they thought it best to try to unite all "opposition" elements for common action.

Communist strike activities began to attract attention

---

berg group. In March 1927, Ruthenberg died, but factionalism continued. Foster's group, which had been the majority, became the minority, and a new majority was headed by Jay Lovestone. Even the Third International could not find much difference between them and ascribed the intensity of factionalism to general weakness and lack of contact with the masses. In midsummer of 1928 Trotsky's exile from the Soviet Union produced another split. Followers of Trotsky were expelled from the Workers' Party and they formed the Communist League of America (Opposition). Another factor of dissension among the communists was the decision of the fourth convention of the Red International of Labor Unions to give up "boring from within" the old unions, and to form separate communist unions instead. This policy was rejected by the "majority group," but was approved by the "minority group." The Third International again intervened. Most of the leaders of the majority group, including Jay Lovestone and Benjamin Gitlow, were expelled from the party. This group then constituted itself the Communist Party of the United States (majority group). The "minority" group headed by Foster was recognized by Moscow and became the official "Stalinist" Party.

when the National Textile Workers' Union, organized in 1928, became active in Gastonia in the spring of 1929. The communists conducted a vigorous strike for several months, but in the end had to withdraw. Communist ideas were too remote from the Southern workers, who preferred to fight their battles in their own way. For the same reason the communists were unable to keep the leadership of a strike at Bessemer City in the same county the following year and failed in their attempt to take part in the Danville strike.

During 1931 the National Textile Workers' Union was active in New England. It led a spontaneous strike against the American Woolen Company in Lawrence, Massachusetts in February; against the General Fabrics Corporation in Central Falls, Rhode Island in May; and against the Royal Weaving Company in Pawtucket, Rhode Island in June. In the first of these strikes the workers won their demands against the "speed-up" system. State troops were used in each strike, clashes between the police and strikers were frequent, and communist leaders were arrested.

During 1929 the Needle Trades Workers' Industrial Union conducted unsuccessful strikes of furriers, cloakmakers, and dressmakers. In 1932, when the International Ladies' Garment Workers' Union conducted a strike of its dressmakers' locals, the communists organized a strike committee of their own followers and called separate strikes. The two sets of strikers opposed one another, complicating negotiations with the employers' associations for a new agreement.

Perhaps the most dramatic performance the communists staged was in the soft coal fields. In June 1931, owing to the desperate condition of the bituminous coal miners, low wages, short time, and unemployment, the National Miners' Union led by the communists experienced a new lease on life. A number of spontaneous local strikes in the Pittsburgh region were seized upon by communist leaders and organized into a mass movement. The strike wave spread into southeastern Ohio and northern West Virginia. By the middle of June about 20,000 were said to be involved. Both employed and unemployed, including women and children, were drawn upon for mass picketing. In several instances the strikers and their families marched to county seats demanding food. Demonstrations were dispersed by guards of the coal and iron companies and by state police, armed with tear-gas bombs. The National Miners' Union grew overnight from a mere handful to a mass organization.

The communists were unable, however, to profit by their success. Alarmed by their activities, the mine operators turned to the United Mine Workers. The Pittsburgh Terminal Company and several other operators signed contracts with the United Mine Workers for the first time since 1927. In the Scott's Run District of West Virginia a number of companies agreed to the union scale of wages, which was lowered by the United Mine Workers to reconcile the operators and to meet new price conditions.

During 1931 the communists were also active in the mines of Harlan County, Kentucky. The miners' strike in that county was called in February 1931 by the United Mine Workers, after the companies announced a 10 per cent wage cut. There was considerable violence during the strike and on May 5 the "Battle of Evarts" took place. One miner and three deputies were killed. The

United Mine Workers withdrew from the strike and the communists stepped in. The I.W.W. were on the scene also. The strike was lost.

Between 1929 and 1932 the communists set up eleven independent unions.[25] But these were mere skeleton organizations and had more the character of propaganda centers. In addition, they staged unemployment demonstrations, including the Hunger Marches on Washington in 1931 and 1932, and carried on propaganda for unemployment insurance.

B. Socialists

The socialists, at one time the chief opposition within the A. F. of L., changed front during these years, because of the slump in their membership,[26] the decline of the socialist vote, and hatred of the communists. They suspended criticism of the Federation and supported it during its anti-communist campaigns in the unions.

The possibility of a rift between the Socialist Party and the A. F. of L. arose over the Brookwood affair.[27] The *New Leader*, the Socialist weekly in New York, sharply rebuked Matthew Woll and defended the college. However, a break was not allowed to develop, and

[25] The Agricultural Workers' League, the National Miners' Union, the Lumber Workers' Industrial League, the Auto Workers' Industrial Union, the Metal Workers' Industrial League, the National Textile Workers' Union, the Shoe and Leather Workers' National Committee, the Needle Trades Workers' Union; Food and Packing House Workers' Industrial League, the Railroad Workers' League, and the Marine Workers' Industrial Union. The total membership in 1931 was given as 30,485. See *Red International Labor Union Magazine*, December 1931.

[26] The membership of the Socialist Party was 25,000 in 1925; 15,000 in 1926; 10,000 in 1928; and 10,627 in 1930.

[27] See below, pp. 264-65.

the Party continued its friendly attitude towards the Federation.[28]

Discontent with the Party's trade union policy was voiced in 1931 by a group of "militants" in New York. They stressed the importance of restoring socialist influence in the unions. They suggested that an organizer be appointed to make contacts among workers, and to assist wherever possible with organizing, picketing, relief work, legal defense, research, and publicity. However, the majority of the New York socialists feared that such tactics savored too much of attempting to control the unions. The "militants" brought up their program at the national convention of the Socialist Party held in Milwaukee in June 1932. They were defeated. The convention gave its approval to the policy adopted by the New York local conference in 1930, according to which the socialists were not to attempt to force socialist policies on the unions, but were to win the workers by argument and service.

C. The Conference for Progressive Labor Action

The Conference for Progressive Labor Action, known as the C.P.L.A., grew out of the break between the A. F. of L. and Brookwood Labor College.[29] During 1928 several unions withdrew support from Brookwood on the grounds that its teachings were too consistently "left-wing," anti-A. F. of L., and even flavored with

[28] As evidence of its friendship for the A. F. of L. the socialists persuaded Ramsay MacDonald, when visiting Canada in 1929, to address the A. F. of L. convention at Toronto. He had at first refused to do so because of the Federation's anti-socialist attitude.

[29] Brookwood Labor College was organized in 1921 by a group of labor leaders and educators, as a resident school for workers and trade unionists. Its curriculum includes general social subjects and special courses on the history of labor and on trade union tactics and administration.

communism. The participation of four Brookwood students in a miners' conference meeting at Pittsburgh under the auspices of the "Save-the-Union-Committee," which planned to start a dual union in the mining industries, particularly aroused the hostility of President Green. The students, it was charged, had absented themselves from school with the consent and approval of the faculty.

President Green delegated Matthew Woll to investigate Brookwood. His report took the form of an indictment, based on students' analyses of the courses given, and on certain incidents of the school life, such as the celebration of May 1 and the anniversary of the Bolshevik Revolution. The Executive Council decided to recommend withdrawal of support from the institution to its constituent unions, an act which was later endorsed by the convention.

In spite of this official condemnation, Brookwood continued to draw students from A. F. of L. unions. The college became pronouncedly oppositionist in spirit. To strengthen its position it took the lead in summoning a conference of "labor progressives" which met in New York on May 25, 1929. The director of Brookwood[30] presided and took a leading part in drafting a program which was entitled a "Challenge to Progressives." A continuing organization was formed, under the name "Conference for Progressive Labor Action," which was to rally the elements in the American labor movement that could accept neither the leadership of the A. F. of L. nor that of the communists. It was thus made clear that no dual trade union center was proposed.[31]

[30] The director was A. J. Muste, at one time a minister, whose labor activities began with the New England textile strikes of 1919.

[31] The "Challenge to Progressives" outlined a number of specific objectives—social insurance, co-operation, effective methods of collective

In September 1932 the C.P.L.A. held a national conference in New York City attended by 91 delegates. A constitution was adopted and a national executive committee of 25 members was elected. Under this new organization the C.P.L.A. aims to be a "militant rallying center" for the American labor movement. Its outlook is akin to that of the left-wing socialists. It predicates the abolition of capitalism, aims at a socialist planned society, believes in the class struggle, but is opposed to the dictatorial methods of the communists. The C.P.L.A. intends to work within the unions of the Federation. But it refuses to "make a fetish" of the A. F. of L. and organizes new or independent unions when it thinks it necessary.

An illustration of the effects of the opposition on an A. F. of L. union is supplied by the various efforts to reorganize the United Mine Workers. In the spring of 1930 John L. Lewis, the president of the United Mine Workers, instituted proceedings to remove the officers of District 12, embracing the Illinois coal field, on charges of misuse of funds. The latter resisted and secured an injunction restraining President Lewis on the grounds that he had exceeded his constitutional powers. After the district's charter was revoked, the opposition forces early in March issued a call for a convention to reorganize the United Mine Workers. Among the signatories of the call was John H. Walker, president of the Illinois State Federation of Labor, a subdivision of the A. F. of L., which thus became involved in the struggle. Five hundred delegates from eleven districts assembled in

bargaining and workshop control, the five-day week, recognition of Soviet Russia, an international anti-militarist and anti-imperialist program, a labor party, a workers' education movement which would include "recreation and culture with a union label on it."

Springfield, Illinois on March 10, 1930. They formally declared the office of international president vacant; elected Alexander Howat, president of the Kansas district, in Lewis' place; and adopted a new constitution.

Simultaneously with the insurgent convention, a regular convention of the United Mine Workers was summoned to meet at Indianapolis in order to strengthen the constitutional and tactical position of the administration. Both conventions claimed legality for their action under different interpretations of the union's laws. Both sides appealed to the American Federation of Labor for support. The insurgents asked for the good offices of President Green in bringing the two factions together in a harmony convention; the regulars asked that the charter of the Illinois State Federation be revoked. President Green, himself a former secretary of the United Mine Workers, appeared in person at Indianapolis to pledge his support to the suppression of dual unionism.

After a bitter fight which lasted nearly a year, in the course of which both sides called each other the vilest names, most of the officers of the Illinois District made peace with the International Union. The C.P.L.A. then stepped in, and in co-operation with Alexander Howat, tried to rally the discontented elements. A "rank and file" convention was held at St. Louis on April 15, 1931 at which some 30,000 miners were represented, including about 25 per cent of the Illinois miners. It had been the expectation to lay the foundation of a new union, but this plan was abandoned. Instead a policy committee was appointed to continue the agitation and to prepare for a new union "at the proper time."

The relations of the various opposition groups were revealed on this occasion. The communists, with their

National Miners' Union already in the field, stayed away from the Springfield convention, for which they were sharply criticized by the two other communist groups. The Communist League saw a chance here for a "united front" with the rank and file, and urged communist participation in the reorganized union, for the purpose of pushing it to the left and showing up the inadequacy of the "machine" leaders. The same disagreement developed in regard to the St. Louis convention. The Communist Party told its members to boycott the convention, while the communist opposition strongly urged sending delegates to capture it. The National Miners' Union, at the last minute, sent an observer, who was allowed to address the convention and urge it to adopt the program of the communist union. His advice, however, was rejected.

During 1931 the C.P.L.A. took part in the strike in the Kanawha coal fields of West Virginia which resulted in the formation of the West Virginia Mine Workers' Union and the Independent Labor Party of West Virginia. Its members were active in the strikes of textile workers in Paterson, New Jersey and Lawrence, Massachusetts. In these strikes, the C.P.L.A. at one and the same time aided A. F. of L. unions and helped to form unions against the A. F. of L. During 1932 it leaned in the latter direction. It lent its aid to the formation of the National Progressive Miners' Union in Illinois.[32] It also took the side of groups fighting the A. F. of L. officials in several unions, such as Local 3 of the Brotherhood of Electrical Workers in New York. And it carried on vehement attacks on A. F. of L. "bureaucracy" in general.

[32] See Appendix B, pp. 495-97.

D. Summary

The effects of communist and other opposition activities on the A. F. of L. were concentrated in three industries: coal mining, and the manufacture of clothing and textiles. Undoubtedly these activities further aggravated the condition of the main unions in these industries—the United Mine Workers, the International Ladies' Garment Workers' Union, and the United Textile Workers. Internal dissension was increased, strike negotiations were frustrated, and the morale of the workers undermined. But there were also items on the other side of the balance sheet. The United Mine Workers made some capital of the fear aroused by the communists in the mine districts of western Pennsylvania and Ohio. The United Textile Workers were helped by the C.P.L.A. and even profited by the work of the communists in Lawrence. The A. F. of L. in its entirety gained a hearing in the South, partly because it held out promise of undoing the communists.

The A. F. of L. fought the communists hard and showed no leniency towards the "progressives." Partly, this was due to fear of further infection in the unions. In part it was caused by the bitter personalities involved in the factional fights and by the anti-Bolshevik animus inherited from war days. A contributing factor was the influence of the National Civic Federation. Its anti-communist zeal was carried to the A. F. of L. through the intermediation of Matthew Woll, who was serving at the same time as a vice-president of both the National Civic Federation and the American Federation of Labor.

But the small results of the communists and of the C.P.L.A. were due not so much to A. F. of L. measures as to inherent factors. The communists in the United States found the same difficulties in building up trade unions as they had experienced in other countries. Interested in large and spectacular mass movements, they found it much easier to arouse discontented workers than to hold them in permanent economic organizations. Their preparations for strikes were hasty, their leadership faulty. Besides, despite their attacks on the "bureaucracy" of the A. F. of L., they showed but little regard for democratic methods. In various articles during 1931-32 Foster and other spokesmen of the Communist Party gave chapter and verse on the high-handed disregard of the wishes and the interests of the membership by the new "bureaucrats" of the communist unions who formulated demands, called strikes, elected and removed officers without a semblance of democratic consultation. On the national and district committees of the National Miners' Union there was not a single working miner. The communist methods in the unions of the Trade Union Unity League were dogmatic and "mechanical." Everything was cut and dried. Intelligent non-party workers were squeezed out. A few leading communists completely dominated the unions and laid down the programs; there was no real effort toward consulting the rank and file membership.

The C.P.L.A. had neither funds nor men to carry on a real campaign. Its influence was exercised through Brookwood and through a few of its members who had connections with some of the more progressive unions in the A. F. of L. Its miscellaneous membership was in many respects incoherent and its leadership neither consistent nor forceful. To this should be added the internal differences in the opposition groups and their inter-group jealousies and animosities. The Communist Party and the Trade Union Unity League regard the C.P.L.A.

as another manifestation of Social-Fascism,[33] and they have even less respect for the "traitorous Trotskyists" and the "liquidating Lovestoneites."[34] The Communist League (Opposition), while advocating the tactics of the "united front," issued warnings against carrying the united front too far. On the other hand, the C.P.L.A. accused the communists of demagogy, dictatorial methods, and subservience to ideas and slogans from Moscow. Despite these weaknesses the communists and the C.P.L.A. gave substance to some of the internal discontent in the A. F. of L. during 1929-32 and reinforced tendencies which affected the policies of the Federation, as in the case of the demand for unemployment insurance.

VI. LEGISLATIVE ACTIVITIES

Compared to the industrial record, the legislative activities of the A. F. of L. during these years, though limited, were far more successful. Many of the bills favored by the A. F. of L. which were passed were those having interest for particular unions, especially for unions whose members were employed in government service and whose gains had to be secured through legislation instead of through collective bargaining.[35] Other special

[33] The term Social-Fascism was coined by the communists as a designation of the socialist parties whose activities presumably tended to strengthen the evolution of "capitalism" towards a Fascist state.

[34] The tactics which the communist factions use against each other are not much different from the tactics which they use against other opponents. Lovestone was accused of burglarizing the offices of the Central Committee of the Communist Party (*Militant*, Oct. 1, 1929), and the Stalinist Party was accused of slugging a member of the Opposition (the same, Sept. 15, 1929).

[35] Some of the measures of this character passed by Congress between 1925 and 1931 were as follows:

1925: (1) Postal employees wage increase—250,000 employees were granted an increase amounting to about $300 a year each. (2) Pay-

legislation included a federal employees' compensation act passed in 1927, covering longshoremen and harbor workers, and a workmen's compensation act passed in 1928 applying to the District of Columbia. In addition the A. F. of L. secured various amendments reinforcing the restrictive features of the immigration laws.[36] Measures of a wider character included the Watson-Parker Act setting up a system of collective bargaining, mediation, conciliation, and arbitration on the railroads, and the Hawes-Cooper Convict Labor Act passed in 1928.[37]

The A. F. of L. was also successful in helping to defeat measures which it regarded as hostile to labor. One of the bills which came up in Congress repeatedly during these years and which the Federation fought successfully was for the "registration of aliens." Numerous bills designed to weaken the immigration laws were not allowed to pass. Efforts to put the Japanese under the

---

ment of 1.6 million dollars in wages to employees of Bethlehem Steel Co. to cover a wage award by the War Labor Board in 1928. (3) A wage increase for 330 employees of the Bureau of Engraving and Printing, covering painters, carpenters, pressmen, bookbinders, compositors, bricklayers, blacksmiths, electricians, machinists, plumbers, steamfitters, etc.

1926: (1) Modification of the federal retirement law, marking "a substantial step forward." (2) A teachers' retirement law for the District of Columbia.

1927: (1) Provision for a differential in pay for night work in postal service, increasing salaries of 135,000 federal employees. (2) Adjustment of compensation of employees in the customs and immigration inspection service.

1930: (1) Further liberalization of the federal retirement law. (2) Wage increases for low-paid federal employees.

[36] Among the federal acts of social legislation may be mentioned an increase in the compulsory education age of the District of Columbia from 14 to 16 years in 1925; an appropriation of $100,000 for the home care of dependent children in the District in 1926; a new and improved child labor law for the District in 1928; extensions of the Industrial Rehabilitation Act in 1929 and 1930.

[37] For analysis of this law, see Chap. XV, pp. 403-05.

quota law were resisted. Other legislation which was blocked included blue laws for the District of Columbia, a sales tax, and the "Equal Rights" amendment sponsored by the National Woman's Party.

Most of the state labor laws passed between 1925 and 1930 had to do with amendments to workmen's compensation laws, with improving and strengthening the enforcement of these laws, extending the list of compensable diseases, raising the scale of payments, reducing waiting periods, and making better provision for medical and hospital care. A number of states improved their child labor laws and strengthened the laws limiting the working hours of women. Of the newer social legislation the most significant was the passage by several states of old-age pension laws. The Federation hailed as a special victory the abandonment of attempts by state legislatures to pass legislation for compulsory arbitration or investigation of industrial disputes.[38]

The most important item in the legislative program of the A. F. of L. during this period was the effort to obtain relief from the use of the injunction in industrial disputes and protection against the application of the individual contract, commonly called the "yellow dog" contract, which pledges an employee not to join outside labor organizations during his term of service. Ever since the Duplex Printing Press Case[39] the Executive Council of the A. F. of L. had been made aware of the need for further legislation supplementing the Clayton Act. Between 1925 and 1930 the seriousness of the injunction situation was increased by a number of other Supreme

[38] In 1925 the Kansas Industrial Court Act was declared unconstitutional by the United States Supreme Court.

[39] See p. 211.

Court decisions, especially by the Bedford Cut Stone Case. The latter arose out of the fact that members of the Stone Cutters' Union on construction jobs refused to handle stone which had been partially cut in quarries by non-union men. The situation was the result of a strike of stone cutters in a number of Indiana quarries in 1921. Refusing to recognize the union with which they had previously had a collective agreement, about 20 firms in a certain district of Indiana resumed quarrying operations and set up company unions of their employees. These firms then brought suit for an injunction, asserting that the union, in not permitting its members to set stone cut in their quarries under non-union conditions, was engaging in a conspiracy to restrain interstate commerce. After two courts had refused to grant the injunction, the companies appealed to the United States Supreme Court which, in a seven to two decision, ordered the union enjoined. The majority of the court based their argument squarely on the Duplex Printing Case, finding a similar secondary boycott, and a similar intent to restrain commerce. The lawfulness of the ultimate end sought by the union, namely the protection of its members, was conceded, but this was not held to justify an unlawful intermediate means.[40]

Likewise various state courts did much during these years to block the efforts to organize non-union areas. Many union boycotts, strikes, and trade agreements

[40] Justice Brandeis, writing the dissenting opinion, pointed out the unfairness of applying the Sherman Act to a small craft of workmen, engaged in a contest not with a single isolated employer but with an association of employers controlling 70 per cent of the output of the trade, when that Act had been held inapplicable to the United States Steel Corporation, admittedly controlling 50 per cent of the steel industry of the country, and to the United Shoe Machinery Corporation, a virtual monopoly.

were declared illegal and in violation of the Sherman Act, even when the union was merely seeking to protect its own members. No corresponding checks were imposed upon employers' associations, except when they collaborated with unions.[41]

For several years the Executive Council had reported to the conventions that it was trying to devise methods for meeting the injunction issue. But year after year passed and no concrete proposals were brought before the convention. In 1927 a bill was introduced in the United States Senate by Senator Shipstead, which dealt with the injunction problem in simple and sweeping terms. It declared that nothing should be deemed "property" within the cognizance of a federal court of equity unless it was "tangible and transferable." The Shipstead bill had no chance of passage because it would have prevented the issuance of injunctions in many types of disputes other than labor disputes. It was however endorsed in principle by the A. F. of L. convention in 1927.

Union representatives met to consider injunction legislation in Washington on February 7, 1928, and attended hearings on the Shipstead bill before the subcommittee of the Senate Judiciary Committee. The Senate sub-committee, after consultation with experts,

[41] There were also court decisions favorable to labor. One of the outstanding examples was *Interborough Rapid Transit Company* v. *Lavin*, decided by the New York Court of Appeals in 1928, which departed from the doctrine set up by the Supreme Court in the Hitchman Case. The Interborough sought to enjoin the Amalgamated Association of Street and Electric Railway Employees and the American Federation of Labor from attempts to organize its employees, with whom it had entered into an understanding that they would not join the union. The court refused to grant the injunction, holding that the "understanding" was not the equivalent of a contract. It is worth noting that the union briefs in this case were prepared with great care and at great expense.

amended the Shipstead bill by striking out its provisions and substituting a bill of an entirely different character, which attempted once more to regulate the issuance of injunctions in labor disputes. The Resolutions Committee at the New Orleans convention of the A. F. of L. in 1928 reported that the substitute bill was not in accord with the recommendations adopted at the Los Angeles convention of 1927 and should not be endorsed. They felt that the time was ripe for Congress to pass a law which should deny the jurisdiction of the courts over labor injunction cases and repeal or amend the anti-trust acts so as to exempt unions from their provisions.

Following the convention of 1928 a special committee was appointed to re-examine the whole question. This committee, in consultation with eminent lawyers, swung round to the substitute bill after minor changes had been made and reported favorably on it to the convention of 1929. After a lengthy debate it was endorsed.[42] The bill contained several important provisions. Its novel feature was Section 2, which declared that since unorganized workers were helpless to exercise liberty of contract they must have full liberty to associate, and to designate representatives of their own choosing to negotiate terms of employment.[43] It further declared the workers must not be subject to restraint or coercion by employers in their concerted activities for the purpose of collective bargaining or other mutual aid and protection. This was an important declaration as it was to serve as a guide to the courts in interpreting the Act. Section 3 of the bill de-

[42] A single negative vote was cast by Andrew Furuseth, president of the Seamen's Union, who favored the original Shipstead bill.

[43] As first drafted the bill specified "trade union organization," and complaint was made by the A. F. of L. convention in 1930 when these words were left out.

clares that individual contracts—"yellow dog" contracts—are not enforceable at law or in equity before the federal courts. Section 4 sets forth certain forms of conduct in labor disputes, which are explicity declared legal and immune from injunctions. In general it provides that "no persons participating in, or affected by, such disputes shall be enjoined from striking, or from striving for the success of the strike by customary labor union effort, short of fraud or violence." The immunity is extended only to persons engaged "in the same industry, trade, or occupation," but it is a considerable extension of the immunity granted by the Clayton Act, which has been construed to apply only to employers and their own employees. A novel and significant provision applies to cases in which injunctions may still be granted—that is, cases which was one reason or another the Act fails to cover. No restraining orders or injunctions are to be granted to anyone who has failed to comply with any legal obligation in connection with the labor dispute, or who has failed to make every reasonable effort to settle the dispute by negotiation or with the aid of available governmental machinery of mediation or conciliation. The procedure of restraining orders, injunctions, and appeals is minutely regulated in an attempt to remove some existing abuses, particularly with regard to hearings and fact-finding.

This injunction bill was unfavorably reported by the Senate Judiciary Committee on June 18, 1930. The majority of the committee felt that it would be declared unconstitutional; that it trespassed upon states' rights in defining a public policy on industrial relations; and that the principal need for legislation was in the states, because at the time it was found that practically no injunctions were pending in federal courts. But during 1931 the A. F. of L. renewed its efforts, and the bill was passed in February 1932 as the Norris-LaGuardia Act, and was signed by President Hoover on March 20, 1932.

VII. NET RESULTS

Even though the officials of the A. F. of L. after 1925 recognized the need for new policies in view of the new economic situation, most of the unions in the Federation pursued their old ways, making only a few changes in methods and policy. The modifications which most of them adopted provided for less reliance upon strikes and greater efforts to come to terms with employers by impressing upon them the business value of unionism. Of the new techniques which were adopted, the most important were the scheme of union management co-operation sponsored by the Railway Employees' Department,[44] the joint system of industrial councils for the adjudication of grievances,[45] and the increasing interest of some unions in efficiency and in improving processes of production.

The unions of the Federation fared unequally between 1925 and 1930, some losing heavily while others gained. A considerable part of the membership was able to obtain higher wage rates, increased earnings, and shorter hours. The 40-hour week in unionized plants was widely accepted, while about half a million union members obtained the five-day week. This was notable in the building trades, in some branches of the transportation industry, in the printing trades, in government employment, and in some of the professions, such as teaching and acting. But where the unions were unable to meet the new condi-

[44] Chap. XIV, pp. 390-95.
[45] See M. H. Hedges, *A Strikeless Industry*, 1932.

tions they suffered a decline in membership, a loss of income, and a weakening of their benefit systems; and they could enforce their standards over smaller areas.

Of the 105 international unions in the A. F. of L. 36 lost in membership between 1924 and 1929, while 25 remained stationary. This means nearly 60 per cent of all the unions and represented one-half of the total membership of the Federation in 1929. These unions included some of the oldest organizations, which had in the past been the very backbone of the Federation.[46]

There were 44 unions, however, which either held their own or showed a fair growth, 15 of these being in the building trades, 5 in the printing trades, 4 in transportation, 7 in government service, and 3 in the amusement trades. The largest increase in membership was in the building trades and in the unions of government workers. The gains of these unions were due chiefly to favorable conditions—the boom in the building industry, the growth of the printing and publishing trades, and the political situation affecting government employees.

The net effects of the "new era" on the A. F. of L. were far from favorable. The membership reported by the Federation remained stationary. Its income decreased, and many of its activities, such as banking and workers' education projects, had to be curtailed. It lost

[46] Such as those of the cigarmakers, molders, metal polishers, journeymen tailors, brewery workers, and garment workers. Other unions which lost ground were those which owed their rapid rise to war conditions and to government agencies which either helped to bring them into existence or to infuse new life into them. Such were the unions of boilermakers, railway carmen, foundry employees, switchmen, oil-field workers, seamen, maintenance of way workers, and textile workers. A third group particularly affected by the industrial changes operated in the "sick" industries, such as the United Mine Workers and the Ladies' Garment Workers' Union. For the way in which particular unions were affected by these conditions, see Appendix B, pp. 494-524.

the campaign in the South and it failed to break through the barriers of the new mass production industries. Its successes were not big enough to offset these industrial setbacks. There was also a slump in the morale and character of unionism, which manifested itself in the indifference of the membership to union activities, in abuses of officials, in the growth of "racketeering,"[47] and in a general loss of zeal for "the cause."

The depression years 1930-32 could not but bring further economic losses to the workers and decline in union organization. Just how great these have been cannot as yet be determined.

[47] For discussion of racketeering, see Chap. XII.

CHAPTER XI

UNEMPLOYMENT

After November 1929 the activities of the A. F. of L. were gradually over-shadowed by one supreme issue—unemployment. The steady decline in employment opportunities had its effects on wages and wage rates, on hours and earnings, and on general industrial relations. Each union was confronted with the problem of aiding its unemployed members and remaining intact during the course of a deepening industrial depression.

I. TRADITIONAL ATTITUDES

In groping for remedial measures against unemployment, the Executive Council of the Federation was guided in large measure by traditional views. In its early days the Federation took the position that trade unions could not prevent industrial depressions, but tended to stabilize industry.[1] In 1893, when the A. F. of L. faced the first serious business depression since its formation, it declared that the "right to work" was the "right to life" and that "when the private employer cannot or will not give work, the municipality, state, or nation must."[2] In 1894 the Federation endorsed the Coxey bill for the

[1] In his testimony before the Senate Committee on Education in 1883 Adolph Strasser, one of the founders of the A. F. of L., said: "The trade unions try to make their members better consumers, thereby enlarging the home market, and at the same time to make them better producers. If we can make the working people generally better consumers, we shall have no panics." 48 Cong., 2 sess., *Labor and Capital,* Hearings on S. res. (unnumbered) dated Aug. 7, 1882, before Committee on Education and Labor, Vol. I, p. 459 (published 1885).

[2] *Report of the Proceedings of the Thirteenth Annual Convention of the American Federation of Labor,* 1893, p. 37.

building of public roads by the government through the issue of $500,000,000 of Treasury notes, at a time when the prevailing view was that unemployment was the problem of the individual worker, and when programs for dealing with unemployment were still undeveloped.[3]

But after 1896 Gompers began to emphasize the theory that unless wages were raised and working hours reduced to make the wage earners' "power of consumption nearly commensurate with the wonderful productivity of modern labor," industrial activity would be short lived.[4] In 1906 Gompers ascribed the quick recovery of the country from the recession of 1903-04 in large measure to the fact that the trade unions had been able to resist wage reductions. The Federation showed less and less interest in programs of public works.

Meanwhile, labor organizations and governments in other countries had adopted a new course towards the problem of unemployment. In 1900 the Ghent system of insurance, providing municipal subsidies to trade unions paying out-of-work benefits, was begun in Ghent, Belgium and soon spread to France, Italy, Holland,

[3] In 1873 the North American section of the First International urged the unemployed to demand that the public authorities provide work "at the usual wages and on the eight hours plan." In England the government in 1886 and again in 1892 laid upon the local authorities the moral obligation to provide work in times of exceptional distress. In 1893 the first experiment in subsidized voluntary unemployment insurance was begun in Berne, Switzerland. In 1896 the International Labor and Socialist Congress in London for the first time advocated public employment in times of depression. In the United States the first demand for a system of public works to relieve unemployment was incorporated in the platform of the Social Democratic Party in 1900.

[4] See *Proceedings of the Annual Convention of the A. F. of L.*, 1896, pp. 18-19; 1897, pp. 18-19; 1899, p. 6; 1901, p. 15; 1903, pp. 14-15. In 1903 he re-stated it thus: "As a matter of fact, the greater the power of consumption of the great mass of the workers, the larger their wants, the higher is their standard of life, the greater the degree of industrial and commercial prosperity."

Switzerland, and the Scandinavian countries.[5] In England the experience of the 1903-04 depression led to the Unemployed Workmen's Act of 1905, which recognized the responsibility of society for involuntary unemployment and set up public agencies to provide relief and work for the unemployed.[6] In 1906 the first international congress on unemployment was held in Milan, and in 1910 the International Association for Protection against Unemployment was formed to collect statistics on the subject and to promote legislation. In the same year the International Socialist Congress at Copenhagen devoted a special session to unemployment and adopted a program providing for adequate unemployment statistics, employment exchanges, and compulsory unemployment insurance. In England the Labor Exchange Act was passed in 1909 establishing a system of public employment offices, and that was followed in 1911 by the National Insurance Act providing compulsory insurance against unemployment on a contributory basis for about 2,500,000 workers.

In the United States the panic of 1907 and the social awakening which followed it laid their impress on public opinion. Unemployment became a subject of serious interest and discussion.[7] In 1910 the Wainwright Commission was organized in New York State to report on the subject. A movement was set on foot for free employment

[5] See M. Rubinow, *Social Insurance*, 1916, Chap. II.

[6] See A. C. C. Hill, Jr., and I. Lubin, *The British Attack on Unemployment.* (In press.)

[7] The change was summed up by a well-known writer as follows: "The funny-paper jokes about Weary Willy and Ragged Rufus have passed their meridian and now for some time have been declining into twilight. Unemployment has ceased in America to be a joke." William Hard, "Unemployment as a Coming Issue," *American Labor Legislation Review*, February 1912, Vol. 2, p. 95.

offices, and the social reform elements began to interest themselves in unemployment insurance. The Socialist Party embodied the demand for such insurance in its platform in 1912.

The A. F. of L. during these years did not touch on the problem at its conventions. Its leadership was opposed to compulsory state action and had a special dislike for the unemployment program of the day because it was sponsored by socialists and social reformers.

This was also the case during 1913-16, when unemployment became a serious issue and gave the radical and socialist forces ammunition for their propaganda. In 1913 the Federation expressed an assurance that the evils of unemployment could be mitigated by road building "without devising any elaborate program of social justice or economic reform."[8] It sponsored uniform vagrancy laws in the states and was somewhat ironical about bills introduced into Congress for the establishment of a federal employment bureau.[9] The Executive Council admitted that it was not yet prepared to offer a "constructive program" and asked the convention of 1915 to appoint a committee to study the problem. As no appropriation was made for its work, the committee did nothing.

In 1916 the activities of reformers for social legislation reached a climax. There was a concerted movement for health insurance, and the American Association for Labor Legislation promoted in several state legislatures bills for compulsory social legislation. In the same year Meyer London, the socialist congressman from New

[8] *Proceedings of the 33d Annual Convention of the A. F. of L.*, 1913, p. 89.

[9] During 1913-14 free public employment offices were established in many states.

York, introduced a joint resolution in the House of Representatives to provide for a commission which would prepare and recommend to Congress a plan for the establishment of a national insurance fund covering all forms of compulsory social insurance.

Gompers was incensed by the fact that neither the American Association for Labor Legislation nor Congressman London consulted him. He branded them as meddlers in the labor movement, as "barnacles of labor," who were trying to foist a foreign scheme on the American labor movement. He was emphatic in his rejection of social insurance as inimical to the freedom of the workers and as tending to put the worker's life under government control, which presumably was out of harmony with the spirit of trade unionism. This came to be regarded as the traditional stand of the Federation on the subject.

II. DEVELOPING A PROGRAM

It was the depression of 1920-21 that forced the Federation to outline for the first time a more definite program for dealing with unemployment. Public opinion had by this time veered away from the pre-war social reformism. The man of the hour was the engineer. Scientific management and the elimination of wastes in industry were being emphasized. The concept of "business cycles" was passing from economic texts into current thinking, carrying the idea that unemployment was an inevitable product of industrial development and a problem of management. There was a growing demand for public employment offices and for expediting public construction.[10]

[10] President Harding's Unemployment Conference in the fall of 1921 gave these ideas publicity.

Because of its new attitudes[11] the Federation was quite prepared to place responsibility for unemployment and for its relief on management. Accordingly, it formulated three practical demands—the establishment of a federal employment service; national conference boards composed of an equal number of workers and employers in each industry to care for the workers in that industry; and public credit for the expansion of public works, including roads, irrigation, inland waterways, railroads, and housing. Unemployment insurance was receiving but scant attention in public discussion, and the Federation took credit for having helped to shape American policy by "consistently opposing unemployment state insurance or doles."[12]

The Federation gave some consideration to the question in 1924 and again in 1927, owing to business recessions. In September 1927 the Federation began publishing a monthly survey of unemployment based upon reports from some 3,000 trade union locals in 24 cities which showed a considerable degree of unemployment due to the displacement of men by machinery. At the convention of 1928 considerable time was devoted to this question, and "technological unemployment" was declared a serious problem facing American labor.

In its analysis of "technological unemployment," the Federation stressed the point that it was a "new type" of unemployment[13] due to the fact that the increase in

[11] See Chap. IX, pp. 217-18.

[12] *Proceedings of the 43d Annual Convention of the A. F. of L.*, 1923, pp. 40-42.

[13] As a matter of fact the displacement of men by machinery had been discussed repeatedly in the conventions of the Federation since 1894. In 1907 the Federation adopted a resolution to study the subject. In 1913 and again in 1916 the Executive Council was requested to appoint a commission for the purpose.

efficiency and in the power to produce was out-stripping the increase in the purchasing power of the workers. The problem was declared to be impossible of solution except by methods which would simultaneously develop production power, opportunity for employment, and consuming power. The Federation outlined a program. It called for a nation-wide employment service under federal management or control; for the stabilization of industry by management with union aid; and for public works as a "prosperity reserve." The Executive Council was authorized to urge Congress for an appropriation to enable the United States Bureau of Labor Statistics to compile accurate unemployment data.

During 1929, though there was a slight upward trend in employment opportunities, the Federation continued to be concerned about the problem. Some reference was made to the irregularity of employment due to lack of balance in production. Apprehension was expressed that this might turn prosperity into depression unless controlled. As a preliminary basis for such control the Federation instructed the Executive Council to make its major task during 1929-30 the establishment of a coordinated system of municipal, state, and federal employment bureaus which were to place workers in jobs, collect information on unemployment, and help avert depressions.

III. FACING THE DEPRESSION

Despite its preoccupations with the problem, the A. F. of L. was as little prepared as other groups of the American people for the stock market crash of October 30, 1929, and for the depression which followed it. The efforts of the Federation to meet the situation as it developed may be described in relation to the Wagner bills, to relief, to unemployment insurance, and to general plans for recovery.

A. The Wagner Bills

At the time the Federation was formulating its program on unemployment in 1928, there were pending in the United States Senate three bills on the subject, introduced by Senator Robert F. Wagner in 1927. One of the bills concerned statistics of employment and unemployment; another employment offices; and a third a federal stabilization board for the planning of government construction. The Federation supported all three. The bills on the collection of unemployment statistics and on the stabilization board were passed by both houses of Congress. But the bill on employment offices which passed the Senate met with opposition in the House. It was also opposed by the Secretary of Labor, William N. Doak. The Wagner bill proposed that the offices should be under state control, co-ordinated by the federal government with clearing houses at strategic points, and financed by the several states with the aid of the federal government, which was to contribute 50 per cent of the cost. It also made provision for federal and state committees to be composed of employers and employees to guide the activities of the employment offices.

Secretary Doak drew up his own bill, which did not provide for federal and state committees, and invited officials of the A. F. of L. and Senator Wagner to a conference to consider it. As the A. F. of L. convention of 1930 had endorsed the Wagner bill, William Green and his associates refused to approve Secretary Doak's bill, despite the latter's promise to put union men in charge of the various offices, and announced that they would continue to support the Wagner bill.

The House Judiciary Committee substituted the Doak for the Wagner bill in reporting to the House, and it appeared as if the Wagner bill would be defeated. But the Federation increased its lobbying efforts and the Wagner bill passed the House by a large majority.[14] It was, however, vetoed by President Hoover in March 1931. Immediately after the veto, William Green issued a public statement condemning the President's action.

The Federal Employment Service was soon after reorganized by Secretary Doak without civil service provisions. Federal employment directors were appointed for each state. Among these directors were friends of union officials and persons formerly active in the American Federation of Labor. The Vancouver convention of the Federation in October 1931 expressed its regret over the Hoover veto and instructed the Executive Council to make a full appraisal of the Federal Employment Service with a view to its reorganization. The Executive Council did not carry out these instructions during 1932.

B. Wage Cuts and Relief

Immediately after the stock market crash in October 1929, the Federation declared that it would resist wage cuts on the part of employers. The conference of business, labor, and farm leaders, called by President Hoover on November 21, 1929 to "organize against panic," de-

[14] Telegrams were sent to Congressmen by a very large number of local unions and state federations of labor demanding the acceptance of the Wagner bill. On the morning of the day on which the final vote was taken in the House, every member of Congress received a long letter signed by President Green, giving his reasons why the Wagner bill should be passed.

clared against a policy of wage reductions and the Federation recommended that its unions refrain from initiating movements for wage increases. This was heralded as a compact between capital and labor which promised to halt the depression.

For a short time after the November conference employers tried to maintain wage rates and earnings in the hope that such a policy would serve to maintain consumers' demand. But beginning with March 1930 the employers' ranks began to break, and a number of corporations declared themselves forced to adjust wages downward. The discussion as to what was the more desirable policy continued all through 1930 and through the first half of 1931. This discussion may have been one of the factors in slowing up wholesale wage reductions.

In the summer of 1931 President Green continued to warn against wage cuts and expressed the belief that industry would safeguard its own interests by keeping up the wage level. However, after the middle of 1931 wage cutting increased. During 1932 hundreds of thousands of workers on the railroads, in the building trades, and in the printing industry made agreements with employers on a basis of lower wages. Employers now claimed that downward wage readjustments were essential to business recovery.[15]

The effects of the depression on standards of living began to be evident in the winter of 1930-31. Decrease in milk consumption in the cities, congestion in the poorer neighborhoods, the appearance in school of underfed children, and the increased demand for aid from the organized charities all indicated a serious reduction in the standard of living of the masses of the people. The

[15] See *Recent Social Trends in the United States*, 1933, Vol. II, p. 823.

situation became progressively worse during 1932 as employment became more scarce and earnings were further reduced.

Individual unions in the A. F. of L. applied both old methods and new devices to the situation. Out-of-work benefits were paid on a large scale. Special assessments were laid on members at work for the benefit of those out of work. Work was staggered in such a way as to assure each union member a minimum number of working days a week. Overtime was disallowed under any circumstances.[16]

Realizing that the resources of the unions were inadequate to meet the need, the Federation at its Boston convention in October 1930 instructed the Executive Council to request the President of the United States to appoint a national relief committee. Accordingly, the Council lent its support to the President's Employment Committee which was appointed in October 1930 and reorganized in August 1931 as the President's Organization on Unemployment Relief. The Federation called upon all unions to co-operate with the President's committee in local relief campaigns and to volunteer their services to all state and municipal committees appointed for the purpose. In the fall of 1931, when a number of social agencies began to call attention to the inadequacy of private relief funds and to the fiscal difficulties of state, county, and municipal governments, the Executive Council took an active part in urging measures of federal relief. It supported measures for relief and for public works introduced in the Senate by Senators La-

[16] For a description of methods used by different unions and amounts paid out, see the *American Federationist*, June 1932, pp. 640-51. See also pp. 316-19.

Follette, Costigan, and Wagner in 1932 and early in 1933.

C. Unemployment Insurance

In the summer of 1930 the demand for compulsory state unemployment insurance was taken up by individuals and organizations interested in social legislation. The Executive Council opposed the idea, branding unemployment insurance as a "dole," incompatible with American principles. However, at the 1930 convention of the Federation in Boston a number of delegates pressed the issue. The convention evaded commitment by requesting the Executive Council to make a study of the subject and report to the convention in 1931.

During the year the Executive Council indicated repeatedly that it would not relinquish its stand against unemployment insurance. In reporting to the 1931 convention in Vancouver, the Executive Council gave a brief summary of the experience of Great Britain and Germany and concluded that unemployment insurance subsidized idleness, turned the nation's resources to unproductive ends, and in the long run retarded real progress.[17]

The main argument of the Executive Council was that every system of unemployment insurance contemplates supervision and control by both federal and state governments and requires registration of all workers. This, according to the Executive Council, would subject every worker to undue control by the law and deprive him of the freedom to fight for better conditions. Union men would thus be forced to accept jobs in non-union plants by the threat that otherwise their unemployment benefits

[17] *Proceedings of the 51st Annual Convention of the A. F. of L.*, 1931, p. 361.

would be withdrawn. The claim was also made that the employer would be in a position to hold the worker to his job by refusing to issue the proper certificate in case of dismissal. Finally, it was argued that insurmountable constitutional difficulties would arise regarding methods for obtaining the necessary funds.

These arguments of the Executive Council, however, were not accepted by large sections of affiliated unions. In the course of 1931 the Brotherhood of Railway Clerks, the International Association of Machinists, the Teamsters' Union, the Molders' Union, some of the printing trades unions, and a large number of local unions came out for some form of compulsory insurance. The state federations of labor of Illinois, Pennsylvania, and Wisconsin were active in support of proposed legislation on the subject.[18] Many local unions lent their aid to non-labor bodies and to disguised communist groups which advocated a nation-wide system of insurance against unemployment.

The Executive Council of the Federation thus faced a convention in 1931 which had a strong element favoring a turn in policy. The debate was heated. Many delegates who had stood together on most issues for years parted company. President Green finally swayed the vote in favor of the report of the Executive Council, rejecting unemployment insurance by promising a vigorous campaign for immediate relief.

Although on July 2, 1932 the A. F. of L. *Weekly News Letter* still wrote that "labor abhors unemployment insurance," a few days later the Executive Council,

[18] During 1931 unemployment insurance bills were introduced in the legislatures of 16 states. Wisconsin passed the first state law providing for compulsory unemployment insurance.

in session at Atlantic City, instructed President Green to draw up an unemployment insurance bill to be enacted by Congress. The Executive Council ascribed its change of policy to the prolonged depression, to the distress of the unions, and to the growing clamor for action on the part of the workers. The ultimate responsibility for the new turn in policy was placed upon management and the government, which had failed to provide work for all or to give proper relief to the millions of unemployed. Undoubtedly the Federation gave way on this issue to the combined pressure from its own local unions, from the radical elements in and outside its ranks, and from middle-class organizations.

At first it was announced that the Executive Council would demand a federal law on the subject. But to the Cincinnati convention in November 1932 the Council recommended compulsory unemployment insurance by states. The Committee on Resolutions of the convention reported favorably on the recommendation. The delegates in the convention voted overwhelmingly for it, regardless of the fact that a considerable number of them were still skeptical about the desirability of compulsory state insurance.[19] The decision was forced upon the convention by the disturbed state of mind of the country, the exhaustion of union funds, and the distress of workers.

D. Planning for Economic Recovery

During the early stages of the depression the Executive Council shared anticipations of an early return of prosperity. However, as conditions became more serious, the Executive Council presented a general program to

[19] *Proceedings of the 52d Annual Convention of the A. F. of L.*, 1932, pp. 343-60, pp. 442-43.

the convention of 1930 which expressed its conception of the nature of the business collapse and of the road to recovery.

Three basic ideas were emphasized in the report: First, the depression which began in November 1929 was unlike other depressions in many ways and was due to the failure of wages and small salaries to keep pace with the increasing power of industry to produce; secondly, management was responsible for the present breakdown because of its failure to use available information to maintain a balance between production and consumption; and thirdly, the government had a responsibility to provide aid in finding employment and in stimulating management to apply policies that would secure industrial stability and progress.

As ameliorative measures, the Executive Council laid down a program of ten points which included demands for a reduction in working hours; for the stabilization of industry through advance planning; for a national economic council to maintain economic equilibrium; for efficiency in production and sales management; for a nation-wide system of employment exchanges; for adequate unemployment statistics; for public works, vocational guidance and retraining; for a special study of technological unemployment; for a study of all relief proposals; and finally for a general program of education adjusted to the changing needs of industry. The new features in this program were the demands for economic planning and for a national economic council. These proposals did not originate with the A. F. of L., having been advocated for some time by a group of economists and writers. The Federation was, however, the first large organization to endorse these proposals and to incorporate them into a general program for dealing with unemployment.

During 1931 William Green issued several mild statements urging President Hoover to summon an industrial and economic conference. He also supported the proposal to establish a national economic council. But little was done by the Executive Council either to elaborate the meaning and practical possibilities of planning or to promote its application. As the discussion of economic planning developed and it was revealed that planning involved increasing control of economic activities, possibly price regulation, and supervision of the flow of capital, the suspicions of the Federation were aroused. In its report to the 1931 convention the Federation sounded the warning that, while the principles of balance in industry were the key to sustained progress, the facts necessary for control were not available, and that therefore any national economic council which might be created by the federal government should not have any more definite charge than fact-finding.[20]

The Federation further pressed the demands for maintaining wages, staggering employment, and shortening hours of labor. At its session in July 1932 the Executive Council urged management to place American industry on the basis of a five-day week and six-hour day, or a 30-hour working week. The Council again authorized William Green to urge upon President Hoover the calling of a national conference of labor and industry to evolve methods of carrying this program into effect. President Hoover refused to call such a conference, but on August 26, 1932 summoned representatives of Fed-

[20] *Proceedings of the 51st Annual Convention of the A. F. of L.*, 1931, p. 81.

eral Reserve district banking and industrial committees, which groups endorsed the shorter work day as a means of "staggering" employment. The Executive Council approved this suggestion and offered to cooperate in carrying it out.

During the early months of 1933 the Federation urged more actively a large program of public works financed by government credit. It also supported federal legislation for a 30-hour week in industry sponsored by the new Roosevelt administration.

PART V

POLICIES, PROBLEMS, AND PROSPECTS

CHAPTER XII

GUIDING THE AFFILIATED UNIONS

The story of the American Federation of Labor during the half century of its development presents a complex record of success and failure. To make an appraisal of its performance, as well as to indicate current trends and prospects, it is necessary to present a general picture of the Federation with its constituent parts and to analyze the functions which it performs, so as to bring into view its current policies and the problems which it faces. In this chapter we shall describe the character of the constituent unions and the machinery of the Federation for guiding them.

I. THE CONSTITUENT UNIONS

The American Federation of Labor is today essentially what it has been since 1886—a voluntary national federation of autonomous unions loosely held together by rules and principles which fix the relations of the constituent elements to one another and to the central body. The units of the Federation at the end of 1932 were the 106 national and international unions,[1] which were composed of 26,362 locals scattered over the country and claiming about 2,520,000 members. In addition, the Federation had 307 local trade and federal labor unions with over 12,000 members;[2] 619 city central councils;[3] 49 state

[1] National unions include members residing and working in the United States only. The international unions have members in Canada also.

[2] The local trade and federal labor unions are chartered directly by the A. F. of L. in trades in which there is no national or international union. Seven workers in any locality in the same trade may form a local trade union. Where that many workers in one trade are not available, seven workers in different trades may form a federal labor union. Some

federations of labor;[4] and 4 departments. The Federation also has a number of intermediate organizations, such as local and state councils in the building and printing trades, and various district councils.

A. Membership

The Federation publishes the number of votes allotted to each union at the convention, which indicates the average membership on which the union paid per capita taxes during the year. In reporting, some unions exaggerate their membership in order to exercise more influence in conventions; others minimize theirs to save per capita taxes; while still others refrain from giving exact numbers for reasons of strategy in relation to employers. It is impossible to correct fully the figures published by the Federation. But some of the divergences can be established and may be cited. The most striking is that of the United Mine Workers. From 1925 to 1931 they reported to the Federation 400,000 and, in 1932, 308,000 members, but claimed at their own convention of 1932 only 156,000 members. The Typographical Union reported to the A. F. of L. 76,100 members in 1932, and only 66,512 to their own convention in the same year. On the other hand, the Brotherhood of Carpenters and

---

of the local trade and federal labor unions may have, however, hundreds or even thousands of members.

[3] The city centrals, known under a variety of names, such as the New York Central Trade and Labor Council, the Chicago Federation of Labor, and the Denver Trades and Labor Assembly, are composed of delegates from the unions of a town or city who meet to consider common local problems. Five or more local unions in a city belonging to different national or international unions may form a central union.

[4] The state federations of labor are composed of delegates from local unions and city centrals within a state. Their function is to consider trade union matters which have state-wide importance, generally of a political and legislative character.

Joiners in 1929 reported 322,000 members to the Federation, while its report to its own convention of that year claimed 346,000 members. The Hod-Carriers' Union in 1927 reported 70,000 to the Federation and 85,000 to its own convention. Similar discrepancies on both sides of the ledger might be cited for other unions.

Because of these discrepancies the membership of 2,532,261 reported by the Federation in 1932 must be regarded as only approximate. It represents a loss of 1,546,479 or 38 per cent since 1920, but is still larger

REPORTED MEMBERSHIP OF AMERICAN FEDERATION OF LABOR FOR SELECTED YEARS

Year	Total Membership Reported	Change in Membership	*Percentage Change*
1914	2,020,671	—	—
1920	4,078,740	+2,058,069	+*101.9*
1925	2,877,297	−1,201,443	− *29.5*
1929	2,933,545	+ 56,248	+ *2.0*
1931	2,889,550	− 43,995	− *1.5*
1932	2,532,261	− 357,289	− *12.4*

by 510,000 or 25 per cent than in 1914. More than likely the present dues-paying membership of the Federation is under 2,000,000.[5]

The membership of the Federation is unequally distributed among the different industries. In 1920, when the membership of the Federation was at its peak, it was more equally distributed among the different industries than it has been since. For instance, the proportion of the membership in the building trades to the total membership of the Federation increased from 20.5 per cent in 1920 to 34.4 per cent in 1932, while the unions in the metal and machinery trades decreased during the same

[5] See Appendix A, p. 485.

period from 19.5 to 7.8 per cent.[6] About half of the reported membership in 1932, or 1,222,100, was concentrated in the building trades and in transportation. The amusement trades and public service combined represented 10.5 per cent of the membership of the Federation in 1932. This distribution of membership in the A. F. of L. is at variance with the actual distribution of workers in American industries.

The Federation continues to be primarily an organization of skilled and semi-skilled workers. Only a small number of its unions consist entirely of unskilled workers or have a substantial proportion of unskilled.[7]

Also, partly because of organizing difficulties and partly because of racial prejudice, the Federation is a white man's organization.[8] The number of colored workers in the Federation was estimated in 1928 at between 40,000 and 60,000, out of a million or more negro workers in American industry, or between 2 and 3 per cent of the total reported membership of the A. F. of L.[9]

[6] See Appendix A, p. 486.

[7] Unions of unskilled workers are the Hod-Carriers and Common Laborers and the Union of Building Service Employees. Unions having considerable numbers of semi-skilled workers are the United Mine Workers, the International Ladies' Garment Workers' Union, Brotherhood of Railway Carmen, and others.

[8] There are unions in the A. F. of L. which specifically exclude negroes. In 1930 these unions were as follows: The Brotherhood of Railway Carmen; the Switchmen's Union; the Brotherhood of Railway and Steamship Clerks; the Order of Sleeping Car Conductors; the Order of Railway Telegraphers; the Masters, Mates, and Pilots of North America; the Railway Mail Association; the Commercial Telegraphers; and the Wire Weavers' Protective Association. See Stirling D. Spero and Abram L. Harris, *The Black Worker*, 1931, p. 57. The Hotel and Restaurant Workers exclude Orientals.

[9] The Hod-Carriers' Union had over 5,000 colored workers; the Maintenance of Way Employees, 10,000; the United Mine Workers, 5,000; the Federation of Musicians, 3,000; the Sleeping Car Porters' Union, 3,000. See the same, pp. 76-78.

The Federation is also predominantly a man's organization. Women do not work in appreciable numbers in the strongest crafts and trades represented in the Federation, and the large mass industries and "white collar trades" which employ women in large numbers are unorganized.[10] No estimate of the total number of women workers in the Federation can be made since the international unions refuse to supply information on the subject.

B. Structural Types and Administration

Though the Federation is commonly described as a craft organization, the pure craft unions which combine workers of identical skill and training in different trades, or those working on a single specialized process, have been steadily decreasing in numbers and importance in the Federation. Not over 25 unions in the Federation belong to this group.

The dominant type of union in the Federation is the so-called compound craft union, which includes workers engaged in interrelated crafts and processes or in closely allied trades that are competitive or substitutive in character. This type of unionism has developed in the building trades, in the metal and machine trades, and in the food industries. At least 50 of the 106 unions in the Federation fall clearly within this group. The third type, described as amalgamated, semi-industrial, or quasi-industrial, includes unions which organize workers of an entire industry or of a major branch of an industry but which maintain craft lines among the various groups of

[10] The unions in the A. F. of L. which have a considerable proportion of women are the Ladies' Garment Workers' Union, the United Textile Workers, the United Garment Workers, the Brotherhood of Bookbinders, the Cloth Hat, Cap, and Millinery Workers' Union, and the Union of Railway Clerks.

their members. Over 25 of the 106 unions of the Federation belong in this group. Only one or two unions in the Federation represent the fourth type of purely industrial union which combines workers on the basis of product made or materials used, regardless of skill or craft, and in which the plant or establishment is the unit of organization.

Because of the relative strength of the unions belonging to these different groups, the Federation might be characterized as an amalgamated craft organization. The Federation lost its craft character as industry changed and unions reached out for new processes and interrelated trades and became amalgamated organizations. At the same time, however, these unions carried over a keen sense of craft pride opposed to industrial unionism. Thus they impress upon the Federation a character of craft exclusivism while in practice they override narrow craft lines and combine related crafts and occupations in larger units.

Another feature of the Federation is the large number and limited size of its unions. In 1931, 59 out of 105 unions had 10,000 members or less each, and a combined membership of about 225,000 or 7.8 per cent of the total; of these, 18 unions had a membership of 1,000 or less each. Some 32 unions, with a membership ranging between 10,000 and 50,000 each, had a total of 856,500 members or 29.7 per cent of the total; while 14 unions with over 50,000 members each had 1,794,200 members or 62.5 per cent of the total. These figures indicate that, despite the tendency towards union concentration since 1904, the Federation still carries a large heritage of small-sized unions.[11]

[11] See Appendix A, p. 487.

The unions in the Federation also vary in their administrative organization, depending upon size and structure, the character of the industry, the human element involved, and traditions. There are in the Federation a few highly centralized unions in which the powers of the locals are limited and in which control is in the hands of the general executive board, usually composed of a president, a secretary-treasurer, and from three to nine vice-presidents. In these unions even local decisions and rules, especially with reference to trade agreements and strikes, are subordinated to the approval of the international body. Some of the unions in this group are those of asbestos workers, bricklayers, electrical workers, typographical workers, and cigarmakers.

A second group allows locals almost unlimited autonomy. The union of operating engineers, for instance, provides that the locals have power to approve or reject any legislative act, resolution, or constitutional amendment enacted by the convention or promulgated by the general officers. In between these extremes is a third group of unions which aims to maintain a more even balance between the central powers of the international officers and the locals. Generally, the locals are given the right to make trade agreements, to fix rules for the admission of members, to fix their dues and initiation fees, to maintain special benefit funds, and to regulate any other matters which fall strictly within their province. The matter in which the locals are restricted is that of strikes, though in this respect too there are various degrees of local autonomy.

The unions in the Federation present a hierarchy of local, district, and national officers. Each local union has its president, secretary or treasurer, and one or more business agents. In the small locals these officers are not on full time with the exception of the business agent. The president or secretary of a local who gives only part time to his job often is paid nothing or only a small sum. The inducement to hold such offices is interest in union work or a flare for local leadership. The presidents and secretaries of locals are usually elected as delegates to the conventions of their international union, which is a coveted honor and a chance for travel and diversion. Being a delegate brings distinction in a trade or community and may help those who are ambitious for higher office in a union. In the larger locals the president or secretary is generally a full-time officer. Also, several business agents may be employed. International officers in the larger unions frequently perform the functions of administrators and organizers. Considering the fact that there are over 26,000 local unions in the Federation and that many of them are of considerable size and employ more than one business agent, the total number of officials in the Federation, including business agents, shop chairmen, local secretaries, and presidents, amounts to many thousands.

The salaries of organizers or business agents of international unions, with a few exceptions, range from $50 to $75 a week plus traveling expenses. The usual payment to local officers who give only part time ranges from less than a hundred to a few hundred dollars a year. The salaries of the officers of the international unions were considerably increased between 1920 and 1929 and ranged until recently between $5,000 and $20,000 a year, though the majority of the positions paid between $5,000 and $7,500.[12] Since the depression, officers of

[12] The unions of musicians, stage employees, and teamsters pay $20,000 a year; operating engineers and bridge and structural iron workers pay

many unions have accepted deductions from their salaries.

C. Main Functions

The main purposes of the constituent unions of the Federation are to supply their members with jobs which provide a "fair" wage, shorter hours of work, safe and sanitary working conditions, and guaranty against arbitrary discharge; to safeguard dignified treatment in the shop to the worker by means of working rules; and to protect each member individually and all members collectively against any action of employers or management which may be injurious. The unions aim to achieve these ends by collective bargaining. This calls for a signed agreement between a union and an employer or employers' association designating the terms under which work is to be done. All unions in the Federation regard the trade agreement as the embodiment of trade union aims and measure their success or failure by the number and character of agreements which they sign.

Agreements vary greatly in accordance with technical and economic conditions in different industries and with the bargaining power of the unions. Most agreements, however, call for a union or "closed" shop, which means that all the workers in it must be members in good standing of the union. Conditions are usually laid down for the hire of workers through the union office and for proper safeguards against unjust discharge. The time of beginning and ending work, and the period to be allowed for meals and washing and cleaning up are usually speci-

---

$15,000; elevator constructors, mine workers, and garment workers pay $12,000; bricklayers, electrical workers, lathers, plumbers, railway clerks, and commercial telegraphers pay $10,000 each. Deductions from salaries since 1930 have been in different forms as, for instance, receiving three weeks' salary for a month's work.

fied. Nearly every agreement contains articles providing for minimum rates of wages, for regular payment in cash or by check, as well as for special payment for overtime and allowances for official holidays. A number of agreements contain apprenticeship provisions and many of them also have provisions relative to the safety of employees.[13] Trade agreements also vary in the machinery set up for their enforcement. Some provide for a shop chairman, shop steward, or shop committee, either elected or appointed by the local official of the union, and entrusted with looking after the interests of the workers in each shop. Provision is usually made whereby the business agent or other officer of the union is granted the right to enter a union shop at reasonable hours to see that the terms of the agreement are being observed or to settle differences which may have arisen.

Grievances are first considered by the employee affected and his foreman. If they fail, succeeding higher officials or committees of the union and representatives of the employer take up the matter. Grievance committees consisting of an equal number of representatives of employers and employees are sometimes provided to adjust disputes which cannot be settled by the individual employer and employee. Grievances which cannot thus be settled by conciliation are often submitted to boards of arbitration. Such boards may be specially set up for each case, but a number of unions have standing boards of conciliation and arbitration which give all their time to the examination of grievances. In the unions in the garment trades, where changing fashions, production standards, and the seasonal character of the work give rise to

[13] "Trade Agreements, 1927," *U. B. Bureau of Labor Statistics Bulletin No. 468.*

many misunderstandings, an elaborate system of arbitration providing for impartial chairmen and arbitrators has been built up between the unions and the employers' associations in the different cities. Complex systems of conciliation and arbitration have also been developed in the printing industry and on some of the railroads.

Collective bargaining is carried on by most of the unions of the Federation locally. Regional agreements are negotiated by a few unions, for example, by the United Mine Workers in the Central Competitive Field. A few unions, including those of the flint glass workers, the typographers, and the molders, make national agreements for all their locals with national associations of employers.[14]

Much time and energy are spent by the unions in police and judiciary functions connected with the enforcement of agreements and union rules. An enormous number of grievances and complaints arise from different interpretations of trade agreements, from temperamental difficulties, and from changes in industrial processes.[15] On the other hand, some difficulties are caused by employers and union members who try to evade the terms of a collective contract. They undercut the union rate, violate provisions regarding overtime and pay for such overtime, and in other ways stretch the terms of an agreement to promote their immediate advantage. Such violations if practiced on a large scale tend to undermine collective bargaining and make it a sham.

The international unions also help to settle difficulties between their locals and employers. Sometimes a local

[14] See Matthew Woll, *Wage Negotiations and Practices*, published by the American Federation of Labor, 1925.

[15] See Louis Block, *Labor Agreements in Coal Mines*, 1930; also Louis Levine, *The Women's Garment Workers*, 1924.

is tempted to make terms with local employers which give the latter a competitive advantage over outside employers. As international unions hold to the idea of equalizing labor costs throughout a national market, it is incumbent upon them to prevent such discriminatory practices. Another problem of a reverse character arises when a local has achieved a strong position and attempts to impose unduly severe terms upon the employers with whom it deals. Sometimes local unions jeopardize the interests of the union as a whole in attempting to protect a few members.

The varying degrees of bargaining power achieved by different locals in a union is another source of conflict. Some locals of an international union have thousands of members while others have only a few. Some locals have achieved a high degree of discipline and have established favorable wage rates and terms of employment. This tempts union members to shift from localities where employment is less favorable to places where local unions have won better employment conditions. Transfer and permit cards are usually given a traveling member and must be recognized by the union in the new locality. But this practice gives rise to two forms of friction. Members of strong local unions protest against the influx of union men from other cities because they increase the supply of labor and undermine established standards. On the other hand, local union officers are tempted to distribute permit cards freely because of the income thus provided for the local union or because of the benefits which they may derive for themselves.

Straightening out all these problems is an absorbing and expensive part of trade union activity and also a fruitful source of friction and discontent. In the small unions this task usually falls to the international president. He travels from place to place examining grievances, holding court, disciplining members, and laying down the law for locals and employers. In the larger unions this work is assigned to one or two vice-presidents, to special organizers, or to both.

Since the main purpose of a union is to supply its members with jobs under fair conditions, the major part of a union's work is to extend the area of its control over jobs and to exercise control over the supply of labor so as to be able to find jobs for all its members. The fact that each industry is subject to continuous changes in processes, materials, technical organization, and demand for and supply of labor creates a continuous problem of finding the point at which the equation of supply and demand is most favorable to those already in the trade. Also, as a union improves conditions in a trade, more workers are attracted into it or employers move their plants from unionized areas, thus tending to upset the favorable relation between the supply and demand of labor. Explicitly or implicitly unions aim at a relationship between membership and jobs which gives a temporary monopolistic strength. For these reasons some unions in the Federation tend to restrict membership. The unions which can most effectively limit entrance into their trades are the craft and compound craft unions in which specialized skill is important. These unions have strict apprenticeship rules, high initiation fees, and special limits on the number of helpers per journeyman. As a rule such limitations are imposed by the locals. Restrictions of membership are complicated by problems of race and nationality.

Though unions do not desire to enroll all persons in

a trade, they are impelled to seek new members constantly. In part this is due to the fact that turnover in trade union membership is high as a result of death, disability, changes in occupation, internal friction, unemployment, and other causes. Also, each union must extend its jurisdiction because inevitably some of its jobs are lost as a result of the substitution of materials and products. Important also is the desire to help build up funds by increasing membership.

Thus the effort to obtain new members becomes one phase of the problem of organizing. Persuading employers to "recognize the union" is another phase. A union may solicit the good-will of an employer or management as a preliminary step in organizing, or may first carry propaganda among the workers of a plant in order to win supporters among them before approaching the employer. But an organizing campaign is successful only when the union is accepted by both the employer and the workers within the plant. The union may bring this about peacefully by convincing the employer that it is to his advantage to recognize the union, or it may gain the adherence of a sufficiently large number of workers within a plant to make it unprofitable for the employer to resist. Most of the unions in the Federation still rely on strikes as their ultimate method of organizing and for this reason many of them still maintain strike benefit funds.[16]

The unions in the Federation also show considerable

[16] It is impossible to compute the total amount spent for organizing for any one year because of the different methods of accounting used by the unions. The total sum runs into millions of dollars. The International Ladies' Garment Workers' Union spent $225,129 from November 1929 to March 1932; the International Association of Machinists spent $114,970 in 1927. The Machinists' Union had over $391,000 in its strike fund in 1927. For further information on different unions, see Appendix B.

differences in their attitudes towards the larger problems of their industries. For instance, the International Union of Mine, Mill, and Smelter Workers has supported the demand for the remonetization of silver and for an international copper syndicate. The United Mine Workers are co-operating with employers in supporting the Kelly-Davis bill in Congress for the organization of coal-selling syndicates under the supervision of a coal commission as a means of reorganizing the bituminous coal industry. The International Printing Pressmen maintain a special bureau to study methods of improving processes of printing and engraving. The International Ladies' Garment Workers' Union in Cleveland has an arrangement with the employers for the setting of production standards as a basis of fixing wage rates and employment. The Electrical Workers' Union, in combination with electrical contractors, has set up machinery for establishing standards of work in the industry and for settling disputes without recourse to strikes. Union management co-operation for continuous improvement of working conditions and of production is practiced by the railway shop craft unions on several railroads and by unions in a number of plants in other industries. A considerable number of unions are advocating protective measures and special tariffs for their respective industries and have formed the Wage Earners' Protective Conference for the purpose.

Considerable differences also exist in the degree to which the unions of the Federation are interested in such activities as education, recreation, banking, and group insurance. In general all these activities have been greatly reduced in scope since 1929, and some have practically ceased as a result of the depression.

The effects of collective bargaining as practiced by

the unions of the Federation are shown in the fact that these unions comprise some of the most highly paid groups of industrial workers, which also enjoy the most favorable conditions of employment, especially with regard to hours. But in this respect too there are great variations. Trade union organization has also affected the welfare of non-union workers by setting the pace for changes in wages and hours.

D. Benefit Systems and Dues

The unions in the Federation have consistently encouraged the establishment of benefit systems as an effective means for holding membership. Of the 105 unions in the Federation in 1931, only 15 had no benefits. Of these, three—the unions of teachers, letter carriers, and fire fighters—have a membership which usually enjoys protection under state and municipal retirement laws. The other twelve include small unions of craftsmen, such as horseshoers, asbestos workers, and metal engravers; three unions of professional workers—actors, draftsmen, and musicians; and a few unions of unskilled and semi-casual labor—building service employees and longshoremen.

The most common form of benefit paid by the unions is the death benefit. As a rule this is paid by the international unions. The amount of death benefit provided varies from $100 to $500, and in a few cases as much as $1,000 is paid. In some unions the locals maintain additional benefits for which their members pay extra dues.

In addition to death benefits 46 unions pay sick benefits, 30 pay unemployment benefits, 15 pay old-age pensions, and 23 pay disability benefits.[17] In most cases these benefits are financed by locals of the international unions. There is thus great unevenness in their incidence upon union members, the larger and more prosperous locals being more able to provide such benefits.

The unions of the A. F. of L. paid $15,236,971 for all these benefits in 1928; $13,497,711 in 1929; $19,320,873 in 1930; and $23,531,676 in 1931; or $71,587,231 in four years. The largest individual amounts were paid by some of the older unions.[18]

BENEFITS PAID BY UNIONS IN THE AMERICAN FEDERATION OF LABOR, 1928–31[a]

Benefits	1928	1929	1930	1931
Sick	$1,363,377	$1,362,324	$1,596,645	$1,470,977
Death	7,946,983	8,007,099	9,088,565	7,946,777
Unemployment	504,005	262,974	3,311,279	9,099,541
Old-age	2,525,525	2,267,097	3,182,065	3,768,175
Disability	1,054,604	425,556	844,650	347,939
Miscellaneous	1,842,477	1,172,661	1,297,669	898,267
Total	$15,236,971	$13,497,711	$19,320,873	$23,531,676

[a] Compiled from figures published in the *Proceedings of the Annual Conventions of the A. F. of L.*, 1929–32.

Before 1920 the costs of benefits were comparatively low and the amounts paid seemed fairly large to the average worker. As the average age of the membership in most unions increased after 1920, largely because of failure to recruit new and young members, the increased costs of protection made it necessary for many unions to impose assessments upon their members or raise dues.

[17] These figures are for 1930. *Report of the Proceedings of the Fifty-First Annual Convention of the American Federation of Labor*, 1931, pp. 100-03. See Appendix A, p. 492.
[18] See the same.

With the standards of living rising among workers, increased insurance was demanded but could be met by the unions only at higher cost. The unions have been pressed to meet the situation because of the group insurance plans provided by employers to compete for the loyalty of the workers.

A great diversity exists in the unions of the Federation in the matter of finances. The weekly or monthly dues vary not only between unions but also between different locals of the same union. Some of the stronger locals have built up strike funds and special benefit funds by high dues and large assessments. The usual dues are from $1.00 to $1.50 a month. But some unions collect from $1.00 to $2.00 a week which is used to pay administrative expenses, strike costs, and various benefits. In almost all unions there is some variation between the amounts paid by the different members due to the fact that there are usually different types of benefits, some of which are voluntary.

Before 1914 very few unions in the Federation had accumulated large funds. A change took place between 1917 and 1920 when large memberships enabled the unions to accumulate considerable surplus funds. Some unions continued to build up reserves between 1922 and 1929, but the depression since 1930 has seriously depleted the reserve funds of most unions. Many unions have cancelled the arrears due from their unemployed members and have carried a large portion of their membership who could not pay dues. Unemployment benefits have also cut into surpluses, while securities held by unions, as well as real estate and property, have decreased in value.

E. Factions, Cliques, and Rackets

Internal dissensions of one kind or another are not new phenomena in unions. The history of all unions is strewn with factional dissensions, cliques, and internal struggles. American unions have also never been entirely free from charges of graft, violence, and other abuses.

Cliques, factions, and machines spring up in unions as they do in other democratic organizations. Unions bring together workers differing in interest and backgrounds, in beliefs and temperament. Differences of views often assume exaggerated importance because of the very democratic character of local unions and of their ways of doing business.

Friction between the rank and file and the leaders is increased by the difficulty of reconciling democracy and efficiency, stability and change. The success of a union generally means an increase of funds, of responsibilities and obligations, and a greater tendency on the part of officers to temper action by consideration of the stakes involved. Policies and methods which have been tried and found successful over a period of time are accepted as more or less final by the leaders. Thus methods, policies, and leadership tend to become stereotyped despite changing economic and political conditions. The limited opportunities for positions of power and leadership in trade unions and the lack of machinery for smooth readjustments often make it necessary for officers and leaders to try to maintain themselves in power by building up special loyalties among the membership by the usual methods of "machine" politics. This gives rise to contests for control, secession movements, dual unions, and factions which are a perennial and seemingly inevitable part of trade union life.

Factionalism may be and often is entirely unrelated to such abuses as corruption within a union, but often the two are inter-connected. The simplest case of graft in a local union arises when a business agent abuses his power. As he interprets trade agreements, he can use his position to the advantage or to the ruin of one or another employer. There is thus an opportunity for a business agent or for a group of business agents acting together to use their offices for personal gain. Such action need not inevitably affect adversely the interests of the other members. Very often it does not. It is for this reason that in many cases the extra gains made by business agents which may be regarded as illicit are tacitly condemned by union members but not actively objected to.

But business agents practicing illicit methods, in order to maintain themselves, must surround themselves with loyal supporters who must be rewarded for their support in the form of easier, better, or steadier jobs. The result is job favoritism. In view of the scarcity of union jobs, even in the best organized trades there arises an incentive for union members to band together to help each other in finding and holding such jobs. Such special "groups" or "clubs" may be formed on the basis of religion, nationality, or some other characteristic. These "groups" try to elect their own candidates to office. After a business agent or other official has been put in office by a particular clique or group, he has to "play the game" with that group. He and his followers may rely upon persuasion and upon diplomatic methods to keep their position. But when several cliques are at loggerheads in a local union, the tendency is for each clique to have recourse to force if necessary.

The abuses and irregular practices of labor unions are now usually referred to as "racketeering."[19] For the sake of clarity, however, it is necessary to distinguish five main practices which are included under the term. The first and simplest is graft as a result of some collusion between officials or members of a local union and employers to ignore some clauses of a trade agreement or to extend special privileges in return for pecuniary emoluments. The second form is that of abuse of the funds and resources of a local union by business agents or other officers, either acting alone or in collusion with some members of the union. This can be done in several ways. Expense accounts may be padded; funds allocated for organizing may be diverted to personal use; extra large fees and retainers may be paid to lawyers, a portion of which is rebated.

A third form arises when a business agent tries to use his contacts and his position to engage in business of one kind or another. In some of the skilled crafts in several cities the business agents have been engaged in business ventures and have used their power to call or threaten strikes for the purpose of promoting their private business interests.[20] A fourth form of abuse occurs when union

[19] A "racket" in general may be defined as any parasitic method of making money which is usually accompanied by misrepresentation, fraud, coercion, and criminal violence. A "labor racket" in a broad sense is the practice of using a labor organization to obtain personal gains which involve a violation of the principles of unionism.

[20] The cases which have attracted wide attention recently are those of Theodore M. Brandle, business agent of Local No. 45 of the Iron Workers of Jersey City and president of the Building Trades Council

officials have arrangements with professional gangsters and call in such strong-arm men to help them maintain control within the union against opposing factions or cliques or against recalcitrant members.[21]

The fifth form of abuse is racketeering proper of the extreme type. Gangsters and underworld men may try to gain control of a local union either because it has large funds or because it would give them an opportunity in the name of unionism to lay tribute on employers. In such cases professional racketeers may "muscle" their way into a union, become members, and manipulate elections so as to put their own men into positions of authority. As a result a local union may be annexed by professional gangsters, in whose hands it becomes a tool for racketeering purposes. Even in such cases it is quite possible for the gang to give members of the union protection and high wages. In Chicago the most successful labor rackets have been those in which gangsters by threats or promises have insinuated themselves into bona fide labor organizations.

The situation may result also in the establishment of "racketeering unions" proper. When a syndicate of

---

of Hudson County, New Jersey; and of Sam Kaplan, president of the Motion Picture Operators' Local of New York. Brandle engaged in bonding, real estate, and the material supply business. Kaplan sold supplies to motion picture houses.

[21] The coming of the strong-arm man into unions may be traced to the large strikes of 1909-12 in which women workers were engaged, when it became necessary to engage special persons to protect women strikers and pickets against thugs hired by employers. While some of these special persons were union members and did their work because of their devotion to the union, many were men hired for the purpose. Once arrived, the strong-arm man tried to find a permanent place for himself in the union and often maintained his position by threatening the union itself. The difficulties of organizing and anti-union attitudes of employers gave the strong-arm man an opportunity to become a factor in industrial relations.

strong-arm men fail to capture a local or when the union which they captured has been expelled from the international union, the gangsters may establish their own "union." They then begin breaking up the legitimate unions by violent methods, and force employers to deal with them. In New York and Chicago the number of such "racketeering unions" has increased in the last few years because of the very efforts of the bona fide unions to resist the racketeers.

Racketeering in unions reflects in large measure racketeering methods of business in the same industries. Racketeers are often used by employing interests to drive out competition in their industry. Also, many labor rackets are possible only because of prevailing conditions in our municipal politics. But racketeering also reflects the industrial weaknesses of many trade unions, especially since 1925.

The public as a rule has been prone to exaggerate the abuses of unionism, and has lumped various abuses under the general term of "racketeering," hurling this epithet at unions without discrimination. There are a few trades —such as the building trades—in which the seasonality of the work, the method of payment, the possibility of causing great damage by stoppages and strikes, and the conflicting interests of contractors, sub-contractors, supply dealers, etc., enable unscrupulous union agents to abuse their power on a large scale. As a matter of fact most of the glaring cases of racketeering which have come to public notice have occurred in these trades. Other unions which have been especially subject to exploitation by racketeers have been those of the motion picture operators, teamsters, longshoremen, laundry workers, and hotel and restaurant workers. These unions have been affected either because of the nature of competition in the trade, the isolated conditions under which the worker carries on his work, or the interest of racketeering rings in the trade.

Considered in relation to the Federation as a whole, racketeering proper is not as extensive as is usually thought. As a rule only local unions are directly involved, and only occasionally some of the officers of the international unions. There are 26,000 local unions in the Federation employing thousands of agents, secretaries, and presidents. There are many more thousands of shop chairmen and minor officials. The funds received and disbursed by the 26,000 locals and the 106 international unions run into many millions of dollars. Considering all this, the extent of graft and racketeering in unions is not so large as it is often made to appear. However, to the extent to which the unfair and illicit practices of unionism inflict injury upon employers and upon the public, they are bound to be exaggerated. More serious is the fact that these practices cause unionists themselves to doubt the integrity and value of their organizations and that the "racketeering union" proper is a menace to the whole structure of unionism.

II. THE A. F. OF L. MACHINERY

From the preceding discussion it is clear that the national and international unions of the American Federation of Labor differ considerably in structure, methods, composition, powers, and policies. They are held together in the Federation by four common purposes—the desire for mutual aid, the need for adjudicating jurisdictional disputes, political exigencies, and the need for co-operation in meeting the larger economic problems of the worker. To achieve these purposes the unions have given the Federation certain limited powers which are enforced through specially devised mechanisms.

The supreme law of the Federation is its constitution. It fixes the limits within which the Federation must work and contains the rules governing representation, powers and functions of officers, and the interrelations of constituent elements. Final authority, however, is vested in the convention, and the officials and Executive Council are the executors of its instructions.

A. The Annual Convention

The constitution of the A. F. of L. provides that the conventions be held annually on the first Monday in October, or the third Monday in November during years of presidential elections. Each convention selects the place of meeting for the following year. The selection of a city is usually determined by opportunity for promoting trade union ideas, ability to secure convenient hotel accommodations, and the desire to placate local and sectional interests.

The convention assembles delegates from national and international unions, city centrals, state federations of labor, federal labor unions, and the four departments. Representation in the convention is intended to give predominance to the national and international unions, each union being entitled to one delegate for less than 4,000 members; two delegates for 4,000 members or more; three delegates for 8,000 or more; four delegates for 16,000 or more, and so on in the same proportion. The other constituent elements of the Federation—city centrals, state federations, federal labor unions, and departments—are each entitled to one delegate. This arrangement is justified by the Federation because the membership of city centrals, state federations, and departments is represented in the delegations of the national and international unions.

Voting at the conventions takes place in one of two ways. Most questions are decided by division or a show of hands. But one-tenth of the delegates may demand a roll-call, in which case each delegate from a national or international union casts one vote for every 100 members or major fraction thereof which he represents. City centrals and state federations are allowed but one vote each. In practice the system works in favor of the international unions because the international union usually not only sends its full quota of delegates but often is willing to pay per capita taxes to the Federation on a larger membership than it actually has in order to have more votes than it is entitled to at the conventions. Such a procedure is possible because of the way in which unions interpret membership. The Federation is lenient because exaggerated membership may provide a larger income to the A. F. of L., may further the aims of the Executive Council, or may be indulged in by a union which has strong influence in the Federation.

The effects of the composition of the conventions may be seen from an examination of the conventions held in Boston in 1930 and in Vancouver in 1931. The former was one of the largest in the history of the A. F. of L., having 430 delegates. Of these, 277 represented national or international unions, 34 were from state federations, 79 from city centrals, and 36 from federal trade and labor unions. Less than 10 per cent of the 804 affiliated city centrals were represented, and a little over 5 per cent of the 663 affiliated trade and federal labor unions. At the convention of 1931, which was one of the least well attended, there were 329 delegates, of whom 239 came from national and international federations, 23 from state federations, 47 from city centrals, and 16 from trade and federal labor unions.

When voting is by show of hands and each delegate is entitled to one vote only, the distribution of votes is such as to give no single union or group of unions undue dominance. At the 1931 convention, for instance, the five largest unions, with 100,000 members or over—the unions of the miners, carpenters, electrical workers, hod-carriers, and musicians—had 32 delegates out of a total of 329 entitled to vote, or about 10 per cent. The 31 largest unions had 4 delegates or more each, and the combined number of their delegates was 151, or less than half of the total.

But on important issues when a roll-call is taken, the dominance of the larger unions is felt. At the 1931 convention, for instance, the 14 largest unions, with 50,000 or more members each, controlled 62.5 per cent of the votes, while the 59 smallest unions, of 10,000 or less members each, had only 7.8 per cent. The 32 medium-sized unions with memberships between 10,000 and 50,000 controlled 29.7 per cent.[22] But such a distribution of the votes also tends to accentuate the influence of personalities in the conventions, especially of the officers of the larger international unions.

The procedure at the conventions has become somewhat stereotyped. The president opens the convention. After an invocation addresses of welcome are given by the mayor of the town, the governor of the state, other official persons, and local trade union representatives. Thus passes the first morning. During the first two days while the committees are at work, much of the time is

[22] See Appendix A, p. 487.

devoted to reading resolutions introduced by delegates, and the resolutions are referred to the proper committees.

The convention lasts from ten days to two weeks. A large number of addresses by specially invited guests consumes much of the time during the first four or five days. The last week of the convention is devoted more continuously to hearing reports of the committees and to the election of officers.

The conventions of the A. F. of L. used to stage lively debates. In recent years they have tended to become rather lifeless. This has been due in some measure to the absence of an opposition and of younger delegates, but more largely to the development of the committee system. In accordance with the constitution, the president of the A. F. of L. appoints 14 committees[23] of 15 members each. The most important committees are those on Report of Executive Council, Resolutions, Laws, and Organization. Much of the work of the convention is done in these committees. They hold private sessions to hear opposing points of view and to examine conflicting interests. Whatever enlivening performance occurs consequently takes place behind closed doors. The committees hammer out differences in their sessions and present the conventions with unanimous reports which contain summary statements of the issues and skeleton résumés of the arguments.[24]

[23] The committees are: Rules and Order of Business; Report of Executive Council; Resolutions; Laws; Organization; Labels; Adjustment; Local and Federated Bodies; Education; State Organizations; Industrial Relations; Building Trades; Legislation; International Relations; Shorter Work Day.

[24] The 1932 Convention in Cincinnati marked a change in this respect and was much enlivened by the discussion of unemployment insurance and of methods for resisting the deterioration of union standards.

B. The Executive Council

In the interim between conventions the Federation acts through its Executive Council. The Council is supposed to carry out the decisions of the convention, but in executing them it exercises wide discretionary and initiatory powers. In the first place, it has become customary for the conventions to withhold decisions on important matters and "to refer them to the Council" for action. Secondly, the decisions of the conventions may be carried out with varying degrees of energy and interest and lend themselves to varying interpretations. Thirdly, in the performance of its general functions, such as organizing, legislation, and economic policy, though subject to the approval of the convention, the Executive Council is allowed much leeway. Fourthly, the Council considers unforeseen matters which arise between conventions upon which it must act without delay.

In discharging its duties the Executive Council acts both as a general staff and as the cabinet of the president of the Federation. Each year it holds four quarterly sessions at the call of the president. These sessions consider urgent issues as well as routine matters and jurisdictional disputes. They are attended by officials and representatives of different unions who are concerned with issues under discussion.

The makeup and character of the Council are important because of its powers and opportunities. In addition to the president, secretary, and treasurer, the Council has eight vice-presidents, known as first, second, third, and so forth, and whose status is rated accordingly. If a vice-president dies or resigns, the ones lower in rank are moved up and the newly elected candidate becomes the eighth vice-president. Each council member is elected annually by the convention by a simple division or roll-call. The term of office is one year and expires on the 31st day of December succeeding the convention. The personnel of the Council changes infrequently, usually as a result of death or resignation. From time to time there are lively contests for office. Since 1914 there were eleven years when there were no changes in the Council. During 1917-20 the turnover in the Council was large, and again between 1928 and 1930. At present, three members of the Council—William Green, Frank Duffy, and Frank Morrison—have been members continuously since 1915; and six, including these three, have been on the Council since 1924.

The members of the Council are elected on a personal basis and not because they are representative of the unions in the Federation. Members of the Council have come from some of the smallest unions and often from the less organized trades. For instance, the 1933 Council does not represent all the industrial divisions of the trade union world. The unions in street and water transportation, in textiles, leather, food and drink trades, in chemicals, and in personal and public service are not directly represented. On the other hand, two members of the Council are from the metal trades, three from the building trades, one from the railroad unions, two from the printing industries, and the remaining three from mining, the clothing industry, and amusements.[25]

[25] Of the present Council, President Green is a former secretary of the United Mine Workers; Frank Duffy is secretary of the Brotherhood of Carpenters and Joiners; T. A. Rickert is president of the United Garment Workers; Matthew Woll was formerly president of the Photo-Engravers' Union and is now president of the Labor Union Co-operative Insurance Company; James Wilson is president of the

Considered in regard to their claimed voting strength, the unions from which the members of the Council come include some of the largest as well as some of the

STRUCTURAL AND FUNCTIONAL ORGANIZATION OF THE FEDERATION OF LABOR, 1932

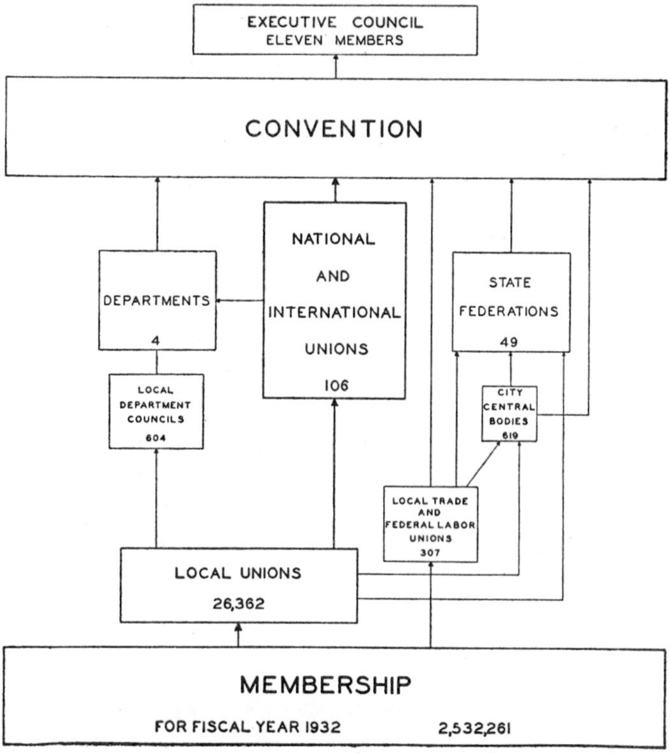

Pattern Makers' League; John Coefield is president of the Plumbers and Gasfitters' Union; Arthur O. Wharton is president of the International Association of Machinists; Joseph N. Weber is president of the American Federation of Musicians; G. M. Bugniazet is secretary of the Brotherhood of Electrical Workers; Martin F. Ryan is president of the Brotherhood of Carmen; and Frank Morrison is a member of the International Typographical Union.

smallest in the Federation.[26] Altogether, in 1931 these unions had 12,864 out of 29,906 votes at the convention, or about 43 per cent of the voting strength of the Federation. This situation is considered inconsequential since the members of the Council are presumed to represent the general membership of the Federation. Practically, however, it means a preponderance of certain types of trade union leaders whose outlook, habits of mind, and methods of action are shaped by experience in their particular trades. Conversely, it also means the absence of influences and ideas which may come from the environment and experience of unrepresented trades and industries. It is also an important factor in the settlement of jurisdictional disputes and in the use of the influence of the Federation on behalf of one or another union or group of unions.

C. Officers and Finances

The leading officer of the Federation is the president. Gompers' vigorous and aggressive devotion to his job gave the office of president great importance in the formative years of the Federation. It became the tradition to regard the president as the real leader and spokesman. Gompers' personality impressed upon the office an authority and prestige which became an inseparable part of it.

The provisions of the constitution are flexible enough to allow for this. Specifically, it provides that the president shall preside at the sessions of the annual conven-

[26] In 1932 the United Mine Workers had a voting strength of 308,000; the carmen 800 votes; the carpenters, 3,020; the electrical workers, 1,420; the photo-engravers, 90; the garment workers 463; the machinists 776; the musicians 1,000; the pattern makers 70; the plumbers 450; and the typographers 775.

tion, sign official documents, call the meetings of the Executive Council and preside over them, and appoint all the committees of the convention. In general he exercises supervision of the Federation throughout its jurisdiction. He is expected to travel in the interests of the Federation and to represent it before the country.

The office of president is thus all that its incumbent can make it. The president's personality is decisive in making the Federation an active factor in American life. The qualities which such an office demand are many and varied, and cannot be fully specified. But above all the office calls for imagination, courage, initiative, a firm grasp of economic realities, and a capacity for inspiring people and reconciling conflicting interests and purposes. As a position of leadership, it is not a job to be filled by a mere "office holder." The salary is $12,000 a year and traveling expenses, which is small compensation on the basis of commercial standards, in view of the qualities desired and the strain of the office, but which is large compared to earnings even of organized workers.

The treasurer is a part-time official whose chief duty is to take charge of the funds of the Federation. He performs his tasks in co-operation with a finance committee of three appointed by the president from among the members of the Council. The treasurer is required to pay warrants drawn on him by the secretary and signed by both the president and secretary or their authorized agents. In practice, this is inconvenient, and a system has been worked out by which the secretary makes payments and then deposits certified warrants with the treasurer. It is also the duty of the treasurer to submit a financial statement to the convention which is examined by a special auditing committee consisting of delegates to the convention appointed by the president. The compensation of the treasurer is $500 a year.

The secretary of the Federation has charge of all its books and records, receives all funds, prints quarterly financial statements, convenes the annual convention of which he is ex-officio secretary, and handles all other matters pertaining to these duties. He furnishes the credentials committee of the convention with a statement of the financial standing of each affiliated union. This is important because no union is entitled to send delegates to a convention unless it has paid its per capita tax. Twice a year, on March 1 and September 1, the secretary prepares a directory of all affiliated unions, with names of secretaries and organizers, which he sends to the secretaries of affiliated unions. The secretary is bonded and receives an annual salary of $10,000.

The office of secretary was meant to be one for handling the routine matters of the Federation.[27] But the exigencies of the situation make demands on the secretary which go far beyond the functions assigned to him by the constitution. He is called upon to supply information, to advise in legislative matters, and to help devise policies vitally affecting the Federation. Because he and the president are the only full-time officers of the Federation in Washington, the secretary is potentially the adviser and collaborator of the president. His opportunities and obligations become even more important when the president is away from Washington. In practice the office thus calls not only for adeptness in keeping records but also for some of the qualities of leadership.

[27] Frank Morrison has filled the office continuously since 1896.

The income of the Federation is derived from per capita taxes and miscellaneous sources. The national and international unions pay a fixed tax of twelve cents per member a year. This tax is paid only for members who are at work and who are paying dues to their union. The local trade and federal labor unions pay a tax of 35 cents a month or $4.20 per member per year. Of this 35 cents, 12½ cents is set aside in the defense fund, 5 cents is paid as a subscription to the *Federationist*, and 7½ cents goes to the Federation's general fund.[28] The city centrals and the state federations of labor pay an annual tax of $10 each. The miscellaneous income of the Federation is obtained from initiation and reinstatement fees, sales of supplies, subscriptions to the *Federationist*, profits on sales of securities, interest on deposits, and a few other items.

Since 1914 the Federation has raised the per capita tax three times, bringing it from 8 to 12 cents per member per year for national unions, and from 15 to 35 cents per member per month for local and federal unions. This and the growth of membership between 1915 and 1920 resulted in increasing considerably the annual income of the Federation. During 1919-20 and 1920-21 the Federation had an annual income of $929,255 and $832,169 respectively, of which per capita taxes were $562,608 and $541,360. Since 1924 the total receipts of the Federation and per capita taxes have been much smaller. In 1932 the total receipts were $466,350, in-

[28] Some writers have made much of the "large" dues collected from these unions. As a matter of fact, the total receipts from all local trade and federal labor unions in 1932, for instance, were $47,725, out of total per capita receipts of $312,809. But it should be kept in mind that the relation of these local unions to the Federation is similar to the position of locals in an international union, and on that basis the dues are comparatively small.

cluding $312,809 in per capita taxes. Since 1920 the per capita tax has remained unchanged because no convention would sanction an increase. The only way in which the Federation can now augment its financial resources is through successful organizing and an increase in membership.

D. Problems of Guidance

The guidance of the Federation is by no means a smooth process. Not every union belonging to it has the same degree of interest in its affiliation or the same reasons for being interested. Also the separate unions in the A. F. of L. are willing to maintain a national federation only as long as their own autonomy is preserved and the powers of the national federation are limited. As the national and international unions are inclined to interpret trade autonomy in a strict constructionist sense, even those powers which the Executive Council and other central bodies of the Federation possess tend to be further curtailed. Fearing undue friction, the Federation avoids raising issues which might put its authority too severely to the test. It relies on persuasion and manipulation to hold its members together and to carry out its policies. It even hesitates to apply its disciplinary powers of temporary suspension or expulsion of a union. Either method has disadvantages involving a temporary or permanent loss of membership, a decrease in revenue, and internal friction. In many situations the Federation is likely to lose more from the application of these disciplinary powers than the union suspended or expelled. This is especially true of the larger unions which can function for a time at least without the Federation.

It is often said that the Federation took as its model

the federal Constitution of the United States and copied the division of powers in the system of American government. Following this analogy, one may say that the Federation carried to an extreme the idea of states' rights in giving the national unions almost complete autonomy. The Federation shows no parallel towards greater concentration of power similar to the growth of the powers of the federal government.

As long as the present principles of voluntarism and trade autonomy persist, the Federation will continue to be faced with the same dilemma. It will either have to be content with more or less dilatory tactics and incomplete fulfilment of its policies by its component unions, or it must increase its moral prestige to such an extent that there will be no need of compulsory and disciplinary powers. At present it is hanging on the first horn of the dilemma.

Because of its loose structure and lack of clearly defined powers, the Federation is peculiarly subject to the influence of personalities. This does not mean, as has often been maintained, that the Federation can be a one-man organization. But its coherence depends upon personal loyalties more than is the case in the national labor movements of European countries. This was clearly shown under Gompers, who maintained his position not only by force of character but also by establishing close personal relations with trade union leaders who found loyalty to him satisfactory and his leadership helpful to them. One of the reasons for the comparative decline in the central power of the Federation since 1925 is the failure of President Green to build up a group of personal followers. The structure of the Federation also offers an opportunity for conflicting leadership within the Executive Council.[29] That often creates personal friction, but it is the policy of the Federation to keep such differences from public view.

[29] This is illustrated at the present time by the third vice-president, Matthew Woll. Woll was considered a candidate for the presidency to succeed Gompers after his retirement. Gompers on several occasions showed his desire to have Woll his successor. In 1917, when Woll was considering a position on the Illinois State Industrial Commission, Gompers urged him in strong terms to stay with organized labor. Owing to his undoubted ability and energy, Woll has maintained an influential position in the labor movement. In the Federation he is chairman of the Resolutions Committee, which is the most important committee of the convention. He is chairman of the Workers' Education Bureau, president of the Union Labor Life Insurance Company, chairman of the League for the Modification of the Volstead Act, and chairman of the Wage Earners' Protective Conference. Some of these organizations collect funds and afford opportunities for extending patronage and building up a personal following. In these various capacities Woll commands attention from legislators and industrialists. As chairman of the Wage Earners' Protective Conference, he has the hearing of the country and the attention and good-will of the industrial interests on tariff questions. Through some labor newspapers with which he is connected he propagates his ideas on international relations. Matthew Woll is also acting president of the National Civic Federation. While the Civic Federation has declined since 1919, its membership still includes many distinguished persons whose public statements are solicited. The Civic Federation in recent years has been particularly active in anti-radical propaganda and in combating the recognition of the Soviet Union. As its acting president Woll from time to time issues statements to the press of the country on communism, on the recognition of Russia, and on such matters as export of capital, tariffs, etc., which often have the appearance of or are publicly interpreted as more or less official A. F. of L. declarations, regardless of the fact that they have not been endorsed either by a convention or by the Executive Council.

CHAPTER XIII

AIDING THE INDUSTRIAL STRUGGLE

One of the main purposes of the Federation is to aid its affiliated unions in their industrial struggles. This involves such specific functions as determining the structure of unionism, organizing the unorganized, and coordinating methods of collective bargaining.

I. SHAPING TRADE UNION STRUCTURE

The form and structure of unions are important because they affect methods of action and the character of inter-union relations. The Federation can shape the form of its trade unions through its power to grant and revoke charters. In its early years the A. F. of L. encouraged a multiplicity of organizations by accepting most unions applying for admission and by granting charters indiscriminately. From 1904 to 1916 the Federation developed the policy of permitting one union to a trade, of using persuasion to settle jurisdictional disputes, and of permitting amalgamation under certain conditions. The Federation adhered to this policy with varying degrees of strictness, tending to show concern for the maintenance of craft unionism and trade autonomy.

Between 1919 and 1921 the Federation was hard-pressed to broaden its policy on trade union structure. Demands were made for the complete reorganization of the A. F. of L. on the basis of plant and industrial unions and for a universal interchange of cards.[1] Between 1922 and 1924 there was agitation for the amalgama-

[1] *Report of the Proceedings of the Thirty-Ninth Annual Convention of the American Federation of Labor*, 1919, p. 348.

tion of trade unions into industrial unions, one for each industry,[2] on the grounds that the craft unions divided the workers and made them unable to resist attacks or to extend organization. Proposals were also made by moderate elements in the Federation for a wider system of card transfers between unions and for the establishment of new departments in the needle trades, the textile industry, the iron and steel industry, the food and distributing trades, the marine transport, and the clerical and office occupations. But along with other radical demands, these met with defeat.

As a matter of fact, the Federation did not seriously consider structural changes during this period or later. The Executive Council supported a few amalgamations of small unions, but did not promote more important combinations. It rejected all applications for new departments. In settling the jurisdictional disputes of these years, the Executive Council tended to conciliate contending parties by demarcating jurisdictional rights rather than to effect larger combinations. At the 1929 convention a resolution was introduced to appoint a committee of 15 to formulate a plan for reducing the number of international unions and for consolidating them. The resolution was voted down, and the convention once more reaffirmed the Scranton Declaration of 1901 as the expression of A. F. of L. policy. Proposals made at the same convention for establishing a Food Department and an Aircraft Department were likewise rejected. In the matter of jurisdictional disputes the Federation followed its traditional policy.[3]

[2] *Proceedings of 43d Annual Convention of the A. F. of L.*, 1923, p. 266.

[3] Between 1917 and 1924 the Executive Council handled about 150 jurisdictional cases, of which about 50 were new disputes arising during

The pressure for changes in the structure of the constituent unions of the A. F. of L. comes from four sources —jurisdictional encroachments, loss of membership by the older unions, efforts to organize new industries, and agitation by amalgamationists and industrial unionists. Jurisdictional difficulties in the Federation arise either between craft unions over borderland processes, tools, and materials; between rival unions having substantially the same jurisdiction; or between an industrial union and a craft union claiming jurisdiction over part of the same industry.[4] They are the result of the way in which charters were granted years ago and of changes in industrial technique and in economic organization. The fact that most unions are constantly seeking to claim new processes and new areas accentuates the importance of these changes as a factor of inter-union troubles. The underlying causes are the scarcity of union jobs and the efforts of American unions to maintain large differentials in wage rates and to extend exclusive control over as wide a job market as possible.

---

these years. The Council ordered seven amalgamations and brought about ten inter-union agreements. In all other cases the disputes were allowed to drag along, the Council calling conference after conference in the hope of bringing about an amicable adjustment. Between 1925 and 1931 the Federation carried through five amalgamations and granted extensions of jurisdiction to six unions, but these did not materially affect its composition. The unions whose jurisdiction was extended were those of the cloth hat and cap makers (including millinery workers); the operating engineers; firemen and oilers; hotel and restaurant workers; maintenance of way workers; and marble and slate polishers. For amalgamations, see Appendix A, pp. 489-91.

[4] These types of disputes are illustrated respectively by the struggles between the Glass Blowers' Union and the Flint Glass Workers' Union for the control of Neon Signs; between the Teamsters' Union and the Railway Clerks for the control of employees in the vehicle department of the American Railway Express; and between the Flint Glass Workers' Union and the International Association of Machinists for the jurisdictional rights over machinists working in glass factories. See **Appendix B.**

The Federation deplores these disputes and is eager to eliminate them because they are costly, because jurisdictional strikes antagonize employers and consume much time, and because they create bitterness in the ranks of organized labor. The Federation claims that its devices—voluntary inter-union agreements, amalgamations, and departmental alliances—tend to mitigate the evil to a considerable degree. To some extent this contention is borne out by facts.[5] However, the relative decrease in the number of disputes since 1925 is more likely due to the general weakening of union organization. In case of industrial revival the devices of the Federation are not likely to appear so effective. The inter-union agreements are generally compromises, either dividing workers of the same class between two or three unions on some arbitrary basis, or dividing jobs of a similar character between unions on the basis of detailed demarcations of processes, tools, and materials. These settlements as a rule do not decrease the number of unions, nor do they tend to set up more compact bargaining units. In fact, they encourage the separate unions to try to lay out as wide claims as possible to get more work for their members. Many of the unions in the A. F. of L. now go into great detail in describing their jurisdictional rights, with

[5] Out of 207 jurisdictional cases between 1917 and 1931, the number considered by the Executive Council and by the conventions decreased from 91 between 1917 and 1920 to 64 between 1921 and 1925, and to 52 between 1926 and 1931. From 1917 to 1931, 80 new disputes arose, but of these only 16 originated after Jan. 1, 1925. Also, of the 74 unions involved in disputes between 1917 and 1931, 42 unions had only one dispute each in these 15 years; 13 unions had 2 disputes; and only 12 unions, mostly in the building trades, had from 4 to 10 disputes. These disputes do not include those which are settled by the departments, as described in Chap. XIV. The unions involved in the largest number of disputes were those of the carpenters, steam engineers, boilermakers, machinists, longshoremen, hod-carriers, teamsters, bridge and structural iron workers, and sheet metal workers.

the result that instead of clarifying the situation they increase the area of potential conflict in related trades and processes.

Neither is the method of amalgamation as practiced by the Federation likely to have a serious effect upon eliminating jurisdictional disputes. Between 1900 and 1931, out of the hundreds of disputes considered by the Federation, only 29 amalgamations were effected.[6] The importance of these amalgamations is much reduced by the fact that, with two or three exceptions, they involved small unions which were absorbed by larger ones and did not affect the interrelations of the larger unions.[7]

The decline of some of the older trade unions, because of technical and economic changes, is another stimulus towards consolidation. The negotiations for the amalgamation of the Cigarmakers' Union and the Tobacco Workers' Union, which have been proceeding for several years, are an illustration. The steady decline of the Cigarmakers' Union, and the difficulties of the Tobacco Workers' Union in making headway in a highly concentrated industry employing large numbers of women, have forced upon both unions the idea that amalgamation might benefit their members. But the amalgamation of such unions is hampered by traditional attitudes, differences in systems of benefits and dues, and the vested interests of officers in their jobs.

The strongest impulse towards structural changes in the A. F. of L. comes from the recurring attempts to organize the basic and newer industries operating under methods of mass production. Organizing attempts in the automobile industry caused the first serious change since

[6] See Appendix A, pp. 489-91.

[7] For the way in which the departments affect jurisdictional disputes, see Chap. XIV.

1914 in the attitude of the Federation towards the question of trade autonomy.[8] It is logical to expect that all future attempts to organize these industries will have a similar effect.

The fourth factor pressing for change is furnished by the advocates of industrial unionism and amalgamation, and is important because it tends to keep the issue alive. Although there is no longer a coherent group of trade unions within the Federation fighting for industrial unionism or amalgamation, propaganda is carried on by scattered locals and individuals and by opposition groups.

Opposing these factors of change, the forces which hold the A. F. of L. to its status quo in structure are still strong. The existing trade unions are largely dominated by the idea of trade autonomy. Sentiment in favor of industrial unionism is weaker than it ever was. Even were it stronger, the difficulty of wiping out existing organizations and consolidating locals, districts, and central offices with their varying systems of dues, benefits, methods of operation, and vested interests of officials would be very difficult.

As a result of its policy, the A. F. of L. has not greatly reduced the number of its constituent elements. The number of national and international unions was 110 in 1914, 112 in 1922, and 106 in 1933. But the number of smaller unions with a membership of less than 5,000 has decreased, being only 38 in 1931 as compared with 56 in 1914 and 68 in 1904. Also, the membership and influence of the small craft unions have decreased, the trade unions proper—based on a combination of crafts—having gained in relative importance.[9]

[8] See pp. 244-46.
[9] See Appendix A, p. 487.

That differences in methods of trade union strategy do not run parallel to differences in structure is indicated by the labor movements of other countries. The politically oriented labor movement of Great Britain rests on a basis of a highly decentralized trade union structure. The British Trade Union Congress is composed of over 200 separate trade union units, many of which are of a narrow craft character. The German Federation of Trade Unions, on the other hand, is highly centralized in accordance with the general character of German industry and is made up of 31 organizations, only a few of which are craft unions, the remainder being large industrial units.[10] Although the labor movement of Austria is as "class conscious" as the German and is socialistic in character, it is based upon a trade union structure, largely craft in character, the Austrian Federation of Free Trade Unions being composed of 49 organizations of which only eight are industrial unions.[11] Similar differences in structure exist between the industrial trade unionism of Belgium and Switzerland and the craft unionism of Denmark and Sweden, regardless of the similarities in the general character of the labor movements of these countries.

Despite these considerations, it still remains true that the method of the A. F. of L. prolongs the life of obsolete unions, and, by extolling the virtue of endless conferences in the jurisdictional disputes of dilatory, obstructionist, or sabotaging unions, hinders the processes

[10] See *Jahrbuch des Allgemeinen Deutschen Gewerkschaftsbund*, 1931, p. 248. It should be kept in mind that the clerical and technical workers of Germany are organized separately in some twelve unions, along more specialized occupational lines.

[11] See *Activities of the International Federation of Trade Unions, 1927-1930*, International Federation of Trade Unions, 1931, p. 121.

of readjustment even where the necessity for more rapid progress towards amalgamation is recognized. However, a demand for amalgamation in general is no solution. What is needed is a realistic approach to the problem and careful study of a possible pattern of organization adapted to the complex structure of American industry, running in the direction of both horizontal and vertical combination. The most promising line of development seems to lie in a structure which would combine plant unionism, amalgamation, and industrial alliances in such a way as to allow for the proper consideration of craft and trade interests where these persist and for wider concerted action where required by modern industrial conditions.

Another problem of structure is the position within the Federation of the city centrals. In the earlier stages in the history of the American labor movement, the city central seemed to offer the logical point of concentration for trade union forces. It was thought that a national federation of labor would be based upon such city centrals as a unit. When national and international trade unions began to display vigor, both forms of organization were considered for a time as co-ordinate bases for a national association. However, with the triumph of the A. F. of L., the national and international union became the dominant form of unionism and the unit for national federation. In the A. F. of L. the national and international unions are regarded as the basic organizations with inherent and inalienable rights which must not be infringed upon. The city centrals and state federations of labor have only such rights and powers as the Federation sees fit to grant them.

As a result, in almost all important matters, the city centrals are used mainly to reinforce the national and international unions. The city centrals are allowed to admit only such locals as are in good standing within national or international unions affiliated with the Federation. As soon as a local is suspended or expelled from its national union, the city central must cancel the membership of that local. This provision is intended to use the city central against secession movements or dual organizations.

Similarly, the city centrals have no power to fix the conditions for the admission of the delegates of whom they are composed. Under the constitution of the A. F. of L. the local unions can delegate any one to the city labor centrals. Some locals have sent lawyers, politicians, and others not working at their trade who held membership cards. At various conventions of the A. F. of L., delegates from the city centrals have demanded that the city centrals have the right to exclude such delegates and to lay down rules governing the qualifications of their membership. But such demands have been uniformly denied. The Federation has taken the stand that trade autonomy implies the absolute right of each local of a national or international union to elect its own representatives to a city central. Also, the Federation has insisted on regulating the method of representation in city centrals. This question was much discussed between 1920 and 1922, the city centrals claiming the right to self-determination in this respect. The Federation won the point with the aid of the international unions.[12]

[12] Under the provisions of the rule adopted in 1922, local unions with a membership of 50 or less are entitled to two delegates in a city central; those with 100 members or less to three delegates; with 250 members or less to four delegates; with 500 members or less to five delegates; and all local unions are entitled to one delegate for each additional 500 members or major fraction thereof.

The Federation has consistently refused the demands of the city centrals that the locals of the national unions affiliated with the American Federation of Labor be required to belong to their respective city centrals. Such demands have been persistently rejected at conventions on the grounds that the Federation is based on the principle of voluntarism, which precludes compulsory membership. The Federation would only advise and urge locals to join their city centrals. The 1930 convention made a concession, recommending that all international unions include a provision in their constitutions requiring local unions to affiliate with the central bodies in their localities.[13] So far this resolution has had little effect. A large number of locals in different cities are not affiliated with their city centrals either because of unwillingness to pay dues, because of indifference, or because of local politics. In many cities the proportion of locals refusing to affiliate with their city centrals is as high as 50 per cent of local trade union membership.

In other ways the Federation has circumscribed the power of the central unions. In 1919 the convention of the Federation amended its constitution so as to prevent central labor unions on penalty of expulsion from calling strikes or taking strike votes for local unions which had a national organization. This provision in the constitution was demanded by the international unions as a means of preventing city centrals from undermining their authority in relation to the control of strikes.

The attitude of the Federation towards the city centrals is contradictory. The Federation has insisted during recent years upon the necessity of making trade

[13] *Proceedings of 50th Annual Convention of the A. F. of L.*, 1930, pp. 272-73.

unionism an important factor in the life of the community, and in its organizing campaigns has emphasized the value of unions to the community. In suggesting ways of making significant the position of trade unions, the Federation has outlined various activities to be performed under the direction of city centrals. It has called upon them to seek representation on boards of education and to become a factor in municipal affairs. At the same time the Federation has a traditional fear of the city centrals, because some of them have tended to become centers of radical opinion and of independent political action and are potential rivals of the national unions. The practical policy of the Federation has thus been to weaken the city centrals financially and otherwise. Only a few city centrals now have sufficient funds and means to make themselves effective. The majority exist largely on paper. Some of them are deeply involved in local machine politics. Their potentialities for unionism, illustrated by the work of the Chicago Federation of Labor, have increased as a result of changes in American industrial and social life. But a new policy towards the city labor centrals on the part of the A. F. of L. is an essential condition for making them effective.

II. ORGANIZING

As formulated in the constitution of the A. F. of L., the function of organizing includes four specific tasks. One is to form local trade and federal labor unions in unorganized industries, and to combine them into national or international unions. A second is to help the organizing efforts of existing national and international unions. A third is to aid the growth of national unions through the work of the departments. The fourth is to form city centrals and state federations of labor to strengthen local and national unions through closer contacts on a community and state basis.

The organizing work of the Federation is determined partly by the demands of its constituent unions and partly by its own planning. The larger and stronger unions generally conduct their own organizing campaigns and only occasionally call for help. The weaker international unions are always in need of aid. Their requests for such aid are a regular feature of the annual conventions. As a rule these requests are nominally granted by the convention. Most of them are not carried into effect by the Executive Council, largely because funds are not available. In some cases the organizers of the Federation are instructed to give whatever aid they can to one or another union as a part of their general work. The international unions thus treated continue to press their claims.

The organizing planned at intervals by the Executive Council is largely opportunistic. The numerous resolutions presented at the annual conventions call attention to many situations, of major and minor importance, and the Executive Council can choose to step into some and to stay out of others. Often the situations arousing the most heated debates in the conventions are let alone. The campaigns most likely to be taken up are either in harmony with traditional policies or those forced on the Federation by events. The union-label campaign of 1925 was of the former type. The Southern campaign of 1929-30 was of the latter. These successive campaigns do not give the impression of continuity but rather of a succession of beginnings which are not followed through.

The machinery through which the A. F. of L. carries on its organizing activities has changed little since 1900. It consists of a staff of regular organizers appointed by the Executive Council, district volunteer organizers, and officials of city centrals and state federations. Some of the regular organizers give full time to their job and maintain branch offices of the Federation in the main industrial centers. Others are paid for part time and hold offices in local or national unions as well. The number of organizers has varied from year to year, in accordance with resources and industrial conditions. In 1919-20 the number was 112 and 125 respectively. Since 1925 it has ranged between 22 and 41.

Each organizer is expected to cover the district assigned to him, the districts varying in area from one to six states. He is expected not only to form new unions, settle shop difficulties, help in strikes, take part in negotiations with employers when called upon by one or another union, but also to represent the Federation in political and legislative questions. In New York City and elsewhere the organizers of the A. F. of L. are members of various municipal and state commissions and give much time to civic affairs and local politics.

From its early years the Federation has issued commissions to district volunteer organizers who, as men working at a trade, are willing to help the work of spreading unionism. The number of these organizers has varied greatly, being over 2,000 during 1920-23 and falling to 1,526 in 1931. Some of these volunteer organizers are paid from $10 to $100 for organizing trade and labor unions or city centrals, and for helping to adjust strikes in which the local trade and federal labor unions are involved. The total annual sum paid volunteer organizers is small; it was $965 in 1924, $386 in 1930, and $558 in 1931. The secretaries and officers of the city centrals, as well as the regular and volunteer organizers, are expected to aid the A. F. of L. in its organizing activities.

Methods of organizing vary from trade to trade and between localities. But in essence all organizing involves a combination of the methods of individual persuasion and collective conversion, and recourse to mass pressure through strikes and to compromise through negotiation. The organizers of the Federation use the method of individual propaganda when they make efforts to win key members in a shop, trade, or industry to build up a nucleus of union men before attempting negotiations with employers. In some recent campaigns they have applied the more spectacular method of collective conversion through mass meetings and circulating literature. In the past the Federation relied largely on strikes as a means of extending organization. In recent years it has stressed converting employers to unionism by promising business gain from co-operative relations with unions.

In addition to union management co-operation the Federation since 1927 has emphasized three other features of organizing technique. One is to make the union a family and social affair; to visit the homes of non-union workers, arrange social meetings, and reach the family through the radio and motion pictures. The second is to make unionism part of the recognized institutional life of the community. The unions are urged to make contacts with citizens' committees and to convince them that unionizing workers by the A. F. of L. is as important for the welfare of the city as for the workers. The unions have been advised to co-operate with chambers of commerce and merchants' associations, and to send representatives to the district boards of these business organizations. Community pride is to be aroused by comparing local labor conditions with conditions in other towns where they are better. College professors and ministers of churches who are presumed to be more generally in sympathy with the aims of labor are to be enrolled in the efforts to win public opinion and to rally the business elements of the community to the labor unions.[14]

Third, the Federation has been urging concerted and planned local campaigns. The city centrals are advised to make systematic surveys of local conditions, map out the plants and districts where workers may be reached, enlist the co-operation of all local unions, zone the city and assign the work to various union members, and obtain the help of organizers from international unions. Such campaigns are expected to arouse general local interest in unionism and to have the advantage of being adapted to local customs.

In accordance with these ideas the Federation has made considerable effort in recent years to change its organizing literature. The leaflets used for circularization are written in a simple style, enlivened with drawings and cartoons, and attractively printed. Their content varies in accordance with the presumed mental attitudes of the workers addressed. Stress is laid in varying degrees on wages, working conditions, the right to have a voice in industry, or the constructive features of unionism.

The criteria for judging the effectiveness of organizing work are not simple. A rise in membership is an index of success, but a fall in membership is not always proof of failure. Organizing activities are often attempts to ward off losses. Also, an organizing campaign which has

[14] For a description of the way these methods were applied, see *Proceedings of 49th Annual Convention of the A. F. of L.*, 1929, pp. 61-65.

failed may have planted seeds which will come to fruition later.

Nevertheless, when all limiting factors are taken into account, the Federation cannot be satisfied with its organizing record. The Executive Committee in its annual reports during the last few years has expressed anxiety over the steady decline in membership. The record of the recent organizing campaigns among women workers, in the automobile industry, in the iron and steel industry, and in the South has been uniformly one of collapse and failure.

It is generally admitted that American economic and social conditions have not favored a high degree of organizability among American wage earners. The belief in unlimited opportunities, in the capacity of the individual to achieve personal success; the hope of rising out of the wage-earning class; the friction between immigrant and racial groups; the difficulties of a polyglot working population; and similar factors have created an especially difficult environment for the building up of strong trade union organizations. In addition, changing technology, the destruction of old skills, the rapid rise of new industries, continuous shifts in the location of old industries, and the drawing of ever new elements into the working population have repeatedly undermined established unions, making it necessary to start work afresh and to carry the doctrines of unionism to new sections of the country.

This industrial environment has also favored speculative habits of mind which are in conflict with group feeling and a sense for collective action. The psychological factors which have been of greatest importance are attitudes of employees and management towards unionism and the prevailing mentality of the workers. American employers have quite generally shown a strict constructionism of the individualistic philosophy of property, a particular insistence on the right of absolute control over their business, and bitterness against any collective efforts to limit such control. The prevailing tone of industrial relations in America has been and is saturated with contempt for and hostility to unions and union officials. Employers of no other country, with the possible exception of those in the metal and machine trades of France, have so persistently, so vigorously, at such costs, and with such a conviction of serving a cause opposed and fought trade unions as the American employing class. In no other Western country have employers been so much aided in their opposition to unions by the civil authorities, the armed forces of the government, and the courts.

These factors have given the worker a sense of fear for his job and have developed in him an individualistic outlook accentuated in recent years by the geographic decentralization of industry, by the growth of suburbs, by the radio and the automobile. The current mode of life makes collective action more difficult, strike-breaking less odious, and reluctance to change greater. Also many non-union mills and factories have introduced union standards to counteract unionism. The workers in such places have found they could enjoy the benefits of unionism without paying dues and without sacrifices.

But in spite of these difficulties the unsuccessful organizing work of the Federation since 1925 must be ascribed also to the shortcomings of its methods and techniques. The Federation has not had the success it anticipated in entering into co-operative relations with employers. It has been forced in its organizing campaigns to engage in large strikes in the South, in Passaic, in Lawrence, and elsewhere, because the inducements which the unions can offer to employers are such as to have but little appeal, while the fear of union rules and of jurisdictional strikes is very real. Employers in industries in which a considerable number of small and medium-sized plants are competing for the better type of worker and for the market will sign up with the union because the union can supply them with more efficient workers, and with a guaranty against strikes. Also the union holds out the promise of helping to extend the employer's market by means of the label, union advertising, and special patronage. However, these inducements limit the extent of organizing. They lose value as they become generalized. If given to all employers, the same opportunities would become of little value. They are worthless to large corporations in basic industries where work is highly mechanized and subdivided and where markets cannot be influenced by union methods.

The Federation assumes that organization can be successful only if the workers are educated to group consciousness, but does not clearly indicate what that involves. The spokesmen of the Federation tend to confuse the group consciousness of the workers with occupational and professional consciousness as exemplified in medical societies, chambers of commerce, lawyers' groups, trade associations, and similar organizations. But such a concept is inadequate to arouse the larger moral and spiritual impulses which the Federation regards as necessary for the success of unionism, because the personnel policies of employers, as well as the limited wage possibilities of many industries, make it impossible for the unions to build exclusively on the basis of material advantages. In other countries the permanence of trade unionism is based on the workers' acceptance of their trade unions as basic organizations which it is their duty to support regardless of temporary or immediate benefits. Such attitude is based on deeper group sentiments such as class consciousness, the aim for political power, or social ideals. The Federation does not emphasize these elements and its organizing literature offers little stimulus to that very state of group consciousness which is its declared objective.

Regardless of the technical changes which it has vividly described and emphasized, the Federation persists in regarding man as a "skill-hungry animal" and continues to cling to the idea that union organization can be based only upon craft skill. By so doing the Federation since 1925 has continuously contradicted itself by emphasizing the destruction of skill by technical changes and yet insisting that the new industrial techniques are creating new kinds of skill which can become a new basis of organization. This strengthens the skilled trades which maintain that unskilled workers and semi-skilled machine hands are largely unorganizable and that it is a waste of money to try to bring them into permanent unions. It also puts the Federation at a disadvantage in its efforts to organize three groups which are of increasing importance in modern industry—namely, the workers in the mass industries, the colored workers, and the women workers.

However, even if the Federation were to evince greater interest in these groups of workers, it would find difficulties in incorporating them in its present structure. This was demonstrated in the campaign among women wage earners in 1924, in the campaigns in the steel and automobile industries where the question of distributing the newly organized workers sharpened jurisdictional jealousies. Efforts to enroll colored workers have largely failed because of the incapacity of the Federation to break through the autonomy of its affiliated unions, which persist in excluding them explicitly or indirectly. In other words, the Federation under its present structural arrangements has no organization device for holding these three groups of workers. The federal trade union, as shown elsewhere, is totally inadequate for the purpose.[15] The international unions so far have shown but little capacity for co-operative effort in this respect because of their mutual jealousies, while the city centrals are not allowed to develop their potential capacities.

The Federation continues to regard organizing as an art in the practice of which native capacity, personality, and intuition are more important than training. Here, too, there is contradiction. On the one hand the Federation advises planning, surveys, and research; on the other it employs people whose methods of organizing are based largely upon intuition, divination, and luck, rather than on training for the job. In addition, many organizing posts are filled by men who have rendered services to the Federation in years gone by, by discarded organizers of international unions, or by persons who have political and other influential personal contacts. They have neither the outlook nor the inclination to develop new methods of organizing or to give the energy which their job requires.

Organizing under American industrial conditions is far from a pleasant and easy occupation. It often in-

[15] See pp. 71-72.

volves danger to the life of the organizer. Unless he can brave his task because of idealistic motives, he must be recruited from the tougher element or must be expected to be easy-going on the job. It is because of the hazards involved that organizers seek alliances with all groups that can afford protection—ward politicians and strong-arm men—thus complicating the problems of maintaining clean and efficient unions.

ORGANIZING EXPENDITURES OF THE AMERICAN FEDERATION OF LABOR, 1899–1931[a]

Period	Total Expenses of A. F. of L.	Organizing Expenses	*Organizing Expenses as percentage of Total Expenses*
1899–1904	$ 736,772	$ 239,227	*32.5*
1905–14	2,130,610	624,400	*29.3*
1915–24	5,388,771	1,557,782	*28.9*
1925–31	3,703,019	851,398	*22.9*

[a] These figures include salaries and expenses of organizers, but do not include expenses from the fund of the local trade and federal labor unions or collections on behalf of strikers.

Though the difficulties and cost of organizing have been on the increase, the expenditures of the Federation for this work decreased from $255,584 in 1920 to $139,526 in 1931 and have formed a steadily decreasing part in its total outlays. This can be only partly explained by the falling off of income, for the Federation has steadily increased its appropriations for salaries and general administration. Also the Federation has given comparatively little time and attention to the study of the problems of organization.

As a rule the organizers of the Federation do not come together to consider common tasks or to exchange experiences. Neither is there any one person in charge of organizing work whose task is to improve methods. The experiences of the affiliated unions have not been studied or utilized as they should have been. Little has been done to mobilize the many millions of dollars spent annually by the various unions so as to make possible concerted organizing campaigns.

III. ASSISTING STRIKES

Closely bound up with organizing are the activities of the Federation involved in aiding its constituent unions in strikes, in carrying on boycotts, and in the sale of union-label goods. Though it has been the contention of trade union leaders and of the Federation that as labor unions grew stronger, strikes tended to decline,[16] the Federation has continuously warned its member unions that success depended on their capacity to build up strong treasuries and to develop fighting strength. For some years also, the leaders of the Federation, especially Gompers, tried to establish a central defense fund in the Federation and to endow the Executive Council with more central power to obtain better co-operation in strikes. Such proposals were repeatedly rejected by the international unions for fear that they would lead to centralized control of strikes. In 1921, as a result of the open shop campaign, the suggestion that a strike insurance department be organized in the A. F. of L. was made but rejected.[17] Since then the matter has not come up for discussion. The Federation has also consistently opposed sympathetic and general strikes.[18]

[16] This theory is questionable. See Paul H. Douglas, "An Analysis of Strike Statistics, 1881-1921," *Journal of the American Statistical Association*, September 1923, pp. 866-77.

[17] By the United Hatters of North America. *Proceedings of 41st Annual Convention of the A. F. of L.*, 1921, p. 391.

[18] In 1928 the A. F. of L. convention rejected a resolution introduced by the Paving Cutters' Union proposing that all member unions

At one time the A. F. of L. made attempts to observe the trend of business conditions so as to counsel member unions when a strike was advisable. Gompers intended to develop a technical information service which would guide unions in industrial negotiations. This scheme never matured. The present research and information service of the Federation only slightly touches upon such problems, though advice in strike matters is given to unions seeking it.

The Federation is an important factor in mediating between striking workers and employers. On a national scale this is one of the tasks of the president and the other members of the Executive Committee. Locally, it is a function of the organizers of the A. F. of L. and of the city centrals. As a rule it is the weaker unions which seek the aid of the A. F. of L. in such matters. In recent years garment workers, furriers, miners, textile workers, and others have hoped to impress employers by invoking the prestige of the Federation. Through its organizers and the officers of the city centrals, the Federation is also of considerable help to striking unions in obtaining police protection and in fighting injunctions.

In addition to these activities the Federation has the power to render financial assistance to its international unions during strikes. The Executive Council either may levy an assessment of one cent per member per week on all member unions for a period not exceeding ten weeks in any one year, or it may issue appeals for funds

---

of the A. F. of L. make provisions in their trade agreements which would reserve the right to declare sympathetic strikes. The reason given for rejecting the resolution was that the provisions of trade agreements were matters over which the national and international unions had sole authority. *Proceedings of 48th Annual Convention of the A. F. of L.*, 1928, p. 297. For effects of departments on strikes, see Chap. XIV.

on behalf of any member union engaged in a protracted strike or lockout. However, the financial assistance rendered its unions through assessments has been negligible. From 1900 to 1931 the total amount has been approximately $250,000. This includes assessments made for strike aid, the $63,750 for legal expenses in the Danbury Hatters' Case, and $51,865 for organizing women workers in 1913-17. The total collected from assessments for purely strike aid in 30 years is thus less than $140,000. The largest single sums collected were $30,357 for the machinists in 1902; $33,680 for the textile workers in 1905; and $56,597 for the typographical workers in 1906-08. How small these sums were at the time may be seen from the fact that the single strike of the Typographical Union in 1906 for the eight-hour day cost the union $1,563,729. The Federation has been reluctant to use the method of special assessment to aid its members.[19] The Executive Council has hesitated to test the financial loyalty of its members too often. Also, assessments must be approved by an annual convention, and as a rule the conventions have not been eager to assume extra financial obligations.

The most effective means of giving financial aid has been the method of appeal. A union on strike in need of help may submit to the Executive Council a statement justifying its request for aid. If the Council approves the request it issues an appeal for funds to all members of organized labor; or it may authorize the union to do so. Authorization by the Federation also enables representatives of the union seeking aid to appear before other unions and city centrals to raise funds directly. In its

[19] Since 1900 it has levied only a dozen assessments. The last one, in 1918, was a war emergency measure, and it yielded about $32,000 which was used to pay the expenses of various labor delegations to Europe. Since 1919 the Federation has levied no assessments.

earlier years, and especially between 1897 and 1907, the Federation issued numerous such appeals because the new international unions could not finance their own strikes. The Federation, however, constantly emphasized the idea that the unions must rely increasingly on their own efforts rather than on the help of fellow workers.[20]

In contrast to its relation to the international unions, the Federation has direct jurisdiction in the strikes of its local trade and federal labor unions. According to the constitution of the Federation, to receive assistance in a trade dispute, the local unions must submit to the president of the Federation for approval by the Executive Council a complete statement of their grievances and must await a reply for 20 days if necessary. After approval has been obtained, the members of the local union involved must cast by secret ballot a two-thirds vote in favor of a strike before it can be declared. A local union is not entitled to benefits unless it has been in good standing for one year. The benefits are $7.00 a week per member for six weeks with a waiting period of two weeks during which no benefits are paid. Every member on strike must report daily to the officers of the local, and there are further rules restricting action in case of a lockout.

[20] Since 1919 the Federation has reported collections through appeals of $1,276,853. In 1919-20 it raised $418,161 for the steel strike. In 1925-26 it collected $200,710 for the anthracite miners. In 1927-28 its appeal for the striking soft coal miners brought in $488,524. In 1929-31 the textile workers obtained $41,530, and $28,725 was raised for the strikers in Danville, Va. Smaller sums were raised for striking cigarmakers, ladies' garment workers, and a few other unions. The Federation in addition between 1919 and 1931 raised about $250,000 for a variety of purposes, such as the promotion of co-operation, publicity, and furnishings for Gompers' room in the International Labor Office in Geneva. In 1924, $27,007 was collected for the German trade unions and in 1926, $83,569 for the British miners. For the Gompers Memorial Fund $115,378 was collected between 1924 and 1931.

The A. F. of L. established a defense fund for its local trade and federal labor unions in 1902. Between that year and 1931 the total receipts in the fund were \$924,489 and total expenditures \$606,183, or 65 per cent. The sums paid out at different times have varied. At first the Federation gave as little as possible in order to accumulate a reserve. Then its payments increased. Since 1925 the percentage paid out has been low as the Federation has not encouraged strikes and has tried to keep a large balance in reserves.

RECEIPTS AND EXPENDITURES OF DEFENSE FUND, 1902–31

Period	Receipts	Expenditures	*Expenditures as a Percentage of Receipts*	Balance at End of Period
1902–07	\$153,473	\$ 50,395	*32.8*	\$103,078
1908–14	108,156	119,384	*101.1*	91,853
1915–19	157,750	94,879	*60.1*	154,725
1920–24	285,663	239,258	*83.7*	201,131
1925–31	219,447	102,267	*46.6*	318,314

IV. THE USE OF THE BOYCOTT

An important function of the Federation at one time was to help unions in carrying on boycotts.[21] However, after the adverse court decisions in the Buck Stove and Range Case and Danbury Hatters' Case in 1908, the Federation discontinued the publication of the "we do not patronize" list in the *Federationist.* Though interpreting the Clayton Act as legalizing boycotting, the Federation did not attempt to revive the "unfair list." The decisions of the United States Supreme Court in the Duplex Printing Case in 1921 and in the Bedford Cut Stone Case in 1927 further discouraged the Federation in the use of the boycott. At its convention in 1929 it abolished the Committee on Boycotts, which had been

[21] See pp. 72-73.

one of the standing committees since 1886, and created in its place a Committee on Industrial Relations.

This new committee, like its predecessor, considers the few boycott cases presented by various unions to the annual conventions.[22] Their number varied between three in 1926 and 15 in 1928, the average for 1925-31 being seven. The assistance commonly requested is that the commodities or services of the firms against which the union has grievance be declared "unfair" to organized labor, and that the fact be widely published. This is the form of boycott which involves the use of the organized workers' consuming power and which is based on the hope that the falling off in the business of the firm will force it to terms. Unions which have asked assistance most frequently in recent years include the bakers (in their fight against the Ward Bakery Company), the hotel and restaurant workers, stove mounters, metal polishers, cigarmakers, tobacco workers, and textile operatives.

In other cases the aid demanded is that a firm or business against which a union is on strike be declared "unfair" and that other workers refuse either to handle the materials made by such firm or to work in plants using its products. This is a form of the boycott which is very closely related to the sympathetic strike. It is practiced most often in the building trades by machinists, sheet metal workers, or carpenters who refuse to handle materials made by non-union men, and in transportation when longshoremen or teamsters refuse to haul or unload non-union made goods.[23]

[22] For definitions of the primary and secondary boycott, see Harry W. Laedler, "The Boycott," *Encyclopædia of the Social Sciences*, 1930, Vol. II, pp. 662-66.

[23] See Edward Berman, *Labor and the Sherman Act*, 1930, p. 191; and also Edwin E. Witte, *The Government in Labor Disputes*, 1932, p. 38.

The Committee on Industrial Relations after hearing such grievances generally recommends that they be referred to the Executive Council for action. The Executive Council is instructed to try to bring about an adjustment between the union and the business firm, and, in case of failure, to grant the union the aid which it seeks. As the Federation no longer publishes an "unfair list," its endorsement of a boycott is made known either at a convention or by means of special circulars published by the union concerned. Such endorsement is of value chiefly in giving publicity to a boycott.

Students of the boycott long maintained that it would become a subordinate weapon in the industrial struggle as trade union organization grew stronger.[24] As a matter of fact the diminishing use of the boycott by American unions has been in no way connected with increase in their strength. It has been due almost entirely to interference by the courts, to the ways in which workers spend their incomes, and to the policy of the Federation. The few cases that come up annually are treated in a more or less routine fashion. Whatever boycotting is still carried on is either local or managed by the international unions. Boycotts involving refusal to handle materials are generally conducted through councils of allied crafts, through local councils of the departments, or by agreement between different crafts. City centrals are active at times in primary or "consumers'" boycotts. Owing to these conditions the boycott has become an obsolete method in the tactics of the Federation.

[24] See Leo Wolman, *The Boycott in American Trade Unions*, 1916, p. 19; Harry W. Laidler, *Boycotts and the Labor Struggle*, 1914, p. 132; and S. Blum, *Labor Economics*, 1925, pp. 395-96.

CHAPTER XIV

CO-ORDINATING INTER-UNION ACTION THROUGH DEPARTMENTS

The A. F. of L. departments have the purpose of coordinating the work of the individual unions, thus helping the Federation to perform its functions. There are four departments. The Union-Label Trades Department differs in its activities from the other three, which are the Building Trades Department, the Metal Trades Department, and the Railway Employees Department.[1]

I. THE UNION-LABEL TRADES DEPARTMENT

The union label, like the boycott, is based on the worker's capacity to use his purchasing power to achieve union aims. By implication and indirectly, the patronage of union-label goods is a boycott of non-union made goods. But legally the label is not considered a boycott and its use is free from the difficulties of the latter.[2]

Because of its legality and seemingly easy application, the label has long been regarded as "organized labor's most powerful weapon." From 1874, when the cigarmakers of San Francisco first used the label in their fight against sweatshops employing Chinese,[3] to 1907, the label was adopted by a large number of unions and be-

[1] The Mining Department organized in 1911 was abolished in 1922.

[2] That the courts might also condemn the use of the label as a violation of the Sherman Anti-Trust Act is shown by the case of the Alden Paper Company, which was enjoined from using the watermark of the International Paper Workers' Union. See *Report of the Proceedings of the Forty-Ninth Annual Convention of the American Federation of Labor*, 1929, pp. 220-21.

[3] *On the Union Label's History*, p. 6. (Leaflet published by the American Federation of Labor, no date given.)

came a distinctive feature of American unionism.[4] After the court decisions of 1907-08 against the boycott, the Federation turned with increased interest to the label. A Union-Label Trades Department in the A. F. of L. was formed in 1909 to provide a central agency for advertising union labels, to interest workers in demanding union-label products, and to promote the union label as a method of advancing unionism.

Like the other three departments in the A. F. of L., the Label Department is subject to the Executive Council of the Federation. Membership in the department is open to all unions affiliated with the A. F. of L. using labels, cards, or buttons to mark products made by their members or to distinguish the members themselves. Most of the trades in the department, consequently, produce consumers' goods or their members come into direct contact with the ultimate consumer. Only a few of the unions in the department make materials to be used in further manufacture, or tools bought and used by workmen.

In 1909, when the department was organized, 37 international unions with a membership of about 420,000 joined. In 1932 the department was composed of 43 national and international unions and of local trade and federal labor unions with a membership of 496,283. The largest unions in the department are those of typographical workers, barbers, garment workers, musicians, stage employees, and bakers. The unions pay a per capita tax of six cents per member per year. Some of the unions pay on their total membership; but others pay only on those members who work under label conditions. The Brotherhood of Carpenters, for instance, with a membership of

[4] The label is but little known as a device of trade unionism in other countries.

over 300,000, paid per capita taxes in 1932 for only 20,000. The department has a president who gives only part-time service; five vice-presidents; and a full-time secretary-treasurer. These officers are elected annually at a convention convening a few days before the convention of the A. F. of L. in the same city.[5]

The activities of the department include holding annual conventions and two executive board meetings per year, distributing literature, sending paid representatives to agitate for the label in certain cities, and occasionally conducting nation-wide campaigns. The literature distributed by the department comprises a directory of manufacturers using labels, which is usually brought up to date once or twice a year, together with reprints of the labels and a list of the commodities upon which they can be found, and leaflets setting forth the aims of the department and the value of the label. The department can no longer afford to circularize individuals or organizations and so literature is sent only upon request. The department also charters local label leagues composed of delegates from local unions affiliated with city centrals. In 1931 the department had 128 such leagues in as many cities, as contrasted with 225 in 1927. These local leagues perform a large part of the work of the department in stimulating demand for labeled goods. The women's auxiliaries which are attached to various unions and the Women's International Union Label League and Trade Union Auxiliary[6] also assist in this work.

The department assumes that it is the duty and obli-

[5] John J. Manning has held the post of secretary-treasurer since 1917.

[6] This organization is not permitted to affiliate with the department because its membership is not confined to actual trade unionists. It receives, however, an annual subsidy of $500 from the department.

gation of the individual trade unionist to obtain information as to where union-label goods may be purchased. A unionist may write to the central labor council for information, and usually directories and other literature are available at local union meetings. Many local unions give certain evenings to the discussion of the label. Some local label leagues undertake house-to-house canvasses. In a few large cities radio programs advertising the label are sponsored. Semi-annual publicity campaigns are arranged to stimulate consumer demand, and officers of the department visit the conventions of international unions to talk on the label.

The most intensive work is done by the paid representatives of the department stationed in the large industrial centers. The New York Central Union Label Council is one of the largest; approximately 150 unions, with 50,000 members are affiliated with it. It publishes a Union Label Directory and Purchasing Guide, and a monthly paper—the *Union Label Advocate.* A union-label store owned by organized labor operates in Brooklyn to provide an outlet for union-label goods and through its competition to stimulate other storekeepers to stock them. This store paid 4 per cent dividends in 1924 and 1925. Since then reports do not indicate a very flourishing condition. In 1926 the Label Council directed a publicity campaign against the Board of Education for purchasing foreign-made chairs for the city schools. In 1928 a state organization for promoting the union label was formed. In that year $4,000 and in 1929 $6,500 was spent on broadcasting publicity. The picture, "Labor's Reward," which had been made for the national campaign in 1925, was shown to classes in economics in

New York schools during 1929. In 1930 the cost of radio programs was increased to $7,320.

The paid representatives in Pittsburgh and Boston spend much of their time visiting merchants to persuade them to stock union-label goods. In Chicago the radio is used for publicity purposes; the Teachers' Union cooperates in bringing speakers into the public schools; and union-label exhibits are staged at public exhibitions.

The work of the Label Department is affected by two main conditions. One is limited finances. The annual per capita taxes of the department were decreased from $48,901 in 1923 to $31,953 in 1931.[7] The department has been living in excess of its income for a number of years, using up its surplus funds. The other limiting factor is the principle of trade union autonomy. Each international union has exclusive ownership and control of its union label, shop card, button, or whatever other insignia it uses. The unions using labels are not prone to delegate power to the department or to entrust it with more than the general work of propaganda. The department consequently does not undertake work unless requested by its international unions and refrains from giving out any information not authorized by the latter.[8]

The Committee on Labels, one of the permanent committees of the annual convention of the A. F. of L., is supplementary to the Label Department. Its main task is to consider requests of different unions for the support of their labels. Through this committee various unions

[7] The salary of the secretary-treasurer is $7,500 a year.

[8] In 1929 the department sent questionnaires to its member unions, inquiring as to the methods used by them and their relative success, and asking for suggestions as to how the department could be of service. Only six unions out of 45 replied, and none appeared desirous of using the facilities of the department.

for a number of years presented their case to the conventions of the Federation. But the work of the committee has now become negligible. At the conventions of 1929 and 1930 only one resolution was submitted to the committee. It was offered by the Union of Retail Clerks and stipulated that workers should buy only in stores employing union clerks. In 1931 and 1932 no resolutions were submitted. This reflects the increasing feeling on the part of international unions that such appeals to the conventions have become useless, and that the reports of the Committee on Labels are little more than "a mere gesture of convention hall formality."

It is impossible to measure the growth of the union label because no information is available concerning the amount of union-label goods distributed from year to year. Manufacturers having agreements with unions to use the label on their products are not forced to do so and often do not use it. The issuance of labels is usually controlled by locals making agreements with employers, and these do not always report fully to their international unions. Furthermore, where the label is imprinted by a stamp there is no check upon the number of articles so stamped.

It is admitted, however, that the results of the propaganda for the union label have fallen short of what had been hoped for. Some of the unions which at one time were most active in pushing the label, such as those of the cigarmakers and brewery workers, have been declining. Other unions which placed much hope in the label, such as the union of hotel and restaurant employees, have not been successful in securing its acceptance. Only a few unions in the A. F. of L., such as the

Boot and Shoe Workers' Union, the Bakery Workers Union, and especially the unions in the printing trades, have had satisfactory results. They have spent large sums of money in advertising their respective labels.[9]

The failure of the A. F. of L. to make the label the "most powerful weapon of unionism" is due to several causes. Union members do not always ask for labeled goods because of indifference,[10] fear to disclose their union affiliations, the inconvenience of finding such goods, or price differentials. The general public has still less interest in union-made goods. Even in working men's families the women are notoriously hard to win over to the cause despite the women's trade union auxiliaries.

Even where the will to buy union-label goods exists, it is not easy to exercise it. Storekeepers do not make any effort to push such articles and often they are not available even if the customer insists. The growth of the chain stores has also proved a serious obstacle, for usually chains do not stock union-made goods. An effort was made to get the Atlantic and Pacific stores to handle union-made bread, but in vain. Union-label advertising finds it increasingly difficult to compete with commercial advertising. Labeled commodities are often slightly more expensive than others and sometimes are of inferior quality.

Suggestions have often been made to make the label more effective by changing the methods of its administration. Under present conditions of trade autonomy it is

[9] The Allied Printing Trades Label has been described as the most extensively advertised label in the world.

[10] An interesting illustration is furnished by the campaign to make all union officials use stationery made of paper bearing the union watermark.

possible for a firm to obtain labels from one union while it is on the "unfair list" of other unions.[11] Furthermore, a worker cannot be expected to know over 57 varieties of labels, cards, buttons, and other insignia used by over 60 unions, and to recognize them from the various spurious and unapproved labels. Besides, the numerous labels and their lax administration often give rise to abuses which weaken even in union members the faith in the label which is necessary for its success.[12]

To remedy these defects it was proposed as far back as 1915 that the A. F. of L. adopt a universal monogram label. In 1922 a scheme was advanced to use the label of the A. F. of L. on all union-made goods as a means of simplifying their recognition. In 1927 a resolution was introduced that no label be issued by a union to a firm unless such firm was fair to all crafts employed in its various departments. But these proposals were rejected by the conventions. The reasons are that a universal label is contrary to many state laws, that it would be impossible to devise a proper design, and above all that a universal label is not in harmony with trade autonomy.

II. THE BUILDING TRADES DEPARTMENT

While the Federation utilizes the Label Department as a means for educating the workers and the general public to the use of union-made goods, its purpose in maintaining the other three departments is concerned more with the industrial struggles of the affiliated unions and with collective bargaining. In the Building Trades

[11] See *Proceedings of 47th Annual Convention of the A. F. of L.*, 1927, p. 232.

[12] At the 1930 convention of the A. F. of L., Weaver, the secretary of the Committee on Labels, summed up the situation by saying that the condition with regard to the label was "a crime." See *Proceedings of 50th Annual Convention of the A. F. of L.*, 1930, p. 231.

Department two problems are involved—the control of local councils and the settlement of jurisdictional disputes.[13]

The structure of the department has not changed much since it was first organized. Membership is open only to international unions affiliated with the A. F. of L. whose members are employed in the erection, repair, or alteration of buildings. In 1932 there were 16 unions in the department, with about half a million members.[14] This represents a considerable decrease in membership since 1929 due to the secession of the bricklayers in 1927, the carpenters in 1929, and the electrical workers in 1931.

The department is governed by a president and a secretary-treasurer elected triennially and six vice-presidents elected annually, forming together the executive council, and by a convention which meets each year immediately before the A. F. of L. convention and in the same city. Each international union is allowed to be represented in the convention by one delegate for 4,000 members or less, and an additional delegate for each additional 4,000 members. On roll-call votes organiza-

[13] The various craft unions in the building trades at an early stage in their development promoted the idea of concerted action to deal with employers. Before 1900 building trades councils composed of delegates from local unions of the trade had been formed in many cities and towns. By means of the sympathetic strike as a weapon in enforcing the closed shop, these councils helped the unions to gain considerable strength. However, the problem of settling jurisdictional disputes in the trades was a major difficulty with which the councils could not cope. For many years the American Federation of Labor attempted to deal with these disputes; but the building trades unions resented the participation of other trades in their affairs. After various attempts the Building Trades Department was organized in 1908 to deal with the problem. See also Chap. IV, pp. 93-95.

[14] These unions were almost all those included in the building trades group given in Appendix A, pp. 476-78.

tions with seven or more delegates are entitled to two votes per delegate, a provision which was inserted to placate the larger unions. Revenue is derived from initiation fees of $100 and a per capita tax of nine cents per member per year. The president and secretary receive salaries of $9,000 a year each. Members of the executive council receive transportation and $15 a day when on departmental business. The department's principal expenses are for salaries, meetings of the executive council, officers' traveling expenses, clerical help, office rent, and other administrative outlays. The department does not contribute to strikes or organization work.[15]

The department functions in part through local and state building trades councils to which it issues charters. Certain rules for the conduct of these councils have been formulated. Some of the rules are that local councils must admit only local unions in good standing in international unions affiliated with the department, and that no local council can enter into an agreement with an employers' association providing for compulsory arbitration, against sympathetic strikes, or for union men to work with non-union men.

Local building trades councils in their turn have certain powers over local unions. Demands for wage increases or for shorter hours must be endorsed by the local councils, as no strike is permitted without the council's consent. When a strike has been declared, the local building trades council is placed in complete charge. Another function of the local council is to distribute quarterly the working cards which are issued by the department to all members in good standing.

[15] The income of the department was $94,902 in 1927-28, $71,853 in 1928-29, and $68,977 in 1929-30.

The local building trades council has been one of the most powerful institutions in the trade union world. Because of this, it tends to limit and undermine the authority of the international unions. The councils have an unusual advantage because uniform national practices are peculiarly difficult to enforce in the building trades owing to the decentralization of the industry and to the fact that competition between different localities plays a small part in the industry.

The national unions in the building trades have consequently had to contend with much antagonistic localism fostered and supported by the local building trades councils. A few of the very strong building trades unions —notably the bricklayers' union—have succeeded in laying down national policies for their locals by fighting the councils. The bricklayers and the carpenters have maintained an independent position, ruthlessly following their own interests and trampling upon the rules and rights of lesser trades. The councils on the other hand have attempted to give the weaker and less skilled trades protection and assistance, but the process has entailed a great deal of warfare between the weak and the strong labor organizations.

The department was expected to eliminate this warfare, but it has not been entirely successful. It has not succeeded in harmonizing the interests of the stronger with those of the weaker unions or in reconciling "nationalism" and "localism." But it has mitigated friction and helped the local councils to stand against the stronger unions. The officers of the department spend a great deal of time assisting local councils in adjusting disputes between local unions, between unions and employers, and between the councils themselves and the international unions. However, inasmuch as its structure recognizes only national unions and gives no representation to the councils, the department in fact strengthens the international unions.

The main business of the Building Trades Department is concerned with jurisdictional disputes between its unions. The persistence and multiplicity of such disputes in the building trades are caused by the changes which have been going on in the industry affecting simultaneously tools, processes, and materials. Structural steel, electricity, concrete, imitation stone, the displacement of wood, changes in decoration and architecture, the assembling of factory-made units on the job, the cement or plaster gun, the paint spray, and other innovations have played havoc with old demarcation lines, long acquired skills, and comparative wage levels. Confusion has arisen because at times well-established unions would resist the introduction of certain processes or materials. New unions would be chartered of workmen who would do the work at less pay. The older unions would then decide that, since they could not ward off the new methods, they would try to control them. A jurisdictional dispute would result which might continue for many years. An even more common cause of dispute occurs when unions reach out to take in new processes or materials which are far removed from the terms of their original jurisdictional claims.[16] Differences in local custom might also flare up into a national dispute.[17] These

[16] The carpenters laid claim to the work of installing metal doors, window frames, and trim when the wooden article began to become obsolete. Carpentering by tradition and skill was a woodworking trade. The sheet metal workers' claim to this work was logically better founded.

[17] In New York, for instance, lathers were accustomed to setting metal rods in concrete for concrete buildings; elsewhere the structural iron workers made good their claim to the work.

internecine fights have been stimulated by the number of specialized crafts seeking work, the short duration of each job, and the highly seasonal character of the industry. These factors offset the advantages of a rapidly expanding industry in which the unions have controlled the number of workers through apprenticeship rules. As a result, competition for the pay envelope has at all times been keen.

During the war, owing to the demand for labor and to the industrial truce between the unions and the government, jurisdictional disputes subsided. Prompted by a desire to perpetuate this truce, the American Institute of Architects in 1918 sent a committee to the Building Trades Department to offer assistance in devising machinery for settling jurisdictional disputes. As a result the National Board of Jurisdictional Awards, a "supreme court of the building industry," was created early in 1919.[18] Its effectiveness, however, was impaired by the withdrawal of the Brotherhood of Carpenters and Joiners after the first year because a jurisdictional award went against it. This meant that some of the more important disputes could not be settled. However, the Board had a decidedly moderating influence on industrial strife and jurisdictional strikes.[19]

Nevertheless, there was much discontent with the Board. In 1922 the American Institute of Architects antagonized the unions by declaring in favor of the open shop. Many of the awards of the Board were said to be

[18] This Board included one representative of the architects, one of the American Engineering Council, two of the Associated General Contractors, one of the National Building Trades Employers' Association, and three from the Building Trades Department. The secretary of the department was made secretary of the Board without the right to vote.

[19] See William Haber, *Industrial Relations in the Building Industry*, pp. 180-90.

ambiguous.[20] The Board also encountered difficulty in getting its awards adopted by employers who hesitated to antagonize powerful unions. The situation was made more difficult in February 1927 when the Board renewed several recommendations (first made in 1922) which tended to strengthen its powers. These were that members of the two professional societies—the architects and engineers—should stipulate in all specifications and contracts drawn up by them that the work be done in accordance with the Board's decisions; that general contractors and employers should require of their sub-contractors the performance of work in accordance with these decisions; and finally that each international union which was a member of the department should instruct its locals not to work with locals of any union refusing to abide by its awards. These recommendations put the Building Trades Department in a difficult position.

The situation was further complicated by the carpenters' offer to reaffiliate, provided the decisions of the Board affecting them be eliminated from the record. The department was thus confronted with the dilemma of either repudiating the Board or again failing to secure the reaffiliation of the carpenters. The department chose the former course. The reason given for withdrawal from the Board was the failure of the employers and professional associations to carry out its recommendations.[21] After relations between the department and the Board had been severed, attempts were made to form local

[20] The bricklayers complained because of the decision granting the operative plasterers the right to set and install certain types of artificial stone which the bricklayers claimed no mere plasterer could successfully perform. Behind such decisions they saw not judicial fairness, but the log-rolling of labor cliques.

[21] See *Proceedings of 21st Annual Convention of the Building Trades Department*, 1927, pp. 77-78.

boards of jurisdictional awards in different localities in order to eliminate jurisdictional strikes. Certain international unions protested against this on the grounds that no two local councils would settle questions in exactly the same way and would thus further confuse the situation.

The number of disputes in the building industry had been declining since 1925.[22] However, in 1929 there was a great increase in jurisdictional disputes. The number of cases increased to 212 involving 44,198 workers. Aside from changes in industry, scarcity of employment due to the decline in building activity was a factor aggravating these disputes. Each trade had to fight for as much work as possible. The need for national machinery to meet the issue was strongly felt. The efforts to settle disputes on a local basis gave the department further incentive to take steps to re-establish national machinery in order to reassert the supremacy of the international unions. Employers in the building trades too were calling for relief from disputes and strikes.

After several conferences during 1930 between contractors, officers of the international unions, and the department, a plan was evolved which resulted in the formation of a Board of Trade Claims. This new Board consists of the Executive Council of the Building Trades Department and an equal number from the National Association of Building Trades Employers. The professional societies, which had made themselves unpopular with the building trades unions, are not represented. The Board may entertain claims sent in by international unions only. Its function is not to arbitrate, but to formulate the question to be arbitrated. Each party to a dispute

[22] In 1928 there were 134 disputes involving 19,965 workers, compared to 194 disputes and 56,249 workers in 1927. *Monthly Labor Review*, July 1928, p. 88; July 1930, p. 130.

names an arbitrator and the arbitrators choose an umpire. If the Board finds that the decision is clear, concise, and in line with the question *as stated*, it approves the award and fixes the date upon which it shall go into effect. If the Board decides the award is not clear, the decision is sent back to the arbitrators. To reconcile the principle of national uniformity with local differences in customs, all decisions are made uniformly effective in all localities. However, the award is not applied in any community where a different state of affairs satisfactory to employers and employees prevails.[23] The effectiveness of the Board has not yet been tested, owing to the unusual industrial situation caused by the depression.

The Board of Claims is weakened by the fact that the three largest unions in the building trades are not in the department. The bricklayers withdrew in 1927 because the convention of that year upheld the strike which the Baltimore Building Trades Council had waged against bricklayers, partly in order to force the bricklayers' local union to join the council, and partly in order to enforce an award of the National Board concerning marble work. The carpenters left in 1929, formally because their demand to reduce the per capita tax was not granted, but really because they preferred freedom of action in jurisdictional disputes. The electrical workers dropped out in April 1931 because they were opposed to the participation of employers, particularly of the general builders

[23] Local boards of claims may be set up in localities where a building trades council and an employers' association exist, to determine claims *temporarily*, between meetings of the National Board. Local boards must meet to hear disputes within 72 hours, and must render a decision within another 72 hours. No local strikes over jurisdictional claims are permitted. Finally, it is recommended to architects and contractors that the decisions of the Board be *observed* in drawing up specifications.

and contractors,[24] in the settlement of jurisdictional disputes. On May 7, 1931 the chief executives of these three unions signed an agreement which provided for close co-operation in any action undertaken by any one of the three unions for the redress of grievances. Their local unions are instructed not to embark on any local action until the matter has been considered by the three presidents. If any of the three unions is attacked in a future jurisdictional dispute, it will have as allies the two other most powerful unions in the industry.

The Building Trades Department is almost entirely occupied with mediating disputes and assisting local councils in disputes with employers.[25] At some of its conventions unionization and the establishment of local building trades councils in the South have been urged, but no action has been taken. The Journeymen Stone Cutters, following the Bedford Cut Stone decision, asked that an assessment be levied for the establishment of a legal fund. The officers of the department investigated the cost of maintaining a legal department and found it would take about $10,000 a year. They decided to recommend the project to the A. F. of L. At the time, al-

[24] The general contractor, in the opinion of the Electrical Workers' Union, is merely a broker, a middleman, often a speculator, interested in obtaining the maximum profit out of both sub-contractor and workers, with no interest in maintaining union standards. The electrical workers maintain that agencies inside the labor movement—the president of the department or the Executive Council of the A. F. of L.—should make decisions in jurisdictional disputes.

[25] It has urged all member unions and local councils to secure the five-day week in their agreements as a means of reducing unemployment. When the National Association of Building Trades Employers in 1929 denounced the five-day week as another instance of arbitrary restriction and asked the department to join in a factual study to determine its wisdom in view of the difficulties of the building industry, the department replied that the question lay outside its jurisdiction and with the international unions exclusively.

though there was a surplus of $100,000 in the department treasury, no further steps were taken to set up a legal fund or to urge the subject on the A. F. of L. Neither has the department taken much interest in the larger questions of the construction industry, such as stabilization or the problem of housing for the people.

Although there is only a small amount of national legislation affecting the building trades, the department plays some part as a lobbying organization. It usually confines itself to supporting the legislative program of the A. F. of L.; but during 1930 and 1931 it was especially active in helping to secure the passage of the Prevailing Rate of Wages Law.

The usefulness of the department in settling internal disputes and in assisting local councils has not been uniform. The department has been unable to keep in line the carpenters—who make up the strongest single union—and the bricklayers and the electrical workers. But the weaker unions lean on the department because of the protection it affords them against absorption by the stronger unions. The effectiveness of the department in helping localities become strong union centers is difficult to judge. It did not prevent San Francisco employers from introducing the open shop and breaking up the power of the building trades council in 1921; it has not played any part in the vicissitudes of collective bargaining in Chicago. Indeed, in Chicago and New York, the building trades councils have gone their own way in defiance of the department.

The withdrawal of the three largest unions has been interpreted by some as a sign of disintegration of the department. The extent to which the department may be injured by their withdrawal will depend on their ability to co-operate. They have weak spots which the department can take advantage of. While they are large in numbers, they perform only a few of the operations necessary in erecting a building. Furthermore, they have rival aspirants for their work among the unions in the department. The iron workers, sheet metal workers, plumbers, and plasterers could manage to perform quite a number of the operations claimed by the "big three." Their position is thus by no means impregnable, and the department is not as ineffective as it might appear.

III. THE METAL TRADES DEPARTMENT

The Metal Trades Department, like the Building Trades Department, includes international unions, local trades councils, district councils, and state councils.[26] Each local, state, and district council has one vote in the annual convention. This leaves control to the international unions, which are represented by one delegate for the first 4,000 members or fraction thereof, and an additional delegate for each additional 4,000 members. Voting power is allotted to the international unions in the ratio of one vote for each 100 members or fraction thereof. The annual conventions are held just preceding the A. F. of L. convention, as are those of the Building Trades Department and Label Department.

The officers of the department are a full-time president, secretary-treasurer, and an executive board elected by the convention. The income is obtained from an initiation fee of $50 and from dues which are now 12 cents

[26] In 1930 the department included 14 unions which paid dues for 223,292 members. The unions were those of the blacksmiths, boilermakers, electrical workers, structural iron workers, machinists, molders, metal polishers, plumbers, and a few others. All these unions paid on only a portion of their membership. More recent figures are not available.

per member per year. The two full-time officers receive a salary of $7,500 each. No paid organizers or representatives are employed.[27]

The Metal Trades Department has been almost free from jurisdictional disputes. Since 1925 only three have been mentioned in the officers' reports, and since 1928 none. One reason why disputes are infrequent is that new unions having claims in conflict with unions already in the department are denied membership until a satisfactory adjustment has been made.

The main purpose of the department is to promote organization and joint action in dealing with employers. It has inaugurated many joint organization campaigns.[28] In 1926 it sponsored the campaign among the Detroit automobile workers. In 1927 it started a campaign in the State of Arizona. The presidents of the unions of machinists, electrical workers, plumbers, boilermakers, and blacksmiths all pledged that their organizations would contribute $100 a month for half a year. This money was given to one full-time organizer to cover both salary and expenses. He spent six months in Arizona, where the workers were scattered over such a large area that he accomplished little. Other proposed projects, such as extensive campaigns in Chicago and in the airplane plants, or for a 44-hour week in the "entire industry," have either been entirely beyond the means and powers of the department or are still under consideration.

The tasks of the department have become increasingly

[27] The income of the department was $22,656 in 1928, $25,235 in 1929, and $27,171 in 1930.

[28] Before the war it launched them in Los Angeles, Erie, Cleveland, and at the Baldwin Locomotive Works outside Philadelphia, but without substantial results.

difficult in recent years. The substitution of machines for both skilled and unskilled labor has made rapid progress, in the metal trades particularly. Semi-skilled operatives and women employed on repetitive operations are supplanting the skilled worker. The wide range of the industry[29] makes uniform tactics in organizing almost impossible. Besides, the efficient national and local associations of metal trades employers, which are for the most part hostile to trade unions and which have widely applied both aggressive and conciliatory methods for keeping their employees out of the unions, have also greatly hampered the work of the department.

The local councils of the Metal Trades Department have not as much power for joint collective action as those of the Building Trades Department.[30] Before 1914 and again after the war, local councils were active in conducting strikes and organizing campaigns. To curb their activities the department ruled that whenever a local council, by a majority vote, determines to inaugurate a general strike, the participating locals must secure the sanction of their international unions before pledging support. To counteract this, the councils have tried to establish the policy that agreements made by the locals affiliated with a council should terminate at the same

[29] The industrial range of the Metal Trades Department includes potentially the manufacture of machinery, locomotives, automobiles, airplanes, ships and battleships, radios, phonographs, stoves and furnaces, refrigerators, tools, hardware, all kinds of recording devices, clocks, gages, automobile accessories; and the erection and installation of machinery, as well as of munition plants and arsenals.

[30] Prior to 1912 efforts were made by the unions to give the local council authority to compel all affiliated locals to join in conducting strikes endorsed by a majority of the council. In 1912 the constitution of the department was altered to permit of such compulsory joint action. The molders protested against it to the A. F. of L. and the department was forced to retract its action.

time. Also, when a council has adopted a policy of general agreements with employers, locals are not permitted to enter into separate agreements without the consent of the council, on penalty of expulsion from the council. However, enforcement of these principles has been lax, as only a few local metal trades councils have been able to negotiate joint agreements with employers.

The Metal Trades Department has achieved its greatest effectiveness in the navy yards. Of about 50,000 metal workers employed in the various mechanical departments of the government, about 40,000 come under the Navy Department, and some 20,000 of these are members of the unions affiliated with the department. The wage rates of these employees are fixed by the Navy Wage Reviewing Board, on which the Metal Trades Department is represented. The Reviewing Board annually receives data collected by local boards in navy yards. Its recommendations to the Secretary of the Navy for the next year's wage scale are based upon these local reports. These recommendations are not mandatory, but they resulted in substantial wage increases for 1926 and smaller ones for 1928. As a result of dissatisfaction with the methods of collecting the wage data in 1928, various changes in procedure were ordered by the Navy Department, in accordance with suggestions made by the Metal Trades Department. Chief among the changes was the provision authorizing representatives of employees to accompany the officers when gathering local wage data and the provision that data should be collected also from private establishments performing strictly comparable work.[31]

[31] The Metal Trades Department has also been active in trying to secure employment for the navy yards. Even before the present depression employment was shrinking because of the limitation of arma-

The system of collective negotiations in the navy yards, on the whole, has worked well. Complaints are made, however, that it has not stimulated an increase in trade union membership. The employees are prone to accept the wage boards without giving the unions proper credit for them. As organized and unorganized workers benefit equally, it has been increasingly difficult to maintain union membership. In the past few years the "company union" has made its appearance in the navy yards, and the Metal Trades Department has had to rule that no local council may permit its members to vote in elections for shop committees which are also participated in by non-union employees. Trade union organization among navy yard employees is far from complete. This means that the unions must struggle continuously to monopolize the channels of representation.

The unions of the Metal Trades Department at one time were active in reducing working hours to ten, nine, and eight a day. But progress apparently halted there. The five-day week is still rare in this group of indus-

---

ments, the government's economy program, and a tendency on the part of the government to let contracts to private firms. In 1929 the government ordered construction on 15 cruisers. Through the efforts of the Metal Trades Department and the A. F. of L., provision was made that eight of the cruisers and all their parts should be constructed in the navy yards. This was later amended to provide that "all work customarily done in navy yards" should be performed there. In 1930, because of the London Disarmament Conference, the construction program was postponed. Two delegations from the Metal Trades Department visited President Hoover, who soon declared himself in favor of a modernization program. The 1930 convention of the Metal Trades Department adopted a number of resolutions bearing on the question. They opposed all forms of propaganda which interfered with a sane, well-balanced program of national defense; favored the full upkeep of all navy yards and arsenals; proposed a modernization program for three battleships; objected to the employment of enlisted men on repair work; and proposed the insertion of a clause in the Naval Appropriations bill which would prohibit the employment of any person not a citizen of the United States on work paid for by the United States Treasury.

tries, though the scarcity of employment is sharpening the demand for a reduction in hours both by the day and the week. Outside of the department's general interest in this movement, its activities in the last five years have been mainly concerned with negotiations on behalf of government employees and with lobbying for more favorable legislation governing the retirement of federal employees. In this work it has co-operated with the A. F. of L.[32]

In the daily business of the department the officers[33] confer with government officials on matters concerning employees in navy yards, naval stations, arsenals, and the Panama Canal Zone. They also confer with other departments of the A. F. of L., other organizations located in Washington, and visiting officials. When Congress is in session much time is devoted to lobbying. A monthly metal trades bulletin is published and distributed free, at an annual cost of $700. It contains articles of general interest to be republished by trade union papers, but does not carry news of the department's activities in detail. The officers do some traveling, attending conventions of affiliated organizations and visiting metal trades councils.

IV. THE RAILWAY EMPLOYEES DEPARTMENT

The Railway Employees Department has fostered more joint action than the other three departments in collective bargaining, in strikes, and in studying the economic problems of the industry, such as stabilizing employment. The department underwent important changes in structure in 1912, and again in 1926. It now consists of nine international unions which are affiliated with the

[32] See Chap. XV.

[33] James O'Connell has been president of the department since 1908. John P. Frey is secretary.

American Federation of Labor and which are divided into three autonomous sections. Section one includes the Switchmen's Union; section two, the six shop crafts—the blacksmiths, boilermakers, carmen, machinists, sheet metal workers, and electrical workers; while section three consists of the firemen and oilers, and maintenance of way employees. The constitution provides that other unions may be admitted to sections one and three, but the membership of section two is final.[34]

The department charters regional organizations known as system federations. A system federation is composed of three or more separate crafts employed on a railroad which is under one general management, such as the Baltimore and Ohio or the New York Central. Each separate craft on a railroad system elects a general chairman, and the chairmen of all the crafts constitute the executive board of the system federation. In addition each system federation elects at its annual convention a president, vice-president, and secretary-treasurer. The purpose of a system federation is to consider the common interests of all the shop crafts on a particular road.

Until 1926 the system federations exercised real power in the department. The delegates to the department conventions were elected by the crafts of the system federations. The executive boards of the various system federations formed a General Conference Committee which had the final decision in the conduct and settlement of strikes. Largely as a result of the experience of the 1922 strike, the center of responsibility was shifted in 1926. The officers of the department felt that the rank and file had forced them into a disastrous strike, contrary

[34] The plumbers, painters, and molders have tried on several occasions to gain admission to the department, but their applications have been consistently rejected to avoid jurisdictional complications.

to their better judgment, and that the department had been handicapped in negotiations for its settlement because ultimate responsibility rested not with them but with the large and unwieldy General Conference Committee. The presidents of the affiliated international unions also objected because the General Conference Committee favored regional interests at the expense of craft interests. They pointed out that most of the shop crafts belonged to international unions, the majority of whose members worked in other industries and were reluctant to vote funds to support the costly wage movements and strikes sponsored by the system federations.

The changes made in the constitution in 1926 gave authority to the international unions. The system federations still elect delegates to the conventions and these delegates vote on all questions. But on roll-call votes the presidents of the international unions cast the votes of their respective unions, after considering the issues in caucus meetings. As the roll is called on important issues, matters of major consequence are thus decided by the action of the crafts and of their international presidents. In taking this step the Railway Employees Department moved away from its original concept of a more or less centralized federation of railway workers towards a federation of autonomous international unions.

The department is governed by a president, secretary-treasurer, and an executive council of nine, consisting of the presidents of the international unions. The officers are elected by the conventions, which were held biennially before 1926 and quadrennially since then.

The unions of the department grew rapidly during 1919-21, but the 1922 strike[35] resulted in a heavy loss

[35] See Chap. IX, pp. 205-10.

of membership. Company unions on a large number of roads increasingly made inroads into membership, which was estimated at about 384,000 in 1926. No figures have been published since then.[36]

The department has not been entirely free from jurisdictional disputes, but as it prohibits all jurisdictional strikes these disputes have not inconvenienced railroads and the public as have those in the Building Trades Department. The settlement of disputes begins locally. A committee of one from each craft employed in a shop decides by a majority vote any dispute which arises; but where there is disagreement the case is taken to the president of the department and to the Executive Council.

During 1919-20, when the United States Railroad Administration operated under a national agreement with the unions, officers of the department represented the component unions before the United States Board of Railroad Wages and Working Conditions. Since the abrogation of that agreement, collective bargaining has been carried on through the system federations. The executive board of each system federation acts as a conference committee with full power to negotiate with the management of its road on wages and other system questions. But before seeking an increase in wages or a change of working rules, the system federation must obtain the

[36] On June 1, 1922 the department adopted a budget of $10,000 a month. In November this was scaled down to $7,000; on Apr. 1, 1923 to $5,000; and on Mar. 1, 1924 to $2,950. However, this budget has not taken care of all expenses, and "emergency bills" have been pro-rated among the component organizations. The maintenance of way employees and the firemen and oilers pay a per capita tax of one and a half cents per month, while the six shop craft unions pay their pro-rated share of the budget plus emergency expenses. No financial statements have been made public since 1926. See *Proceedings of 7th Convention of the Railway Employees Department*, 1926, p. 89.

sanction of the department. Thus the department keeps control over all wage movements. It also undertakes the task of preparing briefs for wage arbitration proceedings. Where a system federation exists, no single craft can make a separate wage agreement without obtaining the consent of the department.

The Railway Employees Department is the chief protagonist of union management co-operation. This form of employer-employee relations was first introduced in 1923 on the Baltimore and Ohio and is now in operation, though in varying degree of completeness, on five roads. The basis of union management co-operation is the willingness of management to regard the union as an integrated part of the industry and to co-operate with it in promoting the welfare of the industry. The policy of co-operation is carried on through a complex machinery. Joint local meetings are held every two weeks or oftener and are attended by an equal number of representatives from local shop committees of workers[37] and from the shop management. Next in order are the joint system conferences. These are held every three months, or on emergency call. The workers are represented by the chairman, secretary, and executive board of the system federation, and the management by the heads of the various departments. Local joint meetings and system conferences do not deal with grievances or disputes but with questions connected with job analysis, standardization of processes, tools and equipment, proper routing of materials, economical use of supplies, conditions of safety and sanitation, improving the quality of work, securing new business for the railroad, and stabilizing em-

[37] In each railroad shop, there is a shop committee composed of elected officers of the various organized crafts.

ployment. The assumption is that the workers can help management to improve production processes, eliminate waste, and increase productivity, and that in return management will not only share the resulting benefits with the workers but acknowledge the collective equality of industrial status which the relationship implies. It is generally admitted that union management co-operation has been effective in improving working conditions on the roads on which it has been tried. It has also focussed attention on the need and methods of stabilizing employment.

Since 1929 the Railway Employees Department has concerned itself mainly with unemployment relief and the stabilization of employment. It has advocated the eight-hour day and the five-day week, changes in the apprenticeship regulations to cut down the supply of trained workmen, and an annual two weeks' vacation with pay for all shopmen. It has also supported the larger program of the Railway Labor Executives' Association.[38]

V. SUMMARY

The departments have not changed the essential character of the Federation, although they have appreciably affected its work and tactics. While they have promoted a few amalgamations, they have not obliterated craft lines. Two of the departments have tended to minimize the extent and severity of jurisdictional disputes. While they do not carry on collective bargaining on an industrial basis, three of them provide a method for strengthening inter-union action. In the Railway Employees Department there is a tendency toward coordinated action on a national scale. All of them allow

[38] See pp. 457-58.

for joint local action through trade councils and otherwise, but their effect is to hold localism in check and to strengthen the hands of the national unions. Larger departmental action is hindered by the insistence of the latter upon their autonomy. Neither is there co-operation between the departments, though it has been advocated. The departments are thus primarily supplementary mechanisms which facilitate and enlarge the work of the Federation.

CHAPTER XV

SECURING REMEDIAL LEGISLATION

Even before the A. F. of L. came into being, American trade unionists were already aware of the importance of laws in influencing their status and problems. The common desire to obtain benefits through special legislation was a factor tending to hold the A. F. of L. together during its early years. Although its industrial program overshadowed its legislative activities between 1899 and 1904, the judicial decisions of 1906-08 and the political developments of 1910-14 reversed the tendency. In recent years the interest of the A. F. of L. in its legislative functions has been steadily growing.

I. SOCIAL RIGHTS AND LEGISLATIVE PROGRAMS

In the constitution of the Federation there are three statements which affect its legislative activities. The preamble asserts that organized workers must unite "to secure the recognition of rights to which they are justly entitled." Section 3 of Article II makes it incumbent upon the Federation "to secure legislation in the interests of the working people." Section 1 of Article IX imposes upon the Executive Council the duty "to watch legislative measures directly affecting the interests of working people, and to initiate, whenever necessary, such legislative action as the convention may direct." These three statements cover the three elements involved in the legislative functions of the Federation—the idea of rights by which it is guided, the kind of measures it advocates, and the methods by which it tries to obtain its ends.

The Federation has not consistently advanced any

particular theory of law or legal development. It accepts some of the concepts of American law based on the theory of natural rights. It makes frequent appeals in the name of the rights enumerated in the first nine amendments of the Constitution of the United States and in the Thirteenth Amendment, emphasizing especially those of free speech and peaceful assembly.

However, in dealing with relations growing out of private property and modern industrial life, the Federation rejects the doctrines of a fixed natural order and of absolute inalienable rights. In these matters it follows the evolutionary concept that rights and justice are relative to changing conditions and must be adapted in harmony with general economic and social needs. As guides in this process of adaptation, the Federation emphasizes the superior rights of human life as compared with the rights of property; group action as contrasted with freedom of individual contract; co-operative relations in industry as contrasted with competition; and the right to a higher standard of living as a practical substitute for the formal right to equality of opportunity.

A contradiction persists in the ideas of the Federation on the value of legal regulation in economic matters. By the logic of its existence, the Federation is a denial of laissez faire. It advocates the intervention of the state over a large area of economic life and calls for the settlement of many industrial questions by legislative methods. In the matters which come under this head the Federation regards the law as a positive and progressive force which may and can be used in developing new relations based upon large social concepts. At the same time the Federation continues to be suspicious of the law, skeptical of its efficacy, and unwilling to push further too rapidly the present limits of legal control of economic relations. Its bias is against the law and legal action as tending to limit "individual liberty" and to become a hindrance to the free growth of economic and social relations. In general terms the Federation continues to maintain that the law can never keep pace with the moral aspirations of mankind and cannot therefore be the main regulator of social relations.

The legislative activities of the Federation reflect these contradictions and have been influenced by them. Broadly, the remedial legislative demands of the Federation have usually fallen into five main groups. The first deals with methods of collective bargaining. The second relates to the protection of the labor market. The third covers the regulation of wages, hours, and working conditions. The fourth is concerned with problems of social insurance. The fifth arises from the fact that the government is itself an employer whose relations to its employees are regulated by Congress and by state legislatures.

A. Legalizing Collective Action

With the passage of the Norris-LaGuardia Anti-Injunction Act,[1] the Federation achieved the specific program to legalize trade union activities which it had begun more than a decade before. However, even assuming that the Anti-Injunction Act will not be declared unconstitutional nor interpreted away by the courts, the legal status of trade unionism still presents many problems. While the right of trade unions of a non-revolutionary character to exist is recognized today,[2] and has been for

[1] See Chap. X, pp. 273-78.

[2] Edwin E. Witte, *The Government in Labor Disputes*, 1932, pp. 12-14.

several decades, and while collective bargaining is generally regarded as lawful and even praiseworthy, the right of trade unions to use the methods they have developed to obtain and enforce collective contracts remains uncertain. The legality of a strike is still contingent on its purpose, which may be declared unlawful according to the judgment of the courts. Sympathetic strikes, picketing, and boycotting have been severely restricted by court decisions, and may still be enjoined. The opportunity of the courts to interpret "threats and intimidation" in relation to the conduct of strikers so as to obstruct the success of a strike remains unrestricted. Damage suits and criminal prosecutions against strikers and active unionists remain a possibility.

The Federation is aware of this situation. Its present program calls for the repeal or amendment of the anti-trust laws, and it regards as important state laws limiting the use of the injunction after the model of the Norris-LaGuardia Act, because the majority of injunctions are issued by state courts.

The suggestion has been often made that the Federation should try to change the substantive law through statutory legislation which would clearly define the legal status of trade unionism and trade union activities. This line of attack was followed by Gompers between 1900 and 1906, and advocated by some labor unions after the war. In 1923 the Portland convention went on record for a constitutional amendment guaranteeing the right of workers to organize and to act collectively. But since 1925 the Federation has ceased to entertain such ideas because of the seemingly insuperable legal difficulties[3] and because such an approach is not in accord with the

[3] The same, pp. 280-81.

philosophy of the A. F. of L. The Federation contends that it is not asking for special privileges or immunities, that it is opposed to "class legislation," and that it only wishes its members to enjoy the rights guaranteed by the Constitution, especially under the Thirteenth Amendment.

When the first avalanche of injunctions was hurled at labor, leaders and officials of the Federation attacked the courts and "judge-made law" in extreme and violent terms. Injunctions were denounced as "judicial piracy." The workers were called upon to ignore them, even to resist them, and to proceed with trade union activities in spite of them. Curbing the irresponsible power of the courts was upheld as the "paramount issue" before the American people.

But since 1925 there has been an increasing moderation in the attitude of the Federation. In 1925 the Executive Council protested against the accusation that labor was hostile to the courts, claiming that organized labor was "attached to every fundamental American institution" and did not propose "to cut down the functions of the courts."[4] In criticizing the injunctive practices of the courts, the Federation shifted to the position that the injunction had become a general problem involving a change from government by law to government by judges and that labor was not alone in seeking redress.[5] The demand for a reform of the judiciary has also been abandoned.

The Federation rejects compulsory arbitration, compulsory investigation of industrial disputes, industrial

[4] *Report of the Proceedings of the Forty-Fifth Annual Convention of the American Federation of Labor*, 1925, p. 303.

[5] *Proceedings of 51st Annual Convention of the A. F. of L.*, 1931, p. 115.

courts, and similar devices which involve limitations upon the right to strike and regulation of relations between employers and employees by law. Such proposals are variously condemned as devices to annul constitutional rights, as denials of "freedom of contract," and as entering wedges towards the "complete domination of the state over industry itself."[6]

B. Protecting the Labor Market

The Federation has given a prominent place in its program to measures intended to limit the supply of applicants for jobs. Among these are the restriction of immigration, the regulation of convict labor, the regulation of apprenticeship, vocational education, license laws, and child labor legislation. The problems falling within this group have social implications which the Federation stresses, thus bringing a popular appeal to measures which have for their primary purpose the control of the labor supply as a means of mitigating competition in the labor market.

On the question of immigration the Federation has been growing continuously more exclusionist since 1917. In 1919 it advocated the prohibition of all immigration for four years. Between 1919 and 1923 it demanded the abrogation of the "gentlemen's agreement" with Japan and the total exclusion of Japanese. During these same years it also opposed the admission of Mexican laborers to the United States and the importation of Chinese workers into Hawaii. In 1924 it supported the National Origins Law as a compromise, though it would have preferred a complete suspension of immigration for five

[6] *Proceedings of 46th Annual Convention of the A. F. of L.*, 1926, p. 38.

years. Since 1925 the Federation has gone on record for applying the quota system to Mexico and Canada, despite the interrelations of the trade unions in these countries;[7] for the exclusion of Hindus and Filipinos; for the reduction of immigration from the Eastern Hemisphere by 50 per cent; for the strict enforcement of the deportation laws; and for similar measures which would extend the area of restriction and tighten the mechanism for enforcing the law.

In contrast to the period before 1914, there are practically no unions in the Federation today which call for a more liberal immigration policy. In 1923 the International Ladies' Garment Workers' Union voiced for the last time some opposition to the extreme demands of the Federation. No such opposition has been heard in a convention of the A. F. of L. since. The technological unemployment before 1929 and the difficulties in which many unions have found themselves since have stimulated sentiment in favor of exclusion. The A. F. of L. now favors a complete cessation of immigration. Aware, however, that such a radical measure cannot be put through, the Federation is proceeding by way of compromise. It is more than ever convinced that "there is no more important question than the protection of the wage earners of the United States from excess immigration," and it is determined to "continue a most vigorous campaign to bring about as great restriction of immigration as possible."[8]

The Federation has also displayed a continuous and growing interest in the problem of contract prison labor. It has fought against the public account and contract sys-

[7] See Lewis L. Lorwin, *Labor and Internationalism*, pp. 374-79.

[8] *Proceedings of 51st Annual Convention of the A. F. of L.*, 1931, p. 407.

tems in prisons; has worked for the application of the principle of paying a fair wage to prisoners for their work; and has advocated "the state-use system" under which prison-made goods are used only by state institutions and departments and do not compete with goods made by free labor. After 23 years of agitation the Federation succeeded in obtaining its objective in the passage in December 1928 of the Hawes-Cooper Act, according to which all goods, wares, and merchandise produced or mined by convict labor come under the laws of the state into which they are shipped. The Act also provides that products of convict labor from state prisons shipped across state boundaries shall in certain cases be divested of their interstate character, thus permitting each state to enact legislation prohibiting the importation of convict-made goods from other states.

The Federation regards the Hawes-Cooper Act as "the most effective legislation secured by labor." While the number of prisoners making goods for the free market is small,[9] it seriously affects a number of trades represented in the Federation. This Act, however, is merely a step towards a solution of the problem. The next task is to achieve legislation in the states establishing the state-use system and prohibiting the importation of convict goods from other states. The Hawes-Cooper Act will become effective on January 19, 1934, and the Federation is now aiming to obtain the desired laws in as many states as possible before that date.

[9] In 1924 the Federation estimated that of 67,000 prisoners in state prisons and reformatories, some 10,740 were working under contract and public account systems making goods for sale in the open market. Over 50 per cent of these were employed in the manufacture of shirts and overalls. Other industries especially affected by prison competition are those manufacturing brooms, furniture, harness, hosiery, whips, shoes, etc.

However, other aspects of the prison problem are now needing attention. Since the passage of the Hawes-Cooper Act there has been an increasing tendency on the part of the federal government and state governments to employ prisoners in the construction of prisons. This has aroused the unions in the building trades. Similarly, the federal employees, printing trades, and garment workers are concerned about the use of prisoners in paper making, printing, and other employments even though their products are for government use only. The unions of the Federation are now forcing it to extend its demand against the employment of convict labor to the extent of denying the principles for which in the past it has stood.

Apprenticeship and vocational training have also been major concerns of the Federation for a long time.[10] In 1917 the Federation helped in securing the passage of the Smith-Hughes Act which provided for federal aid to states undertaking industrial training and which established a Federal Board for Vocational Guidance. In 1920 it supported the Industrial Rehabilitation Act for the refitting of ex-service men for industrial pursuits. In 1924 the Federation demanded that one of the commissioners on the Board for Vocational Guidance be a trade unionist, and this demand was granted by President Coolidge. The Federation has also urged all city centrals and state federations to seek representation on local and state boards of vocational education, and has supported the movement for part-time and continuation schools for workers and evening courses for adults.

Closely related to these issues is the attitude of the Federation on child labor. In 1881 the A. F. of L. de-

[10] In this category belong also laws for licensing men to practice such crafts as mining, plumbing, and barbering.

clared for state legislation forbidding the employment of children under the age of 14. By 1914 some sort of child labor legislation had been passed in most States, but the protection thereby extended to working children was inadequate, both in geographical extent and in respect to the standards set by many of the laws. After a decade of agitation, in 1916 the first federal child labor law was enacted, prohibiting the transportation between states of manufactured commodities on which children younger than 14 had worked, or on which children between 14 and 16 had worked in violation of hour standards fixed by the law. The Supreme Court, by a five to four decision in June 1918, held this law an undue extension of the power of Congress to regulate interstate commerce. The Federation then helped to obtain the passage of a law in 1919 which placed a tax of 10 per cent on the net annual profits of manufacturing establishments employing children in violation of legal standards similar to those in the first law. This law too was declared unconstitutional by the Supreme Court of the United States on May 5, 1922. The Federation was then instrumental in having introduced into Congress an amendment to the Constitution of the United States prohibiting the labor of children under 16. This was modified by the Judiciary Committee of the United States Senate to give Congress the power to regulate or prohibit the labor of persons under 18 years of age. The Federation accepted this as its own program, and the bill to submit this amendment to the states for ratification was passed by Congress the following year.

Since 1925 the Federation has urged state legislatures to ratify this constitutional amendment. But progress has been slow. Ten states—Arizona, Arkansas, California,

Montana, Wisconsin, Colorado, Oregon, Ohio, North Dakota, and Washington—had ratified by May 1933.

C. Wages, Hours, and Social Insurance

The third group of legislative demands dealing with wages and hours of labor includes three distinct parts. One is concerned with regulating the time, method, and place of wage payment, as well as protecting wages through mechanics' lien laws. As these are matters of state legislation, the Federation pursues its aims of improving such laws through the state federations. No general program is advocated in view of the variety of conditions in the several states.

The second part deals with laws fixing hours of labor and wages on government contract work. The traditional demand of American labor for an eight-hour day on all government work is still the major demand today, having been reaffirmed by the Federation in 1925. In March 1931 the Federation succeeded in having Congress pass a prevailing rate of wage law which provides that contractors and sub-contractors doing work on public buildings for the federal government and the District of Columbia in excess of $5,000 in amount must pay the rate of wages prevailing in the locality in which their work is. At present the demand of the Federation is for the application of the law to all government projects.

The third part concerns legislation regulating the hours and wages of women and minors. The Federation early in its career took the position which it holds today that working women, as well as minors, are in need of protective laws to safeguard their health and morals. On these grounds the Federation opposes the "Equal Rights" amendment to the Constitution of the United

States and advocates special legislation for women workers.

At one time the Federation was much interested in minimum wage laws for women. But after the law of the District of Columbia passed in 1918 was declared unconstitutional in 1923 by the Supreme Court of the United States on the ground that it was "a price-fixing law," the Federation did not give the issue much attention. Neither was the Federation very active in pushing federal legislation on the hours of labor of working women. In 1917 and 1918 it favored a law which would prohibit interstate and foreign commerce in articles and commodities on which females 16 years of age or over had been employed more than eight hours in one day or more than six days in any one week. But the fate of the two federal child labor laws and of the constitutional amendment on child labor discouraged the Federation from pursuing this line of attack further. Efforts in this direction, however, are now being resumed in view of recent developments in minimum wage and hours legislation.[11]

The legislative measures covered by the term social insurance include workmen's compensation laws, old-age pensions, maternity and infancy protection, and provisions against loss of wages from sickness and unemployment. It is in this field that the Federation has moved most cautiously and slowly, held back by its *a priori* distrust and fear of state action and resisting

[11] In the older laws, which were declared unconstitutional, the minimum wage was determined with reference to the cost of living. The new type of bill introduced into a number of state legislatures in 1932-33, and recently enacted in New York State, prohibits the payment of oppressive wages, and provides that the wage must be fair and reasonably commensurate with the value of service rendered. It must also be sufficient to meet the minimum cost of living necessary for health.

the impact of forces driving more vigorously in that direction. It took the Federation over two decades to recognize the value of workmen's compensation as against employers' liability laws. The Federation did not come out wholeheartedly for compensation legislation until 1909. At the same time it accepted the principle of old-age pensions and approved an ingenious though bizarre bill which provided that the War Department draft an Old-Age Home Guard Corps composed of men and women 65 years of age and over who had been citizens for at least 15 years, and who were to be paid $120 a year without being required to work.

During the years 1917-23 the Federation fought for the extension of the benefits of workmen's compensation legislation to longshoremen and other water front workers, and to seamen; for a liberal workmen's compensation act in the District of Columbia; for improving the various state compensation laws by raising the benefits, abolishing the waiting period, and bringing occupational disease within the scope of the laws. At its 1923 convention the Federation opposed insurance of industrial risks in private insurance companies and called for exclusive state insurance funds, using the Ohio Workmen's Compensation law as a model. In 1921 and again in 1923 the Federation reaffirmed its approval of old-age pensions, and the Executive Council revived the pension bill of 1909 for reconsideration by Congress. It also supported the Sheppard-Towner Maternity and Infancy Act of 1921, which provided for federal grants of one million dollars a year for five years to states providing for mothers' pensions and the care of infancy. For the first time in its history the Federation also considered the question of health insurance. The Executive Council, in its report to the convention of 1918, urged that the worker should be compensated for loss of income from illness. A special committee was appointed to study health insurance. But owing to serious disagreements on the question of compulsory state health insurance versus voluntary and trade union insurance, the matter was dropped.

The growing interest in social legislation was halted by the 1925 convention. It was declared there that city centrals and state federations were showing a "dangerous" tendency to push social laws too far. They were said to be calling for legislation on questions which properly should be dealt with through trade agreements. According to the Federation, such a tendency threatened to undermine trade union structure and to weaken trade union principles of self-reliance and self-help. This change in attitude did not affect the stand of the Federation on all issues involved in social legislation. The A. F. of L. has registered some of its largest successes in this field since 1925, such as the Longshoremen's Compensation Act of 1927 and the Workmen's Compensation Act of the District of Columbia passed in 1928. The Federation continues to work for liberalizing the federal and state workmen's compensation laws and for exclusive state insurance funds as more economical in cost and more considerate of the workers' interest than private insurance. The Federation is also demanding a restoration of the Maternity and Infancy Act of 1921, which lapsed in 1929.

The A. F. of L. has been cautious in handling the problem of old-age pensions. In 1924 it dropped all bills previously advocated and decided to study the question. In 1928 the Executive Council submitted a preliminary report on the development of old-age pension laws and recommended that the subject be studied by a government commission. In 1929 the Executive Council submitted a more elaborate report which pointed out that the problem of old-age security was "too large for private initiative," and recommended the drafting of a model compulsory state old-age pension law as a basis for an active campaign in the several states. In spite of opposition this recommendation was adopted by the convention. It was reported in 1931 that such a bill had been drafted, but it has not yet been published. Thus, 22 years after first endorsing the principle of old-age insurance and ten years after reaffirming it, the Federation has only formulated its bill. The Federation in trying to take the sting out of its demand for pensions is insisting that the term "old-age pensions" be dropped and "old-age securities" be substituted. The Federation has been consistent in its opposition to health insurance, and was biased against unemployment insurance[12] until forced by its affiliated unions to alter its position in 1932.

D. Programs for Government Employees

Many legislative demands of the Federation arise from the fact that the government is an employer of a considerable number of persons.[13] The government em-

[12] See Chap. XI.

[13] The federal government had over 568,000 employees in 1928, and its total payroll in 1932 was estimated to include over 600,000 wage earners, of whom over 310,000 were in the Post Office Department. About a quarter of a million persons are estimated to be in the employ of the 48 states, and the number of municipal and county employees runs into tens of thousands. See Herman Feldman, *A Personnel Program for the Federal Civil Service*, 1931, pp. 2-3; and also *State Government*, February 1932, published by the American Legislators' Association.

ployees form a substantial and one of the best organized groups in the Federation.[14] Thousands of other members of the Federation are working in the Bureau of Printing and Engraving, in the Panama Canal Zone, in the arsenals and navy yards. They belong to the unions of blacksmiths, boilermakers, machinists, metal polishers, painters, pattern makers, sheet metal workers, and printers. These unions have therefore an interest in the labor policies of the federal government.

The unions of government employees are dependent on legislative procedure for improving their condition for two reasons—their wages and working conditions are usually fixed by Acts of Congress, and they are forbidden to strike. Most of the unions of government workers provide in their constitutions against the use of strikes. As they are also prohibited from engaging in political campaigns, their only recourse is to legislative pressure and lobbying. This they do by maintaining legislative agents in Washington. But in addition they are eager to have the support of the A. F. of L., which adds the weight of its own political influence to their lobbying efforts.

The program of the Federation with regard to government employees includes demands for a shorter work day (such as the seven-hour day and the five-day week), for retirement legislation, for compensation laws, for higher wages and salaries, for a dismissal wage, and for the right to have unions which can voice grievances.

[14] In 1932 the total membership of these unions was 137,800, distributed as follows: International Association of Fire Fighters, 18,000; National Association of Letter Carriers, 55,000; National Federation of Rural Letter Carriers, 1,100; National Federation of Post Office Clerks, 36,000; Railway Mail Association, 20,700; American Federation of Teachers, 7,000. No membership for the newly organized American Federation of Government Employees was reported in 1932.

A large part of the legislative gains reported by the Federation include specific Acts passed by Congress increasing wages for one or another group of government employees or in some other way advancing the position of these employees.[15]

Until recently the Federation and the unions of government employees worked in harmony in their legislative demands. Since 1931, however, a serious conflict has arisen over the question of personnel classification. The Executive Council of the Federation, in its report to the 1931 convention, opposed the classification bill pending in Congress,[16] chiefly because this bill was opposed by the Metal Trades Department on the ground that it would fix the wages of apprentices, helpers, skilled artisans, skilled and unskilled laborers, and navy yard workers—that is of mechanics and laborers—whose wages were already being fixed by wage boards on the basis of trade union rates.[17] It was claimed that this bill, if enacted into law, would eventually eliminate the wage boards, and consequently trade union methods of wage fixing would be abolished. The craftsmen affected would thus be placed at the mercy of a bureau and some would be forced to work at lower rates of wages than others upon the same class of work. The Committee on Legislation at the 1931 convention of the A. F. of L. recommended that the matter be referred back to the Executive Council. However, a minority report recom-

[15] See pp. 271-72.

[16] This bill proposed the repeal of the Classification Act of 1923, the Welch Act of 1928, the Brookhart Act of 1930, etc. It recommends the establishment of an ex-officio board to be known as the Personnel Classification Board, to consist of the Director of the Budget, a member of the Civil Service Commission, and the chief of the U. S. Bureau of Efficiency. The Director of the Bureau of the Budget is to be chairman.

[17] See pp. 388-89.

mending the adoption of the conclusions of the Executive Council was endorsed by the convention.

The representatives of the National Federation of Federal Employees strongly opposed this action of the convention arguing that, in accordance with the majority report of the committee, the resolution should be referred back to the Executive Council. The Federal Employees charged the Executive Council with being unduly influenced by the Metal Trades Department without consulting representatives of their union, which was directly concerned with the legislation and which had jurisdiction over the greater part of the workers to be affected by the legislation. The Federal Employees were willing to exclude the skilled workers from the bill, but they pointed out that the opposition of the A. F. of L. to the bill as a whole endangered the principle of classification in government service. As a result of the controversy, the National Federation of Federal Employees somewhat hastily decided to withdraw from the A. F. of L. in 1932. The Executive Council chartered a new union—the American Federation of Government Employees.

E. Summary

A general survey of the legislative program of the Federation thus indicates that it calls for state action on a large scale. The chief areas of industrial life which the Federation before 1932 refused to bring under legal regulation were wages and hours of adult men workers in private industry. In this respect the Federation has differed from the labor organizations of Europe. In Germany, Austria, Belgium, and other continental countries, the trade unions favor recognition by law of collective agreements, and the legal regulation of employment relations, without giving up the right to strike.

The Federation has also differed from European labor organizations in its attitude toward social insurance. Organized labor in Europe has advocated accident, invalidity, old-age, health, and unemployment insurance. During recent years the main effort of the European labor organizations has been to integrate the laws providing for separate forms of insurance into general and comprehensive social insurance laws, as illustrated by the law passed in Germany in 1927 and in France in July 1930.[18]

The views of the Federation, however, are slowly approaching those of European labor in the matter of social insurance. On the question of old-age pensions the Federation is being forced to support state action because of the incapacity of its unions to maintain their benefits. Despite the large amounts of money spent by the unions, their provisions for disability and old-age are negligible. The increasing average age of union membership, the difficulties of raising dues and assessments, and declining membership during the depression are playing havoc with the insurance schemes of the different unions.[19] The suggestion has been made that the Federation establish a central benefit fund for all unions, but this has been rejected as impractical. The Federation has thus been forced to accept the principle of state-maintained old-age pensions regardless of its anti-state bias.

The Federation has clung with greater tenacity to its policy of opposing the legal regulation of wages and hours—the main objective of collective bargaining. But on this question too the Federation is running into dif-

[18] See Mollie Ray Carroll, *Unemployment Insurance in Germany*, rev. ed. 1930; and Paul H. Douglas, "The French Social Insurance Act," *The Annals*, November 1932, pp. 209-48.

[19] For specific instances, see Appendix B.

ficulties as a result of changing conditions which are forcing its component unions to advocate more state intervention in production and in price relationships. The Federation is thus being pressed by the inconsistencies in the principles on which it operates to revise its traditional ideas on the social functions of the state.

II. POLITICS AND LOBBYING

From its early days the Federation has had to consider the question of the most effective method by which it might obtain the passage of desired laws, establish favorable political conditions for collective bargaining, and win legal recognition and status. The Federation has the choice of several activities. It might confine itself to lobbying activities. It might try to elect trade unionists to office without the formality of a separate political organization, on the assumption that they would favor the aims of the Federation. It might endorse and support the Socialist Party as its political agency. It could form a separate and distinct labor party. It could ally itself with other groups on a common platform and form a larger political organization, such as the People's Party or the Farmer-Labor Party. Or it might pursue the method of supporting candidates of competing parties who promised to vote for the measures sponsored by the Federation.

The Federation wavered for a long time between these different methods. In 1906, after about 25 years of internal struggle, it adopted the policy of rewarding its friends and punishing its enemies. In 1913 it held out a vague promise for a labor party in the future.[20]

[20] The resolution adopted by the convention read: "While our political developments are encouragingly progressive and should be continued, the time has not come when with due regard for the economic movement, still

But between 1919 and 1924, in its fight against the widespread agitation for an independent labor party,[21] the Federation gave greater precision to its non-partisan policy. At the Atlantic City convention in 1919 Section 8 of Article III of the constitution of the A. F. of L. barring partisan politics from the conventions was reaffirmed, and local and state bodies were forbidden to become part of a national political party. Since 1925 the Federation has faced no real opposition to its non-partisan political policy.

A. The Technique of Lobbying

The non-partisan political method of the Federation in practice involves two kinds of activities, lobbying and political campaigning. The former falls largely to the Legislative Committee, which is an integral part of the Federation and is located in Washington. The committee consists of three officers appointed by the Executive Council of the Federation. Its task is to watch bills introduced in both houses of Congress, to analyze and classify them in their relation to the Federation, to lobby against hostile bills, and to obtain the passage of those which the Federation favors.

The task of this committee is by no means simple. Thousands of bills come before Congress each session. Of these several hundred touch on the interests of the Federation. As a rule, one of the three members of the committee devotes most of his time to office work, supervising records and correspondence. The other two spend

---

young and hopeful in organization, a distinct labor political party should be formed. We are confident that when our present political activities have fully matured, a new political party will be the logical result." See *Proceedings of 34th Annual Convention of the A. F. of L.*, 1913, p. 315.

[21] See pp. 191-95.

most of their time at the Capitol, attending hearings and interviewing Congressmen.[22]

The Legislative Committee plans and puts into effect campaigns for the passage or defeat of bills. In these campaigns the committee sometimes drafts a number of bills to be introduced in Congress. Whether supporting its own or other bills, or opposing a bill, the members of the Legislative Committee must see personally individual members of Congress and congressional committees, must appear at the hearings of these committees, and often must provide individual legislators with material bearing upon desired legislation. In all this work the committee keeps in close touch with the president of the Federation, and, in his absence, with the secretary. At the meetings of the Executive Council the work of the Legislative Committee is reviewed, and general directions are issued for its guidance.

Another phase of the lobbying activities of the Federation concerns winning the support of the administration. That large part of the work of the Federation which consists in solicitations for government employees involves the interviewing of heads of government departments and often of one or another member of the Cabinet. When the support of the President of the United States is sought, the task usually falls to the president and secretary of the Federation or to the Executive Council.

In order to increase its lobbying influence, the Federation co-operates with other economic groups. At each session of Congress the Federation supports some of the measures demanded by the farmers' organizations

[22] For a detailed description of the work of the committee, see H. L. Childs, *Labor and Capital in National Politics*, 1930, Chap. VIII.

or by the American Legion. The Federation supported the McNary-Haugen bill in 1927 and agricultural tariffs in 1931 and had the support of the farmers' organizations in defeating the sales tax in 1932.[23]

The efficacy of lobbying is predicated on the capacity of the Federation to reward its friends and to punish its enemies—and also on the assumption that individual Congressmen may be swayed by consideration for the righteousness of labor's cause, by motives of sympathy for the laboring man, or by conviction that the policies advocated by organized labor are in the interest of the entire nation. In all these connections the co-ordination of effort is of considerable importance. There are in Washington a number of international unions which maintain full or part-time paid and unpaid legislative agents, whose business it is to watch legislation for their own organization. In 1921 Gompers conceived the idea of getting these men to work together and organized the Conference Committee of Trade Union Legislative Representatives. After 1925 this committee ceased to function. Recently efforts have been made to revive it.

The legislative committee depends on hired legal advice.[24] The Federation and its unions often employ well-known and high-priced lawyers regardless of their economic or social point of view. Under the present régime of trade autonomy, the Federation cannot and does

[23] The campaign against the nomination of Judge J. J. Parker to the Supreme Court of the United States in 1930 was carried out in co-operation with organizations interested in promoting the interests of the colored people.

[24] The Legal Information Bureau of the Federation is not used for the purpose. It is poorly equipped and meagerly financed. Its total expenses were $13,588 in 1930 and $11,058 in 1931. Its work is to publish bulletins from time to time in which important labor decisions are reprinted, together with a brief résumé of the cases. These bulletins are forbidding in style and dryly written, without comment or interpretation.

not attempt to make more effective the large sums of money spent by its constituent unions for legal advice. At various conventions of the Federation the unions have been advised to see to it that their court cases were thoroughly prepared, and that material thus gathered would be made available at nominal expense to lawyers representing more impecunious unions. But little has been done to make this advice effective.

B. Non-Partisan Tactics

The lobbying activities of the Federation depend in large measure for their success upon the number of persons in Congress favorably disposed towards the aims of organized labor. This is connected with the other major part of the political activities of the Federation—its participation in presidential and congressional campaigns. This phase of the political activities of the Federation is under the direction of a Non-Partisan Political Campaign Committee appointed by the Executive Council. Since 1925 it has consisted of President Green and four or five other members of the Executive Council.

In years of a presidential campaign the president of the Federation appears before the platform committees of the Republican and Democratic Parties and submits to them special labor planks to be incorporated in the party platforms. These planks include the legislative program of the Federation. In the course of the campaign the Federation publishes a pamphlet containing in the form of a comparative table the labor planks submitted to the two political parties and the planks which these parties adopted. This pamphlet is mailed to all the local unions and to newspapers. Statements are also issued indicating the extent to which the different items in the Federation's legislative program have been considered or ignored by the Republican and Democratic Parties. The labor record of the two presidential candidates is examined and tabulated so as to show how many labor laws each has to his credit. Beyond this the Federation makes no effort to pass judgment on the presidential candidates.

With regard to the election of members of Congress the Federation pursues more elaborate methods. The Non-Partisan Political Campaign Committee prepares a list of new candidates and of those seeking reelection, indicating their stand on major labor issues and their general qualifications for office. Every state federation of labor and every city central is asked to appoint a local non-partisan political campaign committee to co-operate with the general committee in Washington. The local committees are requested to urge local trade unionists to take part in the primaries of both parties in order to throw their support to approved candidates. In some cases the non-partisan political committee in each congressional district is asked to write to the candidates to find out how they stand on certain issues. This was done in the congressional elections of 1930 with reference to the anti-injunction bill then pending in Congress. It is part of the task of the local committees to inform the public on the labor issues in the campaign, to obtain the support of farmers and other groups for the candidates approved by the Federation, and to collect funds. During the campaign, statements are issued and speeches made from time to time on behalf of or in opposition to one or another candidate.

Compared to its trade union activities, the political

method of the Federation is simple. It involves neither an elaborate organization nor a large staff nor large sums of money. The total contributions collected by the Federation between the presidential years 1920 and 1930 amounted to $56,770. Most of this sum was collected between 1920 and 1924. Since 1925 no contributions have been reported.

C. Theory and Practice

The Federation defends its non-partisan political method in two ways. In the first place, it is said to rule out partisanship which tends to divide the workers. The leaders of the Federation point to the various labor parties in the past as illustrating the instability of political labor bodies and their destructive effects upon trade unionism. Instead of partisanship to a party, the Federation claims that its method develops partisanship to principles. By ignoring party lines and by concentrating primarily on measures and candidates, the A. F. of L. claims to achieve the purpose of massing the political power of the workers. The workers, it is asserted, are a real unit at the ballot boxes when voting for candidates approved for their stand on labor measures, even though these candidates belong to different political parties and owe their main allegiance to their respective parties. The second argument of the Federation for maintaining its non-partisan method is that it is both practical and effective. With a minimum of cost and effort and without diverting attention from trade union matters, it produces results. The Federation points to the growth of labor legislation in the states and to its record in Congress as proof.

As a matter of fact, the non-partisan method inevitably divides the workers at the polls. In the campaign of 1932 each political party had a labor bureau managed by a prominent union official.[25] Members of the Executive Council of the Federation were out campaigning for opposing presidential candidates, and intensely partisan statements on the labor record of the two major parties appeared over the signature of labor officials pledged to non-partisanship.

Even in regard to candidates for Congress the method of the Federation shows inherent contradictions. It is impossible for the Federation to draw a sharp line on the votes of Congressmen. The usual procedure is to prepare a statistical table showing the number of measures on which the candidate took the side of labor, or vice-versa. This results in a mechanical and schematic summary in which important measures rank equally with minor matters; and in which the political personality of the candidate is blurred. Besides, as very few candidates take labor's position on all issues, compromises have to be made on an arbitrary basis.

Inevitably, the friends whom the Federation endorses are a heterogeneous assortment whose records are a jumble of conflicting political positions and not even in accord with the announced policies of the Federation. Some of the senators who have aided the Federation most in its anti-injunction fight and on other legislative matters have been strongly opposed to the modification of the Volstead Act and to the repeal of the Eighteenth

[25] The Labor Bureau of the Republican Party was in charge of William L. Hutcheson, president of the Brotherhood of Carpenters and Joiners; the labor section of the Democratic Party was managed by Daniel J. Tobin, president of the Teamsters' Union. The Socialist Party had a labor section in charge of Emil Rieve, president of the American Federation of Full Fashioned Hosiery Workers.

Amendment, which have been among the important items in the program of the Federation. Some of the congressmen branded by the Federation as its enemies are advocates of measures which the Federation favors.

The non-partisan method has tended to lend the support of organized labor to local political machines and cliques. This is especially true of city central unions and state federations of labor. The tendency of city centrals and state federations of labor to become identified with one or another of the two major political parties and with their local or state machines is due to two main causes. In the first place, the official positions in many of these labor organizations are unpaid or on a part-time basis, and the labor leaders who fill these positions must seek political appointments as a means of livelihood. Secondly, the presidents and secretaries of these labor centrals can hold their positions in the local labor movements only as long as they are able to render aid to the unions upon whose support they depend. The numerous ways in which political pull can be used to help a union in a strike, to bring public opinion to bear upon wage negotiations, to help place workers in jobs, to throw work on public contracts to union men and so on, are all dependent on the standing of the officer of the labor central with the municipal and state authorities.

At present the demand for independent labor politics in the Federation is slight. The forces which are ready to support an independent labor party are represented by a few international unions, by some of the larger city centrals, and by the radical minorities in the various unions. The non-partisan procedure is in accord with the present spirit of the Federation. It has been fairly effective in obtaining legislation favorable to labor by lobbying. It is a way to screen political disunity. It provides considerable local political influence and patronage to union officers. Also, it is an effective block against the intellectuals and other middle-class people who might climb to the top in political parties and over-shadow the trade union officials.

CHAPTER XVI

MOLDING PUBLIC POLICY AND EDUCATION

Since the employment relationship with which the trade union deals is affected by all the institutions of society, labor movements are inevitably concerned with the large economic and social programs of the day. Labor organizations in all countries have either been connected with political parties or have assumed the task of formulating political and social demands and have been important factors in molding public policy. The A. F. of L. has been no exception to the rule, as is evidenced by its Bill of Grievances of 1906, its Reconstruction Program of 1919, the Portland Manifesto of 1923, and its activities since.

I. SOCIAL OUTLOOK AND ECONOMIC PROGRAMS

A systematic statement of the larger economic and social views of the Federation is even more difficult now than in the past. The Federation has become more pragmatic, its literature more practical, and the ideas reflected in its utterances less consistent. The spokesmen of the Federation increasingly have given vent to doubt in the value of theories, preferring to put their faith in empirical procedure. The rank and file as well as leaders and officials represent a variety of political, religious, economic, and social ideas. Nevertheless, in its activities and in its public statements, the A. F. of L. has tended to proceed, either consciously or by implication, on the basis of certain general principles which together constitute a philosophy explaining its policies and programs.

A. Economic Americanism

Even more than during 1917-19, the Federation of recent years has stressed its Americanism and its devotion to American institutions. It has emphasized that it is working toward the improvement and extension of the principles underlying these institutions, in the evolution of which it sees no necessity for a violent break. American history is viewed by the Federation as a process leading to a greater realization of individual freedom, social justice, and equal opportunity for all, and the labor movement is regarded as the further development of the democratic movement which began with the Declaration of Independence and the American Revolution. Frequent references are made in the current writings and speeches of Federation leaders to the principles of Washington, Jefferson, Jackson, and Lincoln as the sources of the ideas which express the purpose of American labor. The organizing literature of the Federation stresses the American wage, the American system, America as "the greatest country ever established under the most beneficent form of government ever conceived," and its propaganda literature often advances the slogan "Be an American, join your trade union!"

There is also a tendency in the Federation to identify the ideals of trade unionism with those of Christianity. The former are presented as the embodiment of the teachings of Christ and as the social expression of the spiritual ideals of the Church. The Federation claims that its work supplements that of the Church in creating spiritual well-being. Both Americanism and Christianity are presumed to support what may be called the doctrine of the social and moral utility of material welfare. Labor, in the words of the spokesmen of the Federation, seeks to satisfy the physical needs as a means towards the development of spiritual forces. In this view the material and spiritual elements of life are inseparable and the highest attainment of intellectual, cultural, and spiritual values can be reached only through the abolition of poverty and the establishment of humane working and living conditions.

Labor's aim—the life abundant—calls for the fulfilment of the "American standard of living." The Federation has tried to put some definiteness into this rather vague term by insisting that the American standard must provide not only the essentials of life for all members of a family but a steady income and security in the job, a bank account against emergencies, allowances for good housing, for the entertainment of friends, for amusements, for contributions to churches and other organizations, for education, travel, the development of character and personality.

For the worker as producer the American standard implies a status of equality in industry and the right of self-direction. The underlying idea is that the worker has as much stake in his trade or industry as the employer or stockholder. The worker invests his training, his skill, and his whole life in the occupation he follows. He is thus a member of a partnership established objectively by the inherent necessities of production. As a partner in industry he is entitled to an equal voice in shaping industrial destinies.

Equality of industrial status is also based on the worker's right to self-direction, the right to be a free man, which is the basis for the industrial democracy which the Federation interprets as union management co-operation and which it advocates also as a prerequisite and corollary of political democracy. The workers presumably cannot develop the sense of self-respect and dignity necessary for real freedom so long as the "factory boss" has irresponsible powers to hire and fire and can treat his employees as entirely subordinate to his will, without industrial or economic rights.

B. The Worker's Place in National Economy

The primary means of the Federation for the attainment of American standards are high wages and shorter hours. In accordance with the idea of the "social wage," the Federation continues to oppose what it calls the "supply and demand theory of Adam Smith," the "subtle logic of the wage fund theory," and all cost of living theories of wages, which it characterizes as "doctrines of a slave age." The movement for shorter hours is still regarded as the most important and beneficent objective of the labor movement. It is claimed that every reduction in the hours of labor for workers has been followed by an increase in production due to the invention of new machinery and of improved methods. A reduction in the hours of labor thus increases the productive power of the worker, enables him to demand and receive higher wages; and, combined with increased leisure, increases the workers' consuming power and thus further stimulates industry. The Federation is committed to the five-day week and the six-hour day, though it leaves it to each craft to determine how and when they are to be put into practice.

These doctrines on wages and hours have become

part of the larger concept of the importance of the worker in the maintenance of national prosperity. Higher wages, a shorter work day and working week, and progressive living standards are advocated not only in the interests of the wage-earning group but as essential conditions for industrial stability and orderly economic expansion. The theory of the Federation is that productive capacity has the tendency to outrun purchasing power, and that this is a major cause of business depressions. To maintain industrial balance, according to the A. F. of L. a new system of distribution is needed. Mass production demands mass buying and the problem is to enable the millions now living at low levels to buy according to higher standards. In the past employers and managers have concentrated on increasing plant capacity, but now the crying need is for a larger market for consumers' goods. Along with higher wages and shorter hours, continuous employment and security in the job would aid in developing a sustained maximum purchasing power because the workers would be able to plan their expenditures over the year. Specifically, the Federation recommends "annual wages" as a basis for security and steady incomes.

Though putting its greatest emphasis on the proper distribution of the national income, the Federation now accepts the idea that the workers should share responsibility for improving processes and for increasing output. It admits that the welfare of the workers depends upon productivity and that the greater the earnings of industry, the greater the benefits the workers may enjoy. Though approving the general outlook of scientific management, the Federation is still skeptical of the methods applied by industrial management in measuring individual productivity and in apportioning returns, and calls for study and research to develop more accurate procedures.

C. Group Co-operation Versus Class Struggle

As a means towards the end of increasing productivity and maintaining national prosperity, the Federation offers employers the aid and co-operation of trade unionism. The Federation argues that the trade unions are in a new phase of evolution. In their earlier stage they were mainly weapons of industrial war, instruments in the hands of the workers to coerce unwilling employers to consider the human problems of industry. But the trade unions have steadily evolved into organizations trying to gather scattered individuals into a coherent collective force which can utilize the experience and knowledge and good-will of the workers for the benefit of industry and society.

While calling for co-operation between employers and workers, the Federation does not claim that the time can come when there will be no controversy between them over what constitutes a just and equitable division of wealth and income. Such differences of opinion must continue to manifest themselves because they are merely one phase of the general differences in all human activities. But the Federation emphasizes that these differences need not always give rise to conflict. The solution of these controversies can and should be reached through mutual understanding and agreement.

The Federation insists, however, upon one fundamental condition. It is the recognition by employers of the workers' right to organize and to carry on negotiations through trade unions. This is essential to establish a relative equality of economic power between capital and labor, which presumably is the only foundation of industrial peace and co-operation. Labor cannot rely on the good-will of employers. History shows that no group voluntarily limits its privileges or its powers. Neither is there any internal driving force that would impel employers to give the workers the conditions they seek. In the last 100 years, since the coming of modern industrialism, it has been demonstrated that neither the religious ideals of Christianity, the ethical preachings of humanitarians, nor the materialistic urgings of far-sighted economic statesmen have had much effect upon wages and labor policies of employers. What has changed industrial relations in the last 50 years has been the determination of the wage earners and their organized efforts to improve their lot.

Economic power can be exercised only through some definite economic institution. In the case of employers, such power is embodied in property and property rights, and in the corporate form of industrial organization. The workers can have no property power under modern industrial conditions. As the concentration of wealth continues, the tools of labor are more and more alienated from the toilers. Political freedom and equality before the law granted in the Constitution do not give the worker the means for dealing with his employer on a basis of equality. The possessions of the individual worker—his labor power, his willingness to work, and his skill—generate economic power only when combined with the same possessions of other workers in a trade union. In pooling the energies and skill of all workers the trade union develops the collective power of the group based on economic and social interests which may equal the power of property. Because of this, collective action, if allowed to function under proper conditions, holds out the promise of solving group differences through social co-operation.

D. Substitutes for Socialism

These ideas of national solidarity in production, of the partnership of labor and capital in industry, and of co-operation for more equitable distribution modify the doctrine of struggle expounded in the preamble to the constitution of the Federation. That preamble declares that "a struggle is going on in all the nations of the civilized world between the oppressors and the oppressed of all countries, a struggle between the capitalist and the laborer, and will work disastrous results to the toiling millions if they are not combined for mutual protection and benefit." This has a tinge of the doctrine of class struggle. But the Federation does not accept such doctrine in its daily proceedings. On the contrary, it rejects the idea that labor is a separate class within the community, and disavows the social corollary of class struggle—the faith in social revolution. Today, even more than before 1914, the Federation is in opposition to revolutionary socialism. It is vehement in its denunciation of communism as a force that would strike at the very soul of American institutions and substitute a "foreign social creed for the principles of Americanism."

The Federation does not accept, however, the present economic system as a true expression of American ideals. In describing the contradictions of the modern industrial system, the spokesmen of the Federation are often in agreement with socialistic ideas, but they use a terminology which they believe to be in greater accord with American traditions of thought. In their words the present emphasis of society on property rights is destructive of human rights. Large corporations, though organizing capital for greater efficiency, weaken the economic status of the worker and reduce him to a condition of practical servitude. Credit is becoming more and more concentrated in a few large financial institutions managed by a small group of bankers who have become the lords of industry. Mechanical inventions are used in such a way as to deprive large sections of the workers of their chief economic power, their skill, reducing them to the position of unskilled laborers, dependent upon the whim and will of those who control industry. Guided by considerations of profit, employers are entirely concerned with production and ignore the problem of distribution with the result that the economic equilibrium is periodically upset creating unemployment and increasing the insecurity of those who are dependent upon a job for a living. And even at its best, during periods of prosperity, the methods of dividing the products of industry result in great inequalities of income and in the continuance of a large part of the people in a condition of poverty.

The Federation also agrees with the socialists that the lessons of the past indicate that industry, methods of distribution, and financial institutions have changed radically, and that they will continue to change. The course of these historic changes is towards an increasing social control of property in favor of human rights. But the Federation claims that no one is wise enough to foresee the particular changes in economic and social institutions which lie ahead. Therefore it is neither necessary nor desirable to try to visualize new social forms for the future or to construct ideal systems toward which labor should strive. What is important is that social changes should be made as orderly as possible. If the impending changes are revolutionary in character, they should be achieved in a peaceful way by proceeding slowly.

Though the Federation refuses to project its program into the future and to be concerned with social ideals, its general principles and policies, if carried to their logical end, imply a change in present economic and social relations. The general outlook of the Federation is towards a minimum of special privilege and a maximum of equal opportunity. It points to an economic system in which the rights of productive property are limited, in which the profit motive is tempered by considerations of public interest, in which corporate activities are subject to social control, and in which industry is so guided as to provide large purchasing power to the masses as a basis for progressively rising standards of living. The concept is that of an economic society in which industrial activities are carried on through a network of organizations representing employers, management, workers, and consumers. These organizations would fix hours of work, determine wages, and settle other industrial policies, primarily by means of collective contracts.

The Federation does not encourage such a projection. Its spokesmen insist that they prefer to go their way from day to day leaving the future to take care of itself. They wish to confine themselves to making the conditions of life and labor better today than they were yesterday, and "better tomorrow and tomorrow and tomorrow's tomorrow." Such an attitude strengthens their hands in the daily business of collective bargaining, allowing them to stress the fraternity of interests between labor and capital and to reassure employers that no abridgment of property rights or other radical changes are contemplated.

In its earlier period the Federation favored the government ownership of railroads. During 1919-20 it endorsed the Plumb Plan, the nationalization of mines, and government ownership of all public utilities. Between 1920 and 1922 it was also much interested in currency and credit problems, and demanded "credit control by a public agency" subject to Congress. Since 1925 the Federation has dropped all demands for national ownership of railroads or mines and has shown little, if any, interest in government control of credit. Instead of government ownership or nationalization,[1] the Federation is now advocating economic planning nationally and within separate industries which involves a modification of the anti-trust laws and permission to form industrial consolidations for the regulation of production under government supervision. The Federation also favors "taxation aimed at acquired wealth and not at the consuming power of the nation's wage earners." It is in favor of liberalizing credit facilities for the wage earner, small business man, and farmer.

The Federation avoids taking a stand on the protective tariff. But since 1925 an increasing number of its component unions have turned to protectionism as a means of giving aid to their respective industries.

[1] After some hesitation the Federation gave its support to legislation for the government operation of Muscle Shoals and Boulder Dam.

[2] The Federation has neither endorsed nor repudiated the Wage Earners' Protective Conference, which has been formed by affiliated unions

At the request of these unions, the Federation at its conventions has gone on record in favor of high tariffs on various commodities and for embargoes on Russian lumber and on manganese. However, on a number of important issues the Federation holds an uncertain position. It keeps silent while its constituent unions advocate one or another policy, creating the impression that they represent the policy of all organized labor.[3]

E. Research and Propaganda

In most countries of Europe the trade unions develop their social ideas in co-operation with the political parties with which they are affiliated, with trained economists who are in charge of their research departments, and with economic experts friendly to the labor movement. Within recent years the labor movements of Germany and England have relied more and more on the second source.

The American Federation of Labor differs from the European movements in that it has no affiliations with a political party. It has from time to time called in experts, especially on legal and legislative problems, but it has not relied upon them for the formulation of general policies. The spokesmen of the Federation have not much regard for economists, whom they accuse of having been generally wrong on trade union theory and practice, and they have been extremely antagonistic to the so-called "intellectuals."[4]

The development of new policies and the solution of new problems has thus devolved upon Federation

interested in high tariffs and which has worked hand in hand with manufacturers seeking higher tariff rates on their products.

[3] See p. 338.

[4] See pp. 468-69.

leaders. As practical men whose time is chiefly occupied with immediate tasks, they have neither the time nor the opportunity for systematic studies. They rely largely on personal contacts and on intuition. Often they "fall" for ideas which have eloquent defenders or which are "in the air." Sometimes new ideas and policies push their way up from the affiliated unions. For some time, however, the difficulties resulting from this unsystematic procedure have been felt keenly. The large and complex problems of business stability, of finance, of international commercial policies, press in upon the heads of the Federation and call for careful consideration, while the system of traditional ideas which the Federation has inherited gives no clues to many of these questions.

The Federation tries to mold public opinion in favor of its policies through its press, research, and propaganda service.[5] It readily furnishes information in book, pamphlet, and letter form, and material is supplied to the labor and daily press and to all who are interested. The president of the Federation spends considerable time in propaganda tours. Gompers had developed the technique of commenting on every important national and international event through interviews, public statements, or letters to the President of the United States as a means of bringing the Federation before the country. Since 1925 this practice has not been followed as often or as effectively as formerly. Neither has the Federation used the new opportunities of the radio to any great extent. The Chicago Federation of Labor is the only labor organization which has its own radio plant and wave length.

[5] The research work of the Federation is not organized and its statistical methods have been the subject of valid criticism.

II. WORKERS' EDUCATION

To mold the thinking of its own members and to increase their educational facilities, the A. F. of L. has manifested an interest in problems of education. It has concerned itself with such topics as compulsory education, free text books, freedom of expression in the public schools, improving the quality of teachers and increasing their salaries, providing adequate teaching staffs, the development of evening schools, and university extension work.[6] The theory upon which the Federation proceeded was that the public schools supported by public funds belonged to the people and should be reorganized to fit the needs of the workers.

Even in the earlier days there were minority groups in the Federation demanding a type of education which they declared the public schools neither could nor desired to offer. At the A. F. of L. convention in 1902 severe criticism was directed at college professors and teachers in public schools for "their attitude towards the children of the working people." Gompers, however, who at one time had criticized "the professors," adopted a more charitable attitude towards the teaching profession, declaring that the public school could and should be used to meet the educational needs of the working people. In 1904 he stated that the public lecture system in connection with evening schools constituted a potential "workingmen's university." However, in 1905 he was forced to make a concession to the radicals and recommended that the central labor unions establish schools

[6] Between 1897 and 1900 efforts to extend some form of adult education among wage earners led to the formation of the People's Institute in New York, the Breadwinners' College, and the Workers' Education League, and to an attempt to establish a resident labor college at Trenton, Mo. However, it was not until 1906 that a separate workers' school—the Rand School for Social Sciences—was established.

where the principles of trade unionism might be taught. No trade union schools were established and the "workingmen's universities" did not develop. A proposal made in 1905 that the Executive Council establish a lecture bureau did not materialize.

The experiments of a number of unions after 1914 brought the subject of workers' education to the attention of the A. F. of L.[7] At its 1918 convention the Federation appointed a committee to investigate the problem. In reporting the following year, the committee recommended that city central unions should secure representation on boards of education and make every effort to obtain from the public schools liberally conducted classes in subjects which union members wished. If this was not obtainable, the central labor bodies were to organize such classes with as much co-operation from the public schools as could be obtained.

The desire to extend and co-ordinate the movement for workers' education which began to grow rapidly between 1918 and 1920 led to the formation of the Workers' Education Bureau in 1921.[8] The bureau was to serve as a clearing house for workers' classes and colleges and was to focus attention on the need for workers' education. In 1922 the secretary of the bureau made

[7] In 1914 the Women's Trade Union League in Chicago established a school to train women organizers in trade unionism. Between 1913 and 1917, the Ladies Garment Workers' Union established classes for its members and worked out a plan for an educational department, of which Fannia M. Cohn became director. Classes for workers were also organized by trade unions in Boston, by the Chicago Federation of Labor, and by the Los Angeles Labor Union.

[8] A leading part in organizing the bureau was taken by progressive trade unionists, who emphasized the idea that the workers must develop their own educational institutions, and by persons primarily interested in adult education. Among the latter was Spencer Miller, secretary of the bureau since its formation.

overtures to the A. F. of L. and the following year a plan was effected by which the bureau retained its autonomy but became subject to general supervision by the Federation.

Since 1923 the educational work of the Federation has been carried on through its Committee on Education and through the Workers' Education Bureau. The Committee on Education has continued in the main the earlier tradition of the Federation. It has investigated textbooks used in primary and secondary schools and has advocated the teaching of industrial and trade union history in such schools. It has urged city central unions to try to exercise influence in local school matters. Many city centrals and state federations of labor now have local and state committees on education whose function it is to seek special representation for organized labor on school boards and to carry out the general suggestions of the Committee on Education. It has lent its support to the establishment of continuation schools, technical courses, and vocational classes for workers. During the last two years, however, this committee has not held any meetings because of lack of funds.

While the Committee on Education aims to influence the public school system in the interests of the workers, the Workers' Education Bureau has for its purpose the co-ordination of the educational efforts of the unions themselves. The bureau proceeds on two general principles. One is that education must be kept distinct from policy making. The bureau takes no stand on any of the issues with which the unions have to deal. The other is that the educational work of the unions is supplementary to that of the public institutions. It is a phase of adult education, carried on specially for workers, dealing with economic subjects of special interest to them, but also with the general problems of citizenship. Accordingly, the Workers' Education Bureau has sought financial support from sources outside the trade unions and co-operates with other educational agencies in its work.

As at present constituted, the Workers' Education Bureau is an autonomous agency for the purpose of carrying on education for adult workers on a non-partisan basis. In general, however, the bureau does not deviate from the policies laid down by the A. F. of L. It does not admit to membership any labor college or workers' educational enterprise which is not endorsed by the central labor union or other official body of the Federation. Its membership consists of national unions, state federations of labor, and workers' educational enterprises which lend their support because the work of the bureau has the sanction of the Federation. The bureau is governed by an executive committee of nine, to which the A. F. of L. designates three representatives, and the president of the American Federation of Labor is ex-officio its honorary president. The membership at present is uncertain. No figures have been published since 1929.[9] Neither are data available on finances.

During 1930-31 the activities of the Workers' Education Bureau were devoted to promoting discussion on

[9] In 1929 the affiliations included 47 national and international unions; 22 state federations of labor; 132 central labor unions; and 428 local unions. Not all these unions paid dues, however. The total amounts paid by unions in 1927 and 1928 were $9,861 and $8,047 respectively. The total budgets of the Workers' Education Bureau for these years were $38,476 and $24,776. See *Report of the National Convention of Workers' Education Bureau*, 1929, p. 58.

the general topic of unemployment. Since 1931 the bureau has had to curtail most of its activities because of lack of funds. Most of the unions affiliated with the Federation have also either discontinued or greatly reduced their educational work during the past three or four years, first as a result of internal friction and later for lack of funds.

CHAPTER XVII

INTERPRETATION AND OUTLOOK

What lies ahead of the Federation will depend on the course of American economic life and on the capacity of the Federation to make necessary changes in its policies and structure. Certain new economic trends are already discernible which suggest what changes may be called for. But before analyzing these trends and in order that their significance may be more clearly perceived, it is necessary to interpret in a more systematic way than has so far been attempted the factors shaping the character of the Federation as revealed in the story of its past and in the analysis of its present. It will then be possible to evaluate more correctly the manner in which new economic forces are likely to influence the Federation in the near future.

I. THE DYNAMICS OF THE A. F. OF L.

Attempts have been made to explain the course and character of the A. F. of L. by reference to a general law of the development of labor movements. According to this law, trade union structure, policies, and programs have changed with the evolution of modern economic society from merchant to industrial and then to finance capitalism.[1] Small-scale business, and the domination of economic life by the wholesale merchant, presumably gave rise to craft unions and labor movements which advocated co-operation and monetary reform as solutions for most industrial ills. Gradually, as merchant capital-

[1] For one variation of this generalization, see John R. Commons, "The Labor Movement," *Encyclopædia of the Social Sciences*, 1932, Vol. 8, pp. 682-96.

ism gave way to corporations and large-scale industry, larger units of labor were organized and socialistic doctrines sprang up. As credit and finance became increasingly important to our industrial institutions, the financier gained in power and labor unions tended to lose efficacy. In accordance with this generalization, the rise and growth of the A. F. of L. before 1914 coincided with the development of industrial capitalism, while its course since 1920 reveals the complex problems growing out of the predominance of finance capitalism.

This theory, however, is inadequate to explain the American labor movement. It does not account for the persistence of certain features in the A. F. of L. which make it differ from labor organizations of other countries subjected to similar industrial changes. The generalization outlined above needs to be supplemented by the concept that labor movements tend to form types in accordance with variations in the structure of industries and in the rate of their development, and in accordance with changes in social institutions due to historic experience, culture, and tradition.

The features of the A. F. of L. which have distinguished it from the national labor organizations of European countries and which call for explanation are its non-socialist character, its denial of the theory of class struggle, its indifference to the idea of a historic mission of organized labor, its pragmatic outlook and business policies, and its limited economic and political powers. These distinguishing features may be considered the result of five main factors of American economic and social development. One is the dynamic character of American industry, based upon rich resources and on inventiveness, and stimulated by the speculative disposition of the people. This was the factor which prevented the social stratification of wage-earning groups. The abundant employment opportunities offered by rapidly growing industries caused continual shifting in occupations and held out to the working people ever new chances to change status. Many were able to find a new place in economic life where they obtained either greater pecuniary returns or more independence. The successes of the few became a challenge and a temptation to the many and nullified incipient tendencies toward thinking in terms of loyalty to a class.

A second factor having the same effects was the heterogeneity of the American wage earners, who were recruited from various immigrant sources. Differences of race, religion, education, and language acted as further hindrances to the growth of class ideas and class feeling.

A third—and in some ways the most important—factor in influencing the character of the Federation was the peculiar way in which national consciousness developed in the United States as contrasted with its rise in European countries. Nationalism in the industrial countries of Europe developed either as a protest by a rising middle class against a feudalistic monarchy or as a revolt of minority nationality groups against a state dominated by one national group. In either case the national consciousness was formed and strengthened in the political and cultural sense through the struggle against monarchical, feudal, or conflicting national elements. As the workers co-operated with the middle classes in these struggles, they became recognized as an integral element of the nation. Thus in Europe the idea of class and class struggle emerged simultaneously with democratic nationalism. The essence of the class concept was not a denial of nationalism. It was rather the identification of the worker as a member of a rising group which was destined to become dominant in the nation and ultimately to become *the* nation.

The rise of national consciousness in the United States affected the workers differently. The Civil War gave America political unity, but accentuated sectional and racial animosities instead of uniting the majority of the nation against a small economic class. The divisions which ensued and the economic misery of the seventies and eighties bred the concept of class in the organized labor movement, without connecting it with national or democratic ideals. This, however, was reversed in the nineties when the populists who led the agrarian movement of the day put forth a large concept of the solidarity of the people. To the extent to which the organized workers followed the populists, they accepted the idea of being part of the people as opposed to class ideas. The agrarian groups were animated not by opposition to private property in general, but by a desire to protect small against large and monopolistic property, and regarded socialism as "foreign"—not respectable—and out of harmony with the ideals of individual opportunity. These ideas were accepted also by the organized workers. They fitted in with the immediate needs of the trade unions whose weakness made them fearful that by adopting socialist doctrines they would merely give employers an opportunity to turn public opinion against them and make it more difficult for them to obtain economic concessions. Also, the immigrant workers, who had come to America in the hope of finding freedom and opportunity, resented the fact that they were regarded as "foreigners"; they desired to become assimilated—not further alienated from the community by declarations of class and class struggle. To these factors must be added the opposition to socialistic doctrines manifested by the churches beginning with the eighties.

The change in economic and social outlook between 1904 and 1914, which brought the middle class and the workers a little closer together and which gave the workers the feeling that they were becoming accepted more and more as part of the nation, resulted in the growth of reformist and socialistic ideas.[2] But that development was interrupted by the World War and post-war developments. The post-Armistice upheaval of 1918-20 disrupted the alliance of the middle class and the workers. The "new era" of 1925-29, though dominated by the outlook of the business group, sailed under the flag of economic solidarity which the wage earners accepted because of their hope to obtain an increasing share of prosperity. At the same time, owing to the limitations on immigration and other social changes, the wage earners more than ever before tended to become merged in the general mass of the nation and to think in national terms as opposed to those of class.

The fourth factor shaping the Federation has been the tendency of the skilled workers to maintain a monopolistic advantage in their respective crafts and trades. This gave rise to the international union as the dominant form of American trade unionism. The international union has as its main concern the protection and advancement of the interests of a selected craft, trade, or industrial group. Because of this group egotism the international unions have aimed to shape the Federation primarily into an instrument for achieving their own

[2] See Chap. V.

purposes. This explains their insistence on trade autonomy and on the limitation of the powers of the Federation.

The group egotism of the international unions has been and still is fostered to a considerable extent by the opportunities which it offers for public activity and a business career. The union officials in the Federation represent the same variety of types, temperaments, and training as may be found in industry and business. To some extent, the aggressive "go-getter" type predominates in the craft unions, the politician type in some of the older industrial unions, and the efficiency expert or administrator type in the unions which depend more upon negotiations with corporate business or which have large financial assets. But whatever the type, the tendency is for these officials to regard themselves as the business executives of their unions whose primary job it is to get results for their members and for themselves. This business-executive attitude, which is a reflection of the national absorption in material development and in money making, makes it difficult for trade union officials to concern themselves with the problems of other trades and of organized labor in general.

This attitude is strengthened by what may be regarded as quasi-feudalistic conditions in the labor movement. The officials of the international unions tend to regard the area mapped out by their charters as domains over which they have supreme rights. For the protection gained by affiliation with the Federation, they owe a tribute and limited loyalty expressed in the obligation to pay dues and to support some of the policies of the A. F. of L. But in exchange for this loyalty they claim an unlimited sovereignty which they mean to exercise in the particular interest of the trade which they represent and serve. As in all feudalistic systems, the tendency is for the feudal chiefs not only to quarrel among themselves and be jealous of one another's domains but to lord it over the central power which they themselves have set up to adjudicate their differences. The difficulty of overcoming such feudalistic attitudes is increased by the fact that the officials of even small craft unions find greater satisfaction in holding first place within a limited area than in occupying a subordinate position in a large organization.

The fifth factor, which explains changes in the Federation rather than its constant features, is the influence of the semi-skilled and unskilled workers. It was largely as a result of their discontent and pressure that the conservative trend of the Federation never became absolute. Before 1914 the unions which tended to force changes in the methods and policies of the Federation were the quasi-industrial unions of the mine workers, clothing workers, and common laborers. During the war it was the influx of semi-skilled and skilled workers into the unions of the war industries that gave the Federation impetus for change. It was also largely owing to these less skilled groups that the Federation was never able to throw off entirely the implications of class coherence. Their pressure caused even the narrowest craft unions to realize that there was danger in a complete rift between skilled and unskilled. It was chiefly the need of reconciling them and incorporating them into the general structure of the organized labor movement that forced the Federation to advocate programs of economic reform which, though less sweeping in character than those of the European unions, were none the less aimed to make property and industry subject to social control. However, to the extent to which the international unions—even of the semi-skilled and unskilled—became strong, they tended to become self-sufficient and to put themselves above the Federation. Also, as they became more firmly established, they became more interested in maintaining the status quo and thus tended to lose some of their dynamic influence.

II. DECLINE OR REORGANIZATION

The interaction of economic changes during 1925-29 and of the factors described had such adverse effects on the A. F. of L. as to raise the question whether the Federation was not entering a state of chronic internal crisis.[3] Nearly four years of industrial depression have inevitably aggravated the situation. Most of the unions of the Federation have felt the destructive effects of unemployment and wage reductions. Standards of work and wages, of hours and of security, established after a generation of hard struggles, have broken down. The facts so far assembled concerning wage reductions, prolongation of hours, and a general deterioration of working conditions are still fragmentary, but they indicate that union standards are being destroyed. At the same time, the number of dues-paying members in all unions continues to fall, while the demands for aid of unemployed members are on the increase. Surplus funds of many unions have suffered from the collapse of security values and from bank failures, and all such funds have been drawn upon heavily.

This condition is responsible for the change in the program of the Federation which finds expression in the advocacy of governmental and compulsory unemploy-

[3] See Chap. X.

ment insurance plans, of the legal limitation of hours of work, of economic planning, and of governmental control of industry. It is also responsible for the radical tone assumed by officers of international unions and by leaders of the Federation who now speak of a possible collapse of capitalism and of an immediate danger of social revolution.

No prognosis of the Federation can be made on the basis of this change. The record of the A. F. of L. indicates that radical phrases and radical programs adopted in times of depression or upheaval have been forgotten under conditions of returning prosperity and calm. A forecast of the future of the Federation can have some validity only if based on an examination of those trends which are likely to affect labor and unionism more permanently.

The first possibility which calls for consideration is that of a prolongation of the present business depression. It seems obvious that in such case the present radical trend in the Federation will become more pronounced. The main question then will be whether other political organizations would not assume leadership in a movement of social discontent. There is also the likelihood of a combination between the Federation and such organizations for political and economic purposes of more far-reaching consequences than those that come within the scope of this book.

The question of the outlook for the Federation must thus be considered on the assumption of a more or less speedy resumption of economic activities on a normal scale. If this takes place without serious modifications in our industrial system, the trends noted before 1930 are likely to resume their onward course. Technological changes will continue to destroy skill, displace workers, and thus undermine the unions based on craftsmanship. Geographical shifts in industry will go on; and they will be accentuated by the efforts of employers who try to escape from the unions in the larger cities and older industrial centers. In some industries this will mean a resurrection of sweatshop conditions and a complete breakdown of long established standards, even in union plants. Other trends, such as changes in habits of consumption, in methods of marketing, and in world economy, will also continue to have dislocating effects on unionism.

The evidence also points to the conclusion that American employers are not likely to change their attitude toward unionism in the near future. There have been no conversions to unionism on the part of employers since 1930. On the contrary, some employers have taken advantage of the depression to break relations with unions. In the process of economic readjustments ahead, employers will claim that union labor is more expensive than non-union labor, that union rules interfere with production, and that, as industry is becoming more specialized and more technically sensitive, such interference is less and less tolerable and permissible. Though many of the employers' welfare schemes inaugurated between 1922 and 1929 have been declining since 1930, they are likely to be reintroduced and efforts are likely to be made to extend employee representation plans.

The unions in the Federation will be affected by these developments in different ways and varying degrees. Those which have been seriously undermined by technical changes are not likely to survive long. They are decaying unions in a real sense. A few unions, including the small and medium-sized organizations in the building and metal trades, which have entrenched themselves in sheltered trades and which are affected only moderately by technical changes, will be able to hold their own by the old devices of unionism but will be unlikely to grow. On the other hand, a number of unions which have systematically tried to readjust their methods and policies and which have shown promise in the process may be able to make progress even under difficult conditions.[4] Altogether, on the basis of these assumptions, it seems inevitable that the Federation as a whole will be reduced in membership and resources and will have to carry on its activities on an even smaller scale than today.

The possibilities outlined above are the basis for the oft-repeated assertion that the A. F. of L. is "on its death-bed." Predictions of a sudden collapse of the Federation have been made by analogy with what happened to the Knights of Labor. Such predictions are in most cases wish-thoughts and are not based on any careful study of the facts. They fail to take into account the differences in the situation and in the position of the two organizations. The Knights of Labor shot up suddenly and declined rapidly. The unions of the Federation have grown slowly, and many of them have deep roots in their trades. The Federation has a position in the political life of the country such as the Knights of Labor never achieved. Neither is a collapse probable as a result of the sudden rise of an opposing organization. There is no evidence that either the communists or any of the radical groups now in existence have either the resources or the capacity for the task. The greatest con-

[4] For concrete illustrations of the problems facing the different unions of the A. F. of L. and for the methods of meeting them, see Appendix B.

tribution which radical and dual unions have made to the American labor movement in the past, and which they may continue to make, has been in stimulating ideas, in evolving new policies, and in bringing forth younger leaders who have little or no opportunity of making a way for themselves in the existing organizations.

A slow disintegration, however, is not an impossibility, though such a forecast must allow for the possibility that the Federation can continue to exist even if some of its unions disband and others continue to lose in membership. A Federation with a decreased membership, say of one or one and a half million, could still perform the main functions which it carries on today, those of a lobbying agency and a publicity department. It could still exercise some political influence because whatever political party was in power would have to heed the Federation to justify the claim that the legitimate interests of all groups of the population are recognized by the government.

But even such an eventuality must be viewed in the light of possible reform within the Federation. The A. F. of L. has shown a remarkable capacity for continuity, readjustment, and survival. It maintained itself and developed for many years, while rival organizations which attempted to supplant it either disbanded or dwindled to a mere shadowy existence. The Socialist Trade and Labor Alliance, the I. W. W., the One Big Union, the Western Federation of Miners, and the American Labor Union are all mere débris in its path. The Federation has been through more than one crisis, and there is the possibility that it may weather the present one too.

III. PROSPECTS FOR A NEW UNIONISM

It is possible to discern some forces which are driving the Federation in a new direction. One of these is the United Mine Workers. This organization is representative of the quasi-industrial unions which have achieved a certain degree of reconciliation of interests between the skilled, semi-skilled, and unskilled elements in their industry. As in the early stages of the A. F. of L., when this union was an important factor in stimulating industrial unionism, it is now coming forward again as a protagonist of new policies and methods. The officials and leaders of the United Mine Workers may not be fully aware of the implications of their new policy, but that is not important. The fact that the union has been forced to advocate industrial stabilization with governmental aid, as embodied in the Kelly-Davis bill, is of paramount significance.[5] The government is thus assigned a positive part in making collective bargaining a recognized policy in the industry. This is a long step from the traditional philosophy of the A. F. of L., which abhorred intervention by the government in collective contracts between employers and unions. The United Mine Workers in supporting this bill recognizes the government as a party to collective agreements, thus making the success of unionism dependent upon governmental support.

A second impetus towards change comes from the

[5] From the point of view of unionism the important feature of this bill is the provision for collective bargaining as a prerequisite for allowing coal companies to consolidate for purposes of exploiting their markets. The bill allows selling agencies and price-fixing under government supervision, provided employers and employees co-operate on the basis of a recognition of minimum standards set by collective negotiations between the union and the employers' associations.

railway unions.[6] The latter are now faced by a difficult situation in view of the fact that the industry must undergo serious reorganization—financial and otherwise—in the next few years. Because of the large public interest in the sound and continued development of the railroad industry, the railway employees realize that they are expected to make sacrifices in wages and working conditions. But as economic groups usually have fought more stubbornly against lowering standards than for raising them, a growing radical attitude on the part of railway employees may be anticipated.

The railway workers have two possibilities for winning their ends. They may threaten strikes as they did in 1916, or they may try to influence the government by political pressure. Either form of action is likely to force the government to take a greater part in regulating industrial relations on the railroads. Also, the extension of union organization under government protection and regulation is likely. Whichever course the railroad workers follow, they will need the support of the other organized labor groups. It is therefore to be expected that they will make an effort to play a greater part in the general labor movement. To the extent to which the railway employees will do so, they are likely to rally other elements favoring governmental action around their program and policy.[7]

[6] The 21 standard railway unions include the four Brotherhoods not affiliated with the A. F. of L., the 7 railway shop crafts combined in the Railway Employees' Department, and 10 other railway unions, some of which are affiliated with the A. F. of L. They are combined in the Labor Railway Executives Association. The negotiations carried on by these organizations during the last two years have been an example of coherent effort which has but few parallels in the history of American organized labor.

[7] Contributing causes which are driving railway employees to lean more

A similar trend is also noticeable in a number of unions operating in the public utilities industries, for example, the Brotherhood of Electrical Workers. Unaided, this union cannot break through the barriers which the companies have erected to oppose unionism. This union would welcome legislation giving public service commissions the power to control the labor policies of the companies on the ground that such regulation is necessary to secure efficient and uninterrupted service. The assumption is that under such regulation the unions would be aided in organizing the employees in these industries.

There is another group of unions in the Federation which is ready to welcome public and governmental aid for unionism. Such are some of the unions in the clothing and textile industries. They are facing a recurrence of conditions that existed before 1910 and are now asking for legislation to regulate conditions in their industries. Industrial labor boards under government supervision, which would facilitate organizing and maintain standards of work, are advocated. The trend is towards what may be designated as quasi-public or governmental unionism, and will require machinery similar to that established during the war. Opposition to this tendency may be expected from some of the older craft unions in the A. F. of L., such as those in the building trades. These unions have played and still play a dominant part in the Federation. Numerically, they have generally been the more important section of the Federation. In organization and finance, they have been the

---

and more on government aid are insurance difficulties brought about by the financial situation and increasing unemployment of the last few years. The four Brotherhoods and other railway unions have been forced to consider a federal retirement law for all railway employees, as well as legislation for unemployment insurance.

most compact and powerful. In method, they have been forceful because they have not hesitated to use all means at their command—even such as were not approved by the Federation. Because of their narrow craft attitudes, most of them have been a conservative factor in the Federation impeding the advance of larger social policies.

But the outlook for the building trades unions is not particularly bright. If the construction industry continues to languish for some years, the building trades unions will be unable to recover lost ground. Their funds will be diminished, jurisdictional difficulties will increase, and they will be seriously undermined by increasing unemployment among their membership. On the other hand, should business recovery be accompanied or stimulated by a large housing program involving such projects as public works, slum clearance and cheap housing for the people, the construction industry, which has thus far escaped a thorough industrial revolution, would no doubt experience rapid industrialization. New types of housing would most likely eliminate many of the old skills and would involve a cheapening of labor Such an eventuality would mean one of two things Either the building trades unions would lose in importance and play a less influential part in the Federation, or they would undergo a modification in policy which would bring them into line with the newer tendency in the other unions.

Should such a quasi-public trade unionism develop it would mean a considerable modification in the functions of the Federation. The need for organizing drives would be reduced to a minimum. On the other hand, conciliation and arbitration between unions and employ ers would be a greater function and the Federation might play an important part as it did during the war. Inevitably, if the government lends its aid to unionism, it will demand in exchange that the unions surrender some of their traditional liberties and adhere more closely to strictly constructive functions in industry. The problems of industrial management will assume primary importance, and the Federation may be called upon to lend greater aid to its unions in considering these problems and in developing national industrial policies.

The trend toward a semi-legal, quasi-public unionism in the United States is a phase of a movement which seems world-wide in character. In all industrial countries, the voluntary or so-called "free" type of unionism is having difficulties in maintaining itself, if it has not been entirely destroyed. Fascism in Italy, nationalism in Germany, and communism in the Soviet Union have all abandoned free unionism and replaced it with other forms. Under these different economic systems the tendency seems to be the same—to make use of the constructive elements of unionism for purposes of industrial administration and to make it a legally recognized agency for the workers' welfare while shearing it of the the power of independent economic and political action.

Such a change is undoubtedly in contrast to most predictions of labor evolution made during the past 50 years. But it seems in accord with facts of economic evolution. The free trade union was a product of competitive capitalism and of a rising democracy. Competitive capitalism made it possible for trade unions to act more or less as a stabilizing factor in industry in relation to labor costs by setting collective minimum standards. Under a system of competitive preoccupation with costs and prices the unions also protected the human element in industry. The economic losses which they caused by strikes and industrial strife, while considerable, were tolerable because they could be localized. Though there was a continuous outcry against these losses, they were accepted as part of the price paid for economic freedom and industrial progress. The price was reasonable under conditions of a developing world economy which allowed industrial countries to obtain increasing returns through the development of world resources and the exploitation of expanding markets.

Competitive and democratic capitalism also had room for a free labor movement. In fact, though developing as a reaction and protest against capitalism, the labor movement was itself part of the capitalistic system. A capitalism which was allied with liberalism and democracy needed a certain degree of opposition for its functioning. For over a hundred years this fact was the basis of a socio-political system which allowed opposition as a legal and constructive factor in its organization. The political party, the trade union, the co-operative movement, the socialist movement were all part of a dynamic system which predicated itself upon the idea of progress as a continuous movement toward higher political forms and higher standards of living and which allowed a certain degree of questioning of its own foundations and a certain degree of modification in its component institutions.

The present trends in economics and politics are seemingly in the opposite direction. Competition in industry is giving way to various forms of combination and monopoly. The growing importance of the credit mechanism and the rapid increase in productive capacity are accompanied by a constantly exaggerated instability of economic processes due to the problems involved by increasing fixed capital, overhead costs, and financial policies. In protest against such instability and against the resulting personal insecurity, demand for collective control and for economic co-operation as opposed to economic conflicts is likely to grow. Politically, the development of social groups with conflicting interests free to carry on their struggles unhindered is likely to result in a continued reaction against representative democracy and in a tendency toward executive forms of government for the purpose of overcoming friction and making speedy action possible. The trend in world economy towards a reorganization on a basis of greater regional and national self-sufficiency will continue to stimulate an economic nationalism which is intolerant of group conflicts and opposition parties.

Under these conditions a free labor movement becomes less and less possible. The tendency will be to reduce the amount of all conflict and to enforce national standards of economic conduct at the cost of limiting individual and group action. Opposition is no longer likely to be valued as a constructive force. The free trade union, based on voluntary group co-operation and achievement, is thus likely to be forced to give way to a new unionism whose features are incorporation in the economic and administrative system of the country and the performance of publicly recognized functions affecting the worker in his relation to industry.

While the trend toward a quasi-public unionism may be world-wide, it—like the free trade union—may have its variations. The American form need not be a mere duplicate of the extreme forms now developing in Europe. There is a probability that it may reconcile government control with many of the elements of the free trade union. This involves a recognition of three principles. First, that certain functions in industry, such as prevention of waste of materials, improving processes, bettering conditions of employment, maintaining morale, and enforcing safety, can be carried out effectively only through the active co-operation of publicly recognized workers' organizations. Second, that the welfare of the workers must be a co-operative function of the workers, employers, and the government. And third, that the reduction of conflict in industry be achieved with a minimum of governmental coercion by developing proper facilities for a rational examination of facts and issues.

Summing up, the course of the Federation and of the American labor movement in the near future will be shaped by the struggle of three tendencies. One will be the efforts of employers to eliminate unionism and to develop a benevolent industrialism trying to meet the human needs of workers through company unions which under the supervision of employers will be used for performing minor administrative functions in industry. However, as no system of employee representation seems able to provide an adequate substitute for unionism, the second tendency will be a continued effort on the part of the workers to revive and extend the present form of trade unionism. But as the difficulties in the path of unionism become aggravated by economic conditions, the third tendency towards a governmentally aided unionism will become stronger and assert itself against the other two.

IV. NEXT STEPS

The analysis of current trends indicates that the Federation will be faced by a complex situation in the near future. Whether the next few years continue to be years of business stagnation or witness economic recovery, there will be a widespread movement towards further wage readjustments. The unions will make efforts to hold their own or to recover lost ground with government aid, if necessary. Combined with continued technical changes, with some chronic unemployment, and with international complications, this cannot but mean difficult industrial readjustments involving much friction and struggle profoundly affecting our economic and social institutions.

The Federation as at present organized is not in a position to meet these problems. Its mechanisms, which have changed but little in 25 years, are totally inadequate to cope either with problems of struggle or with problems of research and investigation, or with the new issues of economic and social policy. The conclusion is that the Federation must reorganize if it is to play an active part in shaping the course of events. No claim is made here either to the right or to the capacity of mapping out a complete program for the Federation. But the study of past and present trends reveals certain persistent ideas of internal reform in the Federation which may be submitted as suggestions for consideration. In view of its declared faith in planful procedure for all economic life, the Federation cannot ignore the responsibility of planning for its own future. Its reluctance to look ahead has been one of the causes of its inability to shape the direction in which labor was going. Also, the disinclination of the Federation towards self-criticism and its intolerance of outside criticism reveal a sensitiveness which cannot be justified in a public body.

First in order is the long recognized need of giving the Federation greater disciplinary powers over its affiliated unions. The principle of trade autonomy has been carried to such lengths as to nullify the capacity of the Federation to perform most of the functions for which it exists. In fact, for some time the Federation has existed on sufferance of its larger and more powerful international unions. This lack of power is one of the reasons for the inability of the Federation to cope with the problem of internal abuse and "racketeering" in those affiliated unions, a "cleansing" of which is recognized as one of the first steps towards reorganization.

To obtain such a grant of power, it is necessary to overcome the vested interests of the affiliated unions, especially the desire of the larger unions to dominate the Federation. This could be accomplished by changing the voting system at conventions and by reorganizing the Executive Council. Perhaps the first step in this direction would be one which has been repeatedly suggested at Federation conventions since 1900—namely, the establishment of a standing committee whose function would be to map out possible combinations and amalgamations of the affiliated unions in order to create a more equal internal balance.

In line with similar suggestions, which likewise have their roots in the experience of the Federation, the Executive Council could be enlarged and made more representative. The structure of the Executive Council has been unchanged since 1904. In 1918 a demand was made for enlarging the Council so as to include two women, and in 1920 another demand was made to enlarge it by adding four more members. At that time the change was sanctioned by the convention; but it was afterwards rescinded for reasons that are not quite clear. At the 1932 convention a proposal was made to increase the number in the Council to 25, but it was defeated by an overwhelming vote, because the small unions rightly feared that the proposal would merely increase the representation of the larger unions.

This, however, can be avoided by arranging the unions of the Federation in 12 or 15 departments according to industrial divisions and by giving each department one representative on the Council. The Council would be sufficiently large to meet the new demands without being unwieldy, and at the same time it would be representative of the different group interests within the Federation. To counterbalance the dominance of the international unions, representation on the Council should also be given to the city centrals and state federations arranged in regional groups. There is also sufficient reason that at least one member of the Executive Council be a woman, who should be in charge of a Woman's Department such as was planned by Gompers in 1924. And some method of renewing a part of the Executive Council every year or every two years should be devised to offset its tendency of becoming a self-perpetuating closed corporation.

Greater co-ordination between the Executive Council and the international unions is necessary if the Federation is to be effective in its three main tasks—the formulation of policy, research, and legislation. Perhaps the Federation is most vulnerable because of its inability under present conditions to co-ordinate its own work and to mobilize to a greater degree the resources of the affiliated unions. At present the Federation is unable to evolve policies in a truly collective manner. The different elements which it represents are not given sufficient opportunity for co-operative planning. The officers of the international unions are absorbed in their own affairs and have little time to consider general policies. The Federation has tried to meet the situation by calling special conferences of all the officers of the international unions. These conferences are generally called on brief notice and cannot act with the necessary deliberation. Seldom has more come from them than general declarations prepared in advance by those who called them.

The Federation now needs more than general declarations. Careful study of economic changes and trends in various industries, and of their bearing upon national life as a whole is called for. This involves continuity of application, organized research, and systematic analysis of emergency problems. If the unions in the Federation should be organized into departments, each department could elect a member to the Executive Council and an alternate, who together would form a Committee on Economic Policy. If this committee had the services of a well-organized and well-staffed Research Department, it could function efficiently and steadily and anticipate problems. The Federation might obviate the expense of a large research staff by using more effectively than it has hitherto the services of the United States Department of Labor, which it was instrumental in creating and which was considered by its early protagonists as an agency for helping organized labor in providing research as a basis for national economic policies.

Many groups within the Federation have long demanded a Department of Organization for the purpose of consolidating the unions now existing and of extending the area of unionization. The unions in the Federation grouped into departments might assign to the general Department of Organization one organizer who would be familiar with the particular conditions of their respective industries. The different organizers would then be able to co-ordinate their activities. Such a department should study the conditions of the workers in different industries, the problems they have to face, and their outlook and attitudes toward union organization, especially in the mass industries. It should also be charged with the task of considering necessary changes in union structure. The Organization Department should be in charge of a person who, while responsible to the Executive Committee, should have large powers to reduce nepotism in appointments and to train young and efficient organizers. Such a department should convene periodically the active organizers of the various unions to compare methods and discuss new techniques.

The Federation needs a Department of Education to promote the study of economic and social problems and to improve the thinking and morale of union members. Such a department might devise ways and means for establishing a national labor college. Such a college has been a demand of many trade unionists for many years. But above all the Department of Education could do what the Federation has so far especially failed to do. It could study new developments in different unions in America and abroad, serve as a clearing house of information for its own members, and help to generalize successful methods worked out by separate unions.

The Federation must make an effort to attract to its service younger men, not only from the labor ranks but also from groups interested in working with and for labor organization. Its capacity to do so depends upon its acceptance of larger national purposes which would supply a stimulus for young men and women imbued with a social spirit. The attitude of the Federation towards the "intellectual" may have been justified in the past to the extent to which the intellectual was dominated by anti-union ideas or tried to dominate the labor movement. There is undoubtedly a certain group difference between the worker and the intellectual, owing to differences of background, ways of thinking, and experience. But these differences are not wider or deeper than those between some economic groups already in the Federation—such as the teachers and actors and hod-carriers—and they are decreasing. The purpose of the Federation is to become inclusive of wage earning and salaried groups and to work out a basis of common action for them. Younger men and women eager and willing to work in the labor organizations could be used in organizing work, in educational work, and in problems of research for which they are more or less trained and where they could utilize their energies and their enthusiasm. A beginning in this direction would be the establishment of standing advisory committees composed of members of the trade unions and of legal, economic, and other experts.

All trends seem to point to the conclusion that the Federation will be called upon in the future to formulate and to promote more effectively general labor policies as distinct from trade union efforts in separate trades. This will mean that the Federation must develop greater political articulation and coherence than it has at present. This may raise the question of an independent labor party, though the recent experience of the European socialist and labor parties indicates that they are not always capable of solving the larger problems confronting labor. But a step towards greater political effectiveness might be taken by establishing a working relationship with the Railroad Brotherhoods, independent unions, and other labor organizations in the form of a labor political council such as has been projected at various times.

The Federation started out on its active career by formulating a philosophy to which it adhered persistently, often despite unfavorable conditions. The experience of the last ten years gradually undermined this philosophy, and the present depression has given it a final blow. The problem before the Federation is to work out a new program of action in which the principles of voluntary collective relations are reconciled with the economic trend towards greater participation of government in the regulation of economic life, and to readjust its structure and methods accordingly. Basically, the problem is whether the American skilled workers can rise above their present group egotism, reconcile their own interests with those of the semi-skilled and unskilled, and evolve a labor organization truly national in scope and character. The capacity of the American Federation of Labor to lead in this direction will determine its importance to the American workers in the near future and its place in the rapidly changing and increasingly complex economic society of the America of tomorrow.

APPENDIXES

APPENDIX A

TABULAR DATA

The tabular and statistical data assembled in this appendix are intended to illustrate and support general statements in various chapters of the book. Cross-references have been made in the text linking the several tables with the discussion. The tables are based on records of the American Federation of Labor, with the exception of Table I, which has been compiled from the *History of Labor in the United States* by John R. Commons and associates, and from the *Documentary History of American Industrial Society* edited by John R. Commons and associates.

I. Trade Unions Formed or Reorganized, 1850-90

1850	International Typographical Union
1853	Journeymen Stone Cutters' Association of North America
1854	International Hat Finishers
1859	The Grand Union of Machinists and Blacksmiths
	International Molders' Union of North America
1861	The American Miners' Association
1862	The National Forge of the Sons of Vulcan (boilers and puddlers)
1863	The Grand National Division of the Brotherhood of Locomotive Engineers
1864	National Union of Cigarmakers
	Ship Carpenters and Caulkers' International Union
	National Union of Journeymen Curriers
1865	Plasterers' National Union
	Carpenters and Joiners' International Union
	Bricklayers and Masons' International Union
	Journeymen Painters' National Union
	National Union of Heaters

	Tailors' National Union
	Coach Makers' International Union
1866	Silk and Fur Hat Finishers' Union
1867	Spinners' Union
1868	Knights of St. Crispin (shoemakers)
	Grand Division of the Order of Railway Conductors
1869	Wool Hat Finishers
	Daughters of St. Crispin (shoemakers)
	Morocco Dressers' Union
1870	International Coopers' Union of North America
	Telegraphers' Union
1871	Painters' Union (reorganized)
1872	Woodworking Mechanics' Union
	Brotherhood of Iron and Steel Heaters
	Rollers' Union
	Roughers' Union
1873	National Union of Iron and Steel Roll Hands of the United States
	Furniture Workers' Union
	Miners' National Association
	Brotherhood of Locomotive Firemen
	German Typographia
1880	Boilerworkers' Union
1881	Bricklayers' Union (reorganized)
	United Brotherhood of Carpenters
1882	Lithographers' Protective and Insurance Association
1883	Bricklayers and Masons' International Union (change of name)
	Brotherhood of Railroad Trainmen
	Wall Paper Machine Printers' Union
	Journeymen Tailors' National Union
	National Wood Carvers' Association
1884	Paper Makers' Union
1885	National Federation of Miners and Mine Laborers
1886	Maintenance of Way Employees
	Order of Railroad Telegraphers
	Brotherhood of Lake Engineers
	Bakers' National Union
	National Union of Brewers of United States

1887 Brotherhood of Painters and Decorators
Stone Cutters' Union
Pattern Makers' League
Order of Railway Conductors (incorporated)
American Brotherhood of Steamboat Pilots
Paving Cutters' Union
1888 United Brotherhood of Carpenters and Joiners of America (result of amalgamation)
United Machinists and Mechanical Engineers of America
Tin, Sheet Iron, and Cornice Workers' Association
Metal Polishers, Knights of Labor, Trade Assembly 252
Brotherhood of Railway Car Repairers
1889 Operative Plasterers' International Union (change of name)
United Association of Journeymen Plumbers and Steamfitters
National Association of Machinists (change of name)
National Progressive Miners' Union
International Printing Pressmen's Union of America
National Association of Letter Carriers
1890 International Brotherhood of Brass Molders
United Mine Workers of America
United Green Glass Workers' Association

11. MEMBERSHIP IN AFFILIATED UNIONS OF THE

Industry	1899[b]
AGRICULTURE	—
International Union of Fruit and Vegetable Workers of North America[c]	—
MINING AND QUARRYING	**40,000**
United Mine Workers of America	40,000
International Union of Mine, Mill, and Smelter Workers	—
International Association of Oil Field, Gas Well, and Refinery Workers of America	—
Quarry Workers' International Union of North America	—
FORESTRY, LUMBER, AND WOODWORKING	**4,200**
Brushmakers' International Union	—
International Wood Carvers' Association of North America	1,200
Coopers' International Union of North America	2,700
International Broom and Whisk Makers' Union	300
International Union of Piano, Organ, and Musical Instrument Workers	—
International Union of Timber Workers	—
Shingle Weavers	—
Upholsterers, Carpet, and Linoleum Mechanics' International Union	—
METAL, MACHINERY, AND SHIPBUILDING	**46,700**
International Brotherhood of Blacksmiths, Drop Forgers, and Helpers	500
International Brotherhood of Boiler Makers, Iron Ship Builders and Helpers of America	2,700
Brotherhood of Railway Carmen of America	—
International Union of Cutting Die and Cutter Makers	—
Diamond Workers' Protective Union of America	—
International Federation of Technical Engineers, Architects, and Draftsmen's Unions	—
International Brotherhood of Foundry Employees	—
Amalgamated Association of Iron, Steel, and Tin Workers	8,000
International Jewelry Workers' Union	—
International Association of Machinists	13,600
International Molders' Union of North America	15,000
Pattern Makers' League of North America	1,500
Pocket Knife Blade Grinders and Finishers' National Union	—
International Union of Metal Polishers	4,800
Sawsmiths' National Union	—
Stove Mounters' International Union	600
American Wire Weavers' Protective Association	—
BUILDING	**33,800**
International Association of Heat and Frost Insulators and Asbestos Workers	—
Bricklayers, Masons, and Plasterers' International Union of America	—
Bridge and Structural Iron Workers' International Association	—
Building Service Employees' International Union	—
United Brotherhood of Carpenters and Joiners of America	20,000
American Brotherhood of Cement Workers	—
Compressed Air and Foundation Workers' Union of the United States and Canada	—
International Brotherhood of Electrical Workers of America	2,000
International Union of Elevator Constructors	—
International Union of Operating Engineers	1,800

American Federation of Labor, for Selected Years[a]

1904[b]	1914	1920	1924	1929	1932
—	—	—	—	—	—
—	—	—	—	—	—
260,300	**375,400**	**438,600**	**416,900**	**408,600**	**313,400**
257,700	334,500	393,600	402,700	400,000	308,300
—	36,900	21,100[d]	9,100	4,000	2,100
—	—	20,900	2,200	1,600	400
2,600	4,000	3,000	2,900	3,000	2,600
23,200	**13,500**	**25,800**	**11,300**	**13,700**	**8,600**
—	200	[e]	—	—	—
2,100	1,100	1,200	1,000	1,200	900
7,100	4,500	4,300	1,500	800	600
1,100	700	1,400	700	500	300
9,900	1,000	3,200	600	500	300
—	—	10,100	[e]	—	—
—	2,500	[f]	—	—	—
3,000	3,500	5,600	7,500	10,700	6,500
150,600	**206,500**	**795,900**	**303,500**	**232,800**	**198,300**
10,500	9,600	48,300	5,000	5,000	5,000
19,000	16,700	103,000	17,500	17,200	15,000
—	28,700	182,100	137,500	80,000	80,000
—	300	200	[e]	—	—
—	300	600	500	400	300
—	—	3,500	600	1,500	1,000
1,000	600	9,100	3,600	3,500	700
13,500	6,400	31,500	11,100	8,900	5,000
2,400	[e]	8,100	1,200	800	800
55,700	75,400	330,800	77,900	77,000	70,700
30,000	50,000	57,300	33,600	23,700	9,500
3,700	6,700	9,000	7,000	7,000	7,000
—	300	[g]	—	—	—
12,800	10,000	10,000	6,000	6,000	700
—	100	100	[e]	—	—
1,700	1,100	1,900	1,600	1,400	2,300
300	300	400	400	400	300
317,900	**460,900**	**836,900**	**850,400**	**969,900**	**870,500**
700	1,000	2,200	2,200	2,900	2,000
—	—	70,000	70,000	90,000	56,700
11,500	10,200	24,200	17,700	20,400	12,000
800	—	—	6,200	9,200	18,000
155,400	212,800	331,500	315,500	322,000	290,000
—	7,300	[h]	—	—	—
—	1,000	[i]	—	—	—
21,000	30,800	139,200	142,000	142,000	139,900
2,200	2,700	3,100	8,100	10,200	10,200
17,600	20,300	32,000	25,000	33,000	34,400

Industry	1899
BUILDING (*Continued*)	
International Hod-Carriers, Building, and Common Laborers' Union of America	—
International Union of Wood, Wire, and Metal Lathers	—
International Association of Marble, Stone and Slate Polishers, etc.	—
Sheet Metal Workers' International Association	1,500
Brotherhood of Painters, Decorators and Paperhangers of America	4,500
Operative Plasterers' International Association of the United States and Canada	—
United Association of Plumbers and Steamfitters of the United States and Canada	4,000
United Slate, Tile and Composition Roofers, Damp and Waterproof Workers' Association	—
International Union of Pavers, Rammermen, Flag Layers, etc.	—
International Paving Cutters' Union of the United States and Canada	—
Brotherhood of Slate Workers	—
International Slate and Tile Roofers of America	—
Ceramic, Mosaic, and Encaustic Tile Layers and Helpers' International Union	—
Tunnel and Subway Constructors' International Union	—
TEXTILES	**2,500**
Chartered Society of Amalgamated Lace Operatives of America	—
Spinners' International Union	—
United Textile Workers of America	2,200
Amalgamated Association of Elastic Goring Weavers	300
LEATHER	**5,300**
Boot and Shoe Workers' Union	4,300
Travelers' Goods and Leather Novelty Workers' International Union	—
United Leather Workers' International Union of America	1,000
CLOTHING	**10,200**
Cloth Hat, Cap, and Millinery Workers' International Union	—
International Fur Workers' Union of the United States and Canada	—
United Garment Workers of America	4,200
International Glove Workers' Union of America	—
United Hatters of North America	6,000
International Ladies' Garment Workers' Union	—
Journeymen Tailors' Union of America	—
FOOD, LIQUOR, AND TOBACCO	**46,600**
Bakery and Confectionery Workers' International Union of America	3,100
International Union of the United Brewery, Flour, Cereal, and Soft Drink Workers of America	10,700
Cigarmakers' International Union of America	27,000
Amalgamated Meat Cutters and Butcher Workers of North America	1,700
Tobacco Workers' International Union	4,100
CHEMICALS, CLAY, STONE, AND GLASS	**20,200**
United Brick and Clay Workers of America	1,000

American Federation of Labor, for Selected Years (*Continued*)

1904	1914	1920	1924	1929	1932
8,500	25,600	42,000	49,000	91,700	90,000
5,900	5,500	5,900	8,000	16,500	16,500
600	4,100	1,200	3,000	6,400	7,700
15,300	17,800	21,800	25,000	25,000	25,000
60,700	74,400	103,100	103,300	108,100	79,600
—	18,000	19,400	30,000	39,200	35,300
16,500	29,700	32,000	35,000	45,000	45,000
—	1,200	1,800	3,000	4,000	4,000
—	1,600	1,900	2,000	2,000	2,000
1,200	3,500	2,600	2,400	2,300	2,000
—	300	[j]	—	—	—
—	600	[j]	—	—	—
—	3,000	[k]	—	—	—
—	1,700	3,000	3,000	[i]	—
10,600	**21,500**	**105,000**	**30,100**	**30,100**	**27,500**
—	1,200	[g]	—	—	—
—	2,200	[g]	—	—	—
10,500	18,000	104,900	30,000	30,000	27,500
100	100	100	100	[e]	—
36,600	**40,800**	**58,400**	**39,200**	**37,400**	**18,000**
32,000	38,100	46,700	37,200	32,400	17,000
—	900	[l]	—	—	—
4,600	1,800	11,700	2,000	5,000	1,000
77,500	**156,600**	**186,900**	**169,100**	**108,600**	**105,600**
2,900	3,600	[g]	—	6,900	4,600
300	800	12,100	8,900	2,800	3,800
45,700	60,700	45,900	47,500	47,500	45,600
2,000	1,100	1,000	200	800	300
8,500	8,500	10,500	11,500	11,500	8,500
2,200	69,900	105,400	91,000	32,300	40,000
15,900	12,000	12,000	10,000	6,800	2,800
127,200	**117,600**	**180,900**	**78,900**	**70,200**	**63,300**
16,200	15,700	27,500	22,200	21,200	17,900
30,500	52,000	34,100	16,000	16,000	16,000
40,500	40,000	38,800	27,700	17,000	15,500
34,400	6,200	65,300	11,500	11,800	11,400
5,600	3,700	15,200	1,500	4,200	2,500
30,300	**51,700**	**52,700**	**43,000**	**38,500**	**30,000**
7,300	3,200	5,200	4,800	5,000	2,000

Industry	1899
CHEMICALS: CLAY, STONE, AND GLASS (*Continued*)	
Window Glass Cutters' League of America	800
Glass Bottle Blowers' Association of the United States and Canada	4,200
Window Glass Cutters and Flatteners' Association of America	600
American Flint Glass Workers' Union	7,500
International Association of Amalgamated Glass Workers	—
National Window Glass Workers	—
Granite Cutters' International Association of America	4,800
National Brotherhood of Operative Potters	1,300
United Powder and High Explosive Workers of America	—
Journeymen Stone Cutters' Association of North America	—
PAPER, PRINTING, AND PUBLISHING	**41,500**
International Brotherhood of Bookbinders	2,800
International Steel and Copper Plate Engravers' League	—
International Metal Engravers' Union	—
International Photo-Engravers' Union of North America	—
Lithographers International Protective and Beneficial Association of the United States and Canada	—
International Brotherhood of Paper Makers	100
International Plate Printers and Die Stampers' Union of North America	400
International Printing Pressmen and Assistants' Union of North America	7,200
Machine Printers and Color Mixers of North America	—
National Print Cutters' Association of America	—
International Brotherhood of Pulp, Sulphite, and Paper Mill Workers of the United States and Canada	—
International Stereotypers and Electrotypers Union of North America	—
International Typographical Union	31,000
International Association of Sideographers	—
United Wall Paper Crafts of North America	—
TRANSPORTATION AND COMMUNICATION	**29,700**
Brotherhood of Railway Clerks	—
Order of Sleeping Car Conductors	—
Brotherhood of Railroad Freight Handlers	—
International Longshoremen's Association	13,000
Brotherhood of Maintenance of Way Employees	—
National Organization of Masters, Mates, and Pilots of America	—
Brotherhood of Railroad Patrolmen	—
International Seamen's Union of America	4,000
Amalgamated Association of Street and Electric Railway Employees of America	3,000
Switchmen's Union of North America	—
International Brotherhood of Teamsters, Chauffeurs, Stablemen and Helpers of America	1,700
International Air Line Pilots Association	—
Commercial Telegraphers' Union of North America	—
Order of Railroad Telegraphers	8,000
Brotherhood of Railroad Signalmen of America	—

AMERICAN FEDERATION OF LABOR, FOR SELECTED YEARS (*Continued*)

1904	1914	1920	1924	1929	1932
g	—	—	—	900	900
6,600	10,000	10,000	6,000	6,000	6,000
g	—	—	—	300	m
s	9,900	9,900	6,100	5,200	3,900
—	1,200	n	—	—	—
—	—	4,800	4,000	e	—
9,900	13,500	10,500	8,600	8,500	6,200
5,800	7,700	8,000	8,300	6,600	5,200
700	200	300	200	200	100
—	6,000	4,000	5,000	5,800	5,700
81,700	**110,300**	**163,600**	**153,000**	**163,100**	**161,800**
6,500	9,400	20,700	13,400	13,600	11,900
—	—	200	100	—	—
—	—	—	100	100	500
—	4,700	5,900	6,800	8,600	8,900
—	2,800	6,100	5,500	5,800	5,600
8,800	4,400	7,400	6,200	4,000	4,000
1,000	1,300	1,400	1,200	1,200	1,100
16,000	19,300	35,000	38,700	40,000	40,000
—	500	500	p	—	—
300	400	400	p	—	—
—	3,500	9,500	5,000	5,000	5,000
2,400	4,500	5,900	6,500	7,700	8,100
46,700	59,400	70,500	68,800	76,400	76,100
—	100[q]	100	100	100	100
—	—	—	600	600	500
212,000	**197,500**	**623,500**	**420,900**	**434,400**	**351,600**
600	5,000	186,000	88,400	96,900	60,800
—	—	1,200	2,300	2,300	2,100
—	2,900	r	—	—	—
50,000	25,000	74,000	30,500	37,700	27,000
12,300	6,500	g	38,300	32,200	37,100
—	—	7,100	4,100	3,000	3,000
—	—	2,600	g	—	—
20,100	16,000	65,900	18,000	15,000	9,700
30,000	54,500	98,700	100,000	99,700	81,700
—	9,800	14,000	9,300	9,300	7,200
84,000	51,100	110,800	75,000	95,500	82,000
—	—	—	—	—	500
—	1,000	2,200	3,700	3,800	3,500
15,000	25,000	48,700	43,300	39,000	37,000
—	700	12,300	8,000	g	—

Industry	1899
PUBLIC SERVICE	—
National Federation of Federal Employees	—
American Federation of Government Employees	—
National Association of Letter Carriers	—
National Federation of Post Office Clerks	—
Brotherhood of Railway Postal Clerks	—
National Federation of Post Office Clerks	—
Railway Mail Association	—
National Federation of Rural Letter Carriers	—
American Federation of Teachers	—
International Association of Fire Fighters	—
PERSONAL SERVICE AND TRADE	**13,500**
Journeymen Barbers' Union	4,000
Retail Clerks' International Protective Association	7,500
Hotel and Restaurant Employees and Beverage Dispensers' International Alliance	2,000
Laundry Workers' International Union	—
AMUSEMENTS AND PROFESSIONS	**9,000**
Associated Actors and Artistes of America	—
American Federation of Musicians	6,000
International Alliance of Theatrical Stage Employees and Moving Picture Machine Operators of the United States and Canada	3,000
MISCELLANEOUS	**3,100**
International Brotherhood of Stationary Firemen	1,100
International Alliance of Bill Posters and Billers of America	—
International Union of Journeymen Horseshoers of the United States and Canada	2,000
National Marine Engineering Beneficial Association of the United States and Canada	—
Carriage and Wagon Workers	—
Sheep Shearers' Union of North America	—
UNCLASSIFIED[w]	**43,122**
TOTAL AVERAGE MEMBERSHIP	**349,422**

[a] This table is based upon data published in the reports of the proceed-
ported by the A. F. of L. show voting strength on the basis of one vote for
annual membership reported to the American Federation of Labor by the
or withdrew from the American Federation of Labor are not included in 1899
[e] Organized in 1922 with a membership of 1,900; disbanded in 1923.
banded. [f] Merged with timber workers in 1918. [g] Suspended.
carriers. [j] Merged with composition roofers in 1920.
elers' goods merged with the leather novelty workers in 1917. [m] Amal-
[n] Merged with painters, decorators, and paper hangers in 1915.
[p] Amalgamation of National Association of Machine Printers and Color
America and change of title to United Wall Paper Crafts of North America.
[r] Amalgamated with Brotherhood of Railway Clerks in 1915. [s] With-
Clerks and National Federation of Post Office Clerks merged in 1917.
1911 became known as White Rats' Actors' Union of America; organized
rectly affiliated local unions and differences due to methods of computing

American Federation of Labor, for Selected Years (*Continued*)

1904	1914	1920	1924	1929	1932
—	**4,300**	**133,300**	**110,200**	**149,100**	**137,800**
—	—	38,500	20,800	30,500	[s]
—	—	—	—	—	[t]
—	—	32,500	32,500	45,000	55,000
—	—	16,200	20,000	32,000	36,000
—	1,505[g]	—	—	—	—
—	2,800[u]	—	—	—	—
—	—	14,400	17,900	19,800	20,700
—	—	300	300	800	1,100
—	—	9,300	3,700	4,200	7,000
—	—	22,100	15,000	16,800	18,000
129,500	**111,100**	**132,100**	**99,300**	**105,500**	**82,400**
23,600	34,300	44,200	45,300	52,200	39,900
50,000	15,000	20,800	10,000	10,000	8,700
49,400	59,000	60,400	38,500	37,800	28,300
6,500	2,800	6,700	5,500	5,500	5,500
27,600	**86,000**	**96,500**	**104,500**	**134,800**	**128,500**
1,100[v]	11,000	6,900	7,400	11,500	4,500
22,000	60,000	70,000	77,100	100,000	100,000
4,500	15,000	19,600	20,000	23,300	24,000
23,500	**26,600**	**53,600**	**12,600**	**12,000**	**11,200**
18,000	16,000	29,600	9,000	9,500	9,300
1,300	1,400	1,600	1,600	1,600	1,600
4,200	5,700	5,400	2,000	900	200
—	—	17,000	[s]	—	—
—	3,500	[g]	—	—	—
—	—	—	—	—	100
167,700	**28,171**	**195,040**	**22,899**	**67,945**	**23,761**
1,676,200	**2,020,671**	**4,078,740**	**2,865,799**	**2,933,545**	**2,532,261**

ings of the conventions of the American Federation of Labor. The figures re-
100 members or fraction thereof. The voting strength is based on the average
affiliated unions. [b] Some unions which later disbanded, amalgamated,
and 1904 industrial groups. Figures for all other years are complete.
[d] Previous to 1917 known as Western Federation of Miners. [e] Dis-
[h] Merged with operative plasterers in 1916. [i] Merged with hod-
[k] Not recognized in 1919. [l] Leather workers on horse goods and trav-
gamated with Window Glass Cutters' League of America, 1931.
[o] Merged with International Plate Printers and Die Stampers' Union.
Mixers of the United States with National Print Cutters' Association of
[q] Known as Steel Plate Transferers' Association of America prior to 1914.
drew. [t] Organized in 1932. [u] Brotherhood of Railway Postal
[v] Organized in 1901 under name of Actors' National Protective Union; in
under present name in 1919. [w] Accounted for by membership of di-
voting strength and average annual membership.

III. Reported Average Membership of the American Federation of Labor, 1897–1932[a]

Year	Average Annual Membership	Increase or Decrease over Preceding Year	
		Membership	*Percentage*
1897	264,825	—	—
1898	278,016	+ 13,191	+ 5.0
1899	349,422	+ 71,406	+25.7
1900	548,321	+198,899	+56.9
1901	787,537	+239,216	+43.6
1902	1,024,399	+236,862	+30.1
1903	1,465,800	+441,401	+43.1
1904	1,676,200	+210,400	+14.4
1905	1,494,300	−181,900	−10.9
1906	1,454,200	− 40,100	− 2.7
1907	1,538,970	+ 84,770	+ 5.8
1908	1,586,885	+ 47,915	+ 3.1
1909	1,482,872	−104,013	− 6.6
1910	1,562,112	+ 79,240	+ 5.3
1911	1,761,835	+199,723	+12.8
1912	1,770,145	+ 8,310	+ 0.5
1913	1,996,004	+225,859	+12.8
1914	2,020,671	+ 24,667	+ 1.2
1915	1,946,347	− 74,324	− 3.7
1916	2,072,702	+126,355	+ 6.5
1917	2,371,434	+298,732	+14.4
1918	2,726,478	+355,044	+15.0
1919	3,260,068	+533,590	+19.6
1920	4,078,740	+818,672	+25.1
1921	3,906,528	−172,212	− 4.2
1922	3,195,635	−710,893	−18.2
1923	2,926,468	−269,167	− 8.4
1924	2,865,799	− 60,669	− 2.1
1925	2,877,297	+ 11,498	+ 0.4
1926	2,803,966	− 73,331	− 2.5
1927	2,812,526	+ 8,560	+ 0.3
1928	2,896,063	+ 83,537	+ 3.0
1929	2,933,545	+ 37,482	+ 1.3
1930	2,961,096	+ 27,551	+ 0.9
1931	2,889,550	− 71,546	− 2.4
1932	2,532,261	−357,289	−12.4

[a] *Report of the Proceedings of the Fifty-Second Annual Convention of the American Federation of Labor*, 1932, p. 49.

IV. Average Annual Membership Reported to A. F. of L. Compared with Estimated Membership in Selected Unions, 1931

Union	Average Annual Membership Reported to A. F. of L.[a]	Estimated Annual Average Membership[b]	Difference
Actors and artists	8,300	8,200	+ 100
Bakery and confectionery workers	20,100	20,100	—
Boot and shoe workers	27,500	27,500	—
Bookbinders	13,700	13,900	− 200
Brewery, flour, cereal and soft drink workers	16,000	15,300	+ 700
Broom and whisk makers	400	500	− 100
Railway carmen	80,000	48,500	+ 31,500
Cigarmakers	15,500	10,900	+ 4,600
Cloth hat, cap and millinery workers	5,800	5,800	—
Sleeping car conductors	2,300	1,800	+ 500
Diamond workers	400	300	+ 100
International photo-engravers	9,000	9,000	—
Glass bottle blowers	6,000	6,000	—
Window glass cutters	1,000	700	+ 300
Hod-carriers, building and common laborers	115,000	98,000	+ 17,000
Wood, wire and metal lathers	16,500	12,500	+ 4,000
Lithographers	5,700	5,700	—
Mine, mill and smelter workers	4,000	4,000	—
Mine workers	400,000	150,000	+250,000
Musicians	100,000	126,400	− 26,400
Paper makers	4,000	4,000	—
Paving cutters	2,400	2,400	—
Plasterers	37,700	37,600	+ 100
Post office clerks	36,000	48,000	− 12,000
Plate printers and die stampers	1,200	1,200	—
Stereotypers and electrotypers	8,200	8,200	—
Stone cutters	5,800	4,500	+ 1,300
Teamsters, chauffeurs, stablemen and helpers	92,000	92,000	—
Commercial telegraphers	3,800	3,100	+ 700
Tobacco workers	2,400	2,400	—
Typographers	77,500	77,800	− 300
Wall paper craftsmen	600	600	—
Wire weavers	400	400	—
Total	1,119,200	847,300	+271,900

[a] *Proceedings of 52d Annual Convention of A. F. of L.*, 1932, pp. 29–30.

[b] These estimates are based on correspondence with unions and on reports of the conventions of the unions. They were made by Dr. Leo Wolman for a forthcoming monograph to be published by the President's Committee on Recent Social Trends. The author is indebted to Dr. Wolman for permission to use these figures.

V. Membership of the American Federation of Labor by Industry Groups, 1914, 1920, 1932

Industry	1914		1920		1932	
	Total Membership	*Percentage Distribution*	Total Membership	*Percentage Distribution*	Total Membership	*Percentage Distribution*
Agriculture	—	—	—	—	—	—
Mining and quarrying	375,400	*18.6*	438,600	*10.8*	313,400	*12.4*
Forestry, lumber, and wood working	13,500	*0.7*	25,800	*0.6*	8,600	*0.3*
Metal, machinery, and shipbuilding	206,500	*10.2*	795,900	*19.5*	198,300	*7.8*
Building	473,100	*23.4*	836,900	*20.5*	870,500	*34.4*
Textiles	21,500	*1.1*	105,000	*2.6*	27,500	*1.1*
Leather	40,800	*2.0*	58,400	*1.4*	18,000	*0.7*
Clothing	156,600	*7.7*	186,900	*4.6*	105,600	*4.2*
Food, liquor, and tobacco	117,600	*5.8*	180,900	*4.4*	63,300	*2.5*
Chemicals, clay, stone, and glass	51,700	*2.6*	52,700	*1.3*	30,000	*1.2*
Paper, printing, and publishing	110,300	*5.4*	163,600	*4.0*	161,800	*6.4*
Transportation and communication	197,500	*9.8*	623,500	*15.3*	351,600	*13.9*
Public service	4,300	*0.2*	133,300	*3.3*	137,800	*5.4*
Personal service and trade	111,100	*5.5*	132,100	*3.2*	82,400	*3.3*
Amusements and professions	86,000	*4.3*	96,500	*2.4*	128,500	*5.1*
Miscellaneous	26,600	*1.3*	53,600	*1.3*	11,200	*0.4*
Membership not accounted for above[a]	28,171	*1.4*	195,040	*4.8*	23,761	*0.9*
Total	2,020,671	*100.0*	4,078,740	*100.0*	2,532,261	*100.0*

[a] Membership of directly affiliated local unions and differences due to methods of computing voting strength and average membership.

VI. Unions in the American Federation of Labor, Classified by Size, 1904, 1914, 1932[a]

Membership	1904			1914			1932		
	Number of Unions	Total Membership	*Percentage Distribution of Membership*	Number of Unions	Total Membership	*Percentage Distribution of Membership*	Number of Unions	Total Membership	*Percentage Distribution of Membership*
1,000 or less	30	14,900	*0.9*	22	11,400	*0.6*	21	10,500	*0.4*
1,001– 2,500	27	46,400	*2.8*	14	20,900	*1.0*	11	21,000	*0.8*
2,501– 5,000	11	42,100	*2.5*	20	72,700	*3.6*	13	51,700	*2.1*
5,001– 10,000	16	119,000	*7.1*	16	125,200	*6.2*	18	132,300	*5.2*
10,001– 25,000	20	317,500	*18.9*	16	259,500	*12.8*	15	249,100	*9.8*
25,001– 50,000	12	467,500	*27.9*	10	339,100	*16.8*	13	473,100	*18.7*
50,001–100,000	3	200,400	*12.0*	10	616,400	*30.5*	11	832,600	*32.9*
Over 100,000	2	413,100	*24.6*	2	547,300	*27.1*	3	738,200	*29.2*
Unclassified[b]		55,300	*3.3*		28,171	*1.4*		23,761	*0.9*
Total	121	1,676,200	*100.0*	110	2,020,671	*100.0*	106	2,532,261	*100.0*

[a] Compiled from *Proceedings of Annual Convention of A. F. of L.*, 1904, 1914, 1932.

[b] Membership of directly affiliated local unions and differences due to methods of computing voting strength and average annual membership.

VII. Number of Constituent Units Affiliated with the American Federation of Labor, 1899–1932[a]

Year	National and International Unions	State Federations	City Central Unions	Local Trade and Federal Labor Unions	
				Number	Membership
1899	73	11	118	797	[b]
1900	82	16	206	1,051	[b]
1901	87	20	327	1,149	[b]
1902	97	26	424	1,483	[b]
1903	113	29	549	1,747	[b]
1904	120	32	569	1,271	[b]
1905	118	33	599	1,046	[b]
1906	119	36	538	759	24,500
1907	117	37	574	661	28,900
1908	116	38	606	583	[b]
1909	119	39	565	551	18,971
1910	120	39	632	647	20,951
1911	115	38	631	680	28,579
1912	112	41	560	590	27,945
1913	111	42	621	659	28,847
1914	110	43	647	570	27,194
1915	110	44	673	489	23,763
1916	111	45	717	705	35,163
1917	111	45	762	845	58,416
1918	111	45	782	854	66,453
1919	111	46	816	884	65,227
1920	110	46	926	1,286	86,784
1921	110	49	973	941	68,165
1922	112	49	905	666	31,258
1923	108	49	901	523	23,426
1924	107	49	855	458	22,755
1925	107	49	850	436	21,150
1926	107	49	833	380	22,317
1927	106	49	794	365	24,237
1928	107	49	792	373	25,286
1929	105	49	803	388	21,704
1930	104	49	804	348	18,150
1931	105	49	728	334	14,531
1932	106	49	619	307	11,368

[a] Compiled from *Proceedings of Annual Convention of A. F. of L.*, 1899–1932.

[b] Data not reported.

VIII. Union Amalgamations Effected by the American Federation of Labor Between 1900 and 1932[a]

Year	Unions Amalgamated	New Union Formed
1900	Window Glass Cutters' League of America; Other Glass Workers	Window Glass Cutters' League of America
1901	National Union of Textile Workers of America; American Federation of Textile Operatives	United Textile Workers of America
1903	Iron Molders' Union of North America; Coremakers' International Union	International Molders' Union of North America
	International Brotherhood of Blacksmiths; Directly affiliated local of Blacksmiths and Helpers	International Brotherhood of Blacksmiths and Helpers
	International Team Drivers' Union; Teamsters' National Union	International Brotherhood of Teamsters (*Now* International Brotherhood of Teamsters, Chauffeurs, Stablemen and Helpers of America)
	Order of Commercial Telegraphers; International Union of Commercial Telegraphers	Commercial Telegraphers' Union of North America
	International Watch Case Makers; International Jewelry Workers	International Jewelry Workers' Union
1904	Northern Mineral Mine Workers; Progressive Union of North America; Western Federation of Miners	Western Federation of Miners (Now International Union of Mine, Mill, and Smelter Workers)
	International Association of Allied Metal Mechanics; International Association of Machinists	International Association of Machinists
1912	Amalgamated Woodworkers' International Union; United Brotherhood of Carpenters and Joiners of America	United Brotherhood of Carpenters and Joiners of America
1913	International Tin Plate Workers' Protective Association of North America; Amalgamated Association of Iron, Steel, and Tin Workers	Amalgamated Association of Iron, Steel, and Tin Workers
1915	Brotherhood of Painters, Decorators, and Paperhangers of America; Amalgamated Glass Workers' International Association	Brotherhood of Painters, Decorators, and Paperhangers of America
	Brotherhood of Railroad Freight Handlers; Brotherhood of Railway Clerks	Brotherhood of Railway Clerks

VIII. Union Amalgamations Effected by the American Federation of Labor between 1900 and 1932 (*Continued*)

Year	Unions Amalgamated	New Union Formed
1918	Operative Plasterers' International Association of the United States and Canada American Brotherhood of Cement Workers	Operative Plasterers' International Association of the United States and Canada
1917	United Brotherhood of Leather Workers on Horse Goods Travelers' Goods and Leather Novelty Workers' Union of North America	International Union of United Leather Workers
	Brotherhood of Railway Postal Clerks National Federation of Post Office Clerks	National Federation of Postal Employees
1918	International Union of United Brewery and Soft Drink Workers International Union of Flour and Cereal Mill Workers	International Union of the United Brewery, Flour, Cereal, and Soft Drink Workers of America
	International Brotherhood of Bookbinders International Brotherhood of Tip Printers	International Brotherhood of Bookbinders
	International Hod-Carriers, Building, and Common Laborers' Union of America Compressed Air and Foundation Workers' Union	International Hod-Carriers, Building, and Common Laborers' Union of America
	International Brotherhood of Maintenance of Way Employees Railway Shop Laborers	United Brotherhood of Maintenance of Way Employees and Railway Shop Laborers (Now Brotherhood of Maintenance of Way Employees)
	International Union of Timber Workers International Shingle Weavers of America	International Union of Timber Workers (disbanded, 1923)
1919	International Brotherhood of Blacksmiths and Helpers Independent Unaffiliated Drop Forgers	International Brotherhood of Blacksmiths, Drop Forgers, and Helpers
	International Slate and Tile Roofers' Union of America International Brotherhood of Composition Roofers, Damp and Waterproof Workers of United States and Canada	United Slate, Tile, and Composition Roofers, Damp and Waterproof Workers Association
1923	National Print Cutters' Association of America National Association of Machine Printers and Color Mixers of the United States	United Wall Paper Crafts of North America

VIII. Union Amalgamations Effected by the American Federation of Labor Between 1900 and 1932 (*Continued*)

Year	Unions Amalgamated	New Union Formed
1924	United Brotherhood of Carpenters and Joiners of America; Amalgamated Society of Carpenters and Joiners	United Brotherhood of Carpenters and Joiners of America
1925	International Plate Printers and Die Stampers; International Steel and Copper Plate Engravers' League	International Plate Printers and Die Stampers Union of North America
1927	International Brotherhood of Steam Shovel and Dredgemen; Operating Engineers	International Union of Operating Engineers
1929	International Hod-Carriers, Building, and Common Laborers' Union of America; Tunnel and Subway Constructors International Union	International Hod-Carriers, Building, and Common Laborers' Union of America
1930	Window Glass Cutters' League of America; Glass Flatteners' Association of North America	Window Glass Cutters League of America

[a] Compiled from *Proceedings of 51st Annual Convention of A. F. of L.*, 1931, pp. 36–57. This report also contains a summary of amalgamations of unions not now affiliated with the A. F. of L. and the dates of organization of unions in different trades.

IX. BENEFITS PAID BY SELECTED UNIONS OF THE AMERICAN FEDERATION OF LABOR, 1931[a]

Union	Total	Sick	Death	Unemployment	Old-Age	Disability	Miscellaneous
Bakery and confectionery workers	$170,894	$126,379	$ 28,783	—	—	—	$15,732
Journeymen barbers	384,985	273,400	111,585	—	—	—	—
Bricklayers, masons and plasterers	921,856	—	303,675	—	$618,181	—	—
Railway carmen	195,900	—	131,700	$ 30,000	—	$ 9,200	25,000
Carpenters and joiners	1,732,359	—	628,328	—	1,052,685	50,750	596
Railway clerks	383,050	—	373,050	—	—	—	10,000[b]
Electrical workers	421,102	—	367,550	—	53,552	—	—
Operating engineers	152,625	—	152,625	—	—	—	—
Photo-engravers	2,095,217	55,650[c]	127,088[c]	1,665,826[b]	—	2,000	244,651
Machinists	471,108	32,500	231,358	166,500	—	5,000	35,750
Mine workers	1,500,000	—	500,000[b]	1,000,000[b]	—	—	—
Molders	657,883	162,341	288,058	191,158	—	16,325	—
Painters, decorators and paperhangers of America	347,704	—	260,763	—	—	51,075	35,866
Plumbers and steamfitters	2,358,259	179,430	126,443	2,000,000[b]	—	—	52,386
Printing pressmen and assistants	1,315,542	64,142[b]	242,391[c]	881,623[c]	108,890[c]	10,733[b]	7,762[b]
Street and electric railway employees	1,139,119	95,498[b]	902,921[c]	—	122,400	18,300	—
Typographers	4,592,241	50,505	697,332[c]	2,175,183[b]	1,574,461[c]	—	94,758

[a] Compiled from *Proceedings of 52nd Annual Convention of A. F. of L.*, 1932, pp. 88–91.
[b] Paid by local unions.
[c] Includes local benefits.

X. Total Receipts and Expenditures of the American Federation of Labor, 1914–32[a]

With Income from Per Capita Taxes and Outgo for Organization Work

Year	Receipts		Expenditures	
	Total	From Per Capita Taxes	Total	For Organization Work
1914	$263,166	$180,653	$265,737	$ 79,713
1915	271,625	176,372	303,985	72,342
1916	334,275	196,447	315,047	80,983
1917	412,047	251,758	402,440	107,146
1918	303,463	182,239	277,110	76,892
1919	654,687	358,817	587,518	165,609
1920	929,255	562,608	917,765	285,584
1921	832,169	541,360	857,888	279,605
1922	583,120	417,171	562,588	170,935
1923	687,880	515,626	662,398	187,518
1924	512,397	366,504	500,028	131,168
1925	509,702	372,057	533,294	132,305
1926	518,451	360,207	519,113	105,151
1927	524,284	343,300	485,033	114,778
1928	545,437	336,291	496,971	111,658
1929	609,633	432,168	575,181	125,357
1930	560,603	377,597	531,442	122,623[b]
1931	569,105	357,201	561,985	139,526[b]
1932	466,350	312,809	468,747	112,076[b]

[a] Compiled from *Proceedings of Annual Convention of A. F. of L.*, 1914–32.

[b] In addition the American Federation of Labor spent the following sums on the Southern organizing campaign headquarters office: 1930, $12,460; 1931, $14,769; 1932, $5,777.

APPENDIX B

PRESENT STATUS AND PROBLEMS OF SELECTED UNIONS AFFILIATED WITH THE AMERICAN FEDERATION OF LABOR

No attempt is made in this appendix to present either a history or an exhaustive analysis of the unions considered. The data are intended to illustrate some of the problems with which the unions in the A. F. of L. are confronted, and to direct the attention of students to a more thorough study of them.[1]

I. AGRICULTURE

In agriculture the Federation has no unions at present. The Fruit and Vegetable Workers' Union of North America which affiliated with the A. F. of L. in 1922 disbanded in 1923.

II. MINING AND QUARRYING

In the mining and quarrying industries the Federation has four unions, three of which are considered here.

The International Union of Oil Field Workers owed its rise to the War Labor Board. In 1921 it had a membership of 24,800 including workers in oil fields, natural gas wells, and refineries. The membership declined rapidly in 1922 when employers of the Pacific Coast formed the Better American Federation and declared

[1] The material for this appendix has been drawn from reports of proceedings of the conventions of the different unions and from first-hand investigations. For brief summaries of the structure of the unions described, see "Handbook of American Trade Unions," *U. S. Bureau of Labor Statistics Bulletin No. 506*, 1929. The unions are arranged here in the same order as in Appendix A.

in favor of the open shop. In the Middle West the union was faced by a depression in the oil industry between 1925 and 1929 owing to the development of oil fields in Texas. In addition, the oil-bearing districts of the Middle West were overrun by workers from agriculture, lumber camps, and coal mines. In 1932 the union reported 400 members. Its organizing problem is difficult in view of the migratory and unskilled character of most of the workers in the industry.

The International Union of Mine, Mill, and Smelter Workers is a remnant of the once powerful Western Federation of Miners, which at the height of its power in 1911 had a membership of 50,200 and dominated the labor movement of the Far West. It suffered from lost strikes and from attacks of the I. W. W. in 1913-14 and reorganized under its present name in 1916, with a membership of 16,700. During 1918-20 it gained in membership owing to war activities, but was adversely affected by the shutdown of the copper mines in 1921. The union had a revival between 1922 and 1925, but since then has been losing steadily. The chief reasons have been the over-supply of copper, the depreciation of silver, mechanization of the mines, increasing employment of Mexican immigrants, and the hostile attitude of the large mining companies. The International has neither money nor men to carry on organizing. It advocates the restriction of immigration, an embargo on Soviet manganese, the remonetization of silver, the six-hour day, and a four-day week. In 1932 it reported a membership of 2,100.

The United Mine Workers of America, at one time the most powerful union in the A. F. of L., has been losing ground since 1925. Its main strength at present is in the anthracite area where pick-mining still predominates and where the concentrated character of the industry in a relatively small area in central Pennsylvania and the long established collective relations have helped the union to maintain its power. In the soft coal areas the strength of the United Mine Workers has been steadily diminishing since 1927. The union has been faced by three major problems: First, decrease in the total consumption of coal due to improved combustion, competition of oil and other fuels, and the rationalization of processes on the railroads and in the iron and steel industry; second, unemployment due to the increasing mechanization of the mines and over-development; and third, the diversion of orders from union coal fields in the Central Competitive District to the non-union fields in West Virginia, Kentucky, and other states where all efforts to organize the low-paid miners have broken against the stubborn resistance of the employing companies. The union was slow in recognizing these problems and for several years directed its main efforts towards maintaining the wage scale laid down in the Jacksonville agreement of 1924.[2] The failure of the strikes which it conducted and the disorganization of the industry created discontent in the ranks and called forth various opposition groups. The leadership of the union aggravated the situation by its methods of fighting all opposition, by its refusal to make adjustments, and by its methods of maintaining itself in power. Within the last year the leadership has taken a more active interest in the economic problems of the industry. Its program centers

[2] The Jacksonville agreement, which expired in 1927, provided wage rates of $7.50 for a basic eight-hour day and $1.08 per ton for piece workers and included all the districts in the Central Competitive Field. For opposition groups, see pp. 266-69.

around the Kelly-Davis bill which would allow the coal companies to organize selling syndicates on condition that they deal with their workers collectively and that prices be subject to approval by a federal coal commission. The union reported a membership of over 300,000 to the A. F. of L. in 1932, but its dues-paying membership is nearer 150,000.

III. FORESTRY, LUMBERING, AND WOODWORKING

In the group of lumber and woodworking industries, the Federation has five small unions, which include almost entirely workers in skilled crafts. The Federation has not been able to organize the woodsmen, "lumber jacks," and sawmill workers. The Timber Workers' Union organized during the war had 10,100 members in 1920, but collapsed during the depression of 1921 and disbanded in 1922.

Of the five A. F. of L. unions in the industry, the International Wood Carvers' Union embraces highly skilled artisans whose wage rate in 1929 was $11 a day. The union is based largely upon out-of-work and death benefits, and tool insurance. Its membership was about 1,200 from 1920 to 1931, but decreased to 900 in 1932.

The International Union of Coopers, one of the oldest in America, began to decline before 1914, but its decline was accelerated after 1914 by prohibition, the greater use of steel barrels, the introduction of machines, and internal dissensions. Its reported membership of 600 has a large proportion of older men who have claims to death benefits.

The International Union of Piano and Organ Workers is another example of a decaying union. Its decline has been largely due, first to the development of the victrola and then to the falling demand for these instruments because of the radio. The membership, which was over 3,000 in 1920, was about 300 in 1932.

The International Union of Upholsterers, Carpet and Linoleum Mechanics, with 3,500 members in 1914, began to grow after 1922, increasing its membership from 6,500 in 1925 to 10,700 in 1929. The union grew by extending its jurisdiction to include a number of allied crafts—namely, mattress making, measuring and hanging of draperies and awnings, fitting slip covers on automobile bodies, and the laying of linoleum and carpets. In this way it tried to counterbalance losses in one trade by gains in another. When the mattress and bed-spring-making trade was invaded by new machines which threw many workers out of jobs, and when hotel bed equipment, formerly custom made, began to be manufactured in mass production shops owned by large hotels, the union began organizing the linoleum and carpet trades which were rapidly expanding because of the increasing use of their products for floor coverings.

The union finds it difficult to keep up with continuous changes in methods of work, with the increasing influx into the trade of younger men who are disparagingly termed "one-armed mechanics" and who have no interest in unionism, and with inter-city competition which pits the non-union shop against the union shop. The leadership of the international union, although aggressive, has not been able to counteract the indifference of the membership, the increasing cost of organizing, and the abuses of some of its locals.[3]

[3] At the convention of the union in 1928, the president reported that in some locals it was almost impossible for a member to express an opinion or to get any action. In one local conditions had reached a stage where the members didn't dare open their mouths on the floor for fear of being

IV. METAL, MACHINERY, AND SHIPBUILDING INDUSTRIES

In the group of metal, machinery, and shipbuilding industries, the Federation has 14 international unions whose reported membership decreased from 277,700 in 1925 to 232,800 in 1929, and to 198,300 in 1932. Several of these unions are small organizations of highly skilled craftsmen based on membership restrictions, high dues, protective benefits, and strict apprenticeship rules. The American Wire Weavers' Protective Association, for instance, admits only Christians, white, male, 21 years of age or over, who have served an apprenticeship of four years in a union shop. Foreigners applying for admission must declare their intention of becoming American citizens and pay an admission fee of $1,000. Its reported membership in 1932 was 300.

The International Molders' Union of North America, at one time one of the strongest unions in the Federation, has been losing ground because of the profound changes affecting the industry and the workers. The strength of the union was formerly based on the fact that molded castings required skilled hand work. But molding machines have been increasingly introduced into foundries, and today machine operators and handymen aided by machines produce castings by methods of mass production. Machines, the application of electricity, press steel plates, mass production, and specialization have dried up the

---

"knocked down." They were not allowed to enter the meeting room when an election was in order. The money of the organization was being utilized for the exclusive benefit of the business agent. In another local, on the night of the election, the lights were turned out, and everybody tried to find a window. But there weren't enough windows for all, and the result was that they were somewhat crowded in getting out. One fellow even tried to hide in the piano. The local was in the hands of a "small armed crew." See *Proceedings of the Convention of the Upholsterers' International Union*, 1929, p. 71.

sources from which the union used to derive its membership. Apprenticeship rules are becoming obsolete because apprentices are being eliminated by the laborer who is trained to work on the machines. The union shops have also been confronted with the competition of unorganized foundries in the South which employ negroes in large numbers, and with strong anti-union employers' associations. The union has also lost membership as a result of the fact that many stove manufacturers turned to the making of furnaces requiring less skill. As a result of these conditions, even during the period of prosperity, thousands of union members were thrown out of work and under the laws of the union were entitled to out-of-work benefits. As an increasing number of men were also unable to work because of age and called for sick benefits, the funds of the union have been subjected to increasing strain.

The union has attempted to meet these conditions by a number of devices. Special wage adjustments have been made with union employers to enable them to compete with non-union shops. The amount of sick benefit per member has been reduced, and group insurance has been taken out. The local unions have been allowed to declare an "amnesty" and to reinstate expelled and suspended members. The union has also decided to try to organize machine molders on the basis of lower dues and benefits. But so far all these efforts have been of little avail. The reported membership declined from 57,300 in 1920 to 9,500 in 1932. The main strength of the union is in stove foundries and in navy yards. The union has been able to continue because its employed members are willing to pay high dues and assessments in order to be eligible for the benefits which the union provides.

The Amalgamated Association of Iron, Steel, and Tin Workers began to lose ground long before 1914 as a result of unsuccessful strikes and of its inability or unwillingness to organize the unskilled workers in the industry. It is now in a state of decline. Its reported membership in 1932 was 5,000. It has discontinued the payment of sick benefits because of lack of funds. Its death benefit fund is endangered by the increasing claims of a declining membership with an increasing average age.

The International Union of Boilermakers and Iron Shipbuilders had ceased to grow before 1914. However, its membership increased from 18,200 in 1916 to 103,000 in 1920, owing to the war and to the policy of the War Labor Board. With the depression of 1921 the membership was deflated, decreasing to 41,700 in 1922. It declined to 15,000 in 1932, partly because of the slump in the shipbuilding industry.

The boilermakers and their helpers are employed in a variety of trades and plants, such as oil refineries and pipe line companies, railroad shops, copper refineries, iron works, and machine repair shops. During the war the union relaxed its rules and admitted workers from allied trades, including even the unskilled. It has changed its policy since. One of its main efforts now is to enforce apprenticeship rules and to limit the number of apprentices. The union refuses to admit colored helpers, who are becoming numerous in the industry. To increase work for its membership, the union has supported the "modernization" of battleships and has urged the construction of new cruisers. The union carries on continuous organizing campaigns, and maintains an information department which keeps in touch with new jobs advertised in trade journals and with workers who might be persuaded to join the union if given a job. In line with this craft policy, the union inaugurated a policy of providing life insurance for its members by arrangement with private insurance companies.

Despite decreases in membership, the union was thus able for some time to maintain a strong financial condition by increasing per capita dues and assessments. Between 1925 and 1930 its total receipts amounted to over $3,722,000. Per capita taxes rose from $47,100 in 1925 to $151,953 in 1929, and insurance premiums from $33,044 in 1925 to $300,980 in 1929. Since 1930, however, the funds of this union, like those of many others, have been curtailed. Plans for a home for superannuated members have had to be abandoned. An increasing number of locals have declared for old-age pensions and for unemployment insurance.

The Brotherhood of Railway Carmen of America is an amalgamation of many crafts varying considerably in skill. It includes coach cleaners, who are the least skilled, car inspectors, who are highly skilled, and all others who do the work of building and repairing cars. In 1920 the Brotherhood, profiting by the government labor policy, reached its height with a membership of 182,000. Its difficulties began with the shopmen's strike of 1922, and its membership has dwindled steadily since. It reported 80,000 members in 1932, but not more than half of the members were estimated to be in good standing.

The difficulties confronting the Brotherhood arise partly from changes in the railroad industry and partly from the labor policies of the railroad companies. The concentration of repair shops and the mechanization of the industry have greatly reduced the number of carmen employed. Because of resulting unemployment the shopman has been afraid of losing his job and has accepted company welfare schemes and "company unions." The officials of the Brotherhood claim that the old "soap box" oratory method of organizing has ceased to be effective and that they must rely on individual contacts as the only means of winning recruits. But neither this method of organizing nor their strong endorsement of union management co-operation have so far stopped the fall in membership.

During its prosperous years the union paid out large sums in benefits and built up reserves which in 1929 amounted to over two and a half million dollars. Since 1929 the condition of the death benefit fund has been unsatisfactory.

The International Association of Machinists grew by leaps and bounds during the World War, its membership increasing from 75,400 in 1914 to 330,800 in 1920. But it lost heavily in 1921-22 as a result of the depression, and in 1924 as a result of factional troubles. Its membership fell to 71,400 in 1925. It experienced a slight revival between 1925 and 1929, but declined to 70,700 in 1932.

The association includes five classes of membership: (1) skilled machinists who have served an apprenticeship of four years or have worked four years at the trade and who can "with the aid of tools, with or without drawings, make, repair, erect, assemble, or dismantle machinery or parts thereof"; (2) skilled automobile and aircraft mechanics; (3) specialists whose work requires less training, experience, and skill; (4) helpers able to command the minimum rate of wages paid in the locality where employed; and (5) apprentices—mostly persons between 16 and 21 years of age indentured to an employer to serve four years in learning the trade. Women are eligible to membership but there have been practically none in the union since the war period.

At the present time about one-half the membership is employed on railroads, and the other half in contract shops, machine shops, and government plants, as in the Navy and all other governmental departments where machines are used. The association has but few members in the plants of the large corporations in the iron and steel, machinery, and machine tool industries in which there are strong employers' associations and where the company union and employers' welfare plans were developed before 1929. The attempts to organize garage mechanics have not been successful, partly owing to the opposition of the automobile associations, partly to the fact that these workers change jobs often and try to become small employers, and partly also to the craft pride of the old-time machinist who looks down upon the automobile mechanic.

The organizing methods of the association include circularization, industrial exhibits, shop cards, and personal letters. Where locals become delinquent, organizers are sent out to help them. The association has investigated the methods used by other unions but reports that it did not find them very helpful. The organizing expenditures of the association from January 1924 to July 1928 were $463,733.

The structure of the association is that of a craft organization. The international association, called the Grand Lodge, is composed of local lodges. There are separate lodges for the different classes of membership and some mixed lodges which include workers and helpers in railroad and contract shops. The local lodges within a city and its environs form district lodges. The railroad machinists' local lodges are organized into district lodges, there being one district lodge for each system. Railroad machinists may also belong to mixed local lodges. The government employees' local lodges include in their membership all types of machinists. All such lodges belong to one district lodge of government employees. Each district lodge has a paid business agent and usually holds an annual convention.

In its relations with employers the association has relied on the usual devices of the trade agreement. It does not insist on the union or closed shop, but some locals demand the union shop in their agreements. It has taken an active part in initiating union management co-operation as a basis for collective bargaining and participates in the application of this plan on the Baltimore and Ohio Railroad and the Canadian National Railway. The plan is also in effect in the Yoemens Brothers' Pump Company in Chicago and the La France Fire Engine Company and a few other less important plants.

The association has carried on many large and bitter strikes. Between 1919 and 1922 it paid over 3 million dollars in strike benefits to its members; but the amounts paid since have been small. On July 1, 1928, the latest date for which data are available, the association had a balance of over $491,000 in its strike fund.

The association maintains a death and disability benefit for its members on a voluntary basis. Members participating must be over 16 years of age and under 50 at the time of application. The premium cost is $9.00 a year. At death, or in case of total disability, the beneficiaries of the member receive $500. It also has a death benefit fund, for the support of which 14 per cent of the per capita tax is budgeted. Upon the death of a member who has been in good standing for three years $50 is paid to his heirs. The amount increases each year until after 13 or more years of membership $300 is paid. The union's annual expenditures for death benefits have exceeded receipts for this purpose. Between January 1, 1924 and July 1, 1927 the association received $414,294 for the death benefit fund and paid out $508,101. The balance in the fund decreased during the period from $160,414 to $66,277. As a result, meeting the obligations of these benefit provisions has become increasingly difficult since 1927. The question of providing for compulsory life insurance on an actuarial basis has been discussed.

Dues vary among local lodges, but a minimum journeyman's dues of $1.75 per month is specified by the International Association. Women and apprentices may pay dues of not less than one half of those paid by the journeymen, and helpers not less than two thirds. The dues are distributed to the various activities of the International in the following way: 50 per cent goes to the general fund; 20 per cent to the strike fund; 14 per cent to the death benefit fund; 9 per cent to the journal; and 2 per cent to the transportation and convention fund. During the years of prosperity the association collected large sums from its local lodges for these various purposes—$755,030 in 1924; $716,936 in 1925; $729,956 in 1926; $737,019 in 1927; and $368,111 for the first six months of 1928. Since 1930 receipts have fallen off. Under the rules, members may be exempt from paying monthly dues for a maximum of six months out of any consecutive twelve-month period of unemployment. The lodge pays ten cents in dues to the International on all unemployment stamps issued.

The International Association of Machinists has a radical tradition. Its president before 1914 was a socialist. Since 1920 it has advocated public ownership of public utilities, old-age pensions, and unemployment insurance. In 1924 it had a considerable communist element to combat. A rule was adopted that no member could belong to any communist organization and remain a member of the association. However, the union has continued to be troubled by factionalism. In the past the election of officers has caused internal turmoil between "ins" and "outs" and has given rise to accusations of "machine control." To minimize factionalism the constitution provides that each local lodge may discuss subjects of political economy under the heading of "Good and Welfare," providing such discussion does not occupy more than 20 minutes of the time of the meeting and does not include matters sectarian in religion or partisan in politics.

V. THE BUILDING TRADES[4]

There are 18 unions in the building trades affiliated with the American Federation of Labor. Owing to the building boom the membership of these unions increased from 836,900 in 1925 to 969,900 in 1929. Since the depression the membership has appreciably decreased. It was reported as 870,000 in 1932.

As compared to other industries in the United States, the workers in the building trades are highly organized. The building business is subject to keen competition and is full of uncertainties. The weather, a business depression, price fluctuations, high interest rates, or a labor strike may throw it into confusion at any time.

[4] In this summary the author has drawn upon William Haber, *Industrial Relations in the Building Trades*, 1930.

Little capital is usually required to enter the business as compared to other basic industries. The small contractor, operating during the busy season and eager to cut prices in order to get business, the intermittent and seasonal character of building operations, and especially the policy of the building owner to have construction completed at a certain date at all costs greatly enhance the bargaining power of the worker. These factors are also responsible for the jurisdictional disputes and the many abuses which characterize these unions.

The strongest union numerically and the most powerful economically is the United Brotherhood of Carpenters and Joiners. Before 1914 this union expanded largely by eliminating rival competitive organizations and by absorbing their workers. Since 1914 it has concentrated upon organizing the trade and has achieved a fair degree of success. In 1921 the Brotherhood achieved a maximum membership of 352,000. In 1932 its membership was reported as 290,000.

In the early days of the union, the "outside carpenter" who worked with wood alone was the basic group from which membership was drawn. Since then, the Brotherhood has absorbed cabinet makers, carpenters working in mills, furniture workers, box makers, pile drivers, dock workers, and metal trim carpenters. Changes in technical processes and the use of new building materials have had a significant influence on the policy of the carpenters' union. It has reached out to control work effected by changes in the industry. An example of this is the instance when ready-made trim began to displace that made by the carpenter. The union did not oppose the use of machinery nor did it refuse to have its members install machine-made wood products, but it insisted that the factory mill worker be included in the jurisdiction of the carpenters' union. The union declared a "vested interest" in the task and skill required rather than the material with which members worked. The basis for the claim is what may be called the principle of substitution, by which a union is entitled to a new process substituted for an old one. "Once wood, it is always the right of the carpenter to install it no matter of what [*sic*] the material is." In the process of forcing recognition of its jurisdictional rights, the union has been involved in serious, long drawn out disputes with machinists, coopers, bridge and structural iron workers, brewery workers, longshoremen, metal lathers, and sheet metal workers.

The Brotherhood uses the traditional methods of unionism—the strike, the boycott, and the label—to enforce its demands. It collects fairly high dues and maintains various benefits. From July 1924 to June 30, 1928 the total receipts of the Brotherhood were $9,130,000. Its largest expenditure—over $2,842,000—during these years was for death and disability benefits. Strikes and lockouts cost over $683,000. Organizing expenses were over $150,000. The union pays a death donation in sums ranging from $50 to $300. A funeral donation to wives of members ranges from $25 to $75 and disability donations range from $50 to $400. The Brotherhood maintains a home for retired members in Lakeland, Florida, and provides a pension for disabled members over 65 years of age who have been in the union not less than 30 years.

Since the depression the Brotherhood, like other unions in the building trades, has been facing the problem of unemployment. Wage rates have been undermined, organization has been weakened, and funds have been curtailed. The internal problems of the Brotherhood have been largely concerned with apprenticeship rules, clearance cards for members out of work, local abuses, and discipline. Communist groups have been active in a few locals, but have been largely suppressed by the officers of the international union.

The Bricklayers, Masons, and Plasterers' International Union dominates what is known as the "trowel trades" of the building industry. It has developed by reaching out to the stone and plastering trades, and absorbing competing organizations. Today its jurisdiction includes bricklayers, stone masons, stone setters, marble masons, tile setters, mosaic workers, and cement finishers. Its membership was 90,000 in 1929. It still occupies one of the leading positions among the unions in the building industry, although its reported membership fell to 56,700 in 1932. Between 1924 and 1928 the total net assets of the union increased from $1,688,000 to $3,865,000.

This organization has tried to stabilize industrial relations in the industry by controlling strikes. Early in its history it enforced the principle that no question of strike or lockout in its jurisdiction should be acted upon independently by the local unions involved, but must be referred for settlement to a joint committee of an equal number of representatives of union men and employers. This policy of conciliation and arbitration is responsible for the prestige of the union among employers. The bricklayers not only receive high wage rates but are able to maintain the closed shop throughout almost all of the country. In open shop centers, where the unions in the building trades are relatively unorganized, and where union men as a rule work side by side with non-union men in the same or other trades, the bricklayers have secured recognition, collective bargaining, and the closed shop.

The good-will of the employers, however, is often purchased at the cost of disregarding the interests of fellow workers in other unions. The bricklayers have assured employers that if given recognition and a trade agreement they would not join any local building trades council and would not participate in sympathetic strikes. The mason contractors have often reciprocated by refusing to join other employers in a lockout. The same aloofness has been shown by this union towards the A. F. of L. It did not join the Federation until 1916. During recent years there has been discussion in the union whether it should continue in the A. F. of L. in view of the fact that affiliation with the latter results in disputes in which the freedom of action of the union is restrained.

The Bricklayers' Union is beginning to be affected by changes in materials and processes. Its members are also faced with the competition of non-union members. The union tries to restrict membership not only by apprenticeship rules but also by insisting on high standards of workmanship which keep out alleged incompetents, called "boots." Many locals refuse to accept colored workers. A problem affecting membership is the tendency of many members to indenture their children or relatives as apprentices. The union intends to have a journeyman indenture not more than one son, but some journeymen indenture several and some having no sons assume guardianship of boys for the purpose. The union tries to remedy the situation by making the indenturing of apprentices dependent on a joint contract between the local union, the contractor, and the apprentice. The union is also opposed to vocational schools, though it favors special extension courses under the Smith-Hughes Act.

The Bridge and Structural Iron Workers' Union has had a stormy career. The iron workers' trade differs from the other building trades in some aspects. The amount of skill required is considerably less. Whereas the usual period for training apprentices in other building trades is from three to four years, in the iron trades the range is from six to eighteen months. Second, the work of this trade is especially hazardous. Facing danger daily develops in the iron worker a sort of desperate recklessness. Third, the large construction companies erect steel all over the country. Their workmen are migratory and for a long time the kind of men attracted to the trade were noted for their rough and ready tactics. In another respect the history of this union differs from that of every other union in the industry. It has had to contend from the beginning with an effective employers' association which was determined to maintain the open shop. The open shop firms control practically all the bridge work. The union controls construction of buildings.

The membership of the Bridge and Structural Iron Workers' Union has oscillated with the general prosperity of the industry and with the power of the Steel Erectors' Association. An aggressive organization campaign during 1924-28 brought the membership to a total of 20,400. However, it was back at a little above the 1914 level with a total of 12,000 in 1932. Between 1924 and 1932 the union paid $1,025,450 to its members in old-age pensions, and $450,264 in death benefits.

The Elevator Constructors' Union differs from the other building trades' unions in the simplicity of its problems. The Otis Elevator Company produces and erects more elevators than any other firm in the world. About 90 per cent of the membership of the Elevator Constructors' Union is in the employ of this corporation. The union does not have to deal with a horde of "fly-by-night" contractors against whom there must be constant vigilance. The good-will of the one large corporation was secured from the beginning and, with the exception of one large strike called in 1909 when the Otis Company quickly came to terms, relations between workers and employers have been satisfactory. The elevator workers are more effectively organized than any other union in the building industry. The international union has exercised strict control over the locals from the beginning, supervising even the admission of new members. This is done to prevent an increase in union membership and to equalize employment conditions among the different localities. If a strike is declared, the national union takes complete charge, negotiates with the employers, and makes the settlement. At one time the union had a national agreement with the Otis Company, establishing for the whole country uniform working conditions, except that the wage scale was governed by local conditions. The union has maintained a stable membership of 10,200 since 1929. In that year it had triple the membership of 1920.

The Asbestos Workers' Union is one of the smallest in the building trades. Its membership rose from 2,400 in 1925 to 4,100 in 1931, and declined to 2,000 in 1932. The union has no benefits or strike fund, and is primarily a wage negotiating body. Its chief method of enforcing standards is through the limitation of the supply of labor by means of apprenticeship rules.

The union has carried on a fight against poor mechanics known in the trade as "foot men," "lumpers," and "section shooters." A large part of the work in the trade is done by sub-contractors who get their contracts from steam fitters and plumbers and who are subject to such extreme competition that bad work results. The union has co-operated with the contractors in their effort to secure contracts directly from architects and owners. It has set up rules of workmanship with stiff penalties for violations, by means of which it tries to maintain itself. The union, like many others, provides a "superannuated card" which is intended for the protection of aged or incapacitated members, who are allowed to work below the standard wage rate—a condition which is often abused by foremen and business agents. The union advocates old-age pensions by the state and unemployment insurance. Many of the locals of this union are not on a secure financial basis. Having no reserve funds, they have often been in financial difficulties and have tried to meet the situation by fines and assessments.

The International Union of Hod-Carriers and Common Laborers and the International Union of Building Service Employees include almost entirely unskilled workers. Their organizations have been made possible as a result of the rule of other unions in the building trades which prohibits their men from working on a building with non-union men engaged in their own or any other craft. Owing to this willingness of the skilled crafts to support the organization of the unskilled and to the effectiveness of the sympathetic strike, the hod-carriers, common laborers, and helpers in the building trades have secured recognition and have won conditions which in many instances were better than those obtained by skilled crafts in other industries. For many years the unskilled workers in the industry did not wish to be designated as "common laborers," and their local unions were known by the name of the craft they assisted. They were unions of foundation workers, excavation laborers, mason laborers, carpenters' helpers, and plasterers' laborers. These organized separately and refused to affiliate with their respective national unions. Another difficulty in the organization work of the unskilled was the multitude of racial groups among the common laborers. The low dues adopted also proved a bar to intensive organization work. Were it not for the aid of the skilled workers the unions could not have held together long, especially during periods of unemployment. But owing to the building boom during 1925-29 and the conditions described, these unions of the unskilled obtained a strong position in the industry with considerable memberships and large funds.

The Brotherhood of Electrical Workers was a comparatively small organization before the war, its membership in 1914 having been a little over 30,000. Between 1918 and 1920 its membership increased from 51,400 to 142,000. Like many other unions it lost considerable numbers of members who had temporarily joined during the war. In 1932 it reported 139,000 members to the A. F. of L., but the number of dues-paying members in good standing was estimated at 75,000. During the depression many local lodges have been paying to the International for unemployed members the monthly per capita tax of $2.00, which is distributed as follows: 53 cents for general uses, 10 cents for the journal, 3 cents for defense, 37 cents for the pension benefit fund, 7 cents for the convention fund, and 90 cents for the Electrical Workers' Benefit Fund.

The Brotherhood of Electrical Workers may be classified as an amalgamated craft union. It claims jurisdiction over electrical construction, the manufacture of electrical supplies, the radio and movietone business, power plants, the telephone industry, and aviation. The major portion of its membership is engaged in electrical construction. It has a considerable membership in the railroad industry. It holds national agreements with some electric elevator, refrigerator, and movietone corporations. It has few members in the privately owned public utilities, but has agreements in the municipal power plants of Los Angeles, Seattle, and Springfield, Illinois. It has local lodges also in the Panama Canal Zone and in the navy yards.

As a result of its wide jurisdiction, the Electrical Workers' Union has been involved in jurisdictional disputes with the Alliance of Theatre and Stage Employees, with the Union of Elevator Constructors, with the Railroad Signalmen, and others. The Brotherhood of Electrical Workers tries to extend jurisdiction over the installation, operation, and maintenance of electrical devices. It claims all work which involves the application of electrical energy. It opposed the granting of a charter by the A. F. of L. to radio installers, radio repairmen, and radio station operators on the grounds that the radio is entirely electrical in character and that all repairs and adjustments on it properly belong in their jurisdiction. For a similar reason it protested against the issuance of a charter to electrical workers employed in the air transportation industry.

The Brotherhood has encouraged its members to be competent workmen and relies upon craftsmanship as one of the bases of its organization, although it admits laborers in the case of helpers to electrical linemen employed by public utilities. Many local lodges have apprenticeship clauses in their agreements with employers. The locals in the principal cities of the United States operate apprentice classes in connection with public schools. The Brotherhood has also aimed to build up co-operative employer-employee relations in the industry. In 1921, in co-operation with employers it set up the National Council for Industrial Relations in the Electrical Construction Industry, to settle disputes between local unions and employers.

The Brotherhood operates a fraternal insurance association known as the Electrical Workers' Benefit Association which writes a maximum insurance of $1,000 for every member of five years' continuous standing at a cost of 90 cents per month. Its locals and individual members own and operate the Union Co-operative Insurance Association, the first legal reserve life insurance company projected by organized labor, to offset company union activities which were built around group insurance plans. It writes group insurance fitted primarily to union organization needs. It also has a pension system which pays $42 a month to every member who has been in continuous good standing for a period of 20 years, if he has reached the age of 65 and has retired from the trade. The cost to each member for this amounts to 37 cents per month.

The Brotherhood has departmentalized the international office and has revised its constitution, giving greater power to the international union. It has set up standardized agreements for local unions. It stresses the need of internal discipline and business-like procedure.[5] It has a research department which is trying to systematize the collection of information by the local lodges and publishes one of the most intelligent and informative journals in the labor movement.

The industrial problems which the Brotherhood faces are numerous and complex. In the electrical construction industry, especially in the large cities, the biggest problem is the fly-by-night contractor and the small companies which rise, fail, and reorganize, and create excessive competition. As in the clothing industry, the union has at times gone hand in hand with the construction firms against the contractor, while at times it has tried to organize the contractors to offset the power of the big construction firms and of the "electrical brokers." In privately owned public utilities and on some of the railroads, the chief problems of the union are the employee representation plans and the company welfare schemes, which have made organizing by the union impossible. A similar condition exists in the large manufacturing companies such as the General Electric Company. The Brotherhood is thus one of the unions which feels in particularly acute form the problems created by the new mass industries.

Among the internal problems of the Brotherhood are some already described in connection with other unions.

[5] To illustrate, a local union may be penalized if it does not terminate its meeting and have lights out by eleven o'clock. Also, no local lodge may meet more than twice a month, which is considered often enough for "squabbling" with one another. The Executive Board now fills all vacancies between regular elections, which can only be held every two or four years according to the desire of the local. Any increase in wages carries with it automatically an increase in dues. These provisions are aimed to minimize strife in the locals, which has proved so devastating in the past. The assumption is that unions cannot be run by mass meetings and that democracy must be subordinated to business methods.

Such have been the abuses of the permit card, the refusal of the stronger locals to accept traveling cards, factions and "clubs," jurisdictional disputes between different locals, and other difficulties such as attracted wide attention in Local No. 3 of the Brotherhood in New York.

VI. THE TEXTILE INDUSTRY

In the textile group there is only one union affiliated with the A. F. of L., the United Textile Workers of America, which was organized in 1901. By 1914 the union had a membership of 18,000. Owing to the impetus of the war period its numbers increased to 104,900 in 1920; but this membership rapidly dwindled to 30,000, which number was reported to the A. F. of L. each year from 1925 to 1932, when it was reduced to 27,500. About two-thirds of the members of the union belong to the skilled hosiery workers' locals, which are organized as the Full Fashioned Hosiery Workers' Union, forming an autonomous branch of the United Textile Workers. The Hosiery Workers' Union is aggressive and has shown much flexibility in its methods. Organization has been difficult in the textile industry owing to the women and children employed at low wage rates, to great fluctuations in employment, to the great variety of nationalities in the New England mills, and to the opposition of company unions. The officers of the union have carried on organization work in a somewhat routine fashion. The nature of the industry and the character of the workers have made the union a stamping ground for socialists, communists, I. W. W.s and left-wingers. Because of the difficulties of improving the lot of the workers by economic action, the union has often turned to legislative activities.

VII. THE LEATHER INDUSTRIES

There are two unions in the A. F. of L. in this group. The International Union of Leather Workers was organized in 1896. Its membership is largely employed in making saddles and harness and in tanning. In 1920 the union had a membership of 11,700, which declined to 5,000 in 1929 and to 1,000 in 1932. The union pays a death benefit of $80 and a sick benefit of $7 weekly after the first week of illness.

The Boot and Shoe Workers' Union was founded in 1895 on the basis of low dues and no benefits. In 1899 it adopted a new constitution providing for higher dues and benefits. But the union was unable to unite the boot and shoe workers to any great extent. Independent factions, small local unions here today and gone tomorrow, and internal troubles have been especially characteristic of labor organizations in this industry. The mechanized character of the industry is responsible for the large proportion of unskilled workers, difficult to organize. The over-expansion of the industry during the post-Armistice boom, the highly seasonal character of the industry due to changing styles (especially in the manufacture of ladies' novelty shoes), the speeding up of production, and the adoption of new and modern machinery have tended to make employment increasingly irregular and have created in the industry a large reserve of part-time workers. This situation is said to some extent to have been aggravated by the position of the United Shoe Machinery Corporation, which holds a monopoly over shoe manufacturing machinery and leases it to manufacturers. In addition, the union has to meet the problems of prison-made shoes, of large imports of foreign products, and special forms of individual contracts introduced by employers making employment conditional upon a pledge by the worker not to join a union.

The Boot and Shoe Workers' Union relies largely on the label as a method of organizing and maintaining organization. This in a way limits the membership to shops making cheap shoes for men. The union has adopted a system of granting 30-day permits to non-union members who desire employment during the rush season. At the end of 30 days the worker may apply to the union for membership. But these and other devices have not been very effective. The union had a membership of 46,700 in 1920. It decreased to 36,200 in 1925, to 32,400 in 1929, and to 17,000 in 1932. This decrease was due in some measure to internal strife and splits. The possibility of organizing the shoe repairers has been discussed but has been opposed because where it has been tried the owners of shops, not the workers, have dominated the meetings. The union carries on some organization work, but the major portion of its expenses go to sick, disability, and death benefits. It is for a protective tariff.

VIII. THE CLOTHING INDUSTRY

In the clothing industry there are seven unions affiliated with the A. F. of L., with a total membership in 1932 of 105,600. The two largest unions in the group are the United Garment Workers' and the International Ladies' Garment Workers' Union.

The International Ladies' Garment Workers' Union is organized into locals whose membership embraces workers producing a certain class of women's wearing apparel, such as coats, dresses, and raincoats.[6] The union

[6] For a description of the structure and development of the union, see Louis Levine, *The Women's Garment Workers*, 1924.

had a membership of 105,400 in 1920, but it fell to 40,000 in 1932. One of the causes has been the bitter factional fights, especially with communists and "left-wingers." In 1926 the "left-wing" elements among the cloak makers caused the International to become involved in a cloak makers' general strike which lasted 26 weeks and left the union bankrupt. In 1928 a reorganization campaign was launched. It was largely financed by "reconstruction bonds" which were bought by members of the union and friendly individuals and organizations. While the union has made progress in paying off some of its debts, it has not been able to meet all obligations, and the holders of the "reconstruction bonds" are calling for over-due payments. The 1932 convention levied a $10 assessment which produced over $314,000 between November 1, 1929 and March 31, 1932. The per capita dues for the same period were $569,097.

The union has been affected by radical changes in the industry during the past decade. While decentralization has been going on for more than 20 years, the problem has become greatly aggravated in recent years because of the exodus of manufacturers from the larger clothing centers to rural areas. The present increasing demand for cheap garments made from shoddy materials, together with the simplification of styles and work methods, makes it possible to utilize the large supply of unskilled women workers available in rural areas and small towns. Manufacturers are offered cheap and sometimes even free rent in rural communities if they will come and give employment. The rapid development of motor truck transportation facilities has made it practically as easy to ship goods from remote communities in New Jersey and Connecticut to New York as from one part of Manhattan to another.

Among other disturbing problems of the union are the manufacturers who become jobbers in "bad faith." The practice of these employers is to discharge their employees and install contracting shops either on their premises or outside. The entrance of the department and chain store into manufacturing is another complicating factor. The department and chain store will present a manufacturer, contractor, or jobber with materials to make garments at a specified price. Thus the ultimate employer with whom the workers have to bargain is still further removed.

The union meets these problems largely by the methods evolved in former years. It carries on aggressive organizing campaigns and strikes. It spent $242,129 for such purposes between November 1929 and March 1932. It relies on the system of impartial chairmen where agreements with employers are in force. An illustration of the scope of the work of such a chairman is the decree known as the Alger ruling, issued by the impartial chairman of the New York cloak and suit industry on August 2, 1932. It provides that every employer in New York introducing or using electric pressing machines must pay the machine presser a minimum weekly wage of $57 instead of $45, which is the rate for hand pressers. In addition, the employer must pay $8.00 a week into a pressers' unemployment fund for each machine used in his factory, to be distributed among unemployed pressers. This has been heralded as a "mile post in human progress" as the decree assumes that the machine must help support men who lose jobs through it.

IX. FOOD, LIQUOR, AND TOBACCO INDUSTRIES

Five unions affiliated with the American Federation of Labor are in this group. The membership of these unions was 74,900 in 1925 and dropped to 63,300 in 1932.

The Bakery and Confectionery Workers' International Union was organized in 1886. At first the German bakers dominated it, but later this element withdrew to join the Amalgamated Food Workers, a dual union which attempted to control not only the production but also the distribution of food. The Jewish workers in the large cities formed strong locals. The union as a whole grew rapidly between 1900 and 1904, increasing its membership from 4,500 to 16,200. It flourished during and after the war, its membership in 1920 being 27,500. In 1932 the membership reported was 17,900.

The manufacture of bakery products has undergone many changes. As a result the small bakery owner is steadily being forced out of business by wholesale bakers, and these in turn are being swallowed by the big combinations in whose factories there is but little room for skilled bakers. The problem of union organization has been further complicated by the large number of women employed in the confectionery branch of the industry and by the fact that the workers in the industry differ in language and habits. The union employs organizers who adjust local difficulties. The label is one of the main weapons relied upon. The union has spent comparatively small sums in organizing. In 1927-28 organizing expenses were $38,365 out of a total expenditure of $368,513. The union has spent most of its energy in organizing the skilled bakers. It has also spent much time in litigation and in anti-trust agitation. The union has not made progress among the factory workers. It has been indifferent toward organizing the women confectionery workers, among whom some union work has been done by the National Women's Trade Union League. The officials of the union stress the need of strict business methods and greater discipline within the organization, and claim that the desire to give democratic expression to the membership has often been a source of weakness. The union is an employment agency for the skilled bakers and has developed satisfactory contractual relations with small employers through efficiency in carrying out its agreements. Its locals are well administered. In recent years the union has been hampered by communist activities and by jurisdictional disputes, especially with the teamsters.

The Cigar Makers' Union, organized in 1864, was for a long time regarded as a model union. It was one of the first unions to secure the eight-hour day. Its constitution was copied by other unions. Its membership grew rapidly in the eighties and then again from 1899 to 1904, when it increased from 27,000 to 40,500. After 1911, when the peak was reached, it declined steadily, until there were only 23,500 members in 1925 and 15,500 in 1932. The union has refused to organize team and machine workers and to change its structure or method of organization. The funds of the union recently have been inadequate to meet the outstanding claims for sick benefits in spite of the fact that the union members pay $36 per year per capita tax. (The average age of the members is over 50 years.)

X. CHEMICAL, CLAY, STONE, AND GLASS INDUSTRIES

In this group of industries there are eight unions affiliated with the A. F. of L. Their membership decreased from 40,200 in 1925 to 30,000 in 1932. The entire trade union membership in this industrial group—once a powerful aggregation—has greatly declined during the last 15 years. Today its membership is smaller than it was in 1914. Some of this decline may be attributed to the growth of large corporations, but primarily it is traceable to the invasion of labor-saving and skill-destroying machinery. These unions are most frequently cited as illustrations of "decaying" unions unable to readjust themselves to the technical progress of the industry.

XI. PAPER MANUFACTURING, PRINTING, AND PUBLISHING

The A. F. of L. has 12 unions in these trades, which in 1932 had a total membership of 161,800. Skill in these trades has largely persisted in spite of technological changes, so that the high degree of bargaining power once achieved by these unions still maintains.

The most powerful union of the group is the International Typographical Union. Organized in 1852, and one of the founders of the A. F. of L., the Typographical Union experienced steady growth from a membership of 46,700 in 1904 to 77,500 in 1931. In 1932 there was a loss of 1,400 members. Striking features of this union are its centralized character, all local agreements being underwritten by the international officers, and its systematic technique for organizing work. Although stringent apprenticeship rules are applied which act both to increase the efficiency of the journeyman-craftsman and to limit the number of qualified workmen in the trade, organization work is given a place of paramount importance. The president of the union warned the 1931 convention against carrying "exclusivism" too far, saying that if the competent men were not taken into the union when a new plant or "office" was organized, such workers would be forced to create a reservoir of skilled non-union workmen ready to under-cut the organized worker. When a community calls for an organizing campaign, the local situation is usually surveyed. The names of non-union offices are secured and where possible the names of non-union employees are obtained, together with information regarding their craft competency. Thus when an organizer is sent there is some basis for estimating his progress and ascertaining whether he is receiving the proper co-operation from the local union. The International Union makes local officials and rank and file members responsible for the major part of organizing work. The representative from headquarters merely acts in an advisory capacity.

Other outstanding features of this union are its large business and financial transactions. Receipts for its general fund for the fiscal year ending June 20, 1931 were $2,714,034.62, of which 49.6 per cent went into administrative expenses, 18.9 per cent for assistance to local unions and strike benefits, 12.1 per cent to representatives and committees, 15.93 per cent to the *Typographical Journal*, and 3.5 per cent to dues and assessments of affiliated bodies. The union is supported by a per capita tax of 65 cents per member per month and 5 cents for the journal fund. Thirty cents of this goes to the general fund, but this amount has proved inadequate since 1913 and has had to be augmented by special assessments. The strike benefits have been increased from $7.00 and $10 to 25 and 40 per cent of the minimum wage scale. The entire cost of administering pension and mortuary funds has been charged to the general fund since 1925. Increased membership has brought with it an increase in cost of administration, especially as members and local unions call for an ever increasing amount of service. The question has been raised whether a larger per capita tax would not be more advantageous than the present system of special assessments.

More than 90 per cent of the income from the International Union is used each year to pay pensions and mortuary benefits and to maintain the Union Printers' Home, in whose benefits less than 5,000 members participate each year. Less than 10 per cent of the income is thus available for all other purposes. The old-age pension fund was severely taxed during the depression because of the increase in applicants for pensions and the decrease in the fund because of reduced earnings. A deficit was avoided by using the accumulated interest earned on the fund. Also, the death benefits paid in 1931 exceeded the return from assessments. A deficit was again avoided by using interest earnings. The administration of the union discourages agitation for group insurance as in its opinion the union is doing as well by the members as any other plan could. Besides, the unspent money in the fund is an asset to the union.

Amicable relations generally prevail between the Typographical Union and union employers. Expenditures for defense purposes have been lower per capita during the years 1928-31 than during 1915-20. Yet there is a large non-union element in the industry and a strong tendency towards the formation of "company unions." The question of raising a large strike fund has been recently discussed. Also, the growth of chain newspapers has given rise to the question of the advisability of sympathetic strikes by workers in different cities employed by the same chain. The opinion seems to be that since the strongest support during a strike comes from the public and since it would not be easy to get the public agitated by the grievances of some workers in a distant city, sympathetic strikes would not be effective.

In the locals of the Typographical Union, one of the issues is the question of out-of-work benefits. Such benefits are paid by the locals, and the interests of those who pay and those who receive come into conflict. There is no restriction other than that such assessments shall be adopted by referendum vote, and it is possible for the unemployed to become so numerous as to be the deciding factor in assessing members holding positions. During the fiscal year ending April 30, 1932, the locals paid over $2,175,000 in unemployment benefits. To meet the problem of unemployment the Typographical Union has adopted the five-day week in newspaper shops. Also for the present period of unemployment any local union may with the consent of the Executive Council refuse traveling cards to its members.

The International Printing Pressmen and Assistants' Union considers itself "a great volunteer business association with its members stockholders in one of the greatest enterprises that America has ever known." This union was organized in 1899 and experienced steady growth until 1925. Since then it has reported a stationary membership of 40,000. This organization operates a life membership plan which involves payment of a lump sum varying in amount according to the age of the member and by which a considerable saving is effected as compared with monthly dues payments. Among the benefit features supported are an old-age pension plan, a tuberculosis sanitarium, a home for aged members, and an insurance plan. It maintains a technical trade school and trade correspondence courses.

This union takes great pride in the contractual relations it has developed with employers. The procedure in preparing a contract is as follows: The local union considers the demands it wishes covered in the proposed contract; these demands are submitted to the Board of Directors of the International Union; after this body has examined the proposed contract, it is submitted to the employing printer or publisher; thereupon negotiations begin between the parties directly involved. After an agreement has been reached the contract is returned to the president of the International Union to be underwritten so as to give not only the local union's guaranty to the fulfilment of the terms of the agreement but likewise the fullest measure of endorsement of the International Union. The International Union insists on the inviolate and sacred character of contracts and demands a similar attitude on the part of employers.

The printing pressmen have in their organization an engineering department to improve the conditions of the printing department of the newspapers. This service has not been extended to the commercial printing industry because there is no employers' association with which to co-operate in that branch of the industry. The union maintains a statistical department and a patent department which considers suggestions, discoveries, and inventions of the membership.

The union has experienced some difficulty because of the instability of the industry. Frequently plants move from the city to the country and establish non-union conditions in order to profit by cheaper labor.

The International Photo-Engravers' Union of North America was organized in 1900 and joined the A. F. of L. in 1904. Its growth was steady—from a membership of 4,700 in 1914 to 9,000 in 1931. In 1932 it reported a loss of 100 members. This union has established the 40-hour, five-day week, and a maximum of 44 hours a week in the industry for its members. The minimum wage rates range around $55 per week, with an average wage among members of over $70 per week.

The Photo-Engravers' Union maintains a strong defense fund. When the amount in it falls to $35,000, the executive council is compelled to levy an assessment with which to restore the fund to the maximum of $100,000. In February 1930 the fund fell below the minimum and the executive council fixed a per capita levy of $1.00 per month. But, because the executive council was forced to adopt an extremely liberal policy in the payment of strike and lockout benefits and expenses, the $1.00 tax was not sufficient to restore the defense fund to its maximum strength; nor was it sufficient to meet the current obligations charged against the fund. The amount of strike benefits paid during the first six weeks is $15 and $20 but some locals have been paying more. Since difficulties have arisen from lack of uniformity in strike benefits, it has been advocated that the amount be raised to $25.

This union for some time maintained amicable relations with the American Association of Photo-Engravers. During 1931, however, all connections between the two organizations were severed. The employers' association adopted what it called a policy of "strict neutrality in all matters pertaining to industrial relations and employment." The union interpreted this move as a bait by the employers' association for the membership of non-union firms. A result of this development was the abolition of the Joint Industrial Council, which had long been in existence. The officers of both the employers' and the workers' organizations were members of the council. Discontinuing the council meant that practically all existing agreements had to be modified because they contained arbitration clauses referring difficulties to the council.

Other problems with which the union is faced are price-cutting tactics of employers, and the increasing number of shops that are being opened on a "shoestring." Workers out of employment think they can solve their problem by opening a small shop. This has led to an accentuation of competition in the trade which has resulted in disregard for union standards relative to wages, hours, and overtime. The union has increased its out-of-work payments to unemployed men to remedy this condition.

Serious problems are also raised by new processes and developments which are replacing photo-engraved printing plates as usually produced by the members of the union. The union has so far met some of these problems successfully. It organized the gravure workers as the use of that process of etching for printing purposes increased. It was thus able to extend protection to members engaged in relief-plate making as well as to those engaged in the intaglio method of reproduction. Most of the new processes are for the purpose of increasing production rather than improving the quality of output. The craft is thus becoming more mechanized and may in time require less individual skill than in the past. Also, the radio is diverting attention from advertising via the printed page. Television is looming on the horizon. The union hopes to meet the situation by supporting all those who object to the use of all air channels for publicity purposes.

The union also tries to restrict the supply of labor in the trade. It objects to the number of technical schools which claim to teach the photo-engraving trade.

The Photo-Engravers' Union has important fraternal and protective provisions. During 1931-32 it spent over 2 million dollars in various benefits, over three-quarters of which was aid to unemployed members paid by its locals. The remainder was paid to members who were locked out or on strike, or who qualified for sick, death, and funeral benefits. Most of the local unions exempt their unemployed from paying per capita dues.

The International Stereotypers' and Electrotypers' Union of North America was organized in 1902. Its membership was 2,400 in 1904, 8,200 in 1931, and 8,100 in 1932. This union has established contractual relations with employers. The purpose of the union has been not only to make a good union man of the apprentice but to make him an all-round competent craftsman. Difficulty has been experienced in some shops because employers will not move apprentices from one job to another but train him to be a specialist.

This international union has encouraged its locals in the same area to co-operate through district conferences and the exchange of information in securing more uniformity in working conditions, wages, the phraseology of laws, and the wording of contracts. Local unions have been requested to have extra copies of their contracts and by-laws on file for the use of other unions desiring them, and the executive board has been asked to furnish a facsimile copy of a well-worded contract for each branch of the trade. The union maintains strict apprenticeship laws which provide that local unions must limit the number of apprentices to be employed so as to supply only enough journeymen to meet the normal demand in its jurisdiction. In New York City, owing to the rapid expansion of the newspaper industry, there was for a time a "doubling up" which meant that one man covered two positions. This was finally eliminated, and the local union's membership was increased from 1,066 in July 1928 to 1,198 in April 1931. Since 1930 the members of the union have complained that the "situation where men were seeking jobs rather than jobs seeking men" was "a new experience to all those who had joined the organization in the last 15 years." On the other hand, employers complain of their inability to compete with non-union shops.

The four unions considered and the Brotherhood of Bookbinders are combined in the International Allied Printing Trades Association, to which each union sends delegates. The chief function of this body is to issue and control the union label of the allied printing trades. The association has local councils which supervise the use of the label locally. The Board of Governors of the association has endeavored to divert into union shops text books and religious and motion picture printing. Some degree of success has been achieved in the motion picture industry and in the field of religious publications, but the text book situation is more difficult. Merit of the product is only one of many factors entering into the selection of school books. Politics, fraternalism, and religion each plays an important part in the placing of contracts. Much anti-union sentiment exists on school boards even though it may not be voiced.

The question of more compact organization of the unions in the printing trades has been much discussed. The Typographical Union has advocated a federation of the unions in the printing trades to strengthen their bargaining power. It argues that closer contact between locals of the different unions must be established. It holds that one union cannot expect to frame its own demands and press them to the point of a strike or lockout without consulting the other unions and then expect support from the others regardless of cost or consequences. The Printing Pressmen's Union, though strongly opposed to amalgamation, has favored federation, but it holds that the aim should be to develop higher and more scientific methods of arbitration and conciliation. All the unions have been influenced by technical changes. For example, the developments in photo-plate making and processes have caused increasing overlapping of work. In a number of places, members of the lithographers' and photo-engravers' organizations are employed at similar work. However, progress towards closer federation is hampered by the same factors which obstruct it in other unions.

XII. TRANSPORTATION AND COMMUNICATION

In this group the A. F. of L. has twelve affiliated unions which in 1932 had a total membership of 351,600. Four of these are railroad unions—the Switchmen's Union, the Union of Maintenance of Way Employees, the Order of Sleeping Car Conductors, and the Union of Railway Clerks. Two are in the communication trades—the Order of Railroad Telegraphers and the Union of Commercial Telegraphers. Three unite workers in water transportation—the longshoremen, seamen, masters, mates, and pilots. Air transportation is represented by the union of air pilots, and two other forms of transportation are represented by the union of street and electric railway employees and the union of teamsters and chauffeurs.

One of the strongest unions in the group is the Brotherhood of Teamsters and Chauffeurs, Stablemen and Helpers. This organization throughout its history has been alert to claim jurisdiction over new operations as modes of transportation changed. For instance, in 1909 when the motor vehicle began to displace the horse and wagon, the union added chauffeurs to its title. Since its early days it has been among the more powerful unions of the Federation, which it joined in 1899. In 1904 it had a membership of 84,000, of which the strongest units were among the milk wagon drivers. By 1914 its membership had declined to 51,100, but the general impetus of the war period brought it to 110,800 in 1920. Because the membership is connected with many industries, all business fluctuations vitally affect the union. The recessions of 1921 and 1924 reduced its membership; but during the era of prosperity, in which the motor trucking industry expanded rapidly, it again rose to 95,500. In 1932 it reported a membership of 82,000.

The membership of the Teamsters' Union represents a conglomeration of wage earners, salesmen working on a commission basis, drivers owning their own vehicles, and unrelated groups of dairy employees, garage workers, and oil station men. The craft idea is maintained by grouping the membership into local unions according to the character of work, each local having an individual agreement with the employer. This mixed membership has been the cause of many jurisdictional disputes. One of the most serious in recent years has been that with the Union of Street and Electric Railway Employees over motor bus drivers. It was finally decided that the railway employees should exercise jurisdiction where motor bus lines were operated by a street railway company as part of its service and equipment, while operators on independently controlled bus lines when organized should hold membership in the Teamsters' Union. However, the teamsters have not been keenly interested in gaining these workers because they feel that the railroads will soon take over most of the passenger bus lines and a new jurisdictional problem will then present itself.

Organizing activities have always been considered of paramount importance. Campaigns have been carried on during periods of depression in order to prepare workers for unionization during prosperity. Organizers have been paid salaries as high as $12,000 a year. The president and secretary of the union are paid $20,000 a year each. Such salaries are justified by the officers on the ground that "these jobs are not Sunday school positions. The officers take their lives in their hands each day in the week. They don't know from day to day whether they are going to be there the next." Organizing in this trade is no easy task in view of employers' opposition, the character of the workers, and threats from gangsters. In a number of cities, notably Chicago, the teamsters' locals have been the special aim of racketeering rings.

In 1930 the union had a cash deposit of almost 2 million dollars. The only benefits paid by the union are strike benefits, though the president of the organization has advocated the adoption of some form of insurance at each convention for 23 years.

Up to 1925 the organizing activities of this union were among drivers of vehicles conveying a wide variety of commodities—milk, tea and coffee, butter and eggs, laundry, bakery, and other goods. Since 1925 the expansion of the motor truck business has diverted efforts to that industry. As a result of the keen competition between the small trucker and the railroads, wages have tended to be reduced. The officers of the union are concentrating on reducing hours of work. Some union members still work the ten-hour day and the seven-day week.

The Brotherhood of Railway Carmen, though usually classified with the metal trades unions, is affected by the condition of the railroad industry and illustrates the problems of some of the railroad unions.[7]

The Brotherhood of Railway and Steamship Clerks, Freight Handlers, Express and Station Employees was organized in 1899 and joined the A. F. of L. in 1908. It grew from an organization of 5,000 in 1915 to about 207,000 in 1920, though it reported 186,000 to the A. F. of L. Its membership fell to 91,200 in 1925 as a result of anti-union policies on many railroads and the withdrawal of discontented express employees. The decrease in the number of employees falling in the class of railway clerks, due to technological changes in the industry, has affected the membership of the Brotherhood since 1925. It reported 60,800 to the Federation in 1932, but it claims about 100,000 members if the unemployed who are exempt from paying dues are included.

The Brotherhood may be classified as an amalgamated craft union. It includes a variety of elements—the "white collar" class of railway employee; office boys; laborers employed in and around stations, storehouses and warehouses; and freight handlers. The Brotherhood embraces two distinct transportation services—the express and the railway. The railway service employees are organized on the basis of local lodges which draw memberships from a single office or department. Where there are not enough employees in a single office to maintain a local, several offices on a given railroad division are combined to form

[7] See pp. 502-03.

a lodge. In larger centers, lodges are formed by employees from one or more departments of large general accounting offices. The local lodges are organized into system, district, or terminal boards of adjustment representing the employees of a given railroad system or of terminal companies. The local lodges representing employees of the express companies are for the most part composed of all employees of the express companies in a given terminal. In the express division the boards of adjustment are designated as district boards and consist of lodges in a given district. The Brotherhood, like a number of other unions, has a ritual, though the "secret work" is not generally regarded as of much importance. In the initiation of new members a simple ritual is gone through, consisting mainly of a pledge of loyalty by the new member.

The policies of the Brotherhood are shaped by the mixed character of the membership, the large differences in their wages and salaries, the competition of women, the traditional notions of "white collar" employees, and the methods of railroad managements. The Brotherhood, like other transportation unions, does not call for the union shop. In its agreements with railroad companies it insists mainly on rating the job, on maintaining seniority rules in promotion, and on proper methods for settling grievances. The seniority, promotion, and force reduction rules are important because of the wide variations in rates of pay corresponding to the variety of duties involved in the different classes of work performed by members of the union. Promotion rules guarantee promotion to the senior applicant, provided he has fitness and ability. When force reductions are necessary, the rules require that employees be laid off in the order of their seniority. This prevents undue favoritism, nepotism, as well as discrimination on account of union membership.

A distinctive rule in the agreements of the Brotherhood is the six-day working week, which means that clerks receive a full week's wage whether they work a full week or not. As a result of the depression, this rule has been waived in some cases in exchange for the promise of the management not to reduce the working force. The settlement of grievances is carried out through a series of local protective committees and higher agencies.

The Brotherhood established a death benefit fund in 1922. Until 1931 the amount of the benefit depended upon length of membership, varying from $100 for one year to $1,500 for 15 or more years. As this plan proved unsound, a death benefit of $300, regardless of length of membership, was established in 1931. Some of the local lodges pay additional death benefits, varying in amount, and most of them are on an assessment basis.

No other benefits are provided by the Brotherhood, partly because of the objection of the membership to high dues and assessments. The minimum dues are $1.25 per month; and the minimum initiation fee is $5.00. The average monthly dues of lodges is between $1.50 and $1.75. A few lodges collect $2.50 a month in dues and as much as $15 and $25 as initiation fees. The system boards fix their own per capita tax, which is paid to them direct by affiliated local lodges. In the two and a half years from July 1, 1928 to December 31, 1930 the Brotherhood collected $1,944,376 in dues and fees, of which $404,623 was per capita tax. During the same period the Brotherhood paid $811,270 in death claims.

Largely because the Brotherhood has no control over jobs and does not use such devices of craft unionism as the sympathetic strike or the insurance method of other railroad unions, it emphasizes general programs of reform. The Brotherhood was one of the first international unions to enter actively into the campaign for unemployment insurance. It has taken a leading part in the movement for the establishment of a federal system of retirement pensions for railroad workers. The Brotherhood has gone on record as favoring at the first practical moment the formation of an American Labor Party, the amalgamation or federation of the 21 standard railway labor organizations, and public ownership and operation of railroads. It has been comparatively free of internal factional disputes in recent years, has fostered a spirit of self-criticism, and has avoided strong-arm tactics. In addition to the conditions indicated above, factors explaining this situation are the higher average of schooling among the members, their fair general knowledge of the industry in which they are engaged, the fact that a large percentage of the members are young men and women, and the influence of a group of younger men who have come into positions of responsibility in the administration. It should be noted that, despite its political progressivism, the Brotherhood is one of the unions which expressly exclude colored workers.

Organization conferences, first held in 1929, are one of the original experiments of the Brotherhood. These conferences are attended by all railroad system board chairmen and by the international officers. Experts on economic subjects are invited to speak to and advise with the conference on urgent questions and to discuss changes in policy. The Brotherhood has a research department which serves the executive office and local lodges in an informational capacity. The *Railway Clerk*, published by the Brotherhood, has a high standing among labor journals.

The outstanding problems of the organization are those affecting most railroad unions, such as labor displacement, unemployment, the competition of the casual worker, the company union, finances, and others already described.

XIII. PUBLIC SERVICE

In this group there are seven unions affiliated with the A. F. of L. having a total membership of 137,800 in 1932. The unions in this group are unique in that each of them has experienced growth during the depressed years between 1929 and 1932. Five draw their membership from federal employees—four from the mail service, and one has jurisdiction over all federal employees not within the jurisdiction of other unions. As the working conditions of these unions can only be changed by legislative action most of their activities are confined to advancing their welfare through lobbying.[8]

XIV. PERSONAL SERVICE AND MERCHANDISING

In the personal service and trade group there are five unions having a total membership of 82,400 in 1932, the strongest of which is the International Journeymen Barbers' Union. The Barbers' Union was organized in 1887 and joined the A. F. of L. the following year. Membership in the union grew steadily from 23,600 in 1904 to 54,500 in 1927, but by 1932 had fallen to 39,900. The union has a handsome office building in Indianapolis for its headquarters and conducts its affairs in a business-like manner.

[8] For a discussion of these unions see Sterling D. Spero, *The Labor Movement in a Government Industry*, 1924.

This union carries on publicity campaigns to persuade the public to accept the union shop card as evidence of good workmanship, hygienic conditions, and satisfactory service. It appeals to barber supply manufacturers and dealers to co-operate in maintaining high sanitary and professional standards in barber shops. The union is also active in establishing license laws and Sunday closing ordinances. It was instrumental in obtaining the law in the State of California establishing a State Board of Barber Examiners, which supervises the inspection of shops, closes shops not up to standards, receives complaints, issues warrants for arrest, revokes certificates, and closes unqualified barber schools. The Board may refuse to renew licenses of shops that do not qualify. The union aims to establish similar boards in other states. To obtain these legislative ends it co-operates with the Association of Master Barbers—the employers organization which it helped to organize.

The problems of the union are due largely to personal and social factors. Older men are difficult to place because employers call for young and "good looking" men. The union has difficulty in convincing employers that the older men are valuable because they add "dignity to the shop." The union regulation regarding the hour of closing shops is one of the principal issues which cause employers to operate non-union shops. The tipping system and the individualism of the men in the trade who hope to become employers themselves are other difficulties. The union pays sick and death benefits, though the problem of financing these is becoming more complex. It also has an apprenticeship requirement which was recently reduced from three to two years. Since 1924 "beauty culturists" have been eligible to the union. These workers are gradually becoming keen competitors of the barbers. But the conditions of employment in beauty shops and the large number of women engaged in this branch of the industry make the problem of organizing them difficult. The Barbers' Union, like the Bakers' Union and some others in the A. F. of L., is unprepared for the task of organizing women and is reluctant to make the changes in its methods which a large influx of women members would involve.

XV. AMUSEMENTS AND PROFESSIONS

The A. F. of L. has three unions in this group, which in 1932 had a membership of 128,500. The Associated Actors and Artistes of America, known as the Four A's, is interesting because of its achievements and methods. It is a union composed of eight groups of actors and artists—the Actors' Equity Association, the Chorus Equity Association, the American Artistes Federation, the Hebrew Actors' Union, the German White Rats, the Grand Opera Choral Alliance, the Hebrew Chorus Union, and the Hungarian Actors. The membership, which was 11,500 in 1929, dropped to 4,500 in 1932, of whom 3,364 belonged to the Actor's Equity Association. As it dominates the international union numerically, the discussion here is confined to its activities.[9]

[9] The jurisdiction of the Equity Association includes all players or entertainers who are individual or independent in their work and do not act exclusively in mass formation, and who appear in any places where representations containing a sustained plot are given in French or English. This includes and means such performances as drama, melodrama, comedy (musical and otherwise), farce, light opera, grand opera principals, and such performances as "revues" and "follies" or entertainments of a similar nature where such performances take up approximately 85 per cent of the time allowed for the performance. But this does not include what is known as "burlesque," a Hippodrome show, or chorus. This jurisdiction also includes all motion picture artists, but not those who appear in "mobs" only.

The Actors' Equity Association gained recognition after a strike in 1919, as a result of which it signed a five-year agreement with the Managers' Protective Association. The union provides a form of standardized contract for practically every type of engagement in its jurisdiction. Members are not allowed to accept terms less favorable than those contained in the standard minimum contracts, though they are free to bargain for more favorable terms. When members are negotiating for engagements within Equity's jurisdiction they may employ in New York only such agents as are accredited by the association. Commissions must be paid promptly or the offender will be subject to discipline according to the discretion of the council of the union.

One of the main purposes of these contracts is to provide greater security of employment. Once a play has gone through the first week of rehearsals, the actors must be given two weeks' employment, or salary therefor. Whenever it is decided to withdraw the play, one week's notice must be given, or full salary paid. In the dismissal of an individual actor, two weeks' notice or salary for that time is required. This clause is reciprocal and thus provides a degree of security for the manager. A manager still may dismiss an actor for cause, but the cause must be sufficiently good to stand the scrutiny of the Equity council.

Contracts further provide for continuity of employment. The Equity Association takes the position that once the season has opened, the actor is entitled to continuous work until it closes. Several exceptions are made to take care of emergencies such as the illness of a star, or the need of re-writing or recasting a play; but these are subject to close examination by the Equity council.

Exceptions are also made to allow lay-offs during hard theatre weeks, for instance the week before Christmas and the week before Easter. In contrast with conditions prevailing before 1919, salaries must now be paid for all time played. If a manager wishes to lay off his company during the two weeks mentioned, if he anticipates a loss, he may do so, but if the play runs, he must pay full salaries. In the face of continually bad business, managers have been permitted to cut salaries with the consent of the players.

The Equity Association has declared that it will not allow the theatre to degenerate into a sweatshop. It has established a standard week of eight performances, and actors are paid extra for all performances in excess of this number. Before 1919 producers made exorbitant demands on actors for free rehearsal time. Today contracts specify that four weeks of unpaid rehearsals are allowed in dramatic productions, and five weeks in musical comedies and revues. Every Equity contract calls for the return of the actor to the point of the opening of the play. When a manager's financial rating is doubtful, he is required to give bond for an amount sufficient to pay two weeks' salary for all members of the company and return fares from the farthest point of the proposed tour. Under these conditions, when strandings occur, funds are immediately telegraphed and the actors are brought home. Equity then proceeds to collect from the manager of the stranded company through the forfeiture of the bond or otherwise. Contracts also specify the wardrobe which must be provided by the actor and producer respectively.

A more recent demand made by the union is that any Equity actor taking part in the broadcasting of any scene or part of a scene from a play currently appearing or rehearsing must be paid for at the rate of one-eighth of his week's salary for each broadcast. In any television performance in which an Equity member appears, all members of the company must be members of Equity in good standing. Every alien actor who secures an engagement within the jurisdiction of Equity must acknowledge indebtedness to the association of an amount equal to 5 per cent of his weekly salary (not less than $10 per week) and must authorize his manager to pay that amount to the association out of his salary when earned.

According to a rule which went into effect on August 16, 1932 every newly elected member is received on probation for a period of two years contingent upon attendance at specified meetings and lectures and ability to answer a questionnaire on the subjects of these lectures. If the candidate for membership fails to qualify at the end of his two-year probation period, he is allowed an extension of twelve months on payment of $100. If at the end of that period he should still fail, his opportunity to become a member will terminate. The lectures during the winter of 1932 included a series of talks on the early days of the drama, the history of the theatre in the United States, and the importance and necessity of certain clauses in the standard minimum contracts. In other ways Equity maintains a strict discipline over its members. Its monthly journal prints "Do's and Don'ts" and the membership is often commanded to read such notices, or perhaps an article from beginning to end, under penalty of discipline by the Council if found ignorant on the subject. The purpose is to have a membership knowing something of the history of its craft and also familiar with the work of its union.

REFERENCES FOR FURTHER READING

In the preparation of this book, the author has drawn upon documents and unpublished records of the American Federation of Labor and of government boards and departments, as well as current periodicals of the various labor groups to which no reference is made here. Books and articles quoted or cited in the text are omitted from these references.

GENERAL REFERENCES

American Federation of Labor, *History Encyclopedia Reference Book,* Washington, Vol. 1, 1919; Vol. 2, 1924.

American Federationist, 1894-1933.

American Labor Yearbook, 1917-32, Rand School.

Monthly Labor Review, U. S. Bureau of Labor Statistics.

Proceedings of the Annual Conventions of the American Federation of Labor, 1881-1932.

CHAPTERS I-II

Bimba, Anthony, *The Molly Maguires,* International Publishers, 1932.

Buchanan, Joseph R., *The Story of a Labor Agitator,* Outlook Co., 1903.

Hollander, Jacob Harry, and Barnett, G. E., *Studies in American Trade Unionism,* Holt, 1906.

McMurry, Donald LeCrone, *Coxey's Army,* Little, 1929.

CHAPTERS III-V

Adams, Thomas S., and Sumner, Helen L., *Labor Problems,* Macmillan, 1905.

Bimba, Anthony, *The History of the American Working Class,* International Publishers, 1927.

Carlton, Frank T., *The History and Problems of Organized Labor,* Heath, 1920.

Faulkner, Harold Underwood, *The Quest for Social Justice, 1898-1914,* Macmillan, 1931.

Levine, Louis, "The Development of Syndicalism in America," *Political Science Quarterly,* September, 1913, Vol. 28, pp. 451-79.

Mitchell, John, *Organized Labor*, American Book and Bible House, 1903.

Tarbell, Ida M., *The Life of Elbert H. Gary*, Appleton, 1925.

CHAPTERS VI-VII

Bing, Alexander M., *War-Time Strikes and their Adjustment*, Dutton, 1921.

Clarkson, Grosvenor B., *Industrial America in the World War*, Houghton, 1923.

Hines, Walker Donner, *War History of American Railroads* (Carnegie Endowment for International Peace), Yale University Press, 1928.

Lauck, W. Jett, and Watts, Claude S., *The Industrial Code*, Funk and Wagnalls, 1922.

Slosson, Preston W., *The Great Crusade and After, 1914-1928*, Macmillan, 1930.

Watkins, Gordon S., *Labor Problems and Labor Administration in the United States during the World War*, University of Illinois Press, 1920.

Wehle, Louis B., "Adjustment of Labor Disputes Incident to Production for War," *Quarterly Journal of Economics*, November, 1917, Vol. 32, pp. 122-41.

———, "Labor Problems in the United States during the War," *Quarterly Journal of Economics*, February, 1918, Vol. 32, pp. 333-96.

U. S. Department of Labor, "History of the Shipbuilding Labor Adjustment Board," *Bureau of Labor Statistics Bulletin No. 283* (by W. E. Hotchkiss and Henry Seager), Government Printing Office, Washington, 1921.

———, "National War Labor Board," *Bureau of Labor Statistics Bulletin No. 287*, 1922.

———, *Report of the President's Mediation Commission to the President of the United States*, 1918.

CHAPTERS VIII-IX

Barnett, George E., "The Present Position of American Trade Unionism," *American Economic Review* (Supplement), March, 1922, Vol. 12, pp. 44-55.

Bonnet, Clarence E., *Employers' Associations in the United States*, Macmillan, 1922.

Foster, William Z., *The Great Steel Strike and Its Lessons,* Viking, 1920.

Inter-Church World Movement of North America, *Public Opinion and the Steel Strike,* Harcourt, 1921.

Saposs, David J., *Left-Wing Unionism,* International Publishers, 1926.

Soule, George, *Wage Arbitration, Selected Cases, 1920-1924,* Macmillan, 1928.

Wyckoff, Vertrees Judson, *The Wage Policies of Labor Organizations in a Period of Industrial Depression,* Johns Hopkins Press, 1926.

CHAPTER X

American Academy of Political and Social Science, "The Second Industrial Revolution and Its Significance," (P. S. Brown, editor), *The Annals,* May, 1930, Vol. 149, pp. 1-197.

Barnett, George Ernest, "Chapters on Machinery and Labor," *Quarterly Journal of Economics,* May, 1925, Vol. 39, pp. 337-56, 554-74; November, 1925, Vol. 40, pp. 111-33.

Burton, Ernest R., *Employee Representation,* Williams and Wilkins, 1926.

Davis, Eleanor, *Employee Stock Ownership and the Depression,* Princeton University Press, 1933.

Dunn, Robert W., *Labor and Automobiles,* International Publishers, 1929.

Feis, Herbert, "Recent Development in Industrial Relations in the United States," *International Labor Review,* December, 1925, Vol. 12, pp. 776-98.

Foerster, R. F., and Dietel, Elsie H., *Employee Stock Ownership in the United States,* Princeton University Press, 1926.

Herring, Harriet L., *Welfare Work in Mill Villages,* University of North Carolina Press, 1929.

Howard, Sidney, and Dunn, Robert, *The Labor Spy,* New Republic, 1924.

Hunt, Eward E., *Scientific Management since Taylor,* Mcgraw Hill, 1924.

Laidler, Harry W., and Thomas, Norman (editors), *New Tactics in Social Conflict,* Vanguard, 1926.

MacDonald, Lois, *Southern Mill Hills,* A. L. Hillman, 1928.
Mitchell, George S., *Textile Unionism and the South,* University of North Carolina Press, 1931.
Oneal, James, *American Communism,* Rand Book Store, 1927.
Princeton University, Industrial Relations Section, *Labor Banking Movement in the United States,* 1929.
Rhyne, G. J., *Some Southern Cotton Mill Workers and their Villages,* University of North Carolina Press, 1930.
Schneider, D. M., *The Workers' [Communist] Party and American Trade Unions,* Johns Hopkins Press, 1928.
Taylor, Paul S., *Mexican Labor in the United States,* University of California Press, 1928.
U. S. Department of Labor, "Beneficial Activities of American Trade Unions," *Bureau of Labor Statistics Bulletin No. 465,* Government Printing Office, Washington, 1928.
———, "Health and Recreational Activities in Industrial Establishments in 1926," *Bureau of Labor Statistics Bulletin No. 458,* 1928.

CHAPTER XI

American Academy of Political and Social Science, "The Insecurity of Industry," *The Annals,* March, 1931, Vol. 154.
American Federation of Labor, *Trade Unions Study Unemployment,* Washington, 1929.
Douglas, Paul H., and Director, Aaron, *The Problem of Unemployment,* Macmillan, 1931.
Federated American Engineering Societies, *Waste in Industry,* McGraw Hill, 1921.
U. S. Department of Labor, "Unemployment Benefit Plans in the United States and Unemployment Insurance in Foreign Countries," *Bureau of Labor Statistics Bulletin No. 544,* Government Printing Office, Washington, 1931.

CHAPTERS XII-XIII

Blum, Solomon, *Labor Economics,* Holt, 1925.
Catlin, Warren B., *Labor Problem in United States and Canada,* Harper, 1926.
Feldman, Herman, *Racial Factors in American Industry,* Harper, 1931.

Foster, William Z., *Misleaders of Labor*, Trade Union Education League, 1927.

Groat, George W., *An Introduction to the Study of Organized Labor in America*, rev. ed., Macmillan, 1926.

Hoxie, Robert F., *Trade Unionism in the United States*, 2d. ed., Appleton, 1923.

Mathewson, Stanley B., *Restriction of Output among Unorganized Workers*, Viking Press, 1931.

Scrimshaw, Stewart, *Apprenticeship, Principles, Relationships, Procedure*, McGraw Hill, 1932.

Watkins, Gordon S., *An Introduction to the Study of Labor Problems*, Crowell, 1922.

CHAPTER XIV

Helbing, Albert Theodore, *Departments of the A. F. of L.*, Johns Hopkins Press, 1931.

Proceedings of the Conventions of the: Label Trades Department, 1908-32; Metal Trades Department, 1909-32; Building Trades Department, 1908-32; Railway Employees Department, 1910-32.

Wood, Louis Aubrey, *Union Management Co-operation on the Railroads*, Yale University Press, 1931.

CHAPTER XV

American Federation of Labor, *Legislative Achievements of the American Federation of Labor* (pamphlet), Washington, 1929.

Fine, Nathan, *Labor and Farmer Politics in the United States, 1828-1928*, Rand School, 1928.

Frankfurter, Felix, and Greene, Nathan, *The Labor Injunction*, Macmillan, 1930.

McCracken, Duane, *Strike Injunctions in the New South*, University of North Carolina Press, 1931.

Seidman, J. I., *The Yellow Dog Contract*, Johns Hopkins Press, 1932.

CHAPTER XVI

Foster, Frank K., *Has the Non-Unionist a Moral Right to Work, How, When, and Where He Pleases?* (pamphlet), A. F. of L., Washington, 1926.

Gompers, Samuel, *The American Labor Movement: Its Make-up, Achievements, and Aspirations* (pamphlet), A. F. of L., Washington, 1914.
Green, William, *A Great American Institution,* A. F. of L., Washington, 1930.
———, *For Better Understanding,* A. F. of L., Washington, 1930.
———, *Labor's Message to the South,* A. F. of L., Washington, 1930.
———, *Labor Proposes Co-operation,* A. F. of L., Washington, 1930.
———, *Labor Seeks Life More Abundantly,* A. F. of L., Washington, 1925.
———, *Modern Trade Unionism,* A. F. of L., Washington, 1925.
———, *The Purpose of the Labor Movement,* A. F. of L., Washington, 1930.
———, *The Superiority of Trade Unions over Company Unions,* A. F. of L., Washington, 1926.
———, *Wage Theories,* A. F. of L., Washington, 1926.
McNeill, George E., *The Eight Hour Primer: The Fact, Theory, and the Argument,* Eight Hour Series No. 1, A. F. of L., Washington, 1927.
Saposs, David J., *Readings in Trade Unionism,* Doran, 1926.
Thornton, Sir Henry, *The Partner; The New Labor Era.* A. F. of L., Washington, 1930.

CHAPTER XVII

Hardman, J. B. S., *American Labor Dynamics,* Harcourt, 1928.
Perlman, Selig, *A Theory of the Labor Movement,* Macmillan, 1928.
Tannenbaum, Frank, *The Labor Movement,* Putnam, 1921.

APPENDIX B

Baker, E. F., "Technological Change and Organized Labor in Commercial Printing," *American Economic Review,* December, 1932, Vol. 22, pp. 669-90.
Barnes, Charles B., *Longshoremen,* Russell Sage, 1915.
Barnett, George E., "American Trade Unionism and Social

Insurance," *American Economic Review*, March, 1933, Vol. 23, pp. 1-15.

Commons, John R., "The New York Building Trades," *Quarterly Journal of Economics*, Vol. 18, pp. 409-36.

Craig, David R., *The Economic Condition of the Printing Industry in New York City*, New York Employing Printers' Association, 1925.

Deibler, F. S., *Amalgamated Wood Workers' International Union of America*, University of Wisconsin Press, 1912.

Galster, A. E., *The Labor Movement in the Shoe Industry*, Ronald, 1924.

Goodrich, Carter, *The Miners' Freedom*, Boston, 1925.

Haber, W. G., "Workers' Rights and the Introduction of Machinery in the Men's Clothing Industry," *Journal of Political Economy*, August, 1925, Vol. 33, pp. 404-05.

Harding, Alfred, *The Revolt of the Actors*, Morrow and Co., 1929.

Hoagland, H. E., "Trade Unionism in the Iron Industry: A Decadent Organization," *Quarterly Journal of Economics*, August, 1917, Vol. 31, pp. 647-89.

McIsaac, A. M., *Order of Railroad Telegraphers*, Princeton University Press, 1933.

McMahon, Thomas F., *United Textile Workers of America*, Workers' Education Bureau, 1926.

Marsh, Charles F., *Trade Unionism in the Electric Light and Power Industry*, University of Illinois Press, 1928.

Montgomery, Royal E., *Industrial Relations in the Chicago Building Trades*, University of Chicago Press, 1927.

Norton, T. L., *Trade Union Policies in the Massachusetts Shoe Industry, 1919-1929*, Columbia University Press, 1932.

Palmer, Gladys L., *Union Tactics and Economic Change: A Case Study of Three Philadelphia Textile Unions* (Wharton School of Finance and Commerce, Industrial Research Department Research Studies 19), University of Pennsylvania Press, 1932.

Robbins, E. C., *Railway Conductors*, Columbia University Press, 1914.

Squire, B. M., "Marine Workers' Affiliation of the Port of New York," *Journal of Political Economy*, December, 1919, Vol. 27, pp. 840-74.

Stockton, Frank T., *The International Molders' Union of North America*, Johns Hopkins Press, 1921.

U. S. Department of Labor, "Apprenticeship in Building Construction," *Bureau of Labor Statistics Bulletin No. 459*, Government Printing Office, Washington, 1928.

———, "Collective Bargaining by Actors," *Bureau of Labor Statistics Bulletin No. 402* (by Paul Fleming Gemmill), 1926.

———, "Collective Bargaining in the Anthracite Coal Industry," *Bureau of Labor Statistics Bulletin No. 191*, 1916.

———, "Joint Industrial Control in the Book and Job Printing Industry," *Bureau of Labor Statistics Bulletin No. 481* (by Emily Clark Brown), 1926.

Whitney, N. R., *Jurisdiction in American Building Trades Unions*, Johns Hopkins Press, 1914.

INDEX